THE OXFORD ILLUSTRATED HISTORY OF THE VIKINGS

THE OXFORD ILLUSTRATED HISTORY OF THE VIKINGS

EDITED BY PETER SAWYER

Oxford   New York

OXFORD UNIVERSITY PRESS

1997

Oxford University Press, Great Clarendon Street, Oxford OX2 6DP

Oxford New York

Athens Auckland Bangkok Bogota Bombay
Buenos Aires Calcutta Cape Town Dar es Salaam
Delhi Florence Hong Kong Istanbul Karachi
Kuala Lumpur Madras Madrid Melbourne
Mexico City Nairobi Paris Singapore
Taipei Tokyo Toronto
and associated companies in
Berlin Ibadan

Oxford is a trade mark of Oxford University Press

Published in the United States
by Oxford University Press Inc., New York

© Oxford University Press 1997

British Library Cataloguing in Publication Data
Data available

Library of Congress Cataloging in Publication Data
The Oxford Illustrated History of the Vikings
Edited by Peter Sawyer   p. cm.
Includes bibliographical references and index.
1. Vikings.   2. Vikings—Pictorial works.   I. Sawyer, Peter.
DL65.094   1997
948'. 022—dc21   97—16649 CIP

ISBN 0-19-820526-0

1 3 5 7 9 10 8 6 4 2

Printed in Great Britain
on acid-free paper by
Butler & Tanner Ltd., Frome

EDITOR'S FOREWORD

As readers will discover, the contributors to this book do not agree on all matters. That is not surprising: differences of interpretation, which occur in all periods, are perhaps more prominent in discussions of the Vikings than in most topics in medieval history. There are several reasons for this degree of uncertainty. In the first place, the vast range of Viking activity means that our knowledge of it depends on a great variety of sources that were produced in very different circumstances, at different times, and in Old Irish, Old English, Old Norse, Arabic, and Byzantine Greek, as well as Latin. As few, if any, scholars have mastered all these languages, any discussion of Viking activity as a whole depends to some extent on translations that are themselves interpretations and may be unreliable. What is more, apart from runic inscriptions no texts were written before the eleventh century in Scandinavia or in many of the areas in which Scandinavians settled in the Viking Age. Great weight has, therefore, been put on the histories written in Scandinavia and the Scandinavian colonies in the twelfth and thirteenth centuries that are discussed in Chapter 10. Until recently the history of the Viking Age was largely based on Icelandic sagas, the history of the Danes written by Saxo Grammaticus, the *Russian Primary Chronicle*, and the *War of the Irish with the Foreigners*. Although few scholars still accept these texts as reliable sources of information about the Viking Age, traditional accounts of the period that have been based on them continue to influence discussions of the subject.

Historians of Scandinavia, the Atlantic Islands, and Russia in the Viking Age now rely more on archaeology and numismatics, disciplines that have in recent decades made remarkable contributions to our understanding of the period, even in parts of Europe that are relatively well provided with contemporary texts, for they cast light on many topics about which the texts are silent. Both material remains and coins can also furnish valuable dating evidence. Remains of timber structures can, in suitable circumstances, be closely dated by the pattern of annual growth rings in the wood. This has made it possible, for example, to discover when some ships were built, and to date the various stages of the construction of Danevirke. The legends of Islamic coins, many of which reached Scandinavia in the ninth and tenth centuries, indicate the year they were struck; and from the end of the tenth to the beginning of the twelfth century the types of English coins were changed frequently and can therefore be dated within at most six years. Such coins provide date limits for the buildings, graves, or other contexts in which they are found. Such evidence cannot, however, provide the continuous chronological framework based on the chronicles and other contemporary texts produced in Frankia, England, and Ireland. The lack of contemporary texts particularly affects Orkney, Shetland, and the Hebrides; there is, for example, disagreement about when the Scandinavians began to occupy these islands.

Even in well-documented parts of Europe the written sources say very little about the Scandinavian settlements. Place-names provide the best evidence for this colonization but, as emphasized in Chapter 3, they can be interpreted in very different ways. The main problem is that the names reflect the influence of the Scandinavians on language and do not necessarily indicate places in which Scandinavians settled. The fact that Scandinavian influence on place-names in Normandy and Ireland is much less than in England cannot be taken to prove that fewer Scandinavians settled in those colonies than in England.

Discoveries made in the future and the re-examination of familiar evidence may help to settle some disagreements; they will certainly enlarge our understanding of the period in ways that cannot be foreseen.

CONTENTS

LIST OF COLOUR PLATES

LIST OF MAPS AND FIGURES

LIST OF CONTRIBUTORS

PETER SAWYER, Professor Emeritus of Medieval History, University of Leeds

JANET L. NELSON, Professor of Medieval History, King's College London

SIMON KEYNES, Reader in Anglo-Saxon History and Fellow of Trinity College, University of Cambridge

SVEINBJÖRN RAFNSSON, Professor of History, University of Iceland, Reykjavík

DONNCHADH Ó CORRÁIN, Professor of Irish History, University College, Cork

THOMAS S. NOONAN, Professor of Medieval History, University of Minnesota

NIELS LUND, Lecturer in Medieval History, University of Copenhagen

JAN BILL, Research Fellow, Centre for Maritime Archaeology, National Museum of Denmark, Roskilde

PREBEN MEULENGRACHT SØRENSEN, Professor of Old Norse Philology, University of Oslo

LARS LÖNNROTH, Professor of Scandinavian and Comparative Literature, University of Gothenburg

NOTE ON PERSONAL NAMES

The forms of personal names vary in contemporary texts. To avoid confusion most are here given in the uninflected forms commonly used in modern English. The main exceptions are in Chapter 4 where Irish forms of both Scandinavian and native personal names are used. For example, the Old Norse names *Ívarr* and *Óláfr*, which appear as *Inwær* and *Anlaf* in Old English, are in most chapters and in the Chronology standardized as Ivar and Olaf (but Olof Skötkonung), but in Chapter 4 the Irish forms *Ímar* and *Amlaíb* are used. Such different forms are identified in the index. In Chapters 9 and 10 Old Norse forms are used for names that do not occur in other chapters.

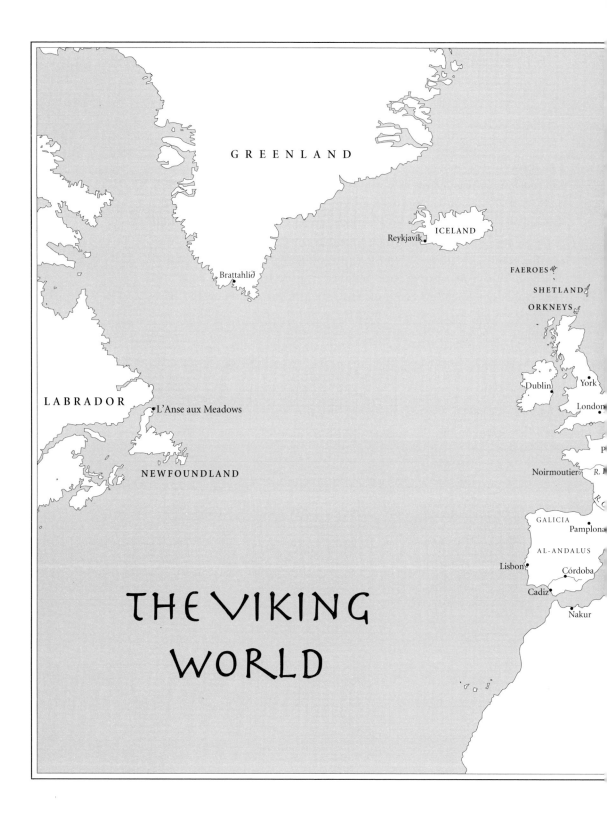

GREENLAND

ICELAND

Reykjavik

Brattahlið

FAEROES

SHETLAND

ORKNEYS

LABRADOR

L'Anse aux Meadows

Dublin

York

London

NEWFOUNDLAND

Noirmoutier

R.

GALICIA

Pamplona

AL-ANDALUS

Lisbon

Córdoba

Cadiz

Nakur

THE VIKING
WORLD

North Cape

NORWAY

White Sea

Lake
Ladoga

ondheim

ergen

Oslo
Uppsala
Birka

Staraja
Ladoga
Beloozero

Novgorod

Iaroslavl

Lund

Gotland

Bulghar

Gnezdovo

Hamburg

orestad

R. Elbe

Kiev
R. Dnepr

R. Rhine

R. Danube

R. Volga

Itil

TRANSOXANIA

Rome

KHWARAZM

Constantinople

Jerusalem

Baghdad

1000 miles

2000 km

1

THE AGE OF THE VIKINGS AND BEFORE

PETER SAWYER

From the eighth century to the eleventh, Scandinavians, mostly Danes and Norwegians, figure prominently in the history of western Europe as raiders, conquerors, and colonists. They plundered extensively in the British Isles and the Frankish empire and even attacked the Iberian peninsula and north Africa. In the ninth century they gained control of Orkney, Shetland, and most of the Hebrides, conquered a large part of England, and established bases on the Irish coast from which they launched attacks within Ireland and across the Irish Sea. Men and women from west Scandinavia emigrated to settle, not only in the parts of the British Isles that were then under Scandinavian control, but also in the Faeroes and Iceland, Atlantic islands that had previously been uninhabited. In the last years of the tenth century they also began to colonize Greenland, and explored North America, but without establishing permanent settlements there. The Scandinavian assault on western Europe culminated in the early eleventh century with the Danish conquest of the English kingdom, an achievement that other Scandinavian kings attempted to repeat later in the century, but without success.

Other Scandinavians, mainly Svear from what is now east Sweden, were active in eastern Europe in ways that were very similar to those of their contemporaries in western Europe, despite the great differences between the two regions. In the east there were no churches or well-established towns to plunder, but the invaders exploited the wealth of the region, principally furs and slaves, by seizure or by exacting tribute. Some of their leaders were able to gain control of centres of power, and Scandinavians emigrated to settle in what is now north Russia.

The peoples these Scandinavians encountered gave them a variety of names: the Franks normally called them Northmen or Danes, while for the English they were generally Danes or heathens. The Irish described the early raiders as pagans or gentiles, but by the middle of the ninth century they began to call them foreigners, the Norwegians and Danes being distinguished as 'white' and 'black' foreigners, *Finngall* and *Dubgall*. In eastern Europe the Slavs called the Scandinavian invaders Rus, a word derived from the Finnish name for the Svear, which itself came from a word meaning 'rowers' or 'crew of oarsmen'. It was 'Rus', variants of which were used in Arabic and Byzantine Greek texts, which eventually gave Russia its name. In the ninth century it was only the English who, occasionally, called the invaders Vikings, a Scandinavian word that now has a wider meaning, and is used to describe many aspects of Scandinavian society in what is commonly called the Age of the Vikings.

The first Viking raids reported in western Europe were in the last decade of the eighth century, on monasteries in the British Isles. In 793 Lindisfarne, an island monastery off the coast of Northumberland, was plundered; a

Some of the early eighth-century silver coins found in Ribe. They were apparently modelled on English coins, but it is uncertain whether they were made in Frisia or in Denmark.

year later another Northumbrian monastery, probably Jarrow, was attacked. In 795 Vikings attacked undefended island monasteries in the west:
on Skye and Iona in the Hebrides, and on Rathlin off the north-east coast of
Ireland. The first recorded raid on the Continent, in 799, was also on an
island monastery, St-Philibert's on Noirmoutier, near the estuary of the
Loire. One early incident that did not involve a church took place in the
reign of Beorhtric, king of the West Saxons (786–802). The crews of three
ships, later described as from Hordaland in Norway, landed in Portland on
the south coast of England and killed a royal reeve who mistook them for
merchants.

There must also have been raids on south-east England at this time,
although none is reported until 835. As early as 792 the churches of Kent
were obliged to contribute to defences against pagan seamen, and in 804 the
nunnery of Lyminge, an exposed site near Romney Marsh, was granted land
within the walls of Canterbury as a refuge. Across the Channel, in 800,
Charlemagne organized defences along the coast north of the Seine estuary
against pirates who 'infest the Gallic sea'. As no attack on that coast is reported before 810 it is not possible to say when the raids began: Scandinavian pirates may have been a nuisance there for many years. It is, however,
clear that by the last decade of the century their raids had become so serious
that rulers on both sides of the Channel took action against them.

Why the Raids Began

It has often been suggested that the main cause of Viking activity was the
pressure of increasing population in Scandinavia and the consequent short-
age of land there. That may have been partly true of western Norway, where
there were few reserves of land, but in other parts of Scandinavia there is no
hint of population pressure on the eve of the Viking period. Most of the first
generations of Vikings were seeking wealth, not land. It is true that during
the Viking Age many Scandinavians emigrated, but few did so out of necessity. It is more likely that most of those who settled in the British Isles, Iceland, or Russia were attracted by the prospect of having more land than they
could ever hope to own or rent in Scandinavia.

A key factor in the outburst of piracy was, in fact, the commercial expansion in north-west Europe that had begun over a century before the first
reported raids. Towards the end of the seventh century a significant increase of trade between the Continent and England led to the development
of several relatively large trading centres: Dorestad on the Rhine, Quentovic
near Boulogne, and, in England, *Hamwic* (the precursor of Southampton),
Fordwich (the port of Canterbury), London, Ipswich, and York. This trade

3

Winter view of Birka, from the north-east. In the background Lake Mälaren is covered with ice and to the left the fort overlooks the site of the settlement which was surrounded by a wall, part of which can be seen beyond the cemetery in the foreground.

grew even faster after about 700, when the Frisians obtained a very large stock of silver from an unidentified source and produced from it a huge supply of coinage that quickly spread throughout the Continent and in England.

Scandinavia and the lands round the Baltic were soon affected by this development, for the produce of that region, particularly its furs, was highly prized in western Europe. The best-quality furs came from areas with the coldest winters, and for western Europe Scandinavia and the lands east of the Baltic were an ideal source. Merchants could sail into the Baltic in the summer to buy furs, skins, and other produce, such as amber, eiderdown, and good-quality whetstones, in trading centres that were established during the eighth century. Already in the first years of that century such a centre had been founded at Ribe on the west coast of Jutland, and by mid-century there were others around the Baltic, the most important being Hedeby at the head of Schlei fjord in south-east Jutland, Birka in Lake Mälaren, and Wolin near the estuary of the Oder.

Most of the produce offered for sale in such places had been gathered as tribute from the Saami, Finns, and Balts who inhabited the best fur-producing areas. The exaction of tribute in Scandinavia is described in a ninth-century English text that includes some information provided by

Ottar, a Norwegian who visited the court of the English king, Alfred. Ottar
lived in the far north of Norway and took tribute from the Saami:

That tribute consists of the skins of beasts, the feathers of birds, whale-bone, and
ship-ropes made from walrus-hide and sealskin. Each pays according to his rank.
The highest in rank has to pay fifteen marten skins, five reindeer skins, one bear-

Left: The main wall of
Danevirke, seen from
the south-west. About
ten kilometres of this
barrier defending Jut-
land was constructed
in or soon after 737.

Below: Timber foun-
dations to support the
face of Danevirke in
marshy ground. Some
of the wood was so
well preserved that it
has been possible to
determine that it
came from trees felled
in 737.

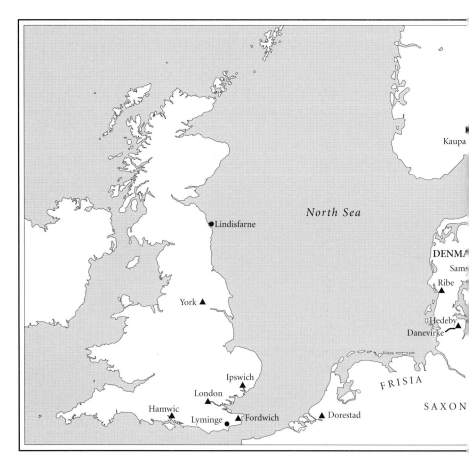

North Sea

Kaupa

Lindisfarne

DENMA

Sams

Ribe

Hedeby

Danevirke

York ▲

Ipswich

London

Hamwic

Lyminge ● ▲ Fordwich

▲ Dorestad

FRISIA

SAXON

skin, and ten measures of feathers, and a jacket of bearskin or otterskin, and two ship-ropes. Each of these must be sixty ells long, one made of walrus hide, the other from seal.

He also hunted walrus for their tusks, which were a valuable substitute for elephant ivory, as well for their skins. He apparently took what he gathered, as tribute or by hunting, to sell in markets such as Hedeby in south Scandinavia, or possibly in England.

Over a century before Ottar's time, Scandinavians had gathered similar tribute in Finland and north Russia, which continued to be the main source of high-quality furs in Europe for centuries. By AD 750 at the latest a base for this activity, with a mixed population of Finns, Slavs, and some Scandinavians, had been established at Staraja (Old) Ladoga on the River Volkhov, some 8 kilometres from its estuary in Lake Ladoga.

The commercial links between northern and western Europe had consequences that in their turn prepared the way for the Viking raids. First, increased familiarity with western European sailing-ships was an important

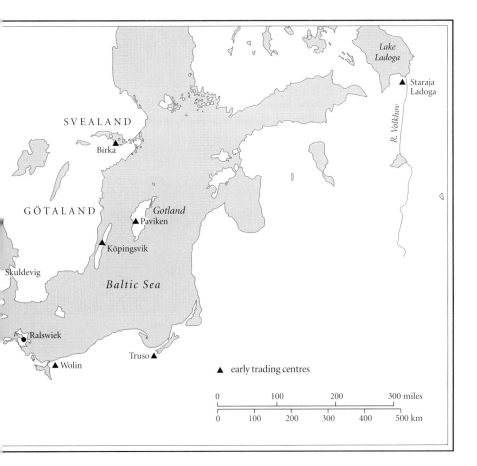

SVEALAND

Birka ▲

GÖTALAND

Gotland
Paviken ▲

Köpingsvik ▲

Skuldevig

Baltic Sea

Lake
Ladoga

Staraja ▲
Ladoga

R. Volkhov

Ralswiek ●

Truso ▲

Wolin ▲

▲ early trading centres

0		100		200		300 miles

0	100	200	300	400	500 km

factor in the adoption of sails in Scandinavia, a development discussed in Chapter 8. Secondly, their contacts with western merchants enabled Scandinavians to learn about Europe's wealth and about the conflicts between, and within, European kingdoms from which they were later able to profit. Thirdly, merchant ships in the Baltic provided opportunities for pirates who were in time tempted to extend their activities into the North Sea. There were also political consequences. Those rulers and chieftains who were best able to exact tribute gained wealth and power, as did those who controlled the trading centres, or the routes leading to them. The Danish kings, whose central territory was in Jutland and the adjacent islands, benefited most, for they controlled the entrance to the Baltic and could offer security to ships passing through the Great or Little Belts. They were thus able to attract merchants to Hedeby, conveniently close to the land route between Jutland and Saxony. The alternative channel into the Baltic, Øresund, was less attractive, partly because of strong currents, but also because of the threat of piracy; it was not directly controlled by Danish kings until the end of the tenth century.

7

THE KANHAVE
CANAL. Made in 726,
it enabled the Danes
to control the main
routes to the Baltic.
Ships based in the
sheltered waters of
Stavns Fjord could
quickly cross the
island to intercept
vessels sailing across
its west coast. The
shaded circle shows
the limit of visibility
in clear weather from
the highest point
(26 m) on Hjortholm
in Stavns Fjord. From
higher ground on
Samsø (over 50 m)
both Jutland and
Sjælland can be seen.

There are various indications that in the first half of the ninth century Danish kings were acknowledged as overlords by many of the local rulers and chieftains in the lands round Skagerrak and Kattegat. Any who were unable to resist Danish power and were unwilling to submit to it could choose exile, a prospect made more attractive by the opportunity to win fame and fortune by taking part in, or leading, Viking raids. The Danes were particularly eager to have hegemony over Viken, the land flanking Oslo Fjord. This district was of great value, for it was there that the Danes could obtain the iron that was produced in Norway. If, as seems likely, the word Viking originally referred to the inhabitants of Viken, it could explain why the English, and only they, called Scandinavian pirates Vikings, for England was the natural objective for men from Viken who chose exile as raiders rather than accept Danish overlordship.

Vikings in the West

At first most of the Vikings who operated in the north and west of the British Isles were from Norway. There is no contemporary record of Scandinavian activity in Orkney, Shetland, or the Hebrides in the early ninth century, but archaeological evidence suggests that there were contacts between Norway and Orkney as early as the seventh century. By the mid-ninth century there were extensive Norwegian settlements in the Hebrides as well as in the Northern Isles, a colonization that could only have been possible after any resistance by the native inhabitants had been overcome, presumably by force. It is therefore likely that the Scandinavian conquests in the Northern and Western Isles began with the establishment of bases by the leaders of the earliest raids. The Danes initially concentrated on the southern North Sea and the Channel coasts. Although the distinction between these Danish and Norwegian zones was blurred in the middle of the ninth century when Danes challenged Norwegians in Ireland, archaeological and linguistic evidence clearly shows that it was predominantly Danes who settled in eastern England and that most of those who occupied land in Ireland, the Hebrides, and the Northern Isles were from Norway.

For several decades the Vikings mounted what were, in effect, hit-and-run raids, rarely venturing far inland. The defences organized by English and Frankish rulers were apparently effective; most reported raids were in Ireland until the 830s, when the scale and extent of Viking incursions increased dramatically. Dorestad, a major trading centre about 80 kilometres from the open sea, was raided in 834 and in each of the next three years. In 835 the Isle of Sheppey was ravaged and in 836 the West Saxon army was defeated by Vikings who landed on the north coast of Somerset. In the same year Vikings began to plunder monasteries in the interior of Ireland and the monks of St-Philibert abandoned Noirmoutier to seek shelter in the Loire valley.

This extension of Viking activity was made possible by the conflict between Louis, the Frankish emperor, and his sons, one of whom, Lothar, welcomed the support of a Viking fleet led by an exiled Danish king. Scandinavians also took advantage of internal conflicts elsewhere in western Europe. In 838 Vikings supported the Britons of Cornwall against the West Saxons, and in 844 a deposed Northumbrian king was restored to power after his usurper was defeated and killed by Viking invaders. In Ireland too there were alliances between Vikings and Irish kings, certainly from 842 and probably earlier. It was, however, Frankia that offered Vikings the most rewarding opportunities. In 841, during the war that broke out between the sons of Louis after his death, churches and towns in the Seine valley were

A ship-burial of *c.*900 in the cemetery at Borre, near Tønsberg, west of Oslo Fjord, contained numerous gilt-bronze harness mounts, some of which are illustrated here. This cemetery, which was in use from the seventh century to the beginning of the tenth, originally had nine monumental mounds, the largest concentration in Scandinavia. The implication is that Borre was a power centre before and during the first part of the Viking Age. The Borre style of Scandinavian art, widely spread in the early Viking Age, is named after the decoration on these mounts.

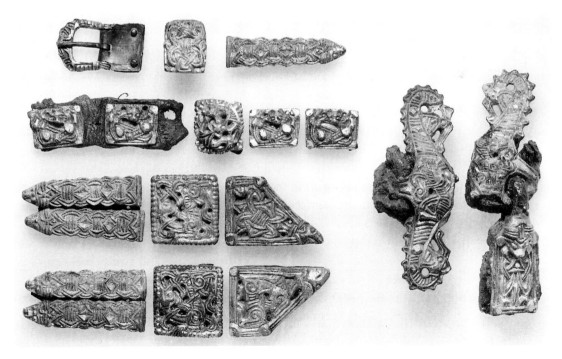

raided and in 842 Quentovic was sacked by a fleet which then crossed the Channel to attack *Hamwic*. When in 843 the war ended with the division of Frankia into three kingdoms, the Vikings had discovered that monasteries and towns on navigable rivers were vulnerable and that the Franks were sometimes prepared to pay large sums for the sake of peace. In 845 an attack on Paris was prevented by the payment of bullion worth 7,000 pounds of silver: for the Vikings an unprecedented tribute. It is not surprising that before long many new bands of Vikings were attracted to Frankia. A Viking fleet wintered in the Seine valley in 852, and a year later another did so in the Loire valley. By the end of the decade all the main rivers of the west Frankish kingdom were being exploited by Viking fleets. Even the Rhône valley was plundered by a fleet that sailed into the Mediterranean in 859 and established a base in the Camargue on the south coast of Frankia. The West Frankish kingdom suffered most; the others were not so seriously disrupted by Vikings, despite the existence of many promising targets in the valleys of the Rhine and Meuse. These rivers were, in effect, protected most of the time by other Vikings who were based near their estuaries as allies of the rulers of that part of Frankia.

Although the main arena of Viking activity in the middle years of the century was Frankia, the British Isles continued to suffer raids. In England one of the main objectives was the estuary of the River Thames. In 850 a fleet wintered on Thanet, near its mouth, and for several years Vikings were based there or further upstream on the Isle of Sheppey. Vikings began to winter in Ireland earlier than they did in England, first in 840 on Lough Neagh and a year later in Dublin, in one of several defended ship enclosures that were constructed in that year. Before long there were Viking bases at Wexford, Waterford, Cork, Limerick, and elsewhere, from which the surrounding areas were plundered. The booty included ornaments and elaborate caskets, but Irish monasteries were not so rich in gold, silver, and gems as those of Frankia and England. Captives, who could be sold to Muslims in Spain or north Africa were far more valuable. The Vikings in these bases were, of course, not land-bound: the Dublin Vikings launched several expeditions across the Irish Sea and in 870, after a siege of four months, captured Dumbarton, the capital of the British kingdom of Strathclyde. The victors returned to Dublin with 'a great multitude of men, English, Britons, and Picts in captivity', a reminder of the importance of human booty. The Vikings based in Ireland were far from united, and rivalry between them was complicated by the arrival of Danes in 851 to challenge the Norwegians in Dublin and elsewhere. In subsequent years Irish annalists recorded with great pleasure many battles between these invaders.

By 870 there had been profound changes in Frankia and England. In 862

Charles, king of West Frankia, began systematically to defend the heart of his kingdom. He had bridges built across the Seine and Loire to hinder the passage of enemy ships, and he fortified towns and abbeys. The lower reaches of those rivers, together with other coastal areas, were, in effect, left to the mercy of the raiders, some of whom remained in the Loire valley for many years. Most of the religious communities and many bishops in the exposed regions sought safety in other parts of Frankia. These changes encouraged many Vikings to concentrate on England instead of Frankia. Several Viking leaders joined forces in the hope of winning status and independence by conquering England, which then consisted of four kingdoms. In 865 a fleet landed in East Anglia and was later joined by others to form what a contemporary chronicler described, with good reason, as a 'great army'. Five years later this army, by conquering two kingdoms, Northumbria and East Anglia, and dismembering a third, Mercia, controlled much of eastern England, from York to London. Only one kingdom, Wessex, remained intact and independent.

For several years after 870 the Viking army made determined, but unsuccessful, efforts to conquer Wessex, and between 876 and 880 its leaders began to grant estates in the conquered areas to their principal followers, who in turn distributed land to any of their men who wished to settle. These colonists had a profound effect on dialects and place-names in the areas in which they settled; their influence on the farming vocabulary and field-names confirms that many were, indeed, farmers.

At much the same time as members of the 'great army' were settling in England, other Scandinavians, mainly Norwegians, began to colonize Iceland. The existence of this island had long been known, but nobody lived there before the ninth century, with the possible exception of a few Irish Christians, who may have established religious communities, as they did on other Atlantic islands. Icelanders later claimed that their ancestors emigrated in order to escape the tyranny of Harald Finehair, who was traditionally remembered as the first king of a united Norway. This explanation is unsatisfactory because the emigration to Iceland began before Harald's time. Although lack of reliable evidence makes it impossible to say what part earlier developments in Norway played in the movement to Iceland, Irish annals suggest that Scandinavians based in Ireland had reason to look for new homes in the second half of the ninth century. By establishing permanent bases in Ireland the Vikings lost the advantage of mobility, and disputes between different groups meant that they were unable to present a united front of the kind that proved so effective in England. They suffered many defeats. In 866 they were expelled from all their strongholds in the north of Ireland and a Viking base at Youghal in the south was destroyed.

Towards the end of the century the Vikings of Limerick, Waterford, and Wexford all suffered defeats and in 902 the Dublin Vikings, weakened by factional conflict, were overcome by the Irish and expelled. Some of the Dublin Vikings settled across the Irish Sea in the Wirral and possibly on the Isle of Man, but other Vikings who left Ireland at that time settled in Iceland.

Whether the colonization was begun from the British Isles or from Norway, reports of the opportunities offered by that unexploited land must have spread rapidly and tempted many to look for new homes there. After about sixty years most of the land suitable for settlement had been claimed. Later arrivals had to be content with less attractive sites, for example in the steep-sided fjords of north-west Iceland. For such people the discovery in the tenth century of apparently better sites in south-west Greenland was welcome, and towards the end of that century some began to move on, to found the most remote permanent Scandinavian settlement in which there were, eventually, some 300 farms.

According to later Icelandic sagas some of the early settlers in Greenland reached North America and discovered a fertile region they called *Vínland* (Wine-land). Several voyages to it are reported, but the natives proved to be unfriendly and permanent settlement was not possible. Remains of buildings of this period with traces of temporary occupation by Scandinavians, found at L'Anse aux Meadows near the northern tip of Newfoundland, appear to have been a base camp for exploration. There is, however, no reliable evidence to show how much further south or up the St Lawrence river Greenlanders went.

The break-up of the 'great army' after its failure to conquer Wessex coincided with renewed succession disputes in Frankia. Vikings were quick to take advantage of such dissension, and from 879 to 891 several Viking armies were active on the Continent, occasionally combining forces. At first they concentrated on the area north of the Seine, including Flanders, where cities and monasteries had not been fortified, and in 881 there was a major incursion up the Rhine to Cologne and Trier. This led the Franks once again to protect that river by allowing a Viking army to control its estuary. Another, more effective, response was to build fortifications. These measures had some success. In 885 the main army divided into two and each part returned to an area of earlier Viking activity, the Thames estuary and the Seine valley. After the former group had failed to take Rochester, some returned to the Continent, while others joined forces with Danes who had earlier settled in East Anglia. The Seine Vikings besieged Paris that winter. Although the city's defences held, the Franks were unable to prevent the invaders spending the next two winters further inland. During these campaigns huge quantities of plunder and tribute, and many captives, were taken, but the Vikings also suffered some defeats in pitched battles, in 881 at Saucourt, in 890 against the Bretons, and in 891 near Louvain.

Following the defeat of 891 the army returned to England to renew the attempt to conquer the West Saxons. It failed. Alfred had learned the lesson of the campaigns in Frankia and had constructed a network of fortifications and built a fleet. In 896 the Vikings, having failed to gain even a foothold in the areas of England not already under Scandinavian control, abandoned the attempt. In the words of the contemporary *Chronicle*: 'The Danish army divided, one force going into East Anglia and one into Northumbria; and those that were moneyless got themselves ships and went south across the sea to the Seine.'

Little is known about Viking activity on the Continent after that reversal. It is, however, clear that in 911 the West Frankish, or French, king granted Rouen and the surrounding territory in the lower Seine valley to a Viking leader called Rollo in the hope that he would deny other raiders the passage of the Seine, an arrangement similar to those made earlier to protect the Rhine. Another group of Vikings was allowed to settle in the neighbourhood of Nantes in 921, apparently to protect the Loire, but that arrangement lasted only sixteen years. The Viking occupation of Rouen proved permanent and was the basis of the later duchy of Normandy, which at its full extent included the Cotentin peninsula in the west. Place- and personal names show that some of the Scandinavians who settled in the west of Normandy came from Celtic regions, probably Ireland, and there are indications that some had spent some time in England.

The other main development in the first half of the tenth century was the conquest of the Scandinavian areas of England by the descendants of Alfred who ruled Wessex and the English part of Mercia. The main resistance came from Northumbrians, who tried to preserve their independence by recognizing Scandinavians as kings of York. With the expulsion and death of the last of these kings, Erik Bloodaxe, an exiled Norwegian king, in 952 or 954, the English were at last permanently united in one kingdom. The earlier Scandinavian kings, none of whom ruled York for long, had all been members of the dynasty that regained control of Dublin in 917. They claimed to be descendants of Ivar, the king of Dublin, who, on his death in 873, was described by an Irish annalist as 'king of all the Scandinavians of Ireland and Britain'. Whatever justification there was for such a title, the fact that his descendants were so closely associated with York lends some support to the suggestion that he was one of the leaders of the 'great army' that seized the city in 866.

During the tenth century the Scandinavians who ruled Dublin and those who retained control of other bases on the Irish coast became increasingly integrated in Irish politics, in which they played a minor role as allies of Irish kings in their struggles for supremacy. They could, however, act independently overseas, and were responsible for the sporadic Viking activity that that continued around the Irish Sea.

For most of the tenth century the opportunities for Vikings in western Europe were limited. The Scandinavians who had settled in the British Isles and Normandy did not welcome newcomers, unless they had money. In Iceland the first settlers had taken the best land. The most promising targets for raids were well defended by fortifications or relatively well organized armies. Vikings could still hope to profit from hit-and-run raids, but few of these are reported until the last two decades of the century. Only large-scale invasions offered any hope of significant gains, but for most of the century no large Viking armies operated in western Europe. One reason was probably that potential leaders were then engaged in internal conflicts in Scandinavia.

The East

The decrease in Viking activity in western Europe may also have been partly because there were better opportunities to gather wealth in the east, where there had been great changes since the eighth century. Staraja Ladoga controlled the river Volkhov, which was one of the most important routes between the Baltic and the interior of Russia. That control was made all the more effective by the rapids above the town that could only be navigated safely with the help of pilots supplied by the townspeople. A hoard of Islamic coins deposited there in about 790 suggests that the resources of the region were by then being exported to the Caliphate. For over 200 years exports from Russia to the Muslim world, either directly across the Caspian Sea, or through markets on the rivers Don and Volga, were paid for mainly in silver coins, huge numbers of which have been found in eastern Europe.

Scandinavians also had dealings with the Byzantine empire. In 860 they attacked Constantinople and by the tenth century that city was an important market for Rus traders. The Rus had, however, already reached Constantinople by 839. In that year the Frankish *Annals of St-Bertin* report the arrival at the court of the Frankish emperor of envoys from Theophilus, the Byzantine emperor. They were accompanied by Svear 'who said that they—meaning their whole people—were called Rus [*Rhos*] and had been sent to him by their king whose name was Khan [*Chacan*], for the sake of friendship, so they claimed'. Theophilus asked the Franks to grant them safe con-

Facing: A hoard of over 2.5 kg of gold, deposited at Hon, south-west of Oslo, in the second half of the ninth century, vividly illustrates the range of Viking activity. It contained Arabic, Byzantine, English, and Frankish coins, a magnificent trefoil brooch from Frankia, and large neck-rings that were probably made in Russia.

duct and help to return home because 'fierce and savage tribes' made the route by which they had reached Constantinople dangerous.

It is suggested in Chapter 6 that the Khan who sent these Rus to Constantinople was the ruler of the Khazars, a Turkish people who occupied the valleys of the lower Don and Volga and who, from the seventh to the early tenth centuries, ruled a huge empire between the Caspian and Black seas. However, as earlier Frankish annals used Khan to describe rulers of both Slavs and Huns, it is more likely that the Rus were sent by their own ruler, possibly from the new base that, by the middle of the century, had been established on an island in the Volkhov where the river flows out from Lake Ilmen, about 200 kilometres above Staraja Ladoga. This was the Holmgarð of later Icelandic sagas, but in Slavonic it was later called Gorodishche (Old Town or Fort), in contrast to Novgorod (New Town or Fort), founded about a century later 2 kilometres downstream. Gorodishche, with both Slav and Scandinavian inhabitants, soon became an important centre for the growing trade in Russian produce in both western and eastern markets.

The amount of Islamic silver reaching Russia increased dramatically in the tenth century thanks to the discovery of huge silver deposits in the Hindu Kush. This enabled the Samanid rulers of Transoxania to produce a vast quantity of coins, many of which were used to buy goods in Russia. This commerce, and the silver acquired by it, offered tempting opportunities to Vikings who found western Europe less rewarding after 900 than it had been earlier. Archaeological evidence for the presence of Scandinavians in Russia is much more abundant for the early tenth century than for the ninth, and significant numbers of Scandinavian graves have been found in the cemeteries of bases or trading centres on the main rivers of the forest region, for example at Pskov, Chernigov, on a tributary of the Dnepr, Timerevo, near Iaroslavl on the upper Volga, and Murom, on its tributary, the Oka. The largest of these cemeteries was at Gnezdovo, on the upper Dnepr, near Smolensk, with 3,000 or more graves dating from the late ninth to the early eleventh centuries, some of which certainly house men and women of Scandinavian descent, and which include boat-burials of people of high status.

The most significant extension of Scandinavian activity was to Kiev on the middle Dnepr, which by the end of the ninth century was ruled by a dynasty of Scandinavian descent, whose members at first paid tribute to the Khazars. Although the rulers of Kiev, and many of their retainers, were of Scandinavian descent, by the end of the century they had been slavicized, a change that is clearly reflected in their names. The prince of Kiev from about 913 to 945 was Igor and his wife was called Olga, names derived from the Scandinavian Ingvar and Helga, but their son, prince from 964 to 971,

Facing, above: Remains found at L'Anse aux Meadows on the northern tip of Newfoundland are good evidence that Scandinavians who had settled in Greenland reached North America early in the eleventh century. Traces of several turf-built houses were found, on which these reconstructions are based. L'Anse aux Meadows was apparently a base for the exploration of the region, but was abandoned after a few years.

Facing, below: Jeufosse in the river Seine, about halfway between Paris and Rouen, seen from the south. Vikings wintered on this island in 853 and 856.

15

Part of a tenth-century silver hoard from Gnezdovo, on the upper Dnepr, near Smolensk. It contained a great variety of jewellery, mostly in Scandinavian and Slav styles. The iron sword and bronze oval brooches seen here probably came from graves discovered in 1868 at the same time as the hoard.

was named Svjatoslav. Nevertheless, he and his successors continued to be considered Rus, a term that was by then no longer used specifically for Scandinavians.

Coin hoards in Scandinavia show that many Samanid coins were reaching the Baltic region by the early years of the tenth century. It has generally been supposed that their existence reflects a favourable balance of trade, although it is not clear what was bought with them. The fact that for some twenty years after about 965 very few Islamic coins were imported into Scandinavia, although they continued to reach Russia, if in smaller quantities than before, suggests that in the first half of the century much of the silver reaching Scandinavia was acquired in ways that were not possible later. The most satisfactory explanation is that much of it was gathered as tribute or plunder in eastern Europe by bands of Scandinavians operating independently, and that the decline in silver imports reflects the success of Rus princes in resisting such incursions. If so, that success was partly due to the Scandinavian warriors, called *varjagi* in Slavonic (Varangians in modern

English) who were recruited by Rus princes in the tenth century. According to later Kievan tradition, Svjatoslav's son, Vladimir, prince from 978 to 1015, reduced his retinue of *varjagi* early in his reign by sending many of them to the Byzantine empire. This is confirmed by Byzantine evidence that a large force of warriors, later called *varaggoi*, sent by Vladimir in 988, enabled the emperor to crush a serious rebellion. Thereafter Varangians, Slavs as well as Scandinavians, played an important role in the Byzantine army, and later formed the imperial bodyguard, the Varangian Guard. One of the most famous members of this élite force was Harald Hardrada before he became king of Norway in 1046.

The Conquests of England

Increasingly effective opposition in the east may well have been a factor in the renewal of Viking raids in western Europe towards the end of the tenth century. Another incentive for Scandinavians to seek profitable exile as Vikings was the revival of Danish power under Harald Bluetooth and his son, Sven Forkbeard. It is unlikely to be a coincidence that the two main periods of Viking activity in western Europe began towards the end of the eighth and the tenth centuries, when Danish kings were extending their authority to neighbouring parts of Scandinavia.

Raids on England reported in the 980s may have been the work of Vikings from Ireland, but ten years later fleets from Scandinavia began once again to threaten western Europe. Many places along the coast of the Continent, from the Elbe to northern Spain, were attacked, but the main target was England, which was then a rich kingdom with large and expanding towns and a great quantity of silver in circulation in the form of coins of high quality. Vikings soon discovered that the English under their king Æthelred were able and willing to pay large sums for the sake of peace, however temporary.

The leaders of several, apparently independent, Viking armies that operated in England after 991 are named in the *Anglo-Saxon Chronicle* and in Swedish runic inscriptions, but the most important was Sven Forkbeard. There is little doubt that he led the first major raid on England in 991, and he returned several times to extort ever larger sums of tribute before conquering the kingdom in 1013. He died soon after this triumph and the English recalled Æthelred from exile in Normandy. Sven's son Knut returned in 1015 to regain what his father had won. By the end of the following year, after Æthelred's death, he was recognized as king by the English, The Danish conquest of England did not put an end to the threat of Viking attacks, but the fleet that Knut maintained proved to be an effective deterrent. No attacks are reported after 1018 when the crews of thirty pirate ships were killed by Knut's forces.

Knut died in 1035 and was succeeded in turn by two sons. In 1042, after both were dead, the English chose Æthelred's surviving son, Edward, as king. Nevertheless, several later Danish and Norwegian kings believed that they had a claim to England. Many Scandinavians were willing to encourage such ambitions and hoped at least to have the opportunity to gather some of England's wealth as plunder even if conquest was not possible.

When Edward died childless in January 1066, his successor, Harold Godwinesson, was challenged by the Norwegian king, Harald Hardrada. He invaded England, but was killed in a battle at Stamford Bridge, near York, on 25 September. Three weeks later Harold Godwinesson was himself killed in a battle near Hastings against William, duke of Normandy, who was crowned king of the English on Christmas Day. It was, however, several years before he had firm control of the whole kingdom, and English magnates who were unwilling to accept him were prepared to support the claim of the Danish king, Sven Estridsson. He arrived in the Humber in 1070, but William's vigorous defensive measures were effective and Sven withdrew in the summer, although he and his men were able to keep some of their booty. Five years later a Danish fleet, led by one of Sven's sons, Knut, set sail to support a rebellion against William, but it had been crushed before they arrived. The Danes returned home after plundering York and its neighbourhood. In 1085 Knut, now king of the Danes, planned to conquer England, a threat that William took very seriously, but the assembled fleet never sailed. There were a few later expeditions by Norwegian kings to the Northern and Western Isles, but England never again suffered a large-scale attack by Scandinavians. The Viking Age was over.

2

THE FRANKISH EMPIRE

JANET L. NELSON

Northmen Meet Franks

'In the year of our Lord 845, the vast army of Northmen breached the frontiers of the Christians. This was something that we never heard or read of happening before.' This is how a monk of the monastery of St-Germain-des-Prés described the first Viking attack on the Paris region. The prophet Jeremiah had foretold that divine punishment on the chosen people for their sins would come from the north. In calling the intruders Northmen (the Franks' usual name for those labelled Vikings in modern English), ecclesiastical scholars not only identified their geographical origin but invested them with prophetic significance. Frankish sins did seem to merit punishment in the years after 840 when Louis the Pious's death was followed by civil wars. Violence previously directed outwards to enemies beyond the empire's frontiers now erupted within. The powerful and their followers fought each other; they also oppressed the powerless whom kings were too distracted to protect. Clergy and monks were victims too, as kings needing support granted monasteries to laymen and allowed church land to be distributed to warriors. Churchmen themselves were drawn inexorably into military involvements, sharing the sins of the laity. The monk of St-Germain thus saw God's vengeful hand in the chastisement of Christians by pagans. How else could a learned connoisseur of Christian history explain why the mighty kingdom of the Franks, once so favourable to the church, 'had been laid so low, defiled by the filth of such enemies'?

Such ecclesiastical responses, however understandable, hardly constituted objective analysis and were not wholly shared by lay contemporaries. The appearance of Northmen was not sudden in 845, nor had they always been stigmatized as 'filthy'. Franks who knew their Bible less well than the monk of St-Germain were aware of a prehistory of contacts with the northern world. Thanks to the trade between the Baltic and western Europe that developed in the eighth century, Scandinavians frequented Dorestad and other Frankish trading centres. They left no first-hand written evidence. Yet in 834, a fugitive Frankish bishop going northwards, probably into Frisia, 'found help from certain Northmen who knew the route and the harbours of the sea and the rivers that flow into it'. Knowledge of the Frankish coastline and of Frankish purchasing power underpinned Scandinavians' commercial contacts with the Franks.

Other contacts had resulted from the expansion of Frankish military power. The early medieval equivalent of international relations entailed constant tension as every ruler strove to extend his territory and exploit wealth beyond his frontiers. A successful kingdom surrounded by a ring of satellite states needed to keep well informed about border affairs. 'If a Frank is your friend he's certainly not your neighbour', was an eighth-century proverb among neighbours of the Franks. 'Friends' of the Franks were often to be found on the other side of their neighbours: for instance the Abodrites, a Slav people to the east of the Saxons, were the Franks' traditional allies. By the 770s, with Frisia firmly under Frankish rule, Charlemagne's armies were conquering Saxony. As Saxony's northern neighbours entered the field of Frankish force, Denmark ('Nordmannia') and Danes ('Nordmanni', 'Dani') first appeared in the *Royal Frankish Annals* written at Charlemagne's court: in 777 the defeated Saxon chieftain Widukind fled with his warband to seek refuge with 'Sigfred king of the Danes'. In 782, envoys from Sigfred appeared at Charlemagne's court: Widukind's reappearance soon afterwards in Saxony may have been the result. When Charlemagne renewed the Saxon wars in 798, he sent an envoy to Sigfred, no doubt to forestall any offer of refuge to Saxons. A letter written by the Northumbrian Alcuin (d. 804), Charlemagne's scholar-in-residence, commiserating with the monks of Lindisfarne after Northmen

The Annals of Xanten, compiled in the lower Rhine region, possibly at Ghent, and perhaps by Gerward, former court librarian of Louis the Pious, give contemporary reactions to Viking attacks in the middle decades of the ninth century. Only one manuscript, of the eleventh century, is extant: shown here is the account of the attack on Paris in 845, alleging that 'more than 600 Northmen died in Gaul'.

attacked their monastery in 793, reveals further contacts. Alcuin hints that Charlemagne might secure the return of 'boys' (noble children offered by their parents to the monastery?) carried off as hostages, presumably to Denmark.

The final conquest of Saxony in 804 inevitably attracted Danish interest. The Saxon population of an area beyond the Elbe was removed into Frankia, and the vacated lands given to the Abrodrites. 'At this point', say the *Royal Annals*, 'Godfred king of the Danes came with a fleet and with all the cavalry of his kingdom to Schleswig on the Danish–Saxon border. He promised to come to talks with Charlemagne but his men advised him not to go in person but to send envoys, which he did.... Charlemagne then sent him envoys about returning fugitives.' Godfred's Danes then attacked the Abodrites and forced them to pay tribute. Godfred further upset the carefully constructed Frankish diplomatic system east of the Elbe by allying with the Wilzes, another Slav people who were the Abodrites' neighbours and ancestral enemies. Before returning to Denmark, Godfred destroyed Reric, a trading centre in Abodrite territory, and transferred its traders to Hedeby in Denmark, anticipating 'a healthy income from tolls'. He built a rampart to protect this settlement, 'dividing responsibility for the work among the commanders of his forces'. In 809, as 'many things were reported . . . about the boasting and pride of the Danish king', the Abodrite leader was assassinated by Godfred's men. Charlemagne was already planning an expedition against Godfred in 810 when he learned that 'a fleet of 200 ships from Nordmannia had attacked Frisia and ravaged all the Frisian islands, defeated the Frisians in three engagements and imposed tribute on them, and the Frisians had already paid 100 pounds of silver'. Charlemagne had collected a large army when news came that Godfred had been killed by one of his retinue. His nephew and successor Hemming 'made peace with the emperor'.

Godfred had seriously threatened Frankish control of Saxony and the alliances that underpinned it. He possessed cavalry; he could muster a very large fleet; he understood the value of merchants and tolls and was capable of transplanting an entire trading centre onto his own territory; he could undertake public works, mobilizing teams under his subordinates to carry them out; he could plausibly challenge the Franks to a pitched battle. Denmark was a passable early medieval kingdom. But Hemming did not last long. Other royals 'greedy for power' engaged in succession disputes, promising rewards to warriors. The aristocracy whom Godfred

This Frankish silver vessel was found in Fejø in Jutland, together with five smaller cups. Apparently of eighth-century manufacture, it could have got to Denmark by trading or raiding or diplomatic gift in the eighth or ninth century.

raised up had acquired an appetite for status and wealth. Temporarily disappointed men were driven to recoup their losses elsewhere.

And where better than in the Frankish empire? In the generation or so after Charlemagne's death in 814, the amount of visible, readily available Frankish wealth continued to grow, stimulating commercial exchanges, attracting the precious goods that constituted the wherewithal of imperial glory, lordly gift-giving, ecclesiastical splendour, and aristocratic display. Coinage oiled the wheels; and it was produced in increasing quantities from a growing number of mints, managed by royal agents and centrally directed. Charlemagne's heir Louis the Pious had some success in maintaining peace throughout a Christian empire. When the archbishop of Sens demolished the walls of his city to get stone to rebuild his church, when landlords increasingly demanded payments in cash rather than kind from their peasantry and annual fairs and weekly local markets thus proliferated on

ecclesiastical and secular estates in the provinces of Gaul, when the boats of traders plied the great rivers far into the interior, there was clearly some confidence in public order. In Denmark, though, Louis was no peacemaker, but instead fomented conflict. When the sons of Godfred drove out a rival named Harald, Louis welcomed the exile, and 'sent' him to Saxony. An attempt to restore Harald to the Danish throne failed in 815, when 'a Danish fleet of 200 ships' menaced Saxony, but in 819 Harald became co-ruler alongside two of Godfred's sons. The next year, the *Royal Annals* recorded well-directed attacks of 'pirates from Nordmannia', in 'thirteen ships', on Flanders, the mouth of the Seine, and western Poitou. All these places would have been familiar ports of call to Danish traders in previous decades. Now that familiarity was put to new uses, whether by losers or winners (the *Annals* do not clarify) in preceding dynastic disputes in Denmark. Though thirteen ships was a small flotilla, and there was vigorous resistance in the first two places attacked in 820, the 'pirates' were successful in Aquitaine and 'returned home with much booty'. War-lords began to eclipse merchants in the Franks' view of Northmen.

Louis reacted by sending Archbishop Ebo of Rheims to mount a missionary drive on the Danish frontier, but the Franks were unable to control events in Denmark. In 826 Harald, his wife and son, were received with great ceremony at the palace of Ingelheim near Mainz. The Danish royals were baptized and Louis, with apt symbolism, became Harald's godfather. He also granted Harald the county of Rüstringen in north-east Frisia as a bolt-hole should he be driven out of Denmark again, as indeed happened in 827. Now just one of Godfred's sons, Horik, emerged as 'the king of the Danes', and remained so until his death in 854. An attempt to restore Harald failed in 828, and subsequent Frankish missionary efforts spearheaded by Bishop Anskar of Hamburg suffered a near-fatal setback in 845, when Horik attacked Hamburg and destroyed Anskar's cathedral there. The Danish–Saxon frontier remained fraught, though not until 880 was there another large-scale military engagement, when a Saxon army suffered very heavy losses. Interestingly, Frankish annalists from the 830s to the 880s called these Danes in Denmark 'Northmen', just like their confrères who were busy ravaging Frankia, and making what bid fair to be permanent settlements in Frisia.

Frisia was the Frankish empire's Achilles' heel. Stretching along the North Sea coast from Denmark to the modern Netherlands, Frisia was impossible to police or defend without an effective fleet, which the Franks lacked. Godfred had shown Frisia's vulnerability to attack from the sea. Other Danes would hit the same target, once Louis the Pious's political position had been undermined by his sons' revolts in the early 830s. Though Louis recovered power in February 834, only weeks later 'the Danes attacked Dorestad and destroyed everything, slaughtered some people, took others away captive, and burned the surrounding region', according to the so-called *Annals of St-Bertin*, a continuation of the *Royal Annals*. Again, in 837, 'Danes fell on Frisia, slaughtered many people on Walcheren and plundered even more, levying as much tribute as they wanted, and then fell on Dorestad with the same fury and exacted tribute in the same way'. Despite Louis's defensive efforts, there were new attacks on Frisia in 839. Perhaps generalized anxiety about Scandinavians that year explains Louis's reaction when Svear (*Sueones*) calling themselves *Rhos* were sent by the Byzantine emperor to the Frankish court for onward transit home: Louis feared they might be spies and decided to keep them with him pending further enquiries (see Chapter 1).

One of the pirate chiefs attacking Frisia was none other than Harald. In 833/4 Louis's rebellious eldest son Lothar had apparently encouraged Har-

Facing: Louis the Pious is depicted in richly classicizing martial costume as *miles Christi* ('warrior of Christ') in this manuscript of Hrabanus Maurus' *In Praise of the Holy Cross*, perhaps made at the author's behest for presentation to the emperor. The cross-staff born by Louis symbolizes victory over visible as well as invisible enemies. In the halo encircling the emperor's head are the words: 'You, Christ, crown Louis': an attractive image of the restored Christian Empire.

ald to add to Louis's difficulties by raiding Frisia. Harald may well have continued his activities even after Louis's restoration. In 836 King Horik, killing
two birds with one stone, sent envoys to Louis declaring that he had had
nothing to do with the attacks on Frisia, claiming, moreover, to have captured and killed those responsible (the executed men did not include Harald, however), and asking Louis for a reward. In 838 Horik asked that 'the
Frisians be given over to him'—a request that Louis angrily scorned. All this
throws a lurid light on the vastly increased output of the Dorestad mint in
Louis's last years. Among the chief beneficiaries of all this coin were the
Danish 'pirates' who took their toll on Frisia and its traders. The *Annals of
St-Bertin*, after reporting the destruction of 'everything' in the 834 attack on
Dorestad, noted that Dorestad was 'looted savagely' in 835 and 'devastated'
in 836. This is not mere rhetoric: it was of the essence of a trading centre to
be annually restocked. Dorestad presumably continued to perform its crucial role in supplying Louis's court, though archaeological evidence suggests that a losing battle against silting was already under way. Frisian trade
was beginning to run, literally, through other channels.

Frisia was arterially linked to the political centre of the Frankish empire,
especially after *c*.800 when Aachen became the empire's effective capital.
Two other regions, however, had made exceptional contributions to keeping that empire rich and powerful. One was Neustria, the West Frankish territory between the Loire and the Meuse, the old heart of the Merovingian
realm. Here were concentrated the richest monasteries, the best-exploited
estates, of the Carolingian world. By the early ninth century a lively wine
trade was plied along the Seine; and dotted along the river-bank between
Paris and the sea were a whole series of landing-stages, small ports. From the
early eighth century to the 840s and 850s, Carolingians were willing to shed
blood to control Paris and the Seine basin. A second key region also had a
proud past and a rich heritage: Aquitaine, relatively self-contained in the
ninth century, was politically important because its resources offered
provincial pickings to Frankish kings and aristocrats. Louis the Pious had
reacted quickly when sea-raiders attacked the island monastery of Noirmoutier in 835, authorizing the building of defences. Aquitaine's long
Atlantic coastline made it vulnerable to waterborne attackers; the Loire, the
Charente, the Dordogne, the Garonne also gave ready access to its hinterland.

Franks Divided, Vikings Ascendant

After Louis's death in June 840 his sons, Lothar, Louis the German, and
Charles the Bald, and their nephew Pippin II, immediately began a vicious

succession dispute. In 841 Lothar granted 'the pirate Harald' the island of
Walcheren and the neighbouring regions as a benefice. Partisans of Lothar's
brothers were outraged that a Christian population in Frisia should now be
ruled by a pagan Dane. Lothar's policy was not really so different from his
father's—the client was even the same man!—yet it marked the beginning
of many decades during which Frisia was in the hands of Danish warlords.
As for Aquitaine, its aristocracy's huge casualties in the battle of Fontenoy
(25 June 841) were thought by some contemporaries to have fatally weakened the region's defensive capacity for the coming generation. In short, the
wealth of the Franks had increased, along with Danish familiarity with that
wealth and Danish desire and capacity to lay hands on it, while the Frankish
empire's ability to defend its wealth had diminished. This was a critical con-
juncture.

As in the 830s, Frankish civil war was soon followed by attacks by Northmen on rich and vulnerable places. The brunt fell on the western lands
ruled, or at least claimed, by Charles the Bald after 840. First Rouen and the
nearby monastery of St-Wandrille (841), then the trading centre of Quen-

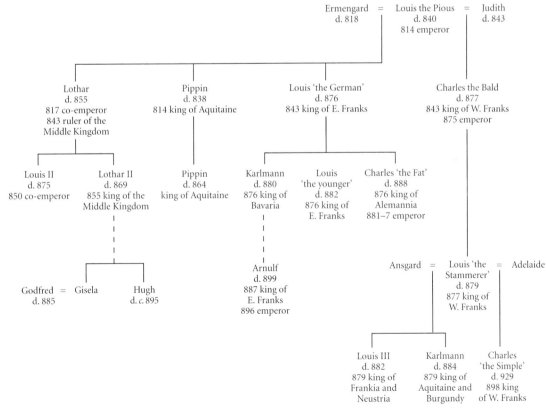

SOME DESCENDANTS OF LOUIS THE PIOUS

25

The Utrecht Psalter was made at Rheims *c.*830 under Archbishop Ebo. The illustrations blend Late Antique models with contemporary Frankish verve and vision. Psalm 44 (Vulgate 43)'s references to God's people being 'scattered among the heathen' and 'counted as sheep to the slaughter' (verses 11, 22) evoked this depiction of an attack on a walled city.

tovic (842), and finally Nantes (843) were ravaged even before the warring Carolingians formally made peace in July 843, agreeing a threefold division of the Frankish empire (excluding Pippin). Frankish writers noted the attackers' interest in ransoms and protection money paid in silver. St-Wandrille paid 6 pounds of silver for the monastery itself to be spared looting, while monks from St-Denis arrived to hand over 26 pounds in ransoms for sixty-eight captives (monks and others, the latter perhaps special friends of St-Denis). Nothing was left unscathed in Quentovic 'except for those buildings which [the Northmen] were paid to spare'. At Nantes the attack fell on St John's Day when the city would have been full of wealthy people: many captives were taken. Further devastation followed in western Aquitaine. An Aquitanian source named these raiders as *Westfaldingi*, that is, from Vestfold, west of Oslo fjord. 'Finally [the Northmen] landed on a certain island [probably Noirmoutier], brought their households over from the mainland, and decided to winter there in something like a permanent settlement' (*Annals of St-Bertin*). Here was a base for further operations along the Atlantic coast. There would be Northmen on the lower Loire until the close of the century and beyond.

The taking of prisoners for ransom remained characteristic of Scandinavian activity in the Frankish empire. Captives included a Breton count, sev-

26

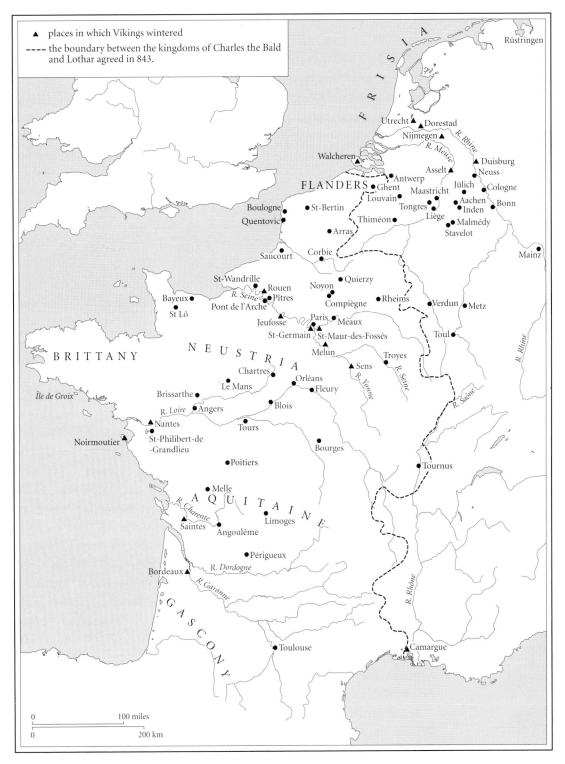

places in which Vikings wintered

---- the boundary between the kingdoms of Charles the Bald
        and Lothar agreed in 843.

FRISIA

Rüstringen

Utrecht ▲ ▲ Dorestad
Nijmegen ▲
R. Rhine
R. Meuse
Walcheren ▲
Antwerp ▲ Asselt ▲ Duisburg
FLANDERS   Ghent   Neuss
Louvain   Maastricht   Jülich   Cologne
Boulogne   St-Bertin   Tongres   Aachen   Bonn
Quentovic   Thiméon   Liège   Inden
Arras   Malmédy
Stavelot
Saucourt   Corbie
Mainz
St-Wandrille
Rouen   Noyon   Quierzy
R. Seine   Pitres
Bayeux   Compiègne   Rheims   Verdun   Metz
Pont de l'Arche   Jeufosse   Paris   Meaux   Toul
St-Lô   St-Germain   St-Maur-des-Fossés
Melun
BRITTANY   NEUSTRIA   Troyes
Chartres   Sens
Île de Groix   Le Mans   Orléans   R. Yonne   R. Seine
Brissarthe   Fleury
R. Loire   Angers   Blois   R. Saône
Nantes
Noirmoutier ▲   St-Philibert-de   Tours
-Grandlieu   Bourges
Poitiers
Tournus
Melle
A Q U I T A I N E
R. Charente   Limoges
Saintes   Angoulême
Périgueux
R. Dordogne
Bordeaux ▲
R. Garonne   R. Rhône
G A S C O N Y
Toulouse   ▲ Camargue

0   100 miles
0   200 km

THE WESTERN PART OF THE FRANKISH EMPIRE IN THE NINTH CENTURY eral West Frankish bishops (one of them, in the 880s, taken 'across the sea'), and, most famously, the abbot of St-Denis whose ransom in 858 amounted to an astonishing 686 pounds of gold and 3,250 pounds of silver. 'In order to pay this, many church treasuries were drained dry at the king's command.' In places that were likely targets, the lesson was soon learned that flight was the better part of valour. A lively literary genre, accordingly, became the *translatio*, the account of a monastic community's transfer of their saint to safety. The monks of St-Philibert on Noirmoutier had practised such an evacuation from their exposed island every year from 819 until 836, when they uprooted themselves to a succession of refuges further in the interior of France, finally settling in 875 at Tournus in Burgundy. St-Philibert's permanent displacement, though well known in modern historiography thanks to a vivid account of the saint's travels by the monk Ermentar, was in fact unusual. Departure was nearly always temporary, and was followed, once the Northmen had gone, by the saint's triumphant return to his home church. The same rivers that gave Northmen easy access provided escape-routes for potential victims. The monk of St-Germain wrote just such an account of 845: Germain's relics and all the monastery's treasure were successfully evacuated up the Seine. The monks returned six weeks later to find the abbey church only superficially damaged and some outbuildings burnt, but (insult upon injury) the Northmen had got into the monastery's cellar and wreaked predictable havoc with the contents. When St-Germain was attacked again at Easter 858, the community, forewarned, had removed saint, treasure, archives, and library to safety during the winter, leaving only a skeleton staff of monks who had time to take refuge in underground tunnels. The frustrated raiders killed a few of the monastery's peasants and set fire to the cellar, but they left so quickly that the monks could emerge from their hiding-places and put out the fire.

In 860 the monastery of St-Bertin was attacked, but the community had had plenty of warning. According to the author of a *translatio* written a generation later and relying on memory and oral testimony, all the monks fled, save four, 'intent on martyrdom, save that God had to some extent decided otherwise'. The slightly ironic tone is continued in the description of how the raiders—they had been 'hoping to capture some monks'—after subjecting three of the four, who were 'older', 'thin and wasted', to 'painful acts of scorn and mockery' (such as pouring liquid into the nostrils of one of them until his belly was distended) tried to take away the fourth, 'more succulent than the rest'. The idea was surely to take this one for ransoming. He was the only one to be killed. He refused to go quietly, throwing himself to the ground and insisting that he wanted to die on the spot, where he might be buried 'in the cemetery of his ancestors, and his name be entered on the commemoration lists of his brother-monks'. Apparently out of sheer vexation at his obduracy, his captors began 'to beat him with their spear-butts', then 'pierced him with spear-points' . . . and the cruel game got out of control.

Scholars have cited this story as evidence for militant Viking paganism, and positive pleasure in martyring Christian monks. What it shows is the Northmen's clear desire to capture rather than to kill. Brutal humour is not militancy. The sequel further reveals a canny respect for Christian sacred power: the leaders of these Northmen, 'gathering enormous quantities of silver, piled it all on the altar of the church where Bertin lay buried and entrusted it to one of the brethren mentioned above so that it could be guarded and not stolen by anyone'. When some errant Vikings were nevertheless caught planning to steal the loot, their leaders hanged them by the monastery gate. 'Thus does the Lord show, even by such brief punishment by the judgement of infidels, what perpetual torment the power of Christianity inflicts on those who commit sacrilege.' Some (if not all) the six recorded killings by Northmen of West Frankish bishops may be such captive-takings gone wrong. Immo of Noyon was killed while being marched away along with 'other noble prisoners' in 859. Even humbler captives might be taken for ransom. In 866, following an agreement between Charles the Bald and Vikings on the Seine, 'any *mancipia* (unfree peasants) who had been carried off by the Northmen and escaped from them after the agreement was made were either to be handed back [by the Franks] or ransomed at a price set by the Northmen'. The labour of those 'handed back' could have been used immediately by these Northmen. Did they also take human cargoes to sell as slaves? Sometimes, perhaps; but the logistics of that trade cannot have made much sense for ninth-century warriors anxious about their own food supplies and travelling in boats of shallow draught. Well documented, by contrast, is the overland slave-trade from the Slav lands to the Muslim world. The plentiful contemporary Frankish sources have rather little to say about a seaborne slave-trade conducted by Vikings operating in the Frankish empire.

Occasionally Vikings ventured far beyond the Carolingian realms. In 844 Galicia and al-Andalus were raided. In 859 'Danish pirates made a long sea-voyage, sailed through the straits between Spain and Africa and then up the Rhône. They ravaged some towns and monasteries and made their base on an island called the Camargue' (*Annals of St-Bertin*). Muslim sources of the tenth century and later record other episodes on this voyage: al-Andalus was raided, and then the little Moroccan state of Nakur, whose royal women were carried off then handed back after ransoms were paid by the amir of Córdoba; 'more than forty ships' were lost on the way home; and, perhaps a

final success on the same expedition, the king of Pamplona was captured
and ransomed in 861 for 60,000 gold pieces. A basis of historical fact thus
underlies the epic Mediterranean journey described in the later medieval
Hiberno-Norse version of *Ragnar's Saga*. All this was spectacular but exceptional. In the Frankish empire, four regions were frequent Viking targets.
These deserve a closer look.

Varieties of Viking Impact

The first was the Seine basin. Attacks in 841 on St-Wandrille, and in 845 on
Paris and St-Germain, were the beginning. One war-band wintered on the
Seine in 852/3; Viking activity was subsequently continuous there from 856
until 866. From bases at Jeufosse and Oissel, sorties were made upriver as far
as Meaux (862), and Melun (866). Thereafter, apart from a fleet which over-
wintered at the river mouth under Frankish surveillance in 876/7, the Seine
and its tributaries were untroubled by further raids until autumn 885. Paris
then endured a year-long siege and there was widespread ravaging of its
hinterland. In 886/7, Vikings moved up into the Seine's tributaries, the
Yonne, whence the surrounding areas of Burgundy were plundered and
Sens besieged for six months, and the Marne, whence there were overland
raids on Troyes and as far inland as Verdun and Toul. In 890 Northmen
came back up the Seine and then the Oise.

In terms of economic geography, the Seine basin constituted the heartland of the West Frankish kingdom of Charles the Bald (840–77). A ninth-
century writer (a local man) called it Charles's 'paradise'. In the first half of
his reign Charles, distracted by rebellions and Carolingian rivalries, offered
only sporadic resistance to Viking attacks. In the early 860s he applied himself seriously to defending his paradise. A co-ordinated strategy included
tribute payments and hire fees for various Viking contingents, and the construction of fortified bridges, notably at Pont-de-l'Arche upstream from
Rouen and just downstream from the palace of Pîtres, in 862–6. Charles
protected the Seine basin effectively after 866, and even before that he prevented any Viking intrusion up the river Oise, on whose banks his two main
palaces, Compiègne and Quierzy, were located. Following the deaths of
Charles's son (879) and his two grandsons (882, 884), leaving only a 5-year-
old heir, Charles the Simple (the contemporary nickname meant straightforward, not stupid), a new phase of Viking attacks on Paris and its environs
opened in 885. The West Frankish Carolingians' run of dynastic bad luck
was one key factor. Another was the military ineptitude of the East Frankish
king Charles the Fat who ruled a reunited Frankish empire from 884 to 887.
After 888 the West Frankish kingdom was disputed between rival kings,

Facing: The interior
of Charlemagne's
church at Aachen
powerfully conveys
his empire's wealth
and romanizing style.
While the elaborate
bronzework is of
Frankish make, the
marble columns were
brought across the
Alps from Ravenna
and Rome. Viking
raiders are said to
have stabled their
horses in this church
in 881.

30

Odo, who as count of Paris had successfully defended the city in 885–6, and Charles the Simple, who eventually succeeded Odo in 898. Local defence was organized. After the 'pirate chief' Rollo and his men ravaged far inland in the upper Seine basin, local nobles combined to defeat them decisively at Chartres in 911. Following the earlier Carolingian tactic of recruiting one Viking warband to ward off others, and imposing the traditional requirement of conversion to Christianity, King Charles straightforwardly set Rollo up at Rouen to defend 'maritime parts'.

This turned out to be the origin of Normandy. By the mid-tenth century, Charles and Rollo were credited with having made a *foedus*, a formal treaty, and Rollo was said to have been appointed count of Rouen, hence 'officially' incorporated into the West Frankish kingdom. Rollo's position turned out to be permanent. The raiders of 911 may never consciously have renounced their roving life, yet raiding perhaps seemed increasingly unprofitable or risky, while the lower Seine area, historically well exploited, recently part-depopulated, now offered settlement on easy terms. In the 920s, West Frankish kingship became markedly weaker, incapable of effective intervention in Rouen or further west. Rollo himself survived until 927: long enough to secure a defined territory and to pass it on to his son; long enough for the new lordship to be shaped to fit the ecclesiastical province of Rouen. Frankish aristocrats accepted the *fait accompli*. The evidence of personal- and place-names, and of language, indicates relatively small numbers of Scandinavian settlers, and rapid and extensive intermarriage with the Franks. By the mid-tenth century, it was hard to find Norse-speakers in Rouen (though there were some in Bayeux for a generation longer). The few Scandinavian words borrowed into French nearly all pertain, appropriately, to ships and shipping. By the eleventh century Norman traditions had to be invented to entertain the ducal court of Rollo's great-grandson. *Nor(d)mannia*—Normandy—was a French principality, and *Nor(d)manni*, descendants of Vikings, were thoroughly assimilated into Frankish culture: quite simply, the duchy's inhabitants. In hosting permanent Scandinavian settlement, Normandy was the exception that proved the rule.

The second major region to feel heavy Scandinavian impact was Aquitaine. Raiders went up the Garonne as far as Toulouse in 844. In 845 Sigwin, *dux* of Gascony, was killed by Northmen while attempting unsuccessfully to prevent the looting of Saintes. Bordeaux fell into Viking hands in 848 after a long siege. Melle, site of a mint and the most important source of silver in the Carolingian empire, was sacked in 848, and Périgueux in 849. Again, conflict between royal rivals, Charles the Bald and his nephew Pippin, increased the region's vulnerability. Yet Pippin's failure to defend Bordeaux triggered widespread Aquitanian defection to Charles in 848.

Facing: The portrait of the evangelist Matthew in the gospel book made for Archbishop Ebo of Rheims shows the remarkable originality and richness of Frankish manuscript illumination in the reign of Louis the Pious.

Two places exemplify Aquitaine's vicissitudes. One was Poitiers, a Carolingian stronghold, its royal palace probably situated in the suburban monastery of St-Hilary. In 855, when Northmen based on the Loire travelled overland on foot to try to attack Poitiers, 'Aquitanians came up to meet them and beat them so soundly that hardly more than 300 of them escaped'. It was a different story in 857: Pippin, still contending with Charles, 'allied himself with Danish pirates and sacked Poitiers'. In 863 Northmen were bought off from sacking the city but burned St-Hilary. In 865, with Charles the Bald busy on the Seine, 'Northmen based on the Loire made their way on foot to Poitiers without meeting any resistance, burned the city and returned to their ships unscathed'. But in 868 'the men of Poitiers offered prayers to God and St-Hilary and boldly attacked the Northmen. They killed some and drove the rest to take flight. They gave a tenth part of all their booty to St-Hilary.' Poitiers survived to become the centre of a tenth-century principality. Angoulême, quite far inland on the Charente, was another major base of Carolingian power in Aquitaine. Unscathed until the 860s, the Angoumois then suffered Viking ravages; but the city itself remained a centre of resistance under its local count. In 868 Charles the Bald ordered Angoulême to be re-fortified. Evidence of Scandinavian activity in the area ceases from this point. Angoulême emerged with its church archives largely intact.

These two examples show the key importance of royal action. While there was no lack of local will to resist the Northmen, the king pegged local resistance to a wider defence strategy. He could also exploit his influence over the church in Aquitaine, making the archbishopric of Bourges the linchpin of royal power there from the later 860s, and transferring the able archbishop of Bordeaux from his more exposed see. The lack of subsequent documentation for Bordeaux before the eleventh century, and breaks in episcopal lists there and in other Aquitanian dioceses over a similar period, have been cited as proof that the Vikings ruined Aquitaine. All such negative evidence in fact proves is that certain churches suffered a significant loss of resources. Ninth-century papal letters blamed Aquitanian aristocrats. Viking attacks no doubt caused some displacement of ecclesiastical centres. If Bordeaux's record is a blank, later ninth-century Limoges produced manuscripts of glorious plainchant.

Brittany and Neustria constituted a third zone of Viking activity. Northmen were active around Nantes from the early 840s, and raiders thereafter penetrated far up the Loire, attacking such rich monasteries as St-Martin, Tours (853), and St-Benoît, Fleury (865). Successive Breton rulers mounted intermittent defence while competing with Frankish magnates for control of western Neustria. In 862 the Breton ruler Salomon (857–74) and Count

Robert of Anjou each hired a flotilla of Scandinavian ships, Robert paying 6,000 pounds of silver for his. In 866 'about 400 Northmen, allied with Bretons, came up from the Loire with horses, and sacked Le Mans'. On their way back to their ships, these Northmen came upon Robert and three other Frankish counts and their men at Brissarthe not far from Angers. The well-informed chronicler Regino described how the Northmen, outnumbered, found a stone church and barricaded themselves in. Robert had siege engines brought up and, flushed with confidence, took off his helmet and mailshirt. The Northmen immediately rushed out to attack, killed Robert, and disappeared back into the church, dragging Robert's body with them, presumably intending to demand ransom. The Franks, now leaderless, withdrew, leaving the Northmen to reach the Loire.

From the later 860s, Salomon co-operated with Charles the Bald, scoring a notable success in 873 against Northmen who had fortified themselves in Angers 'some time before': the Bretons, in Regino's account, had the bright idea of diverting the river Mayenne so leaving the Northmen's ships high and dry. Hincmar of Rheims wrote in the *Annals of St-Bertin*: 'the Northmen agreed to leave Angers and never return. They asked to be allowed to stay until February on an island in the Loire and to hold a market there.' This the king granted on condition that, come February, they would be baptized 'or depart from his realm'. In a contemporary letter, Hincmar vividly evokes the ongoing situation at Nantes: there was 'no necessity' for the Frankish bishop Actard of Nantes to transfer to a 'safer' diocese. Actard's duty was clearly to stay and minister to his flock and attempt to convert 'the many pagans who live in his city'. Hincmar draws parallels with Jerusalem and Córdoba, where Christian bishops still resided: 'How should it be that a churchman, who is not responsible for wife or children, is unable to live in the midst of pagans when the count and his family continue to live there?'

Salomon's successors sometimes used Viking help against their own Breton rivals, but more often fought vigorously against Vikings. Count Alan (888/9–907) effectively defended Brittany. In 890 'Northmen who had come from the Seine' to St Lô on the Breton–Frankish frontier were driven off, but other Vikings remained on the lower Loire, and after Alan's death Breton resistance collapsed. Alan's

This metal object, 60 cm in diameter, excavated among the remains of a ship some 12 m long in the cremation-burial on Île de Groix (dép. Morbihan), has been interpreted as the ship's 'dragon's-tail' stern ornament. The grave-goods suggest that the dead man was a chieftain from Norway, who perhaps had been based in Nantes and involved in renewed Scandinavian attacks on Brittany and Frankia in the decades around 920. These pagan funerary rites contrast starkly with the evidence for settlement and assimilation in Normandy.

son-in-law and grandson fled to England, and for twenty years Vikings
lorded it over Brittany, until the grandson, Alan II (d. 952), returned to drive
them out for good. Interestingly, the most substantial archaeological evidence for Northmen on the Continent, a pagan ship burial, was found in
Brittany at Île de Groix. There is virtually no name-evidence of Scandinavian settlement in Brittany, however, and church organization, though
severely disrupted, was restored under Alan II.

The Meuse–lower Rhine area is the fourth region to merit detailed attention. In 879 Viking activity here increased dramatically following the arrival
from England of what both Anglo-Saxon and continental writers called 'the
great army'. 'Hearing of dispute among the Franks, the Northmen crossed
the sea', wrote the contemporary monastic annalist of St-Vaast. The 'dispute' followed the death of the West Frankish king and the splitting of that
kingdom. Though Northmen were defeated by West Franks at Saucourt
(881), both western kings died soon after. The East Frankish king Louis
'killed over 5,000 Northmen' at Thiméon (880), but his son was killed, and
when Louis himself died of illness in 882 'the army sent against the Northmen broke off the attack'. The bulk of the 'great army' clearly survived these
reverses.

The devastation of the 880s, recorded in some detail in contemporary
annals, was unprecedentedly severe. After fortifying the royal palace of
Nijmegen and wintering there in 880/1, Northmen ravaged Liège, Utrecht,
Tongres, Cologne, Bonn, Zulpich, Jülich, Neuss, the palace of Aachen
(where 'they stabled their horses in the royal chapel') and the monasteries at
Inden, Malmédy, and Stavelot. Under two 'kings', Godfred and Sigfred,
these Northmen then made a strong fortification at Asselt on the Meuse.
The emperor Charles the Fat gathered forces for a siege, then struck a deal
with Godfred, who agreed to become a Christian in return for a large payment and the grant of 'counties' in Frisia. During the negotiations, some
unwary Franks who entered Asselt, 'some to trade, some to look at the fortifications', were 'either killed or kept for later ransoming' (*Annals of
Fulda*). Sigfred and another Viking chief, Gorm, were paid off with some
2,000 pounds of gold and silver. This did not prevent a series of raids far up
the Rhine in 883, when a fresh Viking contingent from Denmark passed
through southern Frisia with Godfred's connivance and fortified themselves at Duisburg to overwinter.

That same year, the emperor's cousin Hugh, illegitimate son of Lothar II,
hoping to make good his claims to the Middle Kingdom, arranged the marriage of his sister Gisela to Godfred. This posed a direct challenge to the
emperor's authority, and stung him into an attempt to retrieve Godfred's
Carolingian bride. In 885 Godfred was tricked into a meeting with the

emperor's men, separated from Gisela (she too was tricked by the arch-bishop of Cologne with talk of arranging peace), and killed. In 887 Charles the Fat was deposed, after repeated defensive failures. 'The Northmen hear-ing of the dissensions among the Franks and the casting-down of their emperor laid waste places which they had previously hardly touched.' But there is more evidence of successful local resistance now. At St-Bertin, the *bellatores* (fighting-men) of the area defended the unarmed. The redivision of the Frankish empire brought the accession of an able East Frankish king, Arnulf, who in 891 defeated what was left of the great army on the river Dyle near the Viking fort at Louvain. Before the end of that year, 'the great army' had left Frankia for England: 'provided [by the Franks?] with ships' at Boulogne, 'they crossed the sea in one journey, horses and all' (*Anglo-Saxon Chronicle*).

Why were the attacks of the 880s so severe? Increased numbers were cru-cial. No less crucial was their concentration on what had been the Middle Kingdom, Lotharingia. Thanks to the vagaries of Carolingian succession, and the denial of his inheritance to Lothar II's illegitimate son Hugh, the Middle Kingdom had disappeared in 870, split between the kings of East and West Frankia. The result was that, though their successors wanted its resources, Lotharingia was not considered heartland by the rulers of either kingdom. The staying of Northmen in royal palaces here (Aachen, Nijmegen) is not paralleled elsewhere. Lotharingia was no one's 'par-adise'—except in the dreams of Hugh, prepared to ally with Godfred in order to recreate his father's kingdom. Perhaps this also explains why Lothar's daughter Gisela was willing to marry and stay with Godfred as her contribution to perpetuating the royal rank of her branch of the Carolin-gian family.

Why Vikings Kept Coming

Generalizing from such diverse material is difficult. The contemporary sources themselves are uneven, some attempting comprehensive coverage, others local and narrowly ecclesiastical in focus. There were marked differ-ences in the scale and tempo, as well as the location, of Scandinavian activ-ity. These differences are masked when modern historians translate the annalistic sources' *Nordmanni* or *Dani* as 'the' Northmen, 'the' Danes, as if these were homogenous entities. Beneath these labels, lesser yet quite dis-tinct groups can be discerned. The *Chronicle of St-Wandrille* covering the years 841–56, introduces a series of 'pirate chiefs' with their flotillas on the Seine: Oscar, Sidroc, Godfred, and Björn. Charles the Bald's preferred tac-tic of recruiting one Viking group to use against others, would have been inconceivable but for the existence of separate war-bands under their own leaders. Equally, Viking groups often owed their success to their willingness to coalesce when necessary.

Both points emerge from the career of Weland, which can be reconstructed from the *Annals of St-Bertin*. Contacted on the Somme by Charles the Bald in 860, Weland agreed to attack a Viking group at Oissel on the Seine in return for '3,000 pounds of silver weighed out under careful inspection'. A delay in payment led to Weland's departure for England, whence he returned to Frankia in 861 'with 200 ships'. Charles now agreed to pay 5,000 pounds of silver and a quantity of livestock and corn. Weland duly besieged the Oissel Vikings, but eventually accepted 6,000 pounds of gold and silver from them instead and agreed to join forces with them. Weland then got Charles to allow his enlarged fleet, 'split up into their brotherhoods [*sodalitates*]', to winter at various ports along the Seine from the coast as far inland as St-Maur-des-Fossés. Early in 862 these Vikings left the Seine: 'when they reached the sea, they split up into several flotillas and sailed off in different directions.'

This silver-gilt strap-end with stylized acanthus decoration is a northern Frankish sword-harness fitting of the mid- to late ninth century. Though its provenance is uncertain, a comparable example was found at Hedeby.

Weland himself did not leave: instead having become Charles's faithful man he accepted Christianity along with his wife, his sons, and some of his men. The following year, two of Weland's men accused him to Charles of bad faith, and in the ensuing single combat 'according to the custom of their people', in Charles's presence, Weland was killed. Close involvement with Vikings was a dangerous game for a Frankish king, but hardly less dangerous for Vikings themselves.

What lured Vikings was movable wealth. Some payments were in the nature of hire fees, like that paid to Weland in 861. Others constituted protection money, as in 857 at Paris when Northmen were paid by three major churches, St-Stephen, St-Denis, and St-Germain, to be spared the destruction visited on the rest. Charles the Fat in 882 paid several thousand pounds of silver and gold to Sigfred and Gorm 'so that they could go on ravaging the [West Frankish] kingdom'. Sometimes payments were organized locally, as by the monasteries on the lower Seine in 841. In 845, and repeatedly thereafter, tributes were organized by the king. In 884 the West Frankish king Carloman agreed to pay the great army 12,000 pounds in gold and silver. When Carloman then died, and the West Frankish magnates tried to re-negotiate, the Northmen replied that 'the sum had been agreed with the king, and whoever succeeded him must give them the money ... if he wished to hold rule in peace and quiet'.

Contributions are often said to have come wholly or largely from church treasuries. In 866 and 877, however, 'the whole West Frankish realm' contributed: an early experiment in full-scale royal taxation, affecting peasant savings, nobles' hoards, church treasuries, and traders' strong-boxes. In 866 the Northmen, perhaps fearing that the coinage was debased, specified payment 'according to their scales'. Data from contemporary annals suggest that some 30,000 pounds of silver, the bulk of it in cash, was paid over: some 7 million pennies. This is credible from the supply side, for the output of Charles the Bald's mints during his reign was arguably over 50 million pennies. What then happened to those coins? Why have so few—fewer than a hundred—turned up in Scandinavian hoards? Much silver certainly found its way to the north-western British Isles (see Chapter 11). Coins reaching Scandinavia were melted down and reused to embellish buildings, ships, and weapons, and for items of personal display and adornment. Sometimes such items themselves constituted Northmen's loot. Frankish swords were much prized, and Charles the Bald in 864 prohibited their sale to Northmen on pain of death. Also prized were what the *Annals of St-Bertin* call 'those little metal things which are fixed on to sword-belts or on to the equipment of men or horses to adorn them'. Use your imagination on a Frankish strap-end from a sword-harness and you catch the glint of stolen finery that was

Tributes and ransoms in the ninth century

Date	Place	Amount
841	St-Wandrille	26 lb. for 68 prisoners, 6 lb. for monastery
845	Paris	7,000 lb. in gold and silver
853	Seine	sum unknown
854	Brittany	church plate worth 60 solidi gold and 7 sol. of silver for Count Pascwethen
858	St-Denis	686 lb. gold and 3,250 lb. silver for Abbot Louis and his brother Gauzlin
860	Somme	3,000 lb. silver *pondere examinato* upped to 5,000 lb. plus large amount of livestock and corn
862	Loire	6,000 lb. silver
864	Lotharingia	sum unknown; 4d. per manse plus flour, livestock, wine, cider
866	Seine	4,000 lb. silver
877	Seine	5,000 lb. silver *ad pensam*
882	Lotharingia	2,412 lb. purest gold and silver
884	West Frankia	12,000 lb. silver and gold

For comparison

Hoards:	Compiègne: 233d. plus halfpennies; Courbanton: 672d.; Bonnevaux: 5,000d.
Prices:	c. 800: top quality horse 30s.; sword 5s.; 12 wheaten loaves 1d.
Peasant dues:	12–20d. per annum
Disposable wealth:	abbot of St-Wandrille leaves 305 lb. silver in cash in his will c.830; 30 lb. gold paid for abbacy of St-Bertin 866

also the currency of power: this was the wherewithal of prestige display, or
of gifts to retain loyal warriors, and keep their wives sweet.

Vikings acquired such loot because of their success as warriors. Yet their
superiority to the Franks was not obvious in every department. In weaponry, Vikings were inferior: their axes were good but they coveted Frankish
swords. Viking lack of body-armour made their men seem 'naked' compared with byrnie (mail)-clad Franks. If Vikings could use siege engines,
Franks did too. Viking mobility had limits. Their ships enabled them to sail
from Scandinavia, to criss-cross the Channel, and to move from one coast
or estuary to another. Yet to move up great rivers into the heart of the
Frankish empire, it was necessary to row, and that was a relatively slow business even with a favourable wind. Monastic communities usually had
plenty of advance warning of Northmen's moves upriver, plenty of time
therefore to transport their relics and treasures to safety. Travelling far on
foot was risky for Vikings, as the would-be attackers of Poitiers found in 857.
Danish cavalry is mentioned as early as 810; but in Frankia the Danes had
first to get their horses.

On some military skills, however, the Vikings scored heavily. First, good
intelligence. Vikings frequently had advance warning of Frankish moves,
and responded quickly to political changes in the Frankish world, notably
in 878 and 887. Second, adaptability. 'Brotherhoods', having combined into
a great army, could redissolve into groups again. Vikings were willing to
leave their ships and to move around overland on horseback or on foot.
They would travel through woods, as it seems the Franks would not, for
instance to raid St-Bertin. Vikings cornered at Brissarthe used a stone
church as an impromptu fort. Outside Paris in 885 Vikings dug concealed
pits to trap unwary Frankish horsemen. Third, good timing. Attacking on
church feast-days meant finding crowds of potential captives ready-
assembled (though the Franks got wise to such tactics). Vikings sometimes
attacked at night. Fourth, naval skills. There is no doubt about the Northmen's superiority to the Franks as sailors. They could manœuvre their long-
boats around islands, and used island forts adroitly. Frankish efforts to beat
them in naval encounters never succeeded. Fifth, and perhaps most important, siting and building good fortifications. Frankish sources repeatedly
attest to these skills, especially in the 880s. It may well be that, unlike Frankish nobles, Northmen did not mind getting their hands dirty and would all
work together at trenching and throwing up ramparts. Certainly they had
strong motivation to work fast, for it was their forts which enabled Northmen to overwinter in hostile territory, to guard their loot, and to compen-
sate for their relatively small numbers.

That last remark is contentious. Estimating the size of Scandinavians'

Viking ships and crews in the ninth century

Date	Location	Recorded number of Viking ships	Number of Vikings (*=killed)
789	Dorset	3	
820	Flemish coast	13	
836	Somerset	35	
840	Hampshire	33	
843	Somerset	35	
	Loire/Nantes	67	
844	Spain	70/80	
845	Elbe/Hamburg	600	
	Frisia		1200*
	Seine		600*
	Seine/Paris	120	
848	Dordogne	9	
851	Thames	350 (9 captured)	
852	Frisia	252	
853	Loire	105	
855	Poitou		300 survivors
861	Seine	200+	
		60+	
862	Loire	12	
865	Charente		400*
	Loire	40	500*
	Seine	50	
	Seine/Chartres		500+
	Seine/Paris		200
866	Loire/Le Mans		c.400
869	Loire		60*
873	Frisia		500* (800*)
874	England	7 (1 captured)	
876	Seine estuary	100	
877	Dorset	120	
878	Devon	23	800 + 40*
880	Thiméon		5,000*
881	Saucourt		9,000*
882	Avaux		1,000*
	Elsloo	200	
	England	4 (2 captured; 2 surrendered)	
885	East Anglia	16 (all captured)	
885/6	Seine/Paris	700	
891	St-Omer		550*
892	Kent	250 (south coast)	
		80 (north coast)	
893	Devon	c.100 + 40	
894	Sussex		many hundreds*
896	Dorset	6 (5 captured)	all but 5*; 120*

Note: The sole Anglo-Saxon source is the *Anglo-Saxon Chronicle*, fullest for the period 874–896, but seldom giving numbers of men. The best-informed Frankish source, the *Annals of St-Bertin*, is particularly detailed on the 860s. The figures for Vikings slain in 845, 880, and 881 come from other arguably less accurate sources.

forces is difficult: numbers of ships are more often available than numbers
of men. Since ships varied greatly in size, anything from ten to sixty might
be an appropriate multiplier. Early medieval writers used numbers impres-
sionistically. Round numbers are ubiquitous, and often frankly incredible,
but more precise figures may have no greater authority. Taken as a whole,
the evidence suggests war-bands in hundreds, with the obvious corollary
that what contemporaries agreed was 'a great army' numbered thousands.
Until the 880s, the Franks were confronting relatively small forces; but their
own forces were not large. Even Charlemagne's armies have been soberly
estimated as comprising only around 5,000 men.

This chapter began with the Northmen's attack on Paris in 845, when the
monk of St-Germain depicts Ragnar arriving out of the blue. Context and
motive can be explored further. A contemporary saint's life reveals, inci-
dentally, that Ragnar had been in Frankia before: he had been given land
near Turholt in Frisia by Charles the Bald, perhaps in 841, and had then lost
both the land and the king's favour. In this light Ragnar's raid looks like
revenge, and the 7,000 pounds of gold and silver bullion he received from
the king something like compensation. But Ragnar also had another audience in mind. The monk describes how Ragnar, after collecting his payment, returned to Denmark:

Ragnar presented himself at the court of King Horik, and displayed to the king,
the great men and visiting notables the gold and silver which he had brought
back from Frankia. He told them he had gained control of Paris, got into the abbey
of St-Germain, and subdued the whole kingdom of King Charles. He laid before
them part of a beam from the church, and a bolt from the gate of Paris. Then he
boasted of the incredible riches of Frankia, and how easy it had been to acquire
them. Never had he seen, he said, lands so fertile and so rich, nor ever a people so
cowardly.

How could the author of the *translatio* of St-Germain possibly have
known of events at the court of Horik? The story has a pedigree. It just happened that King Louis the German had sent an embassy to Horik's court,
led by Count Cobbo who had subsequently visited St-Germain on pilgrimage. Cobbo was evidently the monk's informant. Further details lend cred-
ibility to the story. Independent evidence dates the death of Ragnar to 845.
The *translatio* reports the fact, with its own explanation: 'Ragnar said that
the only person in Frankia with any courage was an old man called Germain. At that very moment, he fell to the ground like someone struck down.
His body swelled up more and more until he burst, and so died.' The *translatio* adds chillingly that Horik, terrified by what the Franks' gods could do
to his people, ordered all those who had gone with Ragnar to be killed.

Other evidence confirms Horik's anxiety to make his peace with the Franks by punishing raiders.

Ragnar's desire to impress, and capacity to recruit, men at the Danish court threatened King Horik. This orientation of Viking warlords' activities homewards towards *Nordmannia* is especially clear in the middle decades of the ninth century. The organizational and military strength of the Danish kingdom made it a magnet, a prize worth fighting for. In 854 warlords who had ravaged the borders of Frankia for the preceding twenty years returned to Denmark when civil war broke out there. Others returned in 855 'in the hope of gaining royal power'. Even later in the ninth century, other successful Northmen planned to live as great lords in Denmark on the proceeds of their activities in the Frankish empire. In 882, Sigfred and Gorm 'sent ships loaded with treasure and captives' taken in Frankia 'back to their country'. The drive to power and status back home went hand in hand with the quest for Frankish loot. The more warlords visibly profited from raiding, the greater the number of their imitators.

In some cases Northmen clearly sought settlement, and in territory granted them 'officially' by Frankish rulers. Frisia, especially, had attractions for Scandinavian warlords, while the Franks could regard it, perhaps, as something less than an integral part of the Frankish empire. Harald was granted Rüstringen as early as 826, Walcheren in 841. His career on the northern frontier ended in 852 when his Frankish patrons had him killed 'as a potential traitor'. After Rorik, Harald's brother, seized Dorestad in 850, the emperor Lothar decided to 'grant' him 'rule' in southern Frisia 'on condition that he would faithfully handle the taxes and other matters pertaining to the royal fisc, and would resist the piratical attacks of the Danes'. Rorik became a well-established part of the political scene. When Charles the Bald's daughter Judith and Count Baldwin of Flanders eloped in 861, they asked Rorik for a safe haven, while Archbishop Hincmar wrote to Rorik on the king's behalf urging him not to receive the reckless pair.

The Loire valley has been seen as an area where ninth-century Northmen all but succeeded in settling. For a century from the late 830s, various warbands were certainly active in the area. By 868 a kind of symbiosis with the local population had developed. Frankish forces captured 'a former monk who had abandoned Christendom and gone to live with the Northmen'. Salomon made a peace with Northmen in the Angers area for 500 cows so that he and his Bretons could harvest wine, and when Charles the Bald ordered the fortification of Tours and Le Mans, and the Northmen heard about this, 'they demanded a great sum of silver and quantities of corn, wine and livestock from the local inhabitants as the price of peace with them'. But this sort of thing does not differ substantially from what is reported on the

Seine in the mid-860s, when inhabitants of the area around Pîtres were forbidden, on pain of death, to sell weapons and horses to Northmen, and
when Northmen 'sent 200 of their number to Paris to get wine', or on the
Rhine in 864 when Northmen led by Rodulf were paid 'a large quantity of
flour and livestock, wine and cider' by Lothar II. Northmen needed food
and drink, and clearly did not produce those items for themselves. True, the
Vikings remained on the Loire for longer than they did on either the Seine
or the Rhine. One warlord, Hasting, seems to have operated on the Loire in
the late 860s and was still there in 882, though he may not have been there
continuously. More significantly, there is no case of a formal grant of land
or lordship on the Frisian model. Further, those Vikings who evidently
remained for prolonged periods seem to have resided in towns, for example
Nantes and Angers, and probably lived by trading. Finally, there is no
archaeological or name-evidence to suggest Scandinavian landlordship,
still less that Scandinavians worked the land, such as survives later from
Normandy. Settlement in England is well documented from the 870s
onwards. With the exception of Frisia, Viking activities in the Frankish
empire before 911 seem to have been different. This surely indicates the
strength and (for the most part) success of Frankish resistance to the idea,
and hence the fact, of Viking settlement on their territory.

Implications of Contact

Some modern scholars suggest that a phase of Frankish fatalistic passivity
was succeeded by a second active phase of successful resistance. Yet from
the earliest accounts of Viking raids there is evidence for resistance *alongside* reports of payments: the different responses could be simultaneous,
and the resisters were various. In the 830s nobles defended Aquitaine; in 841
a royal vassal tried to defend the lower Seine; 'local people' resisted in Flanders in 864; and royally appointed frontier commanders and counts were
prominent in every decade. Some of the bishops killed by Vikings may well
have died leading resistance, for these bishops were warlords too. In 854
Danes on the Loire gave up plans to attack Orleans and its hinterland when
the bishops of Orleans and Chartres 'got ready ships and warriors to resist
them'. In the East Frankish kingdom, two bishops were among the slain
when Northmen defeated a Saxon force in 880. In the Middle Kingdom, the
exploits of the bishop of Liège were hailed by the Irish poet Sedulius:
'Doesn't the hostile Northman tremble to see your battalions clad in white?
He flees back to his ships . . . wishes he'd never thought of attacking the land
of the Franks!' In the Rhineland in 882, a consortium of lay and ecclesiastical magnates, including Bishop Wala of Metz, was formed to fight off the

Northmen. Wala was slain and his following put to flight. Even monastic leaders sometimes took a muscular view of their responsibilities. The young abbot of Corbie had 'a worrying habit', according to his friend the elderly abbot Lupus of Ferrières, 'of pitching yourself unarmed and regardless into the midst of battle, your youthful energy led on by your lust for winning. Confine yourself, I beg you, to deploying your troops, and leave it to the military men to do the fighting with their weapons!' Peasants resisted too, on their own initiative. In 882 the local tenantry of the monastery of Prüm attempted an unsuccessful defence: 'it was not so much that they were unarmed as that they lacked discipline . . . they were slaughtered not like men but like cattle'. Colder still is another contemporary's epitaph on Neustrian peasants who banded together with oaths to resist Northmen in 859: 'because they had made their sworn band heedlessly they were easily

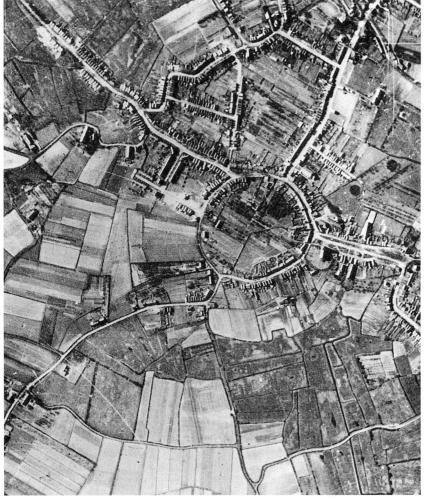

The ninth-century fort at Oost Souburg on the island of Walcheren (on the north side of the Scheldt estuary in modern Belgium) was excavated in the 1970s. It may have been built on the orders of Louis the Pious in the 830s. Alternatively, it may be one of the 'recently built *castella*' of Count Baldwin II of Flanders, mentioned by a writer at the monastery of St-Bertin *c*.890.

slain by our more powerful men.' The Frankish élite might choose to defend their own social position in preference to their own people. No wonder peasants thought the safest defence against the Vikings was flight.

Resistance itself was not a secondary phase. Systematic public defences did take time to organize, however. Charles the Bald's fortified bridges and towns, monasteries and palaces in West Frankia are the best-known examples. But Charles may have belittled parallel efforts of the aristocracy, whose 'unauthorized *castella*' he dismissed as merely a means of oppressing the natives. *Castella* could also be a means of defending them, and those built in the early 860s may well have fulfilled both functions. In the 890s the St-Bertin author noted 'recently built *castella*' in Flanders and south Frisia, apparently planned by Count Baldwin of Flanders. St-Bertin itself was fortified with an imposing tower, as was the monastery of St-Vaast, Arras, on the abbot's initiative. The surviving tenth-century tower of St-Germain in Paris gives an impression of the new defensive capacity. The age of dismantling fortifications was over, and would not return until the seventeenth century. Public power in the interim would depend on the ability to defend and counter-attack.

To assess the Vikings' impact on the Frankish economy we need to stand back from the detail and take a longer-term view. Until the 1960s, eleventh- and twelfth-century monastic scare stories of Viking devastation tended to be taken at face value. They have since undergone historical deconstruction. Where the area covered by modern Belgium is concerned, the scare stories have proven unreliable; they are probably equally false for Aquitaine. Some historians have argued that Viking activities provided a positive stimulus to the Frankish economy. This may go too far in minimizing the Vikings' short-term destructiveness. It may also exaggerate their impact. While it seems likely that demands (with menaces) for payment promoted the release of hoarded wealth in the short-to-medium term, it remains unclear how far the effects permeated what was still only a very partially monetized economy. The fact that the currency of tenth-century Flanders was crude and small-scale neither proves nor disproves a link between Viking activity and commerce. Trade was not necessarily conducted with cash. Northmen probably used coin while in Frankia, where they engaged in local markets to demand Frankish swords, horses, and processed foodstuffs like cider and wine. Northmen in towns like Nantes and Angers must have created a similar demand. Northmen ousted from Angers in 873 sought permission to set up a market, and when the Asselt Northmen opened their gates Franks were eager to go in to trade. Along the coasts and the great rivers in the later ninth and early tenth centuries were genuinely urban developments. On the Rhine, Cologne and Mainz were re-fortified in the 880s. Huy, Dinant,

Facing: The rich, royally endowed monastery of St-Germain-des-Prés on the west bank of the Seine at Paris endured Viking attacks in the ninth century, but remained a major religious centre. Its tenth-century fortified tower still stands, a monument to Carolingian churches' capacity for adaptation and survival.

44

Namur, and Maastricht, all on the Meuse, are first attested as 'ports' and 'burgs' in this period, while in Flanders, Ghent, Bruges, and Antwerp took a new lease of commercial life in the decades around 900. Quentovic was still in the mid-ninth century a place to which monks fled (from St-Wandrille), and it remained the site of a productive mint. On the Seine, Rouen's commercial importance revived and grew from the early tenth century, as, on the Loire and its tributaries, did Nantes, Angers, Tours, and Orleans. All this can hardly have been unconnected with the Northmen's active presence in these regions: but the connection may have been shared exposure to deeper impulses of economic growth.

In some parts of the countryside there was a redistribution of the working population. Peasant flight from the lower Seine valley, for instance, seems to have increased the availability of labour in Champagne, and so encouraged waged work in the vineyards. In order to induce peasant migrants to return, Charles the Bald decreed in 864 that they should be permitted to keep wages earned as wage-labourers. This tilted landlord–peasant relations just slightly in the peasants' favour. Many probably did not return; and the prosperity of tenth-century Burgundy has been attributed in part to their settlement there. The short-term effects of the Vikings' presence could clearly be extremely painful for those who fled, whether nobility, monks, or peasants. People would take with them what movables or livestock they could. Yet there is little evidence for the destruction of buildings themselves, as distinct from their fittings. From churches, books and archives, along with treasures and holy bones, were taken to safety, and returned—which is why with few exceptions the great Carolingian cultural

The pair of oval brooches, each 11 cm x 6.9 cm and weighing 74 grams, found in a grave at Pitres (dép. Eure), may originally have been gilded. Some twenty other examples with this form of stylized animal ornament have been found, all in Scandinavia. They were used to attach the shoulder straps of a woman's sleeveless garment.

centres continued to function, as did St-Germain in Paris, or preserved their manuscripts to be transferred later to new centres, as those of St-Martin in Tours were to Cluny in the tenth century. Given the yearly cycle of agrarian production, and the known timing of raids, it seems unlikely that the Vikings destroyed many harvests. Northmen are never said, as eighth-century Franks were, to have destroyed the vineyards of Aquitaine. Predatory consumers were not imperialists.

For the most part, the Northmen do not seem to have been very different from the Franks: certainly, the Carolingian evidence hardly shows them more savage. The St-Germain monk mentions 111 captives hanged by Northmen on the other side of the Seine from St-Denis, in full view of Charles the Bald and his men; but, to put that in perspective, Charlemagne had had 4,500 Saxon captives executed at Verden in 782. Northmen took and gave hostages, made treaties, and swore oaths 'according to their fashion'. The Franks could make deals with them. Northmen were pagan, but there is no evidence that the Franks considered them militantly so, or attributed their activities to religious fervour. On the contrary, monastic authors sometimes depicted Northmen showing reverence for the saints. Paganism, unlike Christianity, was not intolerant, but eclectic. Harald, Weland, Godfred, and Rollo were willing converts. Normandy, the one case of settlement, is also a case-study in rapid acculturation.

Women provide one test of cultural compatibility. Was the occupant of an allegedly 'Viking' grave found near Pîtres a Viking, or a Frank? All we can say is that she wore jewellery of 'Viking' style. She may have been a Dane (Weland's wife?) who had embraced Christianity. She may have been a Frank who had embraced a Dane. Some Northmen did bring their wives with them (and later saga evidence indicates great respect for deep-minded wives), but others may well have sought Frankish brides, as they certainly did in tenth-century Normandy. Among all the *Annals of St-Bertin*'s references to Viking plunder and pillage, there is no mention of rape, and this is significant, given that these *Annals* twice mention episodes when the followers of Christian Carolingian kings committed rape, in one case, the rape of nuns. It hardly follows that Northmen never raped: it does seem that they were not notorious rapists. Two high-born Frankish women, one of them a queen, considered finding refuge with Viking protectors against Frankish husbands they believed would kill them. The princess Judith, fleeing her father's anger, apparently did find refuge with the Northman Rorik. Gisela, Godfred's Frankish bride, was tricked by talk of 'peace' into unwitting connivance at her husband's murder. Her tragedy hints, though, at more cheerful possibilities which were to be realized in Normandy and elsewhere: of women as peace-weavers and Vikings settling for coexistence.

3

THE VIKINGS IN ENGLAND, c.790–1016

SIMON KEYNES

The rounded head of a ninth-century gravestone from Lindisfarne in Northumbria depicts on one side a procession of seven warriors brandishing axes or swords with apparently hostile intent, and on the other a cross placed between the sun and the moon, towering over two human figures who mourn or bow down before it. The stone was doubtless intended to signify the coming of the Day of Judgement, when nation would rise against nation, when the sun and the moon would be darkened by the appearance of the cross in Heaven, and when all mankind would mourn (Matt. 24: 7, 29–30). It would be mistaken, therefore, to remove the stone from its eschatological context and to identify the warriors as a horde of Vikings in the act of sacking Lindisfarne, but the stone may serve none the less to illustrate a basic truth about contemporary perceptions of the Viking raids on England. The Northumbrian scholar Alcuin was clearly outraged by the desecration of the holy shrine of St Cuthbert by pagans from across the sea, treating it as a manifestation of divine punishment for the sins and immoderate customs of all the people of Britain, and using it as a pretext for urging them to mend their errant ways. A hundred years later, in the late ninth century, King Alfred the Great responded to the Vikings in much the same way, regarding them as instruments of divine wrath and seeking to meet the threat not only by improving defensive systems on the ground but also by restoring the quality of Christian faith and learning among his people. Wulfstan II, archbishop of York, maintained the tradition in the early eleventh century, berating congregations from the pulpit with a diatribe against the sins, crimes, and unjust acts which had arisen among the Eng-

lish, for which the people had incurred divine displeasure and brought
upon themselves renewed punishment in the form of Viking invasions of
unprecedented ferocity. Conceptions of divine judgement were thus insep-
arable in the Anglo-Saxon mentality from experience of Viking invasions;
accordingly, there need be little doubt that the sculptor of the Lindisfarne
stone would have depicted his theme with a Viking raid at the back of his
mind.

Modern perceptions of the Vikings are informed by a greater knowledge
of the Scandinavian peoples in their respective homelands, and by a deeper
understanding of the Vikings who were active in England. If there was once
a tendency to romanticize the exploits of the Vikings overseas, it is now
more fashionable to regard them as the maligned and misunderstood victims of a Christian press, or as creatures of their time whose behaviour was
merely an extension of normal Dark Age activity, or indeed as cultivated
men with elevated thoughts and honourable intentions. We adopt a more
sceptical attitude towards the written sources, accommodate the evidence
of place-names, and listen to the voices behind skaldic verse and runic inscriptions. We admire the ships, the sculpture, and the metalwork, observe
the forms of human activity conducted on farms and in towns, and draw
appropriate conclusions from an array of causeways, earthworks, and forti-

Commemorative
stone at Lindisfarne
(28.5 cm high).
Viking raids were
perceived by affected
parties, from the late
eighth century
onwards, as a warn-
ing (one of the signs
of the impending
Day of Judgement)
or as punishment (an
expression of divine
wrath visited upon
the English for their
manifold sins). The
images on this stone
include a scene which
may have been
suggested by a Viking
raid on Lindisfarne;
but the scene itself
was probably intend-
ed to symbolize
Doomsday.

fied camps. Viking forces active in the late ninth century are compared in their composition and organization with the forces active in the late tenth and early eleventh centuries, and important distinctions are made between them. We debate the impact of the Vikings on the institutions of the English church, and on religious life and culture, and we seek to understand how they might have contributed to the emergence of a sense of common identity among the English people. We may be hugely impressed, or relatively unimpressed, by the nature and extent of Scandinavian influence in eastern and northern England, and we explain what we see in terms of a large-scale peasant migration from Scandinavia, or in terms of members of a conquering army who had been able to establish themselves in dominant positions. We consider how the areas of Scandinavian settlement were brought under royal control in the tenth century, and whether the 'Danes' of the Danelaw retained a sense of identity which under certain circumstances might threaten the integrity of a notionally unified kingdom. We assess the accounts of the Danish conquest of England in the early eleventh century, and judge whether it proceeded from the failure of one and all to respond adequately to a challenge, or whether it should be understood in some other way. These are the kinds of issue which must now be raised in any discussion of Scandinavian activity in England from c.790 to 1016: Alcuin's instruments of divine punishment have become the modern historian's agents of social and political change.

Viking Raids in the Eighth and Ninth Centuries

Some time during the reign of Beorhtric, king of Wessex (786–802), three ships of 'Northmen' arrived at Portland on the Dorset coast. The local reeve (whose name was Beaduheard) appears to have assumed that the visitors had come for purposes of trade, and directed them to a nearby royal estate (probably at Dorchester); but the supposed traders turned out to be raiders, and promptly killed the reeve with all of his men. The significance of the event was not lost on the West Saxon chronicler, writing towards the end of the ninth century, who could see with the advantage of hindsight that 'Those were the first ships of Danish men which came to the land of the English.' In northern England, the Viking Age was recorded in ways which seem to put greater emphasis on churches and holy shrines as the principal targets, though of course one need not imagine that the raiders themselves were quite so selective. On 8 June 793, according to the northern recension of the *Anglo-Saxon Chronicle*, 'the ravages of heathen men miserably destroyed God's church on Lindisfarne, with plunder and slaughter', and in the following year 'the heathens ravaged in Northumbria, and plundered Ecgfrith's monastery at the mouth of the Don', apparently with reference to Jarrow in Northumberland or Hatfield, near Doncaster, in Yorkshire. Alcuin was clearly shocked by what he perceived as an onslaught of pagans against a Christian people, and gave vent to all the patriotic zeal of an expatriate observer in calling his countrymen to order; indeed, it is through his words of power that one can begin to sense the horror which must have been felt by those who found themselves confronted by a hostile force which had appeared from unknown lands beyond the sea, which had no apparent purpose other than to plunder, and which then disappeared whence it came.

It is unfortunate that so little is known of the raiders themselves, of the factors which may or may not have prompted them to leave their homelands, and of the manner in which they conducted their nefarious activities overseas. Some of the earliest raids, in the late eighth century, appear to have originated in Norway, but there is no reason to doubt that the 'Danes' were also involved from the outset. One can but assume, therefore, that from *c.*790 onwards parties of raiders made their separate ways in small groups from Scandinavia down the North Sea littoral, following their respective leaders in search of adventure, fame, and fortune; and that while some crossed over to England, others infested the river systems of continental Europe, or made their way round south-western England into the Irish Sea. It may have been the case that some of the raiders returned home to Scandinavia at the end of the campaigning season, but it is likely that, as time passed, increasing numbers were prepared to stay away for more extended periods, perhaps even for good. There would also have been a tendency for the small groups of raiders to coalesce from time to time into a much larger force, whether for security of numbers or to attack a particular target; and some leaders may have been more successful than others in preventing such large forces from dispersing into their component parts once their objectives had been either frustrated or achieved. The question always arises whether a particular raid recorded in the *Anglo-Saxon Chronicle* originated in Scandinavia, or whether it originated among the Vikings established on the Continent or among those based in Ireland; for one has to bear in mind that the activities of the Vikings in Ireland, in England, and on the Continent, were complementary aspects of a single phenomenon, and that any one raid might have been part of a larger pattern. It follows that we cannot begin to understand the course and the conduct of the raids in England without continual reference to continental and Irish annals (notably the so-called *Annals of St-Bertin*, the *Annals of St-Vaast*, and the *Annals of Ulster*), and one finds that these sets of annals, in their different ways, convey an impression of the impact of the raids, and of the measures taken against them, which by analogy can prove most instructive.

The earliest raids on England, in the late eighth and first half of the ninth centuries, may have been too sporadic to have been seen by contemporaries as a sustained threat to their well-being; indeed, to judge from the silence of the chroniclers, the English appear to have been largely untroubled by the Vikings during the first quarter of the ninth century. It is clear, however, that the raids along the North Sea littoral became more frequent in the 830s, and more penetrating and sustained thereafter; and it may be significant that these developments coincided with increasing degrees of social and political unrest in the affected countries. The activities of the 'Danes' in different parts of southern England may be said to have resumed in 835, when 'heathen men' ravaged Sheppey. Ecgberht, king of the West Saxons, fought against a force of thirty-five ships at Carhampton (on the north coast of Somerset) in 836, and against a combined force of Vikings and Cornish at Hingston Down (Cornwall) in 838; perhaps more significantly, the important West Saxon administrative and trading centre at Southampton (*Hamtun/Hamwic*) was attacked on at least one occasion in the early 840s. However, it may not have been until 850, or thereabouts, that the raids were sustained with a degree of intensity sufficient to make a deep impression on the English people as a whole. The chronicler's remarks to the effect that 'heathen men' wintered on Thanet for the first time in 850/1, and on Sheppey for the first time in 854/5, suggest that these events were considered in retrospect to have marked the next stage in the escalation of Viking activity in England. A Viking force of perhaps unprecedented size, said to have numbered 350 ships, stormed Canterbury and London in 851, putting King Berhtwulf and the Mercian army to flight. Soon afterwards, the same force of Vikings was met by the West Saxons at *Aclea* (apparently in Surrey); and if the West Saxon chronicler exposes his natural bias in recording that King Æthelwulf and his army 'there inflicted the greatest slaughter on a heathen army that we ever heard of until this present day', a less obviously partisan chronicler on the Continent noted in what would appear to have been the same connection that some Northmen who attacked Britain 'were beaten by the English with the aid of our Lord Jesus Christ'. A naval force which had materialized on the Somme in 859 crossed the Channel in 860 and stormed Winchester, but was then put to flight; interestingly, the same continental chronicler took note of the event, adding in this instance that the force returned to the Continent in 861. It is important, therefore, to bear in mind that the intensification of Viking activity in southern England in the 850s might have reflected a greater tendency of combined forces to operate on both sides of the English Channel as much as it must have reflected an increase in the traffic coming to England direct from Scandinavia.

The raids on England escalated further in 865/6, when 'a great heathen

Facing: Map showing the major kingdoms which survived into the ninth century, with a selection of the places mentioned in the text

boundary between England and the 'Danelaw'
as defined in the treaty between Alfred and
Guthrum (*c.* 880)

0		20		40		60 miles

0	20	40	60	80	100 km

- Lindisfarne

R. Tyne
- Jarrow

R. Tees

NORTHUMBRIA

- Whitby

- Brompton
- Middleton

- York

R. Humber

- Cuerdale Hall

- Torksey
- Lincoln

Anglesey
- Penmon

GWYNEDD

MERCIA

R. Trent

- Derby
- Nottingham
- Repton
- Leicester
- Stamford
- Tamworth

- Wrekin

MIDDLE
ANGLIA

- Ely

EAST
ANGLIA

R. Severn

- Northampton

R. Ouse

- Cambridge

- Ipswich

- St David's

DYFED

- Gloucester

- Oxford
- Wallingford

- London

- Maldon

- Wantage

R. Thames

- Sheppey
- Thanet

- Bath

- Reading

- Rochester
- Sandwich

- Enham

- Canterbury

KENT

- Carhampton
- Athelney

- Winchester

WESSEX

- Hamwic

- Dorchester

- Portland

ANGLO-SAXON ENGLAND

army' took up winter quarters in East Anglia. It would be reasonable to assume that the army came to England from Scandinavia, though it is equally possible that it was in fact a composite force, with some elements drawn from among the Vikings active on the Continent and in Ireland. We are not given any indication of its size (beyond the fact that it was considered to be 'great'), and it is only on the strength of its coherence over several years, and on the strength of its recorded achievements, that we might be tempted to suppose that it comprised perhaps two or three thousand men. The leaders appear to have included Ivar the Boneless and his brother Half-dan, sons of the legendary Ragnar Lothbrok, as well as another 'king' called *Bagsecg*, and several 'earls'; and if it is assumed that Ivar is the Ímar who had been active in Ireland in the late 850s and early 860s, it would appear that he had been able to meet up with his brother and assume joint leadership of the army some time after its arrival in England. The annals in the *Anglo-Saxon Chronicle* afford a good sense of the course of the army's campaign in the late 860s, as it moved from East Anglia into Northumbria in 866, from Northumbria into Mercia in 867, and back north into Northumbria in 868, before returning via Mercia to East Anglia in 869. At this early stage the Vikings seem to have been content to allow the East Angles, the Northumbrians, and the Mercians to 'make peace' with them (in the parlance of the chronicler), meaning no doubt that the Vikings took money and supplies from the English in return for an undertaking not to outstay their welcome; there is no mistaking, however, that the Northumbrians in particular suffered mightily at this time, symbolized not least by the death of King Ælla at York in the spring of 867. Soon after their return to East Anglia, in 869, the Vikings killed Edmund, king of the East Angles, and 'conquered' the kingdom, with the implication that they now displaced the existing form of government and established themselves in direct control of the land (perhaps delegating some power to the native kings Æthelred and Oswald, who are known only from their coins). Ivar, if assumed to be Ímar, would appear to have returned to Northumbria at about this time, and was then active on both sides of the Irish Sea from 870 until his death in 873.

It was from their position of strength in East Anglia that the Vikings launched their first offensive against Wessex in the opening weeks of 871. They were soon joined at Reading by a 'great summer army', and after much fighting the West Saxons themselves were induced to 'make peace'. The Vikings were active for some time thereafter in different parts of the extended kingdom of Mercia, wintering successively at London (871/2), Torksey (872/3), and Repton (873/4). Excavations at Repton have shown how the army took up its defensive position in an encampment beside the River Trent, using the ancient church as a form of gateway, and have revealed at

The disarticulated remains of at least 250 people (mainly men in their prime, but also including some women), from the charnel excavated at Repton, Derbyshire, in 1980–6. The 'great army' is known to have wintered at Repton in 873–4; and it has been suggested that the charnel represents the mass burial of members of the army who died at this time from an epidemic of some kind.

the same time that as many as 250 of their own number were buried in the winter of 873/4, in close association with a person of high rank who is presumed to have been one of their leaders. It was from their base at Repton, in 874, that the Vikings drove King Burgred into exile, 'conquered' the kingdom of Mercia, establishing a certain Ceolwulf as king in Burgred's place, and then decided to split into two bands. Halfdan took what may have been the remnants of the 'great army' (865) up into Northumbria, making a base for the next winter (874/5) by the River Tyne. The army duly 'conquered the land', and ravaged further afield; but a year or so later, in 876, Halfdan and his men 'shared out the land of the Northumbrians, and they proceeded to plough and to support themselves', representing the establishment of the Scandinavian settlements in the northern part of the area which came to be known as the Danelaw. Three other kings, named as Guthrum, Oscetel, and Anwend, left Repton in 874 'with a great force', which may have been more or less recognizable as the 'great summer army' of 871, and went thence to Cambridge.

The Viking army which established its base at Cambridge in the winter of

874/5 remained there for the greater part of the next year; but in late 875 it mounted a second invasion of Wessex, maintaining the pressure for two years before taking up its winter quarters for 877/8 at Gloucester, a place by then beginning to emerge as an important political centre in the south-western part of the Mercian kingdom. In 877 the Viking army in Mercia 'shared out some of it, and gave some to Ceolwulf', which appears to represent the establishment of Scandinavian settlements in the east midlands, and the formalization of Ceolwulf's position as king of 'English' Mercia, an area with its centre of gravity in the west midlands but extending down the Thames towards Oxford and London. It must therefore have been a somewhat depleted Viking force, under Guthrum, which staged the third inva-

Lyng and Athelney, Somerset. An aerial view showing (in the foreground) the promontory at Lyng, one of the network of fortifications constructed by King Alfred in the 880s, and (in the middle distance) the raised causeway leading from Lyng across the marshes to the Isle of Athelney (in the background), where Alfred had taken refuge in 878 and where he later founded a monastery under John the Old Saxon. Alfred's place of refuge at Athelney (where he is supposed to have burnt the cakes) was a small fortress on the nearer of the two hills; the monastery was on the more distant hill. The view is essentially that described by Asser in his *Life of King Alfred*, ch. 92.

sion of Wessex, in January 878; and although the Danes enjoyed initial success, occupying the land and driving King Alfred into hiding at Athelney in the Somerset marshes, it was only a matter of weeks before Alfred was able to assemble his forces and to mount the campaign which culminated in his victory over the Danes at the battle of Edington in Wiltshire. Guthrum and thirty of his leading men were promptly baptized into the Christian faith, in an extended ceremony which began at Aller, near Athelney, and which was completed on the royal estate at Wedmore in Somerset; whereupon the Danes retired from the fray, going first to Cirencester (878/9) and thence into East Anglia (late 879), where they 'settled and shared out the land'. Again, the chronicler's remark represents nothing less than the establishment of the Scandinavian settlements in another part of what would come to be known as the Danelaw. It may have been soon after Guthrum had completed the process of the settlement of East Anglia, in 879/80, that the boundary between 'English' England and the 'Danelaw' was formally recognized and duly defined in a treaty drawn up between King Alfred and King Guthrum; for although the boundary leaves London on the 'English' side, and is thus conventionally dated after King Alfred's 'occupation' of the city in 886, it can be argued on the basis of numismatic evidence that London had remained under notionally 'English' control ever since the fall of King Burgred in 874. It need not be imagined, however, that the boundary as defined in the treaty long outlasted the death of King Guthrum in 890, for it is in the nature of boundaries that they are swiftly overtaken by the unfolding course of events.

A third Viking army, which had assembled and encamped at Fulham on the Thames in late 878, appears to have been sufficiently discouraged by the defeat of Guthrum to leave England in the summer of 879, and to transfer its attention to the Continent. It was while this army ravaged and rampaged in France and the Low Countries throughout the 880s that King Alfred undertook the measures calculated in one way or another to ensure that his kingdom and his people would survive any further attack. He would have been able to draw on the experience and practices of his West Saxon, Mercian, and Kentish predecessors, and on whatever he had learnt of the defensive

(i)

(ii)

(iii)

Silver pennies issued in the name of King Alfred the Great (871–99), illustrating the complexity of relations between Wessex and Mercia. (i) 'Two Emperors' type, probably minted c.875. Alfred is here styled *rex Anglo[rum]*, or 'king of the English'. Coins of a similar type were also minted in the name of Ceolwulf, king of the Mercians (874–9), styled simply *rex*. (ii) 'Cross and Lozenge' type. This specimen was minted by the London moneyer Liafwald, probably c.875; Alfred is styled *rex S*, apparently signifying 'king of the Saxons'. Coins of a similar type were minted in the name of King Ceolwulf, styled *rex* or *rex M*. (iii) 'London Monogram' type, reflecting the more formal establishment of King Alfred's authority in London, probably c.880.

Aerial view of Wallingford, Berkshire, sited at an important crossing of the River Thames. The place was one of the network of 'burhs' (including fortified towns and other kinds of fortress) established by King Alfred in the 880s for the defence of his kingdom, and described in a short document known as the 'Burghal Hidage'. Substantial earthworks defined three sides of the town, protecting the rectangular street system laid down within it.

measures adopted by Frankish and other rulers on the Continent; but he would also have drawn strength and inspiration from his own faith, and perhaps above all from his understanding of the kingship of David and Solomon as described in the Old Testament. Alfred built a network of fortresses and fortified towns extending across his kingdom, making the necessary arrangements for their maintenance and defence, and at the same time reorganizing his army in two relays, 'so that always half its men were at home, half on service'; and in addition to these practical measures, he instituted a programme for the revival of religion and learning, driven from the court and intended to ensure that henceforth God would preserve, protect, and defend the English people.

In 892 the 'great Danish army', comprising '250' ships and evidently to be identified as the force which had wintered at Fulham in 878/9 and which had been active on the Continent for over a decade thereafter, came back across the Channel and established itself at Appledore in Kent. Soon afterwards, another army, comprising '80' ships under a renowned and experienced leader called Hasting, came into the Thames estuary and established itself at Milton, also in Kent. It was a moment of great crisis for the English, from which it must have seemed they might not be able to recover. Yet to judge from the detailed account of the warfare in the annals of the *Anglo-Saxon Chronicle* for 893–6, the Vikings were not able to make much of an impression on their intended victims, in the face of determined and concerted resistance; so in the summer of 896 they divided, 'one force going into East Anglia and one into Northumbria, and those that were moneyless got themselves ships and went south across the sea to the Seine'. It was an outcome in striking contrast to the achievements of the Vikings who had ravaged, conquered, and settled their different ways through England from 865 to 880, and one for which the credit from an English point of view belongs, of course, with King Alfred the Great.

When King Alfred reflected on the decline of learning in the ninth century, he remembered 'how, before everything was ransacked and burned, the churches throughout England stood filled with treasures and books'. His statement is, in fact, the only explicit evidence indicating that the Viking raids on England were attended by wholesale destruction. The organization of the church in the areas most directly affected by the Viking raids was certainly disrupted: for example, our knowledge of the succession of bishops of Lindsey, Elmham, and Dunwich breaks down in the late ninth century, and the bishopric of Leicester, serving the east midlands, appears to have been relocated in the 870s to Dorchester-on-Thames. But it is generally (and not unreasonably) supposed that many of the long-established religious houses scattered throughout the country were destroyed by Viking armies on the rampage: their communities slaughtered or scattered, their books and muniments burnt, their treasures looted, and their accumulated endowments of land brought under secular control or taken over by force or default into the hands of the king. It is surprisingly difficult, however, to substantiate this supposition with reference to the fate of particular houses. The Kentish minsters must have been exposed to attack from the late eighth century onwards, and would have been particularly vulnerable in the central decades of the ninth century; and one must assume, of course, that the churches in Canterbury were pillaged during the Viking raid of 851. Some Northumbrian houses might well have succumbed to the 'great army' in the late 860s: excavations at Whitby in Yorkshire and at Jarrow suggest that the sites were abandoned in the latter part of the ninth century, though whether we are necessarily right to assume that the monasteries were ransacked by the Vikings in 867 is perhaps another matter. Other monasteries might have succumbed when Northumbria was conquered and settled in 875–6; most famously, the bishop and community of St Cuthbert are said to have abandoned Lindisfarne in 875, beginning a seven-year wandering which brought them in the 880s to Chester-le-Street in County Durham. Monasteries in eastern England, including Ely, *Medeshamstede* (Peterborough), and Crowland, are presumed to have fallen prey to the 'great army' in 869–70, though again it is not clear that the evidence amounts to much more than a presumption.

Even the most intensely symbolic piece of evidence bearing on the Viking depredations in the ninth century lacks a proper context. An inscription entered not long after the middle of the ninth century in the margins of a mid-eighth-century gospel-book, known as the *Codex Aureus*, indicates that the book in question was found by Ealdorman Alfred (and his wife Werburg) in the hands of a 'heathen army', that the ealdorman and his wife bought it from the army with their gold, and that they presented it for the good of their souls to the community of Christ Church, Canterbury. Unfortunately, it is not known how, where, or when the book had fallen into heathen hands; but since Alfred appears to have held office as ealdorman of Surrey, from the 850s to the 880s, and also had strong interests in Kent, one might suppose that the book was looted from a church during one of the raids which affected Surrey and Kent in the early 850s, and that it was recovered by the ealdorman not long thereafter. Perhaps one should note in this connection that Abbot Beocca, Edor the mass-priest, and ninety monks are said to have been killed by heathen men at Chertsey Abbey (Surrey), presumably some time in the second half of the ninth century, in circumstances which ensured that Beocca and Edor were soon commemorated as martyrs (and registered in an early eleventh-century tract on the 'Resting-Places of Saints'). It is not clear whether this event took place in the early 850s, or in 871/2 (when the Viking army wintered at London, and at about which time one of their number seems to have deposited a hoard of silver coins at Croydon in Surrey, on an estate which Archbishop Æthelred subsequently entrusted to Ealdorman Alfred); but it is interesting that Chertsey Abbey appears to have been thriving again when Ealdorman Alfred drew up his will, probably in the 880s.

It would be mistaken, however, to imagine that the Viking raids were the only factor affecting the quality of religious life in ninth-century England. In King Alfred's view, the raids were not a cause but rather an effect of neglect and decline, or (as he would have put it) a manifestation of God's displeasure with the English people. When Fulco, archbishop of Rheims, wrote to King Alfred in the mid-880s, he wondered whether the perceived decline of the ecclesiastical order was occasioned 'by the frequent invasion and onslaught of Vikings, or through decrepitude, or through the carelessness of its bishops or the ignorance of those subject to them', as if the raids might have exacerbated a process of change which originated among the English themselves. Similarly, when Asser considered what he regarded as a decline in enthusiasm for the regular monastic life, he wondered whether it was because of 'the depredations of foreign enemies whose attacks by land and sea are very frequent and savage, or else because of the people's enormous abundance of riches of every kind, as a result of which (I suspect) this kind of monastic life came all the more into disrespect'. These remarks suggest that the quality of religious life in England had been affected as much by negligence and complacency as by any systematic acts of plunder perpetrated by Viking armies, leading to the sorry state of affairs which prevailed at the time of King Alfred's accession. For one reason or another Ceolnoth, archbishop of Canterbury (833–70), seems to have abandoned the earlier practice of convening regular meetings of the church in southern England; and in so far as this may be symptomatic of an attitude which passed down the ecclesiastical hierarchy, it is hardly surprising that the rot was allowed to set in. If those in positions of authority lacked the ability and the inclination to ensure that standards of religious life were properly maintained, or if they lacked the spirit to resist encroachment on their privileges by secular powers, the result would be a steady decline of the kind of which King Alfred writes in the preface to his translation of Pope Gregory's *Cura Pastoralis*. The decline at Canterbury itself is reflected in the wretched quality of the charters produced at Christ Church in the third quarter of the ninth century; elsewhere, the decline might have been reflected in ways ranging from loss of the ability to understand service books written in Latin to a disinclination to organize communal life in strict accordance with a monastic rule. Latterly, the well-being of religious houses was affected by the activities of the English themselves. Church treasuries would have been depleted of gold and silver whenever it was necessary to raise the sums of money required to 'make peace' with the enemy, and church lands, if they were not sold off in order to raise more money in the same connection, might have been taken over by the secular powers in whatever was perceived to be the overriding interest. For his part, King Alfred appears to have made demands on the church of a kind which incurred the displeasure of Archbishop Æthelred, and which even earned him a letter of reproach from Pope John VIII; and he came to be remembered at Abingdon, in particular, as one who appropriated land from the abbey and used it for his own purposes. It should not be forgotten, however, that episcopal churches, as well as an unspecified number of monasteries and nunneries, maintained their existence in the late ninth and early tenth centuries, and that, whatever might later have been said to the contrary, religious life in England was never snuffed out.

Facing: The Abingdon Sword (surviving length 31.5 cm). The warfare between the English and the Vikings in the late ninth century was perceived by some contemporary commentators as a struggle between Christians and pagans. This sword, of English manufacture, is decorated with a combination of designs best understood in relation to the Christian symbolism of other late ninth-century metalwork, and seems in this way to capture the 'Onward Christian Soldiers' mentality of the age. The sword was found at Bog's Mill, Abingdon, Oxfordshire, in about 1874.

61

Since the Viking raids were perceived by contemporaries as the assault of
heathen men upon a Christian people, it is arguable that this would have
served to heighten the sense in certain quarters that rulers of men had a
bounden duty to seek God's support in the struggle against the invaders.
The example was set in a most conspicuous manner by Æthelwulf, king of
the West Saxons and of Kent (839–58). In 853 he sent a deputation to Rome
(with Alfred, his youngest son); in 854–5, he granted the tenth part of his
lands 'to the praise of God and his own eternal salvation'; in 855 he jour-
neyed to Rome himself, 'with great state' (taking Alfred with him), returning a year later via the court of Charles the Bald; and not long before his
death, in 858, he drew up a testamentary document which included provi-
sion for the support of the poor and for annual payments of money to
Rome. The father's good example may have been followed in one way or
another by his sons Æthelberht (860–5) and Æthelred (865–71); certainly,
the latter earned renown for his determination to complete his devotions
before engaging the enemy at the battle of Ashdown in 871. Above all, however, it was King Alfred (871–99) who made the most sustained, elaborate,
and determined effort to gain God's favour for the English people in their
struggle against the Vikings. Inspired, perhaps, by memories of his two
journeys to Rome in the 850s, Alfred seems to have established particularly
close relations with Pope Marinus (882–4), promising gifts of alms (first
sent in 883), and persuading the pope to free the 'English quarter' in Rome
from taxation; and after 'the good pope' Marinus' death (duly recorded in
the *Chronicle* for 885), Alfred made it his business to ensure that the alms of
the king and his people were taken to Rome each year (as recorded in 887,
888, and 890). Alfred also took it upon himself, in the 880s, to devise and to
implement a programme for the revival of religion and learning, calculated
not least to ensure that henceforth God would give his support to the English people. The programme is best represented, of course, by the series of
translations into English of those books considered 'most necessary for all
men to know', and by Alfred's establishment of a school for the education
of the noble youth in the kingdom; but it is also represented by objects such
as the Fuller Brooch, the Alfred Jewel, and the Abingdon Sword, which are
symbolic in their different ways of the regeneration of the Christian faith in
Alfred's kingdom.

Yet perhaps the most significant aspect of the Viking impact on England
in the ninth century is the impetus which the raids gave to the emergence of
a sense of common identity among the English peoples, and the context
they provided for the formulation of a distinctively Alfredian political order
which lasted for about forty years, from 886 to 927. As we have seen, the
kingdom of East Anglia was 'conquered' in 870, the kingdom of Mercia was

Facing: A page in
the *Codex Aureus*, a
gospel book written
and decorated in
southern England
in the mid-eighth
century, showing
the opening of St
Matthew's Gospel.
The added inscrip-
tion, in Old English,
records how the book
was purchased from
a Viking army by
Ealdorman Alfred
(ealdorman of Surrey
in the mid-ninth
century) and his wife
Werburg, 'because we
were not willing that
these holy books
should remain any
longer in heathen
hands', and how it
was given by them
to Christ Church,
Canterbury.

✠ In nomine dni nri ihu xpi. Ic Ælfred aldormon 7 Werburg min gefera begetan ðas bec æt hæðnum herge
mid uncre claene feo ðæt ðonne wæs mid clæne golde 7 ðæt wit deodan for Godes lufan 7 for uncre saule ðearf

XP AVTEM
GENERATI
SIC ERAT CVM ESSET DIS
PONSATA MATER EIVS
MARIA IOSEPH ANTEQVA
CONVENIRENT INVENTA
EST IN VTERO HABENS

Ond for ðon ðe we noldan ðæt ðas halgan beoc lencg in ðære hæðenesse wunaden, 7 nu willað heo gesellan inn to
Cristes circan Gode to lofe 7 to wuldre 7 to weorðunga, 7 his ðrowunga to ðoncunga, 7 ðæm godcundan geferscipe to brucenne
ðe in Cristes circan dæghwæmlice Godes lof rærað, to ðæm gerade ðæt heo mon arede eghwelce monðe for Ælfred
7 for Werburge 7 for Alhðryðe heora saulum to ecum lece dome, ða hwile ðe God gesegen hæbbe ðæt fulwiht æt
ðeosse stowe beon mote. Ec swelce ic Ælfred dux 7 Werburg biddað 7 halsiað on Godes almehtiges noman 7 on allra
his haligra ðæt nænig mon seo to ðon gedyrstig ðætte ðas halgan beoc aselle oððe aðeode from Cristes circan ða hwile

'conquered' in 874, and the kingdom of Northumbria was 'conquered' in 875. The West Saxons briefly succumbed in 878, but in the years which followed Alfred's victory at Edington the political complexion of 'English' England was radically transformed. Building upon the alliance which had developed between Wessex and Mercia in the 850s and 860s, and capitalizing on his own record and reputation, Alfred seems to have been able in the early 880s to extend his authority over 'English' Mercia; and on his formal occupation and restoration of London in 886, 'all the English people that were not under subjection to the Danes submitted to him'. Henceforth he was hailed as 'king of the Angles and Saxons', or as 'king of the Anglo-Saxons', denoting his position as ruler of a newly conceived polity which embraced 'English' Mercia as well as Wessex (and its eastward extensions); when he died, he was quite accurately described on the same basis as 'king over the whole English people except for that part which was under Danish rule'. No doubt there would have been many who had cause to resent his political self-aggrandizement, just as there were many who would resent the imposition of heavy burdens on the people, or the encroachment of kingship (or royal lordship) deeper and deeper into the fabric of secular society. Alfred had the qualities in abundance which set him above other kings; but it is an essential part of his distinction as a ruler that he saw his opportunities, took them, and turned them to his own advantage.

Scandinavian Settlements in the Danelaw

To judge from the bare record of events in the *Anglo-Saxon Chronicle*, the Scandinavian settlements in the constituent parts of what came to be known as the Danelaw originated when members of Viking armies which had been on campaign in England for several years decided that the time had come for them to abandon one form of activity and take up another: as we have seen, in 876 Halfdan and his men 'shared out the land of the Northumbrians, and they proceeded to plough and to support themselves'; in 877 members of another army 'went away into Mercia and shared out some of it, and gave some to Ceolwulf'; and in 880 Guthrum's army went into East Anglia, 'and settled there and shared out the land'. It is the case that English people remained in the areas affected by Scandinavian settlement, no doubt in large numbers, but under subjection to the Danes. It is also the case that while some members of the Viking army active in England from 892 to 896 settled latterly in East Anglia, or in Northumbria, there is no explicit evidence that the Danes were joined in the late ninth or early tenth century by any substantial number of settlers coming to England direct from Scandinavia. It is otherwise apparent from the *Chronicle* that political power in

Facing: A vast hoard of treasure, comprising about 7,500 coins and 1,000 other pieces of silver, deposited *c.*905 in a lead-lined chest in the bank of the River Ribble near Cuerdale Hall, Preston, Lancashire. The treasure is presumed to represent the accumulated loot of a Viking army, gathered from places far afield (including Scandinavia, Frankia, Italy, Ireland, Pictland, and various parts of England) in the late ninth and early tenth centuries. It was found on 15 May 1840, and is now widely dispersed.

Inset: A necklace made up of silver pennies of King Æthelred the Unready, of the 'Long Cross', 'Helmet', and 'Last Small Cross' types (current consecutively from 997 to 1016), illustrating one of the uses to which the riches collected in England were put. The coins were arranged in a way which suggests that the necklace was worn with the obverses (king's portrait) on the underside, and the reverses (various cruciform designs) on the visible side. The necklace formed part of the Åspinge hoard (Hurva, Skåne, Sweden), deposited *c.*1048.

certain areas of Scandinavian settlement resided not in anyone recognized
as king, but in some other kind of body politic, centred on a borough and
perhaps under the authority of one or more men styled 'earl'. It is unlikely,
of course, that the armies raised by these boroughs in the first quarter of the
tenth century included any surviving members of the Viking armies active
in the 860s and 870s, so one must assume either that they comprised a new
wave of soldier–settlers, or that they comprised the sons and the grandsons
of the first generation.

The evidence bearing on what is perceived in retrospect to be the distinctive complexion of the Danelaw comes in various forms, each beset with its
own problems of interpretation. In general terms, however, one has to
avoid the temptation to fasten on any aspect of 'Danish' influence, and to
judge it in isolation from its wider context. That is to say, it is essential to
bear in mind that we are dealing with the settlement of 'Danes' in an 'English' landscape, and that the nature of the interaction between the two
peoples would from the outset depend on a variety of factors: for example,
the degree of social, economic, and political dependence of one group on
the other; the ability of people to learn how to converse with others brought
up to speak a different language; the implications of intermarriage, or of
social, cultural, and religious assimilation; and changing perceptions of collective identity. At the same time, we must not forget that the evidence as a
whole is the end-product of a long and complex process, with much local
variation, and does not relate directly to the circumstances of the original
settlements in the late ninth century.

The linguistic evidence of Scandinavian influence in the Danelaw is of
the greatest importance, if only because it is so pervasive. It was Snorri
Sturluson, writing in Iceland in the first half of the thirteenth century, who
first observed that some of the places in eastern England have Scandinavian
names; and in the hands of those who have pursued the matter in more
detail, a simple observation has been transformed into a great depth of
understanding. The main categories of 'Scandinavian' place-name are the
hybrids (a Scandinavian element compounded with an English element),
the *by*-names (containing the Old Danish word *by*, meaning a farmstead or
village), the *thorpe*-names (containing what is presumed in most cases to be
the Old Danish word *thorp*, denoting a secondary settlement or hamlet), a
variety of names containing other Scandinavian elements, and a variety of
names containing elements which have been affected by Scandinavian pro-
nunciation; but one also has to take into account the Scandinavian element
in the vocabulary of minor names within parishes, such as field-names,
which in certain areas add considerably to the overall picture. The main categories of names can be examined on their own terms (for example, by

Facing: The distribu-
tion of 'Scandinavian'
place-names in
England is the prod-
uct of two hundred
years of social, eco-
nomic, and political
development, from
the initial settlements
in the late ninth
century to the age of
the Domesday survey
(1086), and it is
hazardous, therefore,
to read too much
between the dots.

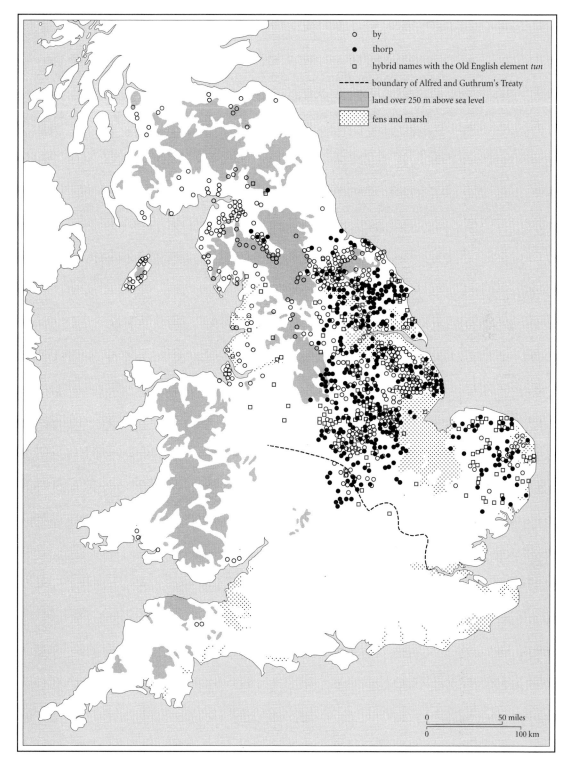

Legend:

○ by

● thorp

▫ hybrid names with the Old English element *tun*

----- boundary of Alfred and Guthrum's Treaty

land over 250 m above sea level

fens and marsh

0   50 miles

0   100 km

assessing the proportion of Scandinavian personal names to English personal names used as the defining element), and also in relation to the quality of the soil, the strategic importance of the site, and the distribution of other Scandinavian place-names in the vicinity; and it is possible on this basis to form an impression of the incidence, density, and relative chronology of the Scandinavian settlements in a particular part of eastern or northern England. It is important to remember, however, that the 'Scandinavian' names were formed over a long period of time (extending throughout the tenth and eleventh centuries, and beyond), and that as a general class they must take their place within the pattern of surviving 'English' names in the same area. Moreover, the place-name evidence is just one part of a wider

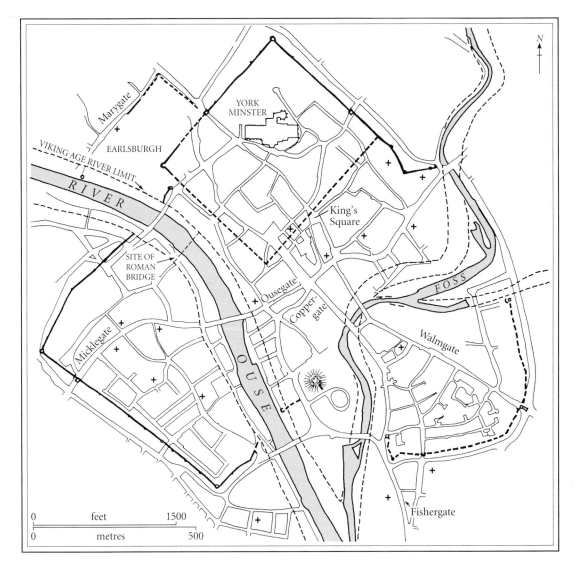

linguistic picture; although the wider picture shows how extensive and profound was the Scandinavian influence on the spoken language of eastern
England, the language which emerged was still recognizably English.

The evidence of material culture is more elusive, suggesting that in certain respects the settlers soon became effectively indistinguishable from the
rest of the population, and reflecting their ability to melt into the landscape;
there are, however, some fine examples of supposedly 'Viking' sculpture
preserved in churches, especially in northern England, while the analysis of
brooches and other small objects suggests that the inhabitants of some parts
of the Danelaw retained a degree of contact with Scandinavia throughout
the tenth century. Excavations at York have revealed much about the material and economic basis of life in the major trading centre of the northern
Danelaw, though perhaps rather less than we should like of the city which
would have been recognized by its Hiberno-Norse rulers in the tenth century, or by the itinerant poet Egil Skalla-Grímsson on his visit to the court
of Erik Bloodaxe. The coinages of some of the earliest of the Scandinavian
rulers in the eastern and northern Danelaw reflect the rulers' desire to furnish themselves with the trappings of respectable royal government, and
happen to provide evidence, at the same time, of their rapid adoption of
Christianity (which may have facilitated the process of assimilation). Similarly, the coinage struck in the names of the succession of Scandinavian and
English rulers of York, in the first half of the tenth century, is central to the
reconstruction of a political process of great complexity; and again, the
coinage includes particular types which project compelling images of Scandinavian kingship in that part of the country. Law codes issued in the names
of King Edgar, King Æthelred, and King Knut cast light on the distinctions
between legal practices in 'English' England and in the Danelaw; and the
records of some of the reformed monasteries of eastern England, such as
Peterborough, Ramsey, Thorney, Ely and Bury St Edmunds, make it possible to enter into the Anglo-Scandinavian societies around these houses.
Finally, the evidence of the Domesday survey (complemented by the evidence of later charters) forms the basis for an understanding of the social,
agrarian, and economic patterns which prevailed in eastern and northern
England in the second half of the eleventh century, establishing a picture of
a landscape inhabited by 'sokemen', 'free men', and others, following practices which seem to be distinctive when set beside those which prevailed
elsewhere in England; the question being, of course, whether this is evidence of a distinctively 'Danish' society in the Danelaw, or whether it is simply symptomatic of the particular kind of society which emerged during the
tenth and eleventh centuries in those areas most directly affected by the disruption and settlement of the late ninth century.

Facing: Plan of
Anglo-Scandinavian
York. It is often
important to main-
tain a distinction
between the political
nerve-centre of a city
and its industrial,
social, or commercial
pulse. Knowledge of
daily life in the most
important trading
centre of the
Northern Danelaw
was transformed by
the excavations
which took place at
Coppergate in 1976–
81. It would appear,
however, that the
Scandinavian kings
of York from the 870s
to the 950s conducted
their affairs from the
area known as King's
Square, and the earls
who governed the
city thereafter oper-
ated from the area
known as Earlsburgh.
The hustle and bustle
of Coppergate should
not, therefore, be
confused with the
York where the
Icelandic poet Egil
Skalla-Grímsson
recited his praise-
poem in honour of
Erik Bloodaxe, and
from which Erik was
driven in 954.

Needless to say, the evidence is capable of different interpretations; but at the risk of some misrepresentation of complex hypotheses, it may be helpful to reduce the competing interpretations to a set of models, which overlap to some extent but which differ from each other in the emphasis given to one factor as opposed to another. We might suppose, quite simply, that the conquest and initial settlement of parts of eastern and northern England was conducted by members of large Viking armies, followed immediately (in the late ninth century) by a veritable peasant migration from Denmark to eastern and northern England, on a scale sufficient to swamp the indigenous population and to produce a distinctively 'Danish' society. Alternatively, we might suppose that the settlements were conducted by the remnants of relatively small Viking armies, whose political dominance enabled them to exert an influence (not least on language, and so on place-names) out of all proportion to their actual number; and that it was the descendants of these old soldiers, in the tenth century, who expanded from the areas of initial settlement by a gradual process of internal colonization. Again, we might suppose that the initial settlements were on a small scale, made by members of the Viking armies who not unnaturally established themselves in the most advantageous positions; and that in the late ninth and early tenth centuries further settlements took place on a much larger scale behind this protective screen, amounting to a secondary migration from Scandinavia to eastern England. Or we might suppose that the settlements in the late ninth century were conducted by the remnants of relatively large Viking armies, in politically dominant positions; that from the outset these settlers mixed and intermarried with the indigenous English population, adopting some of their customs, and influencing or introducing others; and that there is no need to introduce any further settlers from the Scandinavian homelands in order to account for the evidence, since from the early tenth century successive generations of an increasingly integrated population participated in a normal process of social and economic expansion, creating an 'Anglo-Danish' society which none the less retained its notionally 'Danish' identity. It would probably be unwise to express a preference for any one model, since it is obvious that a model which might apply to one part of the Danelaw would not necessarily apply to others; after all, different areas were settled under different circumstances, and the later histories of each area in the tenth century were rarely the same. It should be noted, however, that the important factor is not the size of the 'great' Viking armies of 865 and 871 (whether a few hundred, or a few thousand, men), or indeed the scale of the settlements in the late ninth century. What truly counts in our understanding of the Scandinavian settlements is the fact that the settlers were in the politically dominant position, coupled with the presumption that they would have had good reason to mix with the English from the first generation, and supplemented by the proposition that 200 years of social and economic development passed until we reach the position in the second half of the eleventh century, represented by the Domesday survey. As F. W. Maitland put it, 'we must be careful how we use our Dane'.

If the Viking raids had helped to unite the English people under Alfred's leadership in their struggle against a common enemy, the Scandinavian settlements have to be seen as a major complicating factor in the more down-to-earth process which led ultimately to the political unification of England. King Edward the Elder succeeded his father in 899 as 'king of the Anglo-Saxons', and soon embarked on a campaign to extend his authority over those areas which had been taken over by the Danes. There can be no mistaking that he acted throughout in close co-operation with his brother-in-law, Ealdorman Æthelred, and with his sister Æthelflæd, rulers of the Mercians, who had recognized his superior authority from the outset of his reign; but it is not very surprising to find that the 'West Saxon' and 'Mercian' accounts of the campaign incorporated in the different versions of the *Anglo-Saxon Chronicle* present matters from their different points of view. The West Saxon chronicler traces the stages by which the Danes and the English living south of the River Humber submitted to King Edward, and one can see how the Danes were disadvantaged in this process by the lack of any political coherency among them. In 920 'the king of the Scots and all the people of the Scots, and Ragnald, and the sons of Eadwulf and all who live in Northumbria, both English and Danish, Norsemen and others, and also the king of the Strathclyde Welsh and all the Strathclyde Welsh, chose him as father and lord', signifying that all these parties acknowledged Edward's overlordship but obviously falling short of the achievement of direct rule north of the Humber. It is appropriate to find that Edward's successor, Athelstan (924–39), was styled 'king of the Anglo-Saxons and of the Danes' in a charter issued early in his reign, in effect representing the position established by his father south of the River Humber; but this polity was superseded in 927, when Athelstan 'succeeded' to the kingdom of the Northumbrians and could claim henceforth to be 'king of the English', or even 'king of the whole of Britain'. Numerous earls with Scandinavian names attended meetings of the king's councillors in the years between 928 and 934, presumably as representatives of different parts of the Danelaw; but alas it is not known in any detail how Athelstan brought these men under his control, or how royal authority was enforced on his behalf. Curiously, the 'Scandinavian' earls no longer appear among the witnesses to the king's charters in the last five years of the reign, perhaps because the earls in

A stone cross from St Andrew's Church, Middleton, Ryedale, North Yorkshire (1.17 m high). The face of the stone shows a warrior-lord in a conical helmet, with a knife hanging from his belt, apparently seated on a 'gift-stool' or throne; he is surrounded by other symbols of power, including spear, shield, sword, and axe. The sculpture is thought to date from the late ninth or the first half of the tenth century.

question ceased to attend meetings of the king's councillors, or because their place had been taken by 'English' ealdormen appointed above them, or because the charters were drawn up, latterly, by scribes who did not feel that the earls were of sufficient standing to deserve inclusion in the main body of the king's ealdormen.

It is especially difficult to understand the politics of the Danelaw in the twenty years which passed from the death of King Athelstan in 939 to the death of King Eadwig in 959, not least because so many competing factions and personalities were involved. As a member of the Hiberno-Norse dynasty with interests in Dublin and York, Olaf Guthfrithsson seized the initiative on Athelstan's death, first establishing himself as king of York and then driving the southern boundary of his kingdom down to Watling Street; he was succeeded in 941 by his cousin, Olaf Sihtricsson. King Edmund (939–46) recovered control of the territory of the Five Boroughs (Lincoln, Derby, Nottingham, Leicester, and Stamford) in 942, an act seen by a contemporary chronicler as freeing the 'Danes' from their forced subjection to the heathen 'Norsemen'; and in 944 Edmund drove Olaf Sihtricsson and Ragnald Guthfrithsson from York, and proceeded to reduce all of Northumbria under his rule. There can be little doubt that Wulfstan I, archbishop of York (931–56), played a very significant part in these affairs. He did not attest charters of the English kings from c.935 (which seems significantly 'early') to 941, but he does attest a number of Edmund's charters in 942 (before Edmund's recovery of Northumbria), as if he were already in attendance at the king's court; he is 'absent' again in 943, and, since one chronicler gives the credit for driving the Norse kings from York not to King Edmund but to 'Bishop Wulfstan and the ealdorman of the Mercians', it seems that Wulfstan himself had been instrumental in effecting their discomfiture, leading to his resumption of attendance at Edmund's court in 944. Following Edmund's death on 26 May 946, King Eadred (946–55) immediately 'reduced all Northumbria under his rule', and could thus be described in one of the distinctive series of 'alliterative' charters, in this case a charter issued on the occasion of his coronation at Kingston-upon-Thames on 16 August 946, as ruler of a quadripartite kingdom comprising the 'Anglo-Saxons' (a term now referring loosely, it seems, to all those living south of the Humber), the 'Northumbrians' (presumably the English in the far north, and the Anglo-Danish inhabitants of Yorkshire), the 'pagans' (the Hiberno-Norse element in York), and the 'Britons' (presumably the British of the kingdom of Strathclyde). The evidence bearing on the events of the late 940s and early 950s is open to different interpretations, of which only one is followed here. In 947 Archbishop Wulfstan and the 'Northumbrians' seem to have accepted Erik Bloodaxe, from Norway, as their king;

but in 948 the Northumbrians were forced to desert Erik and to submit again to King Eadred's authority. Eadred certainly ruled the whole of England from a point in 948 to a point in 950; he is described as king of the Anglo-Saxons (or 'English'), Northumbrians, pagans, and Britons in further examples of the 'alliterative' charters, issued in 949 and 950, and the same charters are attested by (among others) Archbishop Wulfstan, Bishop Ealdred of Chester-le-Street, some 'Scandinavian' earls, and Oswulf, high-reeve of Bamburgh. The Northumbrians appear to have reasserted their political independence in 950, taking first Olaf Sihtricsson (again) and then Erik Bloodaxe (again) as their king. It is striking that the ability to make and break kings seems to have been a matter which resided in the Northumbrian people themselves, as if they were still trying to see where their best interests lay; and since Archbishop Wulfstan and the other northerners were absent (appropriately enough) from King Eadred's charters in 951, and since Wulfstan is said to have been imprisoned by the king in 952, it may be that Wulfstan was still playing a significant part in the politics which lie concealed behind this complicated sequence of events. Wulfstan seems to have recovered his standing at Eadred's court in 953; and at about the same time, or in the following year, the Northumbrians took it upon themselves to drive out Erik Bloodaxe, whereupon Eadred 'succeeded to the kingdom of the Northumbrians'. The draftsman of the 'alliterative' charters, who had necessarily reduced Eadred to a deliberately ambiguous 'king of the English' in charters issued in 951, duly restored him in 955 to the dignity of the kingship (in his terms) of the Anglo-Saxons, Northumbrians, pagans, and Britons.

'Hogback' monuments from Brompton, North Yorkshire (1.27–1.36 m long). These monuments, presumed to be grave-markers or some other kind of memorial, are formed in the shape of bow-sided buildings, with muzzled bears at each end. Hogbacks are concentrated in Cumbria and North Yorkshire, and are thought to date from the central decades of the tenth century.

The fact that the polity could still be conceived in this way in 955 (even though 'king of the English', in its all-embracing sense, was the norm in most other charters) serves as a reminder that the political unity of the kingdom of England was not yet taken for granted; so it may be instructive to consider how others appear to have seen the component parts of the kingdom as a whole. For various reasons, the kingdom of England was divided in 957 between King Eadwig (955–9) and King Edgar, along the line of the River Thames. In one of his charters, issued in 958, Edgar is styled 'king of the Mercians, Northumbrians and Britons', as if the Danes, as such, did not feature separately in this conception of his share of the kingdom as a whole. After Eadwig's death in 959, the kingdom was reunified under King Edgar (959–75); and it was during his reign as 'king of the English' that the unity of the kingdom became an enduring political reality. A law code issued in Edgar's name, possibly in 962–3 though perhaps in the early 970s, affords some idea of the complexities which underlie the superficial appearance of unity. The draftsman of this law-code clearly recognized a basic distinction between the customs or rights which applied among the 'English', and the customs or rights which applied among the 'Danes'; but although some measures were to be 'common to all the nation, whether Englishmen, Danes or Britons, in every province of my dominion', Edgar was willing to let the Danes decide certain matters for themselves, adding 'I have ever allowed them this and will allow it as long as my life lasts, because of your loyalty, which you have always shown me'. It might be supposed that the king was rewarding the Danes for their support in 957, by granting them what amounted to a semblance of legal autonomy, and that in this sense it was Edgar who brought the Danelaw into existence; but it would be more natural to suppose that Edgar was pragmatically conscious of the limitations on his own ability to legislate for the 'Danish' part of his kingdom, and regarded the act of acknowledging the diversity of established customs among different peoples as the best way of maintaining the appearance of overall political unity. About thirty years later Edgar's son, King Æthelred the Unready (978–1016), issued one code (at Woodstock) intended to apply to areas under 'English' law, and another code (at Wantage) intended to apply to the territory of the Five Boroughs. The Wantage code is replete with 'Scandinavian' vocabulary, showing the extent to which the customs prevailing in this part of the Danelaw had been affected during the course of the tenth century by the particular conditions arising from the Scandinavian settlements in the late ninth century; the truth remains, however, that the code represents what is essentially royal legislation for an Anglo-Danish society. It might be supposed that Æthelred was trying to bring practices in one part of the Danelaw into line with practices in 'English' England, that the code thus represents an attempt to impose conformity where King Edgar had preferred to grant autonomy, and that in this way Æthelred earned for himself the enmity of the Danelaw; but while the code can certainly be construed as an act of royal government which went much further than King Edgar's, there is no reason why it need be regarded as anything more sinister than evidence of government going about its business, and no reason to think that it would have antagonized the Anglo-Danish inhabitants of the Danelaw.

Another hint of a contemporary perception of the body politic in the late tenth century is encapsulated in a formula found in a vernacular charter, referring to 'all the thegns who were gathered there from far and wide, both West Saxons and Mercians, both English and Danes'. The distinction may have been between the West Saxons, the Mercians, the (Northumbrian) English, and the inhabitants of the Danelaw; but it is more likely that the intention was simply to develop a distinction between West Saxons and Mercians (the English), on the one hand, and the Danes (the inhabitants of the Danelaw), on the other. Whatever the case, the formulation is a reminder that the inhabitants of the Danelaw retained a collective identity as 'Danish', even though they must by this stage have been of very mixed blood, and even though this identity is not likely to have had any residual political connotation. As a prolific draftsman of royal law codes in the first quarter of the eleventh century, Wulfstan II, archbishop of York (1002–23), legislated for the whole of England, recognizing much the same distinction between areas under 'English' law (covering both 'West Saxon' and 'Mercian' law) and areas under 'Danish' law, and respecting the differences which had arisen between them. The differences were, however, accentuated artificially in the twelfth century, when legal antiquaries formulated the notion that English law could be divided in accordance with the division of the kingdom into three parts (Wessex, Mercia, and the Danelaw), and then amused themselves by listing the shires which belonged to each part. In this way the Danelaw came to be defined as an area comprising Suffolk, Norfolk, Cambridgeshire, Lincolnshire, Yorkshire, Nottinghamshire, Derbyshire, Staffordshire, Cheshire, and Shropshire; but it is not, of course, a definition which needs to be taken very seriously.

Viking Raids during the Reign of King Æthelred

The Viking raids which beset the English people during the reign of King Æthelred the Unready (978–1016) can be divided, for the sake of convenience, into four successive phases.

The first phase covers the period 980–91, and witnessed the resumption of raiding activity after the long interlude earlier in the tenth century. Some of the raids seem to have originated in the Irish Sea and others in Scandinavia; and while they do not appear to have been on a scale which occasioned much more than local disruption, they were taken seriously enough to have precipitated a peace process between England and Normandy in 990–1, perhaps implying that some of the raiders were using Normandy as a safe haven. The second phase covers the period 991–1005. It may not seem from a cursory reading of the *Anglo-Saxon Chronicle* that the events of these years deserve to be distinguished as a distinct 'phase' of activity, but it is arguable that they can, in fact, be understood in terms of a sustained threat from a single army; for although its leaders changed, the core of the army appears to have been based in England for a period of several years, representing a threat to the security of the realm comparable with that represented by the 'great army' in England during a period of similar duration, from 865 to 880. A Viking force of over ninety ships, perhaps comprising two or three thousand men, arrived off Folkestone in 991. Its leaders appear to have included Olaf Tryggvason (from Norway) and Sven Forkbeard (from Denmark), both apparently in search of the fame and fortune which would help them to achieve their respective purposes in Scandinavia. The force made its way round the south-east coast, defeating an English army at the battle of Maldon (10 or 11 August 991), and receiving a payment of 10,000 pounds (of money, presumably in gold and silver) 'because of the great terror they were causing along the coast'. The force appears to have remained in the south-east in 991–2, but then sailed north to ravage Northumbria in 993, returning south for an abortive attack on London in September 994, followed by some serious ravaging along the south coast; whereupon the English resolved to make peace, allowing the Vikings to remain at Southampton for the winter of 994/5, and providing them with all the necessities of life, including a payment of 16,000 pounds. At this stage Olaf and Sven seem to have gone their separate ways, but it would appear that the bulk of the Viking army remained in England (perhaps still based at or near Southampton), having undertaken to protect the

A selection of Viking weapons from a hoard found on the foreshore of the River Thames, near the north end of London Bridge. The weapons comprise seven battle-axes and six spearheads; associated with them were a small axe or carpenter's tool, a pair of fire tongs, and a four-pronged grappling-iron. The assembly is presumed to date from the late tenth or early eleventh century, and is a reminder (as if any were needed) that the Viking attacks on London were a fearsome reality.

English from other raiding armies; significantly, no activity is reported in 995 and 996. The Vikings then resumed their previous and doubtless preferred form of occupation, ravaging various parts of the country in 997, 998, and 999, crossing to Normandy for the winter of 1000/1, and returning to England for a further bout of ravaging, before receiving more provisions and a payment of 24,000 pounds in early 1002. Sven Forkbeard appears to have had occasion to rejoin the Viking force in England during the course of 1003, leading his men on campaign first in Wessex, and then in East Anglia; but in 1005 there was a great famine throughout England, forcing the Vikings to make their way back to Denmark.

The third phase of Viking activity during Æthelred's reign covers the period 1006–12, and saw two major invasions, each of which had a devastating effect on the English people. A 'great fleet', possibly led by a certain Tostig, arrived at Sandwich in July 1006, causing disruption wherever it went, and using the Isle of Wight as a base for its further operations in Wessex during the winter of 1006/7. The English sued for peace, and the handsome sum of 36,000 pounds was paid to the army in 1007; whereupon it seems to have returned whence it came. As if that was not enough, an 'immense raiding army', led by Thorkell the Tall, arrived at Sandwich in early August 1009, and proceeded to overrun the greater part of southern England. The campaign culminated with the siege of Canterbury in 1011, leading to the capture of Archbishop Ælfheah and to his martyrdom at Greenwich on 19 April 1012; a payment of 48,000 pounds was made over to the Viking army soon afterwards, whereupon it 'dispersed as widely as it had been collected'.

The fourth phase covers the period 1013–16, and again saw two major invasions; but in this case, each invasion culminated with the conquest of

England, as had doubtless been intended. Sven Forkbeard, king of Denmark, brought the Danish fleet to Sandwich in the summer of 1013, and immediately made his way northwards into the Danelaw, perhaps expecting that he would be able to gather there the support and provisions needed for his campaign; he was not disappointed, and was then able to strike south, eventually gaining recognition as 'full king' and forcing Æthelred into temporary exile in Normandy (1013–14). Following Sven's death on 3 February 1014, his son Knut remained for a while with the Danish army in the heart of the Danelaw (at Gainsborough, in Lindsey); but he was soon driven away by King Æthelred, and made his way back to Denmark. Not to be outdone by his father, and no doubt eager to outdo his elder brother (Harald, king of Denmark), Knut brought his own fleet to Sandwich in 1015, and at once adopted a strategy quite different from that of his father's campaign two years previously. He sailed west, ravaging first in Wessex before striking into the west midlands during the Christmas season; then, in the opening months of 1016, Knut moved steadily eastwards and northwards into the Danelaw, as far as York, before returning southwards to his ships in order to mount his attack on London. The story of the rest of the campaign, of the strenuous resistance orchestrated after Æthelred's death by King Edmund Ironside, and of the circumstances of Knut's accession following Edmund's death on 30 November 1016, can be followed in the *Anglo-Saxon Chronicle*.

In order to understand the impact of the Viking raids on the course of affairs during King Æthelred's reign, it would be necessary to relate each phase of activity to the changing pattern of domestic politics over the same period; and one has to say that this would not make very edifying reading. It must suffice for present purposes to focus attention on certain aspects of the English response to the Viking threat, though we shall have to suspend judgement on how the response might reflect (for example) the incompetence of the king and his advisers, or the incapacity of the English leaders to mount effective resistance, or the social and political conditions of the age, or the overwhelming power of the Danes.

The most distinctive (and seemingly damning) aspect of the English defensive strategy in Æthelred's reign originated in the immediate aftermath of the English defeat at Maldon in August 991, and is symbolized by the successive payments of tribute (*gafol*) made to the Viking armies active in England from 991 to 1012, as part of a policy condemned by E. A. Freeman as the 'senseless and fatal system of looking to gold to do the work of steel, of trusting to barbarians who never kept their promises'. The payments rose inexorably from 10,000 pounds (in 991) to 48,000 pounds (in 1012), reflecting not only an increase in the size of the armies which had to be bought off, but also their escalating demands and the ever-worsening position of the English; payments of a different kind were made under rather different circumstances to the forces of King Sven and King Knut, reaching a staggering 72,000 + 10,500 pounds in 1016 (paid in 1018). The payments, made in gold as well as silver, and doubtless comprising precious jewellery, church plate, and other fine objects, as well as coinage, were presumably distributed in some way by the leaders of the Viking armies among their followers; and it is evident that several of the Danish and Swedish Vikings who brought home a share of the proceeds regarded the matter as a splendid achievement which deserved to be recorded in runes, and thereby advertised to posterity. What became of the treasure itself is another matter: a lot of the precious metal must have been melted down for reuse by native craftsmen, and it can be seen that some of the coinage was turned into necklaces (perhaps showing studied contempt for the English king); but much of the loot would have passed quickly from one hand to another, in such a way that the separate components of the many treasure-hoards found in Scandinavia are often quite far removed from their original source.

A second aspect of the English defensive strategy involved the formal employment of Vikings as mercenaries, for the defence of the country against other marauding Vikings. This policy appears to have been adopted for the first time (in Æthelred's reign) in 994, as part of the treaty drawn up with the Viking army at that time; and it was perhaps in the same connection that King Æthelred gave 'great gifts' to a certain Pallig, 'in estates and gold and silver', apparently in return for a pledge of loyalty. Mercenaries do have a tendency, however, to turn on their employers when favourable opportunities arise. The Vikings who had been bought off and perhaps brought into the king's service in 994, and who had been quiescent in 995–6, seem to have turned against the English in 997; and in 1001 Pallig himself collected some ships, deserted the king, and joined forces with those who may have been his former associates. The treaty made with the Viking army in 1002 may, or may not, have involved a renewal of their terms of employment as mercenaries. Whatever the case, on St Brice's Day (13 November), in the same year, 'the king ordered to be slain all the Danish men who were in England . . . because the king had been informed that they would treacherously deprive him, and then all his councillors, of life, and possess this kingdom afterwards'. The intended victims of this drastic measure can hardly have been the 'Danes' of the Danelaw; and since a charter of 1004, which refers to the king's decree 'that all the Danes who had sprung up in this island, sprouting like cockle amongst the wheat, were to be destroyed by a most just extermination', reveals how it was implemented in relation to Danes living in Oxford, one might suppose that the intended victims were any remaining groups of mercenaries, or paid-off and provisioned members of the army who had now outstayed their welcome. The so-called Massacre of St Brice's Day was not a pleasant act; but given the activities of the Danes in previous years, and in view of their reported intentions, it is easy to understand the strength of anti-Danish feeling at the king's court, and among the English people. After what may have been a ten-year gap, the policy of employing mercenaries was adopted again in 1012, when forty-five ships (led by Thorkell) came over to the king, 'and they promised him to defend this country, and he was to feed and clothe them'. It was evidently in this connection, in 1012, that King Æthelred instituted the form of annual taxation on land known as the *heregeld* (army tax), specifically for the purpose of paying the Danish mercenaries (and to be distinguished in this and other respects from the payments of *gafol*, or tribute); and although the *heregeld* is said to have been abolished in 1051 ('in the thirty-ninth year after it had been instituted'), a change in political circumstances ensured that the tax was soon afterwards revived, coming in its later manifestation to be known as the Danegeld. Thorkell's mercenary army seems to have remained impressively loyal to King Æthelred in 1013–14, especially when in opposition to the forces of Sven Forkbeard; but the conflicts of loyalties which surfaced after Sven's death complicated the situation, and it seems that in 1015 what still remained of the mercenary force (with or without Thorkell) transferred its allegiance to Knut.

A third aspect of English defensive strategy found its most obvious expression in 994, when Olaf Trygvasson was brought 'with much ceremony' from his base at Southampton to Andover (in Hampshire), where King Æthelred 'stood sponsor to him at confirmation, and bestowed gifts on him royally'. This was, of course, no more than an extension of long-established practices in making peace with one's enemies, and it is a useful reminder of one of the ways in which Christianity might be deployed for military or political advantage.

A fourth aspect of the strategy is represented by King Æthelred's marriage to Emma, sister of Richard II, duke of Normandy, in 1002. It is not entirely clear whether the Danish army which went to 'Richard's kingdom' in the summer of 1000, and which seems to have returned thence to England in 1001, had sought and found shelter in Normandy, in defiance of the treaty of 991, or whether it had gone there for further entertainment; but if we may assume that the marriage was intended to be of political advantage to both parties, it would presumably relate in some way to promises of taking action against the Danes. Nor is it clear what, if anything, the English might have owed to the putative alliance during the traumatic events of the following years; but it certainly meant that Æthelred, Emma, and the æthelings

Facing: The text of a law-code of King Æthelred the Unready (978–1016), preserved in a mid-eleventh-century manuscript written probably at New Minster, Winchester. The heading, here displayed in capital letters (line 4), indicates that the code in question (*VII Æthelred*) was issued 'when the great army (*se micele here*) came to the land', probably with reference to the arrival of Thorkell's army in August 1009. The code lays down a programme of public prayer, and ends (in capital letters, bottom line) 'God help us. Amen'.

Edward and Alfred were able to take refuge in Normandy while Sven had the upper hand in 1013–14.

A fifth aspect of English defensive strategy, evidently precipitated by the activities of the Viking army in 1006, was brought into effect following the dispersal of that army in 1007 and following whatever reorganization of administrative structures might be suggested by the appointment in the same year of Eadric Streona as 'ealdorman over the kingdom of the Mercians'. At a meeting of the king and his councillors held at (King's) Enham, in Hampshire, in mid-May 1008, it was specifically resolved, among many other things, that boroughs and bridges should be kept in good repair, that military service should be performed whenever the need should arise, and that ships should be supplied 'so that each may be equipped immediately after Easter every year'. It was perhaps on the occasion of the same meeting at Enham, in May 1008, that the king, in the words of the chronicler, 'ordered that ships should be built unremittingly over all England, namely a warship from 310 [or 300] hides, and a helmet and corselet from eight hides'—a measure which would have produced a brand new fleet of anything between 150 and 250 ships, each (it seems) with equipment for about forty men. The ships were ready in 1009, 'and there were more of them than ever before . . . had been in England in any king's time; and they were all brought together at Sandwich and were to stay there and protect this country from every invading army'. Unfortunately, the good work was soon undone by rivalry between factions of the king's leading thegns, and a large part of the fleet was lost at sea in a storm.

Yet the most remarkable aspect of the defensive strategy adopted by the English, and the one which happens to provide the most moving testimony to the Viking impact on English society, is represented by the law codes and sermons of Wulfstan II, archbishop of York. The earliest of the codes drafted by Wulfstan was issued from the meeting of the king's councillors held at Enham, during the season of Pentecost (16 May) in 1008. The code as a whole is an affirmation of the principle that all should honour one God and hold one Christian faith, under the rule of one king, and its import can be expressed well enough in one sentence: 'But God's law henceforth is to be eagerly loved by word and deed; then God will at once become gracious to this nation.' As we have seen, the fine words and good intentions were matched on this occasion by hard work, even if the hard work itself came to naught. No less striking is the law code issued at Bath, probably in mid-August 1009, following the arrival of Thorkell's 'immense raiding army' at Sandwich at the beginning of that month. The code lays down an intensive programme of fasting, almsgiving, and prayer, to be implemented on the Monday, Tuesday, and Wednesday before Michaelmas (which fell in 1009 on Thursday, 29 September), so that the people may obtain God's mercy, 'and that we may be able through his help to withstand our enemies'. On those three days, everyone (including slaves) would be expected to come barefoot to church, 'without gold and ornaments', and after confession their priest would lead them out in procession with the relics, and they would 'call on Christ eagerly from their inmost hearts'; and in religious houses throughout the country, communities would be expected to sing their psalters together, while each priest separately would celebrate thirty masses and each monk would say thirty psalters. In respect of their daily routine, religious communities were to observe other special practices, 'until things become better': the votive mass 'Against the Heathen' was to be said at matins, and at each of the canonical hours, the whole community, prostrate before the altar, was to sing the psalm 'Why, O Lord, are they multiplied' (Ps. 3), as well as other prayers and the collect 'against the heathen'. The code ends with a reminder that God's dues are to be paid on time, followed by the heartfelt plea 'God help us. Amen.' This picture, albeit formed in our imagination, of what must have happened in England on 26, 27, and 28 September 1009, as the people processed barefoot round town and countryside led by priests bearing relics, and as religious communities recited their psalters, masses, and prayers, all calling out in unison for God's help against Thorkell's army, is without any doubt one of the most powerful and evocative images of England during the reign of King Æthelred the Unready. It is, moreover, a picture which is given a further dimension by the remarkable series of *Agnus Dei* pennies, which seem to symbolize the need to invoke divine assistance in driving away the sins of the earth, and to secure deliverance from all enemies. The coins in question combine a representation of the Lamb of God on the obverse (in place of the king's head) with a representation of the Dove, symbol of the Holy Spirit, on the reverse (in place of more common cruciform motifs). They are thus set apart from the main sequence of types issued before, during, and after Æthelred's reign; and since only fourteen specimens are known (minted at nine different places), and since these specimens appear on numismatic grounds to belong as a group between the king's *Helmet* pennies (c.1003–9) and his *Last*

Silver penny of the exceptionally rare 'Agnus Dei' type, issued in the name of King Æthelred the Unready. These remarkable coins, which show the Lamb of God on the obverse, and the Dove, or Holy Spirit, on the reverse, appear to symbolize a desperate appeal to God for deliverance from the enemy. They were issued probably in the autumn of 1009, and may have been connected in some way with the programme of public prayer represented by *VII Æthelred*.

Small Cross pennies (*c.*1009–16), it is difficult indeed to resist the supposition that they were issued in close association of some kind with the programme of prayer in late September 1009. Alas, of course, it was all to no avail, and matters only went from bad to worse. When Wulfstan issued further legislation for the king soon after the king's return from exile in 1014, he was trying not only to restore a sense of trust in Æthelred's government, after the disasters of the previous year, but also to instil good Christian practices among the people, and to promote an orderly society: 'And let us loyally support one royal lord, and let each of our friends love the next with true fidelity and support him rightly.' Wulfstan's sermons and other writings are infused with the same sense of an urgent need to build a Christian society. The following extract from the 'Sermon of the Wolf to the English', first preached in 1014 'when the Danes persecuted them most', is indicative of Wulfstan's analysis of the situation, and broadly representative of the tone of his remarks:

Things have not gone well now for a long time at home or abroad, but there has been devastation and persecution in every district again and again, and the English have been for a long time now completely defeated and too greatly disheartened through God's anger; and the pirates so strong with God's consent that often in battle one puts to flight ten, and sometimes less, sometimes more, all because of our sins. . . . We pay them continually and they humiliate us daily; they ravage and they burn, plunder and rob and carry on board; and lo, what else is there in all these events except God's anger clear and visible over this people?

Archbishop Wulfstan gave nothing if not powerful expression to a view of the Viking raids which must have been commonplace from the moment that the Vikings first appeared on English shores in the late eighth century, and which would certainly have been well understood at the court of King Alfred the Great. Yet the problem in Æthelred's reign was not that the English used words and prayers, as well as gold and silver, to do the work of steel; it was, of course, that there was more than merely the work of steel to do. The English survived the raids of the 980s without difficulty, and seem to have emerged from the more sustained assault in the period 991–1005 with their spirit and faith intact. It is clear, however, that the very fabric of English society was weakened by the widespread devastation which attended the invasion of 1006–7, and especially Thorkell's invasion in 1009–12; and, when the best efforts of the English people had been further undermined by failures of leadership and internal dissension, the English were finally overwhelmed by the superior forces brought to England by Sven Forkbeard in 1013–14, and by Knut in 1015–16. In the dismal tale of recurrent treachery, cowardice, incompetence, and defeat told in the annals of the *Anglo-Saxon*

Rune-stone from Evje, in Galteland, Norway, raised in memory of a young man who died in Knut's army during the invasion of England in 1015–16: 'Arnsteinn raised this stone in memory of Bjor, his son. He was killed in the *lith* when Knut attacked England'.

Chronicle, the ubiquitous villain of the piece is not King Æthelred but Eadric Streona, who was appointed ealdorman of Mercia in 1007, who appears to have achieved the highest office under the king in the period 1009–12 (while Thorkell's army was on the rampage), and whose activities in 1015–16 (while the king himself was incapacitated by illness) proved the undoing of the English. Eadric's final act of treachery, during the reign of King Edmund Ironside, took place at the battle of *Assandun* (Ashingdon, or Ashdon, in Essex), on 18 October 1016, when he was the first to start the flight, 'and thus betrayed his liege lord and all the people of England'. The chronicler supplies a roll-call of the dead, including the bishop of Dorchester, the abbot of Ramsey, the ealdorman of Hampshire, the ealdorman of Lindsey, and Ulfcetel of East Anglia. We may be interested to note that the men of the Danelaw had done their bit; more to the point, however, is the chronicler's lament that 'all the nobility of England was there destroyed'.

4

IRELAND, WALES, MAN, AND THE HEBRIDES

DONNCHADH Ó CORRÁIN

The Early Raids, 795–836

For in those days shall be such tribulations as were not from the beginning of the creation which God created until now; neither shall be. And unless the Lord had shortened the days, no flesh should be saved; but, for the sake of the elect which he hath chosen, he hath shortened the days

In the Book of Armagh, opposite Christ's prophecy of the destruction of Jerusalem (Mark 13: 19–20), the name 'Cellach' is written. This laconic comment throws a sudden light on a dark landscape: the beginning of the Viking raids on Ireland and Scotland, and the reaction of church leaders to the unforeseen misfortunes of the great island monastery of St Columba at Iona. For them, it was Jerusalem destroyed. Cellach was abbot from 802 to 814. In 795 the Vikings sacked Iona, in 802 they burned it, in 806 they killed sixty-eight of the community. The leadership was so badly shaken that a safer place was sought for its treasures and perhaps senior personnel, and in 807–14 a new inland monastery was built at Kells in Co. Meath. This contemporary comment is much more tight-lipped than Alcuin's eloquent horror at the Viking raid on Lindisfarne in 793, but deep shock is evident.

Iona survived, and another dramatic event is reported by Walafrid Strabo (c.808–49), scholar and favourite of Emperor Louis the Pious, who met Irish émigrés at Reichenau and the imperial court. He wrote a Life, based on their reports, of the martyr Blathmac, killed in 826. For him, Blathmac is a future king who became a monk and, coveting the martyr's crown,

The first Irish church
raided by the Vikings
was on Rathlin Island
where a viking ceme-
tery was discovered
in the nineteenth
century. The best
piece from it is this
putatively tenth-
century brooch.

went to Iona, knowing the danger. Expecting raiders, he advised his fellows
to flee: some did. He buried the shrine of Columba's relics and, when the
Vikings came, refused to reveal where it was, and they killed him. This may
indeed have happened though the whole narrative is overlaid with hagio-
graphical conventions. This story, and the annalistic references to the com-
ings and goings of abbots of Iona (in 818, 829, 831, 849, 865, 878) show that
monastic life continued.

The Viking raids, mainly by Norwegians, began abruptly. The *Annals of
Ulster* report without forewarning 'the devastation of all the islands of
Britain by pagans'. Sudden raids on islands and coasts continued for a generation. The first on Ireland was in 795: 'The burning of *Rechru* by the
pagans, and Skye was plundered and robbed.' *Rechru* is Rathlin, an island
off the north-east Irish coast, rich in monastic foundations, and in the path
of southbound ships. The raiders soon swept into the Irish Sea: in 798 the
annalist reports 'the burning of *Inis Pátraic* by the pagans and they took the
cattle-tribute of the territories and they smashed the shrine of Do Chonna

and they made great incursions both in Ireland and in Scotland'. *Inis Pátraic*
is St Patrick's Island near Skerries, St Do Chonna is its patron.

So far the raids were exploratory—the work of two or three ships, not fleets. By 807 they had rounded the northern headlands and reached the west-coast bays. They burned Inishmurray off Sligo and attacked Roscam, on the inner waters of Galway Bay. Sometimes they met determined opposition from the local lords: in 811 'a slaughter of the pagans at the hands of the Ulaid'; in 812 'a slaughter of pagans' by Fir Umaill at Clew Bay. Meanwhile, they pushed south through the Irish Sea. In 821 they raided Howth and 'took a great prey of women'—for ransom or slaving—and plundered the monasteries on the islets of Wexford Harbour. In 822 they had reached Cork, and in 824 they raided the remote monastery of Skellig, 13 kilometres off the Kerry coast, and captured Étgal, its superior.

Now came a change: Vikings attacked the main monasteries of the northeast and east coasts as far south as the Boyne. First, an attack in 824 on Bangor on the south shore of Belfast Lough, long famous for its schools. They plundered the monastery, destroyed the oratory, shook the relics of St Comgall, its founder, from their shrine, and killed the scholars and bishops. Then they attacked Moville, on Strangford Lough. In 827 they raided Lusk on the Dublin coastline and ravaged the local kingdoms, and in 828 they struck north of the Boyne. Local rulers resisted, and in the south-east the king of Uí Chennselaig and the monastery of Taghmon joined forces to drive them off.

Viking pressure mounted. In 831 the Vikings raided north Louth, and took its king for ransom. The monks of Armagh sent troops to defend their property about Carlingford Lough, but they were badly beaten and many prisoners were taken. This brought the wealth of Armagh to the notice of the Vikings, and early in 832 it had its first raids: three in a month. This was followed by raids on other churches. Tuathal (d. 850), later abbot of Durrow and Lambay, was captured at Donaghmoyne, Co. Monaghan, while on circuit with the reliquary of St Adomnán. Cleric and reliquary were both taken by the Vikings. The cleric was ransomed; the fate of the shrine is unknown.

Raiders began to go further inland, as they did in mainland Europe: in 833 they hit Derry on the north coast, Clondalkin near Dublin, Dromiskin in Co. Louth, and they attacked the great monastery of Lismore on the south coast and slaughtered the local levies that defended it. In 834 they struck Glendalough and Slane on the Boyne 11 kilometres above Drogheda. Next year they sacked Ferns and Clonmore—both patronized by the kings of south Leinster. In 836 they attacked Glendalough from the coast at Arklow, through the Avonmore valley, over 30 kilometres of difficult terrain.

Scotland will have suffered equally but the sources are thin. Recording at

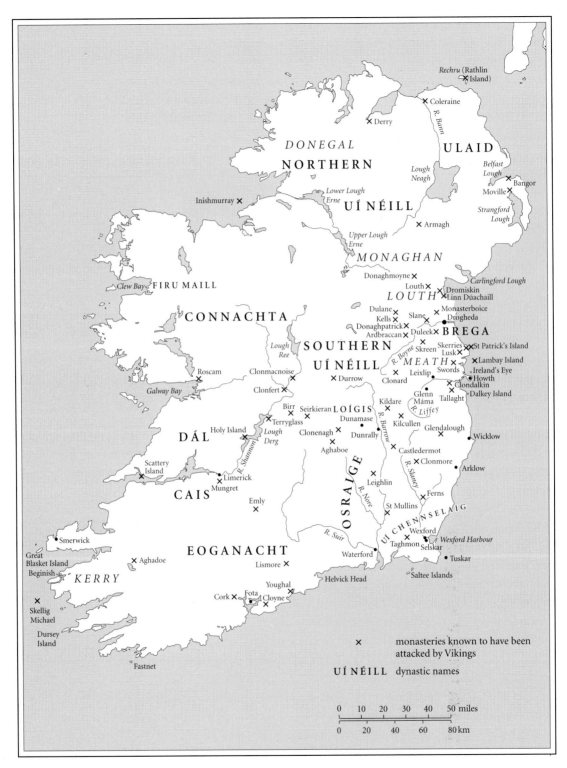

Rechru (Rathlin Island) ✕

✕ Coleraine

✕ Derry

R. Bann

DONEGAL

NORTHERN

ULAID

Lough Neagh

Belfast Lough

✕ Bangor
Moville ✕ ✕

UÍ NÉILL

Strangford Lough

Inishmurray ✕

✕ Armagh

Lower Lough Erne

Upper Lough Erne

MONAGHAN

Clew Bay **FIRU MAILL**

Donaghmoyne ✕

Carlingford Lough

Louth ✕ ✕ Dromiskin
✕ Linn Dúachaill

LOUTH

CONNACHTA

Dulane ✕ Monasterboice ✕
Kells ✕ ✕ Slane Drogheda ●
Donaghpatrick ✕ ✕ Duleek **BREGA**
Ardbraccan ✕

SOUTHERN

✕ Skreen Skerries ✕ ✕ St Patrick's Island
Lusk ✕ ✕

MEATH

UÍ NÉILL

Roscam ✕

Clonmacnoise ✕

✕ Durrow

Clonard ✕

Leixlip ●
Swords ✕ ✕ Lambay Island
✕ Ireland's Eye
● Howth

Galway Bay

Clonfert ✕

Lough Ree

R. Boyne

Glenn Máma ●
Tallaght ✕
✕ Clondalkin
● Dalkey Island

Birr ✕
Terryglass ✕ Seirkieran ✕

LOÍGIS

Kildare ✕
R. Liffey

DÁL

Holy Island ✕

Lough Derg

Clonenagh ✕

Dunamase ✕

Dunrally ✕

Kilcullen ✕

Glendalough ✕

✕ Wicklow

Aghaboe ✕

Castledermot ✕
✕ Clonmore

● Arklow

Scattery Island ✕

R. Shannon

Limerick ✕
Mungret ✕

CAIS

Emly ✕

OSRAIGE

Leighlin ✕

R. Nore

Ferns ✕

R. Slaney

St Mullins ✕

UÍ CHENNSELAIG

Smerwick ●

Great Blasket Island

Beginish ●

KERRY

✕ Aghadoe

Lismore ✕

Youghal ✕

R. Suir

Waterford ✕

Helvick Head

Taghmon ✕
Wexford ●
✕ Selskar
● *Wexford Harbour*

● Tuskar

EOGANACHT

Cork ✕ Fota ●
✕ Cloyne

Skellig Michael ✕

Dursey Island

Fastnet ●

● Saltee Islands

✕   monasteries known to have been attacked by Vikings

UÍ NÉILL   dynastic names

| 0 | 10 | 20 | 30 | 40 | 50 miles |
| 0 | 20 | 40 | 60 | 80 km |

IRELAND

Iona may have stopped after 825: it had hardly begun in Scotland proper. Dál Riata disappears from the record and by 820 its dynasty was ruling to the east in Fortriu. When the 'pagans' defeated 'the men of Fortriu' in 839 this was an attack on central Pictland that suggests that the Western and Northern Isles and the western and north-eastern mainland were already theirs. Here, very likely, is the *Lothlind* or *Laithlinn* of mid-ninth-century Irish sources—the kingdom of Earl Tomrair who fell in Ireland in 848 and of Amlaíb who arrived there in 853. Later, this term is applied to Scandinavia as a whole.

Evidence for Wales comes in scanty native annals. The Welsh coastal monasteries will have been plundered from the Irish Sea before the Vikings attacked the royal stronghold on Anglesey in 853/4 and Rhodri, king of Gwynedd, killed their leader Horm in 856. The Irish annals record that Rhodri fled to Ireland from the Danes in 877 and when he returned he was killed by the English in 878. The Vikings wintered in Dyfed in that year and settlement in south Wales may have begun.

In Ireland, for the first forty years, raids were mostly hit-and-run, by small seaborne forces led by freebooters with ships fast enough to surprise defence. No Viking is named in the Irish records before 837, and no king before the mid-ninth century. They kept to the edge: hardly ever much more than 30 kilometres from navigable water. Coastal defence was difficult—there are 48,000 kilometres of coast, and the raiders moved swiftly. There are no references to coast-guards or forts like the Frankish ones on the Rhine estuary, and it is thought that Irish fleets were not well developed. However, Irish local defence was sometimes effective.

Intensified Raiding and Settlement

In the later 830s the raids became more formidable, in Ireland as elsewhere: from 836 large-scale attacks began with 'the first prey of the pagans from southern Brega [south Co. Meath] and they carried off many prisoners and killed many and took very many captives'. In autumn, there was 'a most cruel devastation of all the lands of Connacht by the pagans', probably by fleets on the Shannon. The monastery of Clonmore was burned on Christmas Eve: many were killed and more were taken captive. Raiding from autumn to mid-winter, and especially slaving, proves that the Vikings were already over-wintering, possibly on islands, and could keep numerous prisoners. The Life of St Fintan of Rheinau indicates that they were slaving, and selling captives in their homeland in the mid-ninth century.

The best evidence for the provenance and activities of Viking raiders in Ireland is the Irish material recovered from Norwegian Viking-Age graves. This three-dimensional stylized cast male figure whose body is inlaid with *millefiori* glass and enamel was found in a grave of the first half of the ninth century in Myklebostad in west Norway.

87

In 837 fleets of sixty ships appeared on the Boyne and the Liffey. These must have come from bases nearer than Norway—very likely from the Scottish settlements. They ravaged the vale of the Liffey and eastern Meath and robbed monasteries and fortresses. The Uí Néill routed them, but this was soon followed by a battle in which the Uí Néill were defeated 'in a countless slaughter'. The Vikings now began to appear regularly on the inland waterways. In 837 they were on the Shannon and burned Holy Island on Lough Derg together with neighbouring churches; they were on the Erne and the Boyne, plundering inland monasteries.

In 839 they put a fleet on Lough Neagh, the largest Irish lake, linked to the north coast by the navigable lower Bann, and 'they plundered the kingdoms and monasteries of the north'. The first entry of the Ulster annalist for 841 reads: 'Pagans still on Lough Neagh.' He expected them to be gone: his surprise proves they over-wintered there for the first time in 840/1. Now came the building of *longphoirt*, permanent fortresses that also protected their ships. In 841 the annalists report a *longphort* at Linn Dúachaill (Annagassan, Co. Louth) and another at Duiblinn (Dublin). From Annagassan they plundered the midlands, from Dublin Leinster and the Uí Néill kingdoms as far as Slieve Bloom; they also robbed churches and lay settlements.

The annalist had not expected the *longphort* at Dublin to be permanent, and notes in his second entry for 842: 'Pagans still in Dublin.' But they had come to stay, they were there in big numbers, and well-defended fortresses were set up. Some are mentioned in the annals—Lough Ree on the Shannon (845), Cork (848), Dunrally on the Barrow (862), those on the north coast (866), Youghal (866), and Dún Amlaíb at Clondalkin (867); others not noticed in the literature are identified by archaeologists. Vikings were on Lough Ree in 844 and from here they plundered Connacht and Meath and rifled the rich midland monasteries. Very likely it is they who captured Forannán, abbot of Armagh, on circuit in Munster, and carried him (and the halidoms of St Patrick) off to the ships. He returned next year with his relics intact, probably ransomed at great expense. This event is likely to have alarmed his clerical contemporaries and may have prompted a royal reaction. The Viking Turges, perhaps a leader of the Lough Ree fleet, was put to death by the king of Tara in 845, but the fleet remained active.

The onslaught of the mid-ninth century was so violent that it seemed to some that Ireland was being overrun. This is conveyed by the Irish *émigré* sources behind the *Annals of St-Bertin* for 847: 'After they had been under attack from the Vikings for many years, the Irish were made tributaries to them; the Vikings have possessed themselves without opposition of all the islands round about and have settled them.'

The greater kings had not united against the attackers: they were too busy with their feuds. The annalists record the raids and killings laconically with the wry detachment of administrators of great church institutions inured to contemporary violence. And the churches supplemented their prayers with self-help: clerics took the field. In 845, the abbot of Terryglass and Clonenagh and the deputy abbot of Kildare were killed at Dunamase leading their monastic levies. Dunamase is about 13 kilometres from Clonenagh, 24 from Kildare—near enough to show they were engaged in local defence. In 842 the first explicit (and cryptic) reference to Viking–Irish co-operation occurs: Commán, abbot of Linn Dúachaill, was killed and burned by Vikings and Irish. The annalist gives no explanation, and expresses no opinion. An ironic comment on prayers for defence occurs in the notice of a raid on Armagh in 895:

> Alas, holy Patrick!
> unavailing your orisons—
> the Vikings with axes
> are hacking your oratories.

Belatedly the major kings turned on the Vikings—and found they were well able to cope. In 845 Niall Caille, king of Tara, defeated them in Donegal. In 846–7 Cerball, king of Osraige, celebrated in the twelfth century as a great ancestor of upper-class Icelanders, ably defended his territory and killed over 1,200 of his enemies. In 848 Mael Sechnaill, the next king of Tara, defeated them in battle near Skreen (Co. Meath), and killed 700. In the same year, Ólchobar, king of Munster, and Lorccán, king of Leinster, joined forces and overthrew them at Castledermot (Co. Kildare). Here fell Earl Tomrair whom the annalist calls *tanise righ Laithlinne* (heir-designate of the king of *Laithlinn*), and 1,200 of his troops. These were significant successes, even if we take the annalists' figures simply to mean large numbers, and there were others. These victories lie behind an embassy to Charles the Bald in 848, reported in the *Annals of St-Bertin*: 'The Irish attacked the Vikings and with the help of our Lord Jesus Christ they were victorious and drove them out of their territory. For that reason, the king of the Irish sends ambassadors with gifts to Charles for the sake of peace and friendship.' The first Viking attempt to take Irish territory had almost spent itself.

From the mid-ninth century the Vikings become accepted in Irish life; what began as fortresses with a subject hinterland gradually became coastal kingdoms, competing lordships. Despite their best efforts, they took no large territories—quite unlike their fellows in Scotland, England, and Frankia. The Irish kings now made war on them, now used them as allies and mercenaries in the shifting web of alliances at the centre of which lay the

In Kilmainham/Islandbridge there is solid evidence for trading: four ninth-century bronze balance scales and nine lead alloy weights with decorated mounts, some of Irish design. These scales have a bird on top and a folding cross-beam. The pans, decorated externally and internally with rows of concentric circles, hang by three chains from a cast three-legged element.

Uí Néill attempt to make themselves kings of Ireland. Soon, however, there was a more menacing Viking presence.

In 849 an expedition of 120 ships arrived in Ireland—a fleet of 'the people of the king of the Foreigners' that came to exact obedience from the Vikings of Ireland and upset the whole country, says the annalist. To add to the disorder, fierce struggles broke out in 851–2 between the Vikings in Ireland and incoming Danes who were finally driven off. In 853 'Amlaíb, son of the king of *Laithlind*, came to Ireland and the Foreigners of Ireland submitted to him and he received tribute from the Irish'. A lot has been written about the supposed Norwegian background of this Amlaíb, but it is most likely that he belonged among the rulers of the Viking kingdom(s) of Scotland, an area in which he and his successors would have vital interests for over a century to come. For the next twenty years or so, he and two others—Ímar and Auisle, who are called his brothers or kinsmen—became the most prominent of the Dublin-based Viking leaders. In 866, leading 'the Foreigners of Ireland and Scotland', they attacked and overran all Pictland, took hostages and captives and, apparently, put it under tribute. Their dramatic siege and capture of Dumbarton on the mouth of the Clyde in 870–1 (mentioned even in the Welsh annals) smashed the Britons of Strathclyde. They returned to Dublin with 200 ships, treasure, and large numbers of English, British, and Pictish captives. This opened most of Scotland to raiding, slaving, and tribute—and probably Viking domination. In 875 Danes and Norsemen were competing: the Picts were defeated by Danes from the south, and Constantine, king of what remained of Pictland, was killed by the Vikings in 877.

When Aed Finnliath, king of the Northern Uí Néill, destroyed *longphoirt* all along the north coast (including Lough Foyle) in 866 he was winning back the littoral from Viking control and settlement—a reaction to growing Viking power on both sides of the North Channel. But they held on, and in his obit in 873 Ímar is called 'king of the Northmen of all Ireland and Britain'—meaning overlord of the Vikings in Ireland and in Scotland, including Pictland and Strathclyde, and possibly Wales.

Elsewhere in Ireland the Vikings were independent adventures. There was a fleet at Waterford—and this implies a settlement—that raided along the Nore in 860. The king of Loígis and his uncle, Cerball of Osraige,

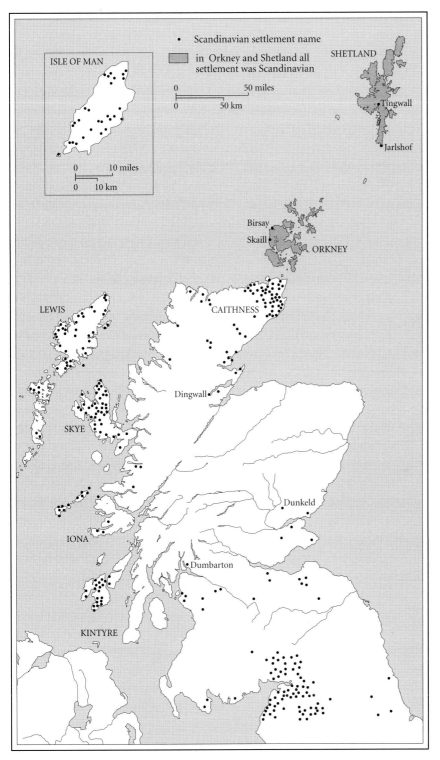

SHETLAND

Tingwall

Jarlshof

Scandinavian settlement name

in Orkney and Shetland all
settlement was Scandinavian

ISLE OF MAN

0   50 miles

0   50 km

0   10 miles

0   10 km

Birsay

Skaill

ORKNEY

LEWIS

CAITHNESS

Dingwall

SKYE

Dunkeld

IONA

Dumbarton

KINTYRE

NORTH BRITAIN AND THE ISLE OF MAN

destroyed a great Viking *longphort* and its fleet at Dunrally on the Barrow in September 862. The same Vikings were still active further south two years later when Cerball crushed them after a raid on the monastery of Leighlin. Settlements still survived on the north coast: Vikings from Lough Foyle attacked Armagh in 898 and a fleet appeared on Lough Neagh in January 900. There was another settlement on Strangford Lough. Yet another at Youghal on the south coast had its fleet defeated in 866 and its *longphort* destroyed. A year later, Gnímbeolu, leader of the Cork Vikings, was killed in battle. The raiders who killed the abbot and deputy abbot of Cloyne in 888 may have belonged to Cork. There were Limerick Vikings who were defeated by the Connachta in 887. The south midlands suffered attack from the Vikings of Waterford, Wexford, and St Mullins, who were finally defeated in 892. These operated independently, like Earl Tomrar, who plundered Clonfert in 866 and died within days of reaching his *longphort*—killed by a vengeful St Brendan, says the annalist with satisfaction.

In the later years of the ninth century the history of Dublin becomes sketchy: it was unstable and its leadership divided. The Irish successfully counter-attacked: they burned Amlaíb's fortress at Clondalkin in 867, defeated the fleet, and attacked the city itself. But Amlaíb was back in business in 869: he plundered Armagh, burned its oratories, and killed or captured 1,000 of its inhabitants. Dublin was fought over by three families. At this point Amlaíb disappears from the records; his son Oistin was murdered by Danes in 875; Barid (perhaps another son of Ímar) is called 'a great Viking tyrant' by the annalist who ascribes his death and burning in Dublin in 881 to God and St Cianán. There were more dynastic feuds and killings in 883, 888, and 893 when the Dubliners divided into two camps, one led by a son of Ímar and the other by Earl Sigfrith. In 896 his fellow Vikings killed Sitric, son of Ímar, and the Irish his brother. They still could raid deep into the hinterland: in 890–1 they plundered Ardbraccan, Donaghpatrick, Dulane, Glendalough, Kildare, and Clonard, and in 895 they attacked Armagh and took 710 prisoners. But the power of Dublin was ebbing fast. Defeat came in 902 when Brega to the north and Leinster joined forces: 'The pagans were driven from Ireland, i.e. from the fortress of Dublin and they abandoned a good number of their ships, and escaped half-dead after they had been wounded and broken.' The first Viking settlement of Dublin had come to an end.

Ireland offered no rich pickings like the Frankia of Charles the Bald. Easy settlement was not to be had, and in the late ninth century secondary Viking migrations were taking place to Iceland and the north-west of England. The aggressiveness of the Irish reaction and opportunities in Iceland and England took the pressure off Ireland. The so-called 'forty years' rest'—often discussed by historians—that supposedly marks the end of the first Viking Age derives from a twelfth-century literary source, and ultimately a biblical topos (Judg. 3: 11, 5: 32, 8: 28 etc.) that is not to be taken literally.

The Impact of the First Viking Age

The effects of the first Viking Age on Ireland are difficult to measure. In the case of the church and monastic culture the Vikings have been held responsible for a calamitous decay, but the notion that the attacks had dire effects on the resilient Irish churches, that they led to abuses and a general decay and secularization in a society that was coarsened and demoralized by violence from the Vikings (and their Irish imitators), goes too far. The ninth-century Irish scribe of the Reichenau Bede fragment, who may have belonged to a community much exposed to attack, that of Mo Chua at Clondalkin near Dublin, expressed the sentiment of many: *Di thólu aech-trann et námat et geinte et fochide di phlágaibh tened et nóne et gorte et galrae n-ile n-écsamle* ([Save us] from a flood of foreigners and foes and pagans and tribulations; from plagues of fire, famine and hunger and many divers diseases). He sets Viking attacks in their context—amongst the other nasty things in early medieval life for which the remedy was most often prayer and the mercy of God. He would have had the same weary reaction to Irish royal plunderers of monasteries.

One must not exaggerate the frequency or extent of monastic raiding. In the period 795–806 four Irish monasteries were plundered and Iona and Skye, between them, were the victims of four attacks. In 807 there were two plunderings; no more are recorded until 822. From 822 to 829 fifteen monasteries were despoiled. This adds up to twenty-five monastic raids in thirty-four years. Even if we argue that the annalists record only a quarter or less of the major attacks, the count is still very low given the number of monasteries and churches in Ireland.

From c.830 to 845 the raids on monasteries were severe: the annals list some fifty victims of specific attacks, and nine times they add a notice of raids 'on peoples and churches' in large areas, such as north Leinster and the Uí Néill kingdoms. It seems that the Vikings concentrated on big monasteries where there were things to steal and notables worth taking for ransom. There was little in the local churches, and these and their communities may have escaped disruption.

Attacks were not equally severe. Some well-known churches escaped for a long time: the first plundering of the royal monastery of Emly did not take place until 847. Seirkieran and Birr were raided once. Aghaboe, Kilcullen, Kells, and Coleraine seem to have escaped unscathed throughout the ninth century though they were attacked in the tenth. Others raided in the ninth century (for example Swords, Skellig, Mungret, Moville, Monasterboice), as far as we can tell, seem to have escaped the assault of the next century. Still others are never mentioned as victims. We must infer that many raids have gone unrecorded, but we must be careful not push this too far and make the Vikings out to be more effective than they were. Clearly they concentrated on the greater monastic towns: Armagh, Glendalough, Kildare, Slane, Clonard, Clonmacnoise, Lismore, and a few others. These were the leaders of the Irish church before the Viking period; they emerged from it in the same position, perhaps even more influential. Hardly any houses disappeared, not even those near and within Viking territories. The annalists' record is partial: their coverage is dispassionate, laconic, and obviously uneven geographically and chronologically, but it is the best guide to events as seen by the victims. And they rarely complain of the cruelty of their attackers.

Viking disruption has been blamed for specific 'abuses' such as pluralism, the use of lay abbots, clerical marriage, and the practice of hereditary succession in church. However, these long predate the Vikings. The upsets may have sometimes worsened behaviour and coarsened monastic life, but the opposite may also be true: martyrdom strengthens devotion and, for some at least, the crisis may have stiffened discipline and tightened administration.

It is often said that the raids caused an exodus of Irish scholars, poets, and teachers to Frankia and a consequent impoverishment of Irish schools. One well-known *émigré* is the poet Sedulius Scottus, who arrived at the court of Charles the Bald in the mid-ninth century. To his circle belongs the St Gall Priscian, heavily glossed in Old Irish, written in Ireland about 845 and brought to the Continent. A famous quatrain on the Viking raids occurs in its marginalia:

Is acher in gaíth innocht
fu-fuasna fairggae findfholt
ni ágor réimm mora minn
dond láechraid lainn ua Lothlind

[The wind is fierce tonight
It tosses the sea's white hair
I fear no wild Vikings
Sailing the quiet main.]

Sedulius' lines to bishop Hartgar have been taken to show that he and his like fled Ireland to escape the Vikings:

Facing: Among the larger Viking gravefields known outside Scandinavia are those at Kilmainham and Islandbridge, a mile upstream from tenth-century Dublin. They were uncovered unsystematically in the course of building in the mid-nineteenth century. While there were some domestic and some female finds, weaponry dominated. This watercolour by James Plunkett (dating to 1847), records some of the finds: swords with ornamented silver-inlaid hilts, an axe, spearheads and arrowheads, shield-bosses, four gaming pieces, and women's bronze brooches.

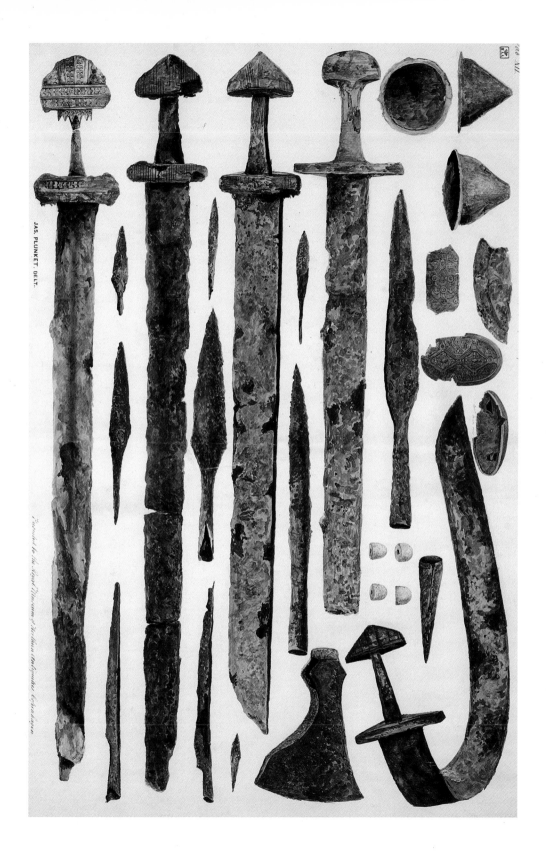

JAS. PLUNKET. DELT.

Furnished by the Royal Museum of Northern Antiquities, Copenhagen.

The swollen North Wind ravages us—piteous to see—
Learned grammarians and holy priests
For the rushing North Wind spares no persons
Lacerating us with his cruel beak
Therefore, a helper of the weary, O flourishing prelate Hartgar,
Receive with kindly heart us learned Irishmen

Sedulius indeed refers to the raids, but these hardly drove him into exile. Irish scholars were influential at the Carolingian court and elsewhere long before the Viking attack became significant, and well after the worst had blown over. Sedulius was a scholar–courtier: the Frankia of Charles the Bald was under severe attack and he was well able to use the experience of the Franks to win sympathy for himself and his fellows by pleading that they, too, were victims. Irish scholars were not driven out by the raids: they were attracted by the lavish patronage of the Carolingians when Frankia itself was more troubled than Ireland.

The Irish monastic schools flourished. The outstanding works of vernacular literature—lyric and religious poetry of great delicacy, building on metrical forms already established in the seventh century, and the narrative prose of the Ulster cycle and the king tales, heir to over two centuries of stylistic development—belong to the ninth and tenth centuries. Elaborate genealogies, law texts, and historical tracts were written at the same time and, in European terms, the Irish monastic scholars provide the most detailed and dispassionate annals of the Viking wars. If one leaves out of account the expatriate Irish scholars in the Carolingian empire, Latin writing of the late ninth and tenth centuries is mostly workaday hagiography and devotional texts. There was no decline in metalwork but a change in style, and the silver made available by the Vikings was much used. Figure-carving in stone is impressive. The high cross at Kinnitty was erected for Mael Sechnaill, king of Tara (d. 862), and inscribed with his claim to the kingship of Ireland. What seems to be a representation on the cross of Samuel calling David to the kingship (1 Kgs. 16: 1–13) is a suitable symbol of the church's acceptance of his position and a statement of his priorities. The magnificent Cross of the Scriptures at Clonmacnoise was erected for his son, Flann Sinna, king of Tara (879–916). The Gospel of Mac Durnan and the tenth-century psalters show that the tradition of manuscript illumination continued. The monastic churches and their schools came through the wars and survived even within Viking areas.

Some hold that the raids caused a growth in violence towards the churches and ended clerical immunity. This is questionable. Attacks on monasteries preceded the Viking wars, persisted during them, and continued long after they had ended. The causes are complex; structural, social,

Facing: A group of Viking-Age finds from Fishamble Street and Christchurch Place, Dublin. This spectacular assemblage includes a bone trial piece, a bone needle, bronze ring pins, a magnificently carved wooden crook (for a walking stick or whip handle), a leather shoe, coins, a knife, and assorted pieces of amber. Over 3,000 pieces of Baltic amber have been found in Dublin.

and economic reasons made the monasteries vulnerable—the breach of sanctuary by a violent aristocracy, the close kinship of churchmen and kings that made monasteries royal centres and drew the church into political conflicts, rivalry between church lineages, and the raiding of church stores in times of famine.

Reliquaries to hold the bones of saints and other relics were common in early Christian Ireland. This eighth-century example is made of yew and covered with copper alloy, tin, and enamel. It is ornamented in the Irish style with triple spirals in relief and there are recesses that once held red enamel. The base has a tenth-century runic inscription: *Ranvaik a kistu thasa* ('Ranvaik owns this casket').

The Vikings did not attack monasteries for religious reasons (they had none), but because they were places of concentrated wealth, were used as safe-deposits, and because monastic farms were well stocked. Unlike the Irish, they deliberately plundered altar plate, shrines, and halidoms. The evidence comes from the annals and from the survival of looted artefacts in Norway. But they did not limit themselves to these. Once raided, monasteries could not replace precious vessels and shrines quickly; besides, their worth as bullion was low—their value depended on the religious and artistic perceptions of their owners, and it is likely that the Vikings soon learned that they fetched more ransom than their crude worth in precious metal.

The Vikings quickly discovered the profits to be made from people as a commodity: slaves and prisoners for ransom. Slave-taking was a regular feature of early raids; large-scale slaving came later. Amlaíb killed or took captive 1,000 people in Armagh in 869. Other major slave-raids are reported in Duleek in 881 when many were taken; in Kildare in 886 when 280 captives (including the deputy abbot) were seized; and in Armagh in 895 when 710 people were carried off. It is not clear how these slaves were marketed, but some found their way to Scandinavia and to Iceland. Slaving of this kind was new to Ireland: the Irish used it against the Vikings, but not against one another.

On the political level, it has been held that pre-Viking Ireland was tribal and ritualistic, and that archaic Irish institutions—legal and political—crumbled under attack. This 'old order' is not found in historic Ireland. It comes, rather, from too narrow a reading of the Irish laws, coloured by a mistaken interpretation of saga texts, some written in the ninth century or later when the society they are imagined to describe had presumably collapsed. In fact, the literature betrays current concerns. The Irish mythological tale *Cath Maige Tuired* has clear reference to the Viking threat (perhaps even a contemporary political message), and the annals and genealogies

96

reveal an Ireland ruled by power-hungry kings and lords very like their European peers. Some of these claimed to be kings of Ireland and were long engaged in violent power-struggles. They were not deflected by Viking raids.

The Second Viking Age

By the early tenth century there was a long-established Hiberno-Viking area on both sides of the North Channel—in Ireland but much more significantly in Scotland and Man. Colonists came from Dublin and its dependencies in a great movement that led to dense settlement, at an unknown date, from the Dee to the Solway and beyond, and extending to Yorkshire north of the Humber, as shown by place-names ending in -*by* compounded with Irish personal names (for example Melmerby <*Máel Muire*, Melsonby <*Máel Suthain*, Duggleby <*Dubgall*). Ingimund, who occupied part of Anglesey in 903 and was driven on into Mercia leading a mixed force of Vikings and Irish, is one of the few named refugees. The exiled Dublin leaders settled in their Scottish dependencies and immediately tried to subjugate the Picts. In 904 two 'grandsons of Ímar' killed the king of Pictland in battle, and Ímar ua hÍmair (king of Dublin until 902) was killed by the Picts at Strathearn. Another kinsman, Ragnall ua hÍmair, won a victory over the English and Scots at Corbridge in 914 and granted lands to his followers. This expanding Scandinavian power in north Britain threatened all its neighbours. In 913 a sea-fleet of the Ulaid was defeated on the English coast by the Vikings—evidence that north-east Ireland felt vulnerable and had joined the English in trying to contain Ragnall. In 914 he extended his activities to Man.

In Ireland the second Viking Age began suddenly with 'the arrival of a great sea-fleet of pagans in Waterford Harbour' in 914. It came originally from Brittany, made an attack on the Severn estuary and sailed for Ireland in the autumn. It arrived before 1 November, and probably went into winter camp—the annals say nothing of its doings in 914. The next year more Vikings arrived in Waterford and ravaged the kingdoms and churches of Munster. In 917 two leaders of the exiled Dublin dynasty joined in the renewed attack. Their relationship to the Waterford fleets of 914/15 is not clear, but they took control of Viking activities in Ireland. Ragnall, who is called *rí Dubgall* (king of the Danes) because he ruled Danish Northumbria, arrived with a fleet at Waterford. His kinsman, Sitric Caech, occupied Cenn Fuait, on the border of Leinster.

The arrival of large forces under well-known leaders led to war with Niall Glúndub, king of Tara since 916. A northerner, he was keenly aware of

Ragnall's threat to Ireland, Scotland, and England. In August 917 he marched to Cashel 'to make war on the pagans'. The leaders played safe: there was no decisive engagement, though the campaign lasted three weeks or more. Niall persuaded the Leinstermen to attack Sitric's encampment at Cenn Fuait. They were heavily defeated: the king of Leinster, its bishop, and many of its leaders fell, and Sitric retook Dublin. In 918 Ragnall led his Waterford fleet to north Britain and to campaigns that made him king of York and ruler of Northumbria. He had won nothing worthwhile in Ireland.

Soon Niall Glúndub and Sitric of Dublin were at war. In September 919 Niall marched on Dublin. He was heavily defeated at Islandbridge (near Dublin), and he and many Uí Néill leaders fell. An annalist notes ironically that Céle Dábaill, abbot of Bangor and Niall's confessor, who had incited him to battle, gave the king viaticum in exchange for his horse so that he could flee. (That prudent and learned abbot died in retirement in Rome in 929.) Never before had so many Irish notables been killed by the Vikings, and contemporaries were shocked. Then, suddenly, Sitric left Dublin to lay claim to York.

Ragnall had returned to north Britain in 918. On the way, he attacked Scotland and sacked Dunblane. At Tynemouth, he defeated the English and Scots. He took York in 919, and then submitted, as king of Northumbria, to king Edward. York and Dublin were now ruled by a single dynasty, and this had important political and cultural consequences. Ragnall died in 921 and in his obit he is called *rí Finngall 7 Dubgall* (king of the Norse and the Danes)—an accurate description of his mixed Scandinavian kingdom. Sitric of Dublin succeeded him and ruled York until his death in 927. He met King Athelstan in conference at Tamworth in 926, became a Christian of sorts, and married the king's sister.

Dublin was ruled by Sitric's kinsman, Godfrid, a raider and slaver. In 921 he attacked Armagh on the eve of the feast of St Martin (11 November), when it was full of food and well-loaded pilgrims, but he spared the church and the charities. He also harried the countryside to the east and north of Armagh. This was part of a tenacious Dublin campaign from *c.*921 to 927 (and again later) to create a Scandinavian kingdom like that on the other side of the Irish Sea. This was foiled by Muirchertach, king of the Northern Uí Néill. When Sitric died, Athelstan took Northumbria. Godfrid hurried to claim York, but he was driven out. In his absence, Tomar mac Ailche, the powerful, independent Viking lord of Limerick since 922, struck up an alliance with Godfrid's enemies and took Dublin briefly; this was part of a longer Dublin–Limerick struggle. Limerick put fleets on the western and northern lakes, and its forces were a menace there and a serious threat to

Dublin. In 934 Godfrid died: his obit describes him, unusually, as *ri crudelissimus Nordmannorum* (a most cruel king of the Norsemen).

His successor was his son Amlaíb, who carried on a vigorous struggle with the Irish and dealt with Limerick: in August 937 he defeated the Limerick leader on Lough Ree, smashed his fleet, and brought him prisoner to Dublin. Now Amlaíb turned to York and to a north British alliance that led first to his defeat at Brunanburh, and then to the kingship of York. On the English side were Athelstan and his brother Edmund, and the troops of Wessex and Mercia; on the other were Amlaíb with the Vikings of Dublin and the north of Ireland, Constantine, king of the Scots, and the king of Strathclyde. The result was a great victory for Athelstan, but Amlaíb escaped, and returned to Dublin in 938.

Underlying the battle of Brunanburh was the insecurity of the kingdoms of northern England and Scotland (including the Scandinavians) in the face of Athelstan's growing power. Conditions were ripe for a revolt of the periphery, but how this came about is obscure and, to judge from the annals, at the heart of the darkness is the ringleader, Amlaíb of Dublin. He must have been in a position to lead the alliance before his local victory over Limerick, and this suggests that he was the foremost Viking figure in the British Isles. The English chronicler Florence of Worcester calls him 'the pagan Anlaf [Amlaíb], king of the Irish and of many islands'. We must infer that Dublin held real power in the north Irish Sea, Man, the Hebrides, Scotland, and northern England and had formidable resources. It was a sea-kingdom, the centre of economic and political interests at some remove from the observers in Ireland and England, and thus poorly documented. When Athelstan died in October 939 Amlaíb sailed for England, reached York before the year's end, and was made king by the Northumbrians. He followed this success with a campaign south of the Humber, accompanied by Wulfstan, archbishop of York. The result was a negotiated settlement with Edmund, Athelstan's successor, by which Amlaíb was recognized as king of York and ruler of Danish Mercia—almost half the kingdom of England. He died in 941.

York was soon lost by his successor, Amlaíb Cuarán, who returned in 945 to an Ireland where Irish–Viking warfare had reached a new intensity. Muirchertach of the Northern Uí Néill won many victories but was killed by the Vikings at Ardee in 943. Next year, Congalach, king of Brega and Bróen of Leinster, united against Dublin in a pincer movement and sacked the city with a new ferocity:

The destruction brought upon it was this: its houses, house-enclosures, its ships and its other structures were burned; its women, boys and common folk were

The Gaelic-speaking Isle of Man was heavily settled by Vikings. It was a dependency of Viking Dublin and its overlords in the eleventh and twelfth centuries, and belonged to the kingdom of Man and the Isles. Odd's cross-slab from Kirk Braddan is carved in the Jellinge style—and this may betray direct artistic contact with Norway among artists in the Irish Sea area.

enslaved; its men and its warriors were killed; it was altogether destroyed, from four persons to one, by killing and drowning, burning and capture, apart from a small number that fled in a few ships and reached Dalkey.

The victors plundered the city. After this, Congalach was recognized as king of Tara and it seems that authority over Dublin (and profit from its economy) was now a perquisite of that office. Amlaíb Cuarán turned again to England where he held the kingship of York from about 948 until he was driven out in 953. Congalach attacked Dublin again in 948 and killed its ruler, and 1,600 of its troops were either killed or taken prisoner.

Wales was subject to attack from two points on the Irish Sea. The Dublin of Amlaíb Cuarán intervened in Welsh dynastic disputes, drew tribute from Wales, and plundered it. In 961 Amlaíb's sons raided from Ireland's Eye, off the coast of Dublin, and pillaged Holyhead and the Lleyn peninsula. There were other Dublin raiders in Wales in the eleventh century. The second set of attackers were the lords of the Western Isles in the tenth and eleventh centuries who plundered the Irish and Welsh coasts like the Vikings of an earlier age. Magnus, son of Harold, lord of the Isles, raided Penmon in 971. His brother Godfrid took Anglesey and spoiled Lleyn in 980, raided Dyfed in 982, and was back in Anglesey in 987, where he took 2,000 prisoners. There were frequent monastic raids in the second half of the tenth century and opportunistic attacks in the eleventh. To judge by place-names, there were Viking settlements all along the south coast of Wales from Newport to Fishguard (Pembrokeshire seems to have been a Viking colony) and perhaps in the north, from Anglesey to Flint.

From about 950 to 980 Dublin behaved politically much like a powerful local kingdom as the Irish kings struggled to build up power bases. Mael Sechnaill, king of the Southern Uí Néill, crushed the Dubliners at Tara in 980 (the annalist calls it 'a red slaughter'), where Amlaíb Cuarán commanded the troops of Dublin and the Hebrides. Everything suggests a long-planned attack on Mael Sechnaill that went disastrously wrong and greatly weakened Dublin. Mael Sechnaill besieged the city and forced it to terms: the

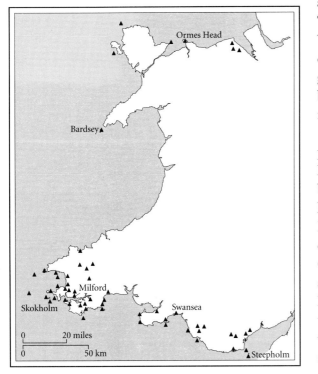

freeing of all Irish hostages including the king of Leinster and the hostages of the Uí Néill; the handing over of treasure and valuables, the freeing of all the lands of the Uí Néill from the Shannon to the sea from tribute. He released all Irish slaves in Viking territory—that, says the annalist with pious hyperbole, was 'the Babylonian captivity of Ireland, second only to the captivity of hell'. Amlaíb Cuarán retired to Iona as a penitent. Mael Sechnaill now ruled Dublin through an underking and reasserted his authority when Sitric Silkenbeard succeeded to Dublin in 989.

In the late tenth century, the Dál Cais (later Uí Briain) rose to power in Munster. Their greatest king was Brian Bórama, who dominated the Viking cities and used their revenues and fleets to make himself king of Ireland: the fleet of Waterford in 984 and 988, the cavalry of Dublin in 1000, and Dublin's fleet in his northern campaigns of 1006 and 1007. He drew on the Vikings' other skills: for example, Osli, grandson of the king of Limerick (whom he had killed in 977), was his adviser and *mormaer* (principal minister) in 1013. His thorough absorption of Limerick betrayed the policy Dublin feared. In 997 Brian and Mael Sechnaill divided Ireland between them, and Brian took the hostages of Dublin and Leinster, and thus Brian became their overlord. Late in 999 Leinster and Dublin, led by Sitric Silkenbeard, revolted. Brian and Mael Sechnaill overwhelmed them at Glenn Máma, south of Dublin, and Brian sacked the city and besieged its fortress. He restored Sitric Silkenbeard as a subject king, and he now had the troops, fleets, and taxes of Dublin for his final and successful effort to become king of Ireland.

There were rumblings of revolt from 1012—Brian fortified Munster and sent troops against Dublin. Early in 1014 the Dubliners built up a defensive alliance, including Sigurd, earl of Orkney, and troops from the Hebrides and elsewhere in the Viking world. Brian and Mael Sechnaill led their armies to Dublin to engage them. The battle, fought at Clontarf, north of Dublin, lasted all day on Good Friday, 23 April. In the end the Vikings and their allies were routed. Losses were heavy and Brian, extravagantly described as 'the Augustus of the whole of north-western Europe', was killed. Though spectacular, this was not a struggle between the Vikings and the Irish for the rule of Ireland, nor did it alter irrevocably the status of Dublin. The Leinstermen had resented the dominance of Brian and joined the Dubliners, the prime movers. These were fighting for their survival as a prosperous, self-governing, and nearly autonomous city-state (with a rich hinterland and large overseas interests) which Brian threatened to absorb. He was about to do to Dublin what Athelstan and his successors had done to York, and Dublin resisted fiercely.

Gradually, the more powerful Irish kings dominated Dublin and as the

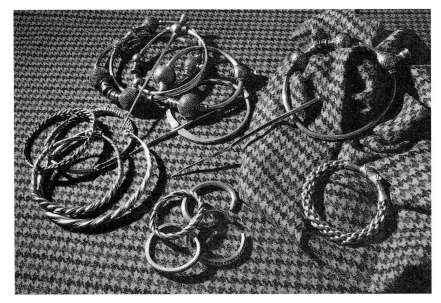

The Skaill Bay hoard, Orkney, deposited *c.*950, is the largest Viking silver hoard from Scotland; it contained about eight kg of silver. There are few coins, but fine examples of neck-rings, penannular arm-rings, and thistle brooches, as well as ingots and hack-silver. The ornamentation on the thistle brooches is close to that of the Manx crosses and the art is that of the Irish Sea area.

struggle for the kingship of Ireland gathered momentum it became an important prize. When Donnchad, son of Brian, marched north against Meath and Brega in 1026, he encamped in peace for three days beside the fortress of Dublin. The Dubliners knew how to bargain, and the king knew how to profit from his position. Control over Dublin passed from one king to another. First was Diarmait, king of Leinster, who led a great expedition to Dublin in 1052, drove its existing king overseas, and seized it for himself. In 1054 and 1057–8 he commanded its army and fleet and installed his son Murchad on the throne. When Murchad died in 1070 the annalists calls him 'lord of the Foreigners and king of Leinster under his father' and, significantly, he was buried in Dublin. When Diarmait himself fell in battle in 1072 the Welsh annalist laments him as 'the most praiseworthy and bravest king of the Irish, terrible towards his enemies; kind towards the poor, and gentle towards pilgrims'; the Irish annalist entitles him 'king of Wales and of the Isles and of Dublin'—clear evidence that Diarmait's influence extended to the overseas territories of the Vikings and to Wales. And Irish dynasts and Irish-based Vikings continued to intervene in Welsh affairs in the eleventh and twelfth centuries.

The royal authority of Tairdelbach, grandson of Brian, was accepted by Dublin, and later Gofraid, king of Dublin, did him homage and recognized his suzerainty. When they fell out in 1075, Tairdelbach expelled him. Soon Tairdelbach's son Muirchertach was enthroned in Dublin at the age of 25 and ruled there until he succeeded his father as king of Munster (and Ireland) in 1086. Dublin remained his capital. In 1094, when a northern alliance challenged Muirchertach, it did so there. He used its fleet against

102

the north in 1100, and its army in 1103. When the abbot of Armagh tried to broker peace between him and his northern enemies in 1105 the negotiations took place in Dublin. In 1111 Muirchertach went to Dublin and held court there from Michaelmas (29 September) to Christmas. When challenged by Leinster interests he defeated them in battle at Dublin in 1115 and made his son Domnall ruler of the city. His authority extended to Man and the Western Isles. Muirchertach dominated the Viking cities (Dublin, Limerick, Waterford, Cork) and he took care to have reform bishops of his choice appointed to them. He dealt craftily with the colourful Magnus Barelegs, king of Norway, who came adventuring in the west in 1098—taking Orkney, the Hebrides, and Man, perhaps even Galloway and Gwynedd, and threatening Ireland. Muirchertach and Magnus made a marriage treaty and Magnus spent the winter of 1102/3 with Muirchertach. The next spring they headed north—Muirchertach to a major defeat, Magnus to his death in a skirmish.

Control of Dublin and its resources was an appurtenance of the kingship of Ireland. This is clear from the annals and from a passage in the laws describing the king of Ireland and very likely dating from the reign of Muirchertach: *do righ Erunn cin freasabra .i. in tan bit na hinbir fui, Ath Cliath Port Lairge Luimniuch olcheana* (to the king of Ireland without opposition, i.e. when the estuaries are under his control: Dublin and Waterford and Limerick besides).

Cultural Assimilation

Cultural assimilation marked the landscape and place-names attest to otherwise undocumented settlement. The name of Scattery, an island monastery in the Shannon estuary, is an Old Norse re-formation of Irish *Inis Cathaig*. In the extreme south-west, the Blaskets (earlier Blasques) contain the Old Norse word *øy* 'island' (the first element is uncertain); the nearby harbour of Smerwick (<ON *Smǫrvík* a re-formation of the Irish *Muirbech*) means 'butter bay', perhaps from the fertile monastic farmlands that lie about it; and at Beginish, on the tip of the Iveragh peninsula, a cross-inscribed rune-stone points to Hiberno-Norse settlers in a monastic context. Norse names on the south coast (Dursey, Fastnet, Fota, Helvick, Waterford, Saltees, Selskar, Tuskar) and on the east coast (Wexford, Arklow, Wicklow, Howth, Ireland's Eye, Lambay, Skerries, Carlingford, Strangford) passed from Old Norse into English. Landmarks or settlements in the lingua franca of Viking seamen, they left no trace in Irish. Dalkey near Dublin is a part translation of Irish *Delginis*. Inland purely Old Norse names, as distinct from those formed in the Irish way with Old Norse ele-

ments, are scarce. One of the few is Leixlip, from Old Norse *lax-hløypa* 'salmon's leaping-place'. Names with Old Norse elements are common enough within the kingdom of Dublin, but Norse place-names are infrequent in Ireland as a whole compared with England, Wales and Scotland

Linguistic contact began early and was in full swing by the mid-ninth century. Our datable evidence, however, comes from the literary register, and that is slow to admit borrowings. The earliest ordinary loanword is *erell*, *iarla* from *jarl* 'earl'—the Irish were impressed by these military leaders. There are three important farming terms: *punnann* from **bundan* 'sheaf (of corn)'; *garrdha* from *garðr* originally 'messuage', later 'fenced vegetable garden'; and *pónair* from *baunir* 'beans'. This shows that there were Norse-speaking farmers.

The most significant loanwords have to do with typical Viking activities: shipping (*ancaire* <*akkeri* 'anchor', *bád* <*bátr* 'boat', *scód* <*skaut* 'sheet', *stiúir* <*stýri* 'rudder', *laídeng* <*leiðangr* 'naval forces', *cnarr* <*knǫrr* 'ship'); fishing (*langa* <*langa* 'ling', *trosc* <*þorskr* 'cod', *scatán* <*skadd* 'herring', *dorgha* <*dorg* 'fishing-line'); commerce and traded goods (*margad* <*markaðr* 'market', *pinginn* <*penningr* 'penny', *scilling* <*skillingr* 'shilling', *scuird* <*skyrta* 'shirt, cloak', *cnaipe* <*knappr* 'button', *bróg* now 'shoe' <*brók* 'hose, trousers'); warfare (*boga* <*bogi* 'bow', *elta* <*hjalt* 'hilt', *merge* <*merki* 'battle-standard'). There are a few terms for food, notably *builín*, *builbhín* 'a loaf' probably <*bylmingr* 'a kind of bread', *beoir* 'beer' <*bjórr* (very likely a different kind of ale from what the Irish had). Social terms are limited: *ármand* 'officer, commander' <*ármáðr* 'Norse stewards of royal farms', *lagmann* <*lǫgmaðr* 'lawyer, local aristocrat', *súartlech* <*svartleggja* 'mercenary', *traill* <*þræll* 'slave, servant'. There are only a few verbs: *leagadh* 'lay down, knock down' <*leggja, crapadh* 'shrink, contract' <*krappr, rannsughadh* 'search, rummage' <*rannsaka* (English 'ransack' is borrowed from Old Norse too). The surviving Old Norse contribution to Irish is modest—well under fifty words and Norse loanwords were probably never more than a tiny percentage of the vocabulary.

Irish forms of Old Norse personal names appear early in the ninth cen-

Sarcophagus in Cormac's Chapel at Cashel (the finest Irish Romanesque church, consecrated in 1134). A striking example of Urnes style with deeply carved interlacing animals.

tury: the first is *Saxolb* from *Søxulfr* a Viking leader killed in 836. The most common are *Amlaíb* from *Óláfr*, *Gothbrith*, *Gothfrith*, *Gofraid* from *Goðrøðr*, *Ímar* from *Ívarr*, *Ragnall* from *Rognvaldr*, *Sitriuc* from *Sigtryggr*, but there were others. Irish aristocrats borrowed Norse names only at the end of the tenth century, and commonly in the eleventh and twelfth centuries: we have no idea what the lower classes did. Amlaíb, Ímar, Ragnall, and Sitric—the usual royal names amongst the Viking leaders—are the most common, and these gave rise to Irish surnames. The Vikings borrowed Irish names a little earlier and we find Vikings in the early eleventh century with purely Irish names. This shows that deep intermingling was well advanced long before the middle of the tenth century.

When Amlaíb Cuarán died in 981 the annalist respectfully entitled him 'high king over the Foreigners'. He was a patron of poets and skalds: the poet Cináed ua hArtacáin (d. 975) wrote of him:

> *Amlaíb Átha Cliath cétaig*
> *ro gab rígi i mBeind Étair*
> *tallus lúag mo dána de—*
> *ech d'echaib ána Aichle*

> [Amlaíb of populous Dublin
> who ruled as king over Howth
> I received the reward of my poem from him—
> A steed of the steeds of Achall]

Important twelfth-century literary texts, one in Old Norse and the others in Irish, throw light on this Viking–Irish society. The Old Norse text, an account of the battle of Clontarf, is *Brjánssaga* (Brian's Saga), much of it extant in *Njála* and *Þorsteinnsaga Síðuhallssonar*. It was written in Dublin, probably by a cleric, and before 1118. Brian is presented as an exemplary king—holy, just, powerful, the ancestral saint-king. The battle of Clontarf and Brian's death, it says, were the work of pagans, apostates, and traitors, not the ancestors of the Christian burghers of Dublin, the good subjects of the present rulers, who were themselves descended from the beneficiary of the saintly king's first miracle. This was an astute, if anodyne, interpretation of a part of Dublin's history that had become embarrassing. The political perspicacity of the tale and the accuracy of the Irish names in it show that it was written in Dublin and transmitted in writing to Scandinavia. A literary culture existed in the early twelfth century—in Dublin, in the Orkneys, and elsewhere—and it may go back a century or more to the acquisition of Norse literacy in the Dublin–York axis of the tenth century.

Cogad Gaedel re Gallaib (The War of the Irish with the Foreigners) is brilliant propaganda, contemporary with *Brjánssaga* and written in the interest of the Uí Briain kingship of Dublin and Ireland. It is in two parts: annals detailing the plundering of the Vikings and the miseries they inflicted on Ireland, and a triumphal account of the heroic victories of Dál Cais over the Vikings, culminating at Clontarf, written in the contemporary bombastic style and full of patriotic hyperbole. The Vikings are 'furious, ferocious, pagan, ruthless, wrathful people' who ravish a saintly land, tyrants whose long oppression was ended by Brian, 'the beautiful ever-victorious Augustus Caesar ... the strong irresistible second Alexander'. The Dál Cais are 'the Franks [i.e. the Normans] of Ireland, the sons of Israel of Ireland' meaning that, as God's providential dynasty, they would dominate Ireland as the Normans did England. This rewriting of history is meant to put the Dubliners in their place as subjects, and give the Uí Briain the unique record of achievement that destined them to be kings of Ireland.

If propaganda like this is to be effective it must reach its target audience. How far had integration gone? Very far, if one may judge from disparaging Irish references to 'the broken speech of the Vikings' and the 'cant of the hucksters'. Could the Vikings of Ireland grasp a message conveyed in highly rhetorical and colourful literary Irish that cannot have been the ordinary contemporary register? Could the royal court of Muirchertach Ua Briain appreciate a subtle rewriting of Dublin's history in polished literary Old Norse? It seems so. The royal families were closely related by marriage. For example, both Brian and Mael Sechnaill had been married to Sitric's mother, Gormlaith, and were therefore Sitric's stepfathers. Donnchadh, son of Brian, was the uterine brother of Sitric Silkenbeard and he was married to the daughter of the Viking ruler of Waterford. Two of Gormlaith's three husbands were involved in the battle of Clontarf, Finally, for good measure, her son Sitric Silkenbeard was married to a daughter of her former husband Brian. Brian, then, was stepfather and father-in-law of Sitric Silkenbeard. Meanwhile, Sitric was the brother-in-law of Olaf Tryggvasson, king of Norway. One can conclude that there was widespread vernacular bilingualism in the ruling élite of the eleventh and twelfth centuries—and this extended to the literary registers. It is to be expected that texts in both languages should be written about the most notable military conflict that occurred within this élite, the battle of Clontarf.

This cultural variety is the literary and linguistic correlative of the remarkable interpenetration of Irish and Viking art. Viking styles spread from the cities. A good example is the Cross of Cong, a work commissioned to enshrine a relic of the True Cross, begun in 1123 and finished about 1127. It is inscribed with its patron's name, Tairdelbach Ua Conchobair, king of Ireland, who had seized the kingship of Dublin in 1118. It is a magnificent achievement of the Scandinavian Urnes style. As in art, so in language and literature.

They were united, too, by a common Christian culture. Tenth-century Dublin developed close ties with the rest of Ireland. Major monasteries prospered in areas dominated by Viking Dublin—Monasterboice, Dunleer, Dromiskin, Swords, Clondalkin, Tallaght, and others in the Viking settlement's immediate suburbs—and these will have influenced the Viking settlers from an early period. Great houses like Glendalough and Kildare had new foundations in or near the city. Already in the late ninth century there were Christian Dubliners. The ruling dynasty was Christian in the tenth. Amlaíb Cuarán formally became a Christian in 943; his son Sitric Silkenbeard made a pilgrimage to Rome in 1028, and a diocese of Dublin, suffragan to Canterbury, was founded somewhat later. An elegy, perhaps twelfth-century, offers an image of Christian Dublin, whose people the poet calls 'the seed of Aralt, remnant of the warriors of Lochlainn':

> Unwillingly and willingly I fare to Dublin,
> to the fort of Amlaíb of the golden shields;
> from Dublin of the churches and the graves
> swift and slow will be my going.
>
> O people of Dublin of the bells
> both abbot and bishop
> do not place clay over Tadc in the east
> until I have been able to see him.

An Irish poem on Dublin, of Armagh provenance and dated *c.*1121 × *c.*1129, lists the main churches of the city: St Patrick's, St Michael le Pole, St Michan's, St Paul's, St Peter's, Christchurch, St Mary de Dam, St Bride's, an unnamed church within the fortress (perhaps St Olaf's), and some unidentified churches including a *Cell mac nAeda* that is said to be the first church founded in Dublin. It lists the dues Armagh expected of Dublin—and these reflect the Dublin archaeological finds:

> a horn of mead from every vat
> a comb from every comb-maker
> a shoe from every shoemaker
> a vessel from every glorious silversmith
> a scruple from every moneyer
> a cowl from every merchant ship.

Comb-making, using deer antlers, was a significant activity in the Viking world—important enough in Dublin to be taxed. The raw material came from the rural hinterland, as traded goods. These fine-wrought combs were found in the Dublin excavations.

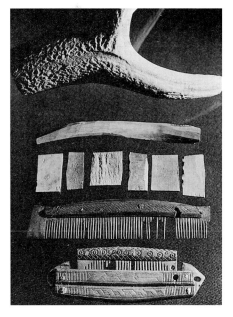

107

And Armagh is entitled to a tithe of all Dublin levies on Viking merchants trading out of Dublin with the interior:

> Every Viking in Ireland
> who is entitled to ply as merchant—
> taxes are due from him
> to the folk of the royal citadel.
>
> The tax that they are required
> to pay over to Dublin:
> a pack-horse load of malt
> and half a pack-horse load of salt meat
>
> Two pack-horse loads of firewood
> with their complement of candles
> are strictly owed to the Vikings of the citadel
> by the trading Vikings of Ireland
>
> Every tenth of these loads
> that reaches the Vikings
> is known to be owed to Patrick [Armagh].

This remarkable twelfth-century crozier from Aghadoe (Co. Kerry) is of walrus ivory and is carved in the Viking Urnes style, strikingly similar to the carving on the jambs of the Romanesque portal of the ruined cathedral of Aghadoe.

The Viking cities were in the vanguard of the twelfth-century reorganization of the church, and Dublin held tenaciously to Canterbury until 1152. Paradoxically, the institution that the pagan Vikings first attacked proved resilient and most adept at absorbing them; and their Christian successors were among the pioneers of an episcopal reform movement that set aside that traditional monastic church in favour of territorial dioceses.

The Impact of the Vikings

What of the political effect of the Vikings? They did shake up the major Irish kingdoms, but no large kingdom was conquered. The territories taken, though small, were strategic, and from the tenth century the cities were very important. The economic changes that came in the wake of urban settlement in the second Viking Age—especially the unprecedented growth of trade, and thus of royal income—provided the greater dynasties with the means to build up their power dramatically and fuelled the struggle for the kingship of Ireland. The example of Athelstan and later English kings was not lost on the Uí Néill or their successors, particularly since the connections of Dublin and York ensured that the leading Irish kings followed closely the changing fortunes of English–Viking relations. The idea that there should be a kingship of Ireland, pursued with great energy in the eleventh and twelfth centuries, owed more to foreign example and to the economic and political changes brought about by the Vikings than to inherited concepts of power. The vigorous warfare of the kings—the use of cavalry, fleets, fortifications, and encastellation—owed much to the Vikings, and later to Norman influence mediated by contact with England through the Viking ports. Above all the Vikings were enablers of communication, ultimately the most effective agent of change in all societies. They brought Ireland into closer political and economic contact with Britain and the European mainland—and this is reflected in twelfth-century vernacular literature—and with the tide of change that flowed strongly in the eleventh and twelfth centuries in government, church, and commerce. This, in the end, was their most important contribution. They lost influence when their cities fell to the Normans, and though they continued as discrete Old Norse-speaking communities at least until the late thirteenth century they were ultimately absorbed by the English colony in Ireland.

5

THE ATLANTIC ISLANDS

SVEINBJÖRN RAFNSSON

Facing: The Cross of
Cong, a processional
cross and reliquary of
the 'True Cross'. Com-
missioned in about
1123 by Tairdelbach Ua
Conchobar, king of
Connacht, it is said to
be 'one of the finest
and liveliest pieces of
ornamental metalwork
ever made in Ireland'.
There are gilt bronze
panels in the Urnes
style and revivals of the
traditional polychrome
style. It is a spectacular
example of the integra-
tion of Viking and
Irish styles.

Inset: One of the
magnificent chessmen
of walrus ivory of the
late twelfth century
from Lewis in the
Hebrides. They have
clear similarities with
material from Trond-
heim and demonstrate
the close connections
between the Western
Isles and Norway.

Classical authors gave the name Thule to the northernmost parts of
Europe. The first person known to have used it was the Greek Pytheas of
Masilia who lived about 300 BC. In the early eighth century AD Bede
described Thule as an island north of Britain, but we do not know what he
meant—perhaps Scandinavia, or parts of it. About a hundred years later
Dicuil, an Irish scholar working in Frankia, mentioned Thule among the
many islands north of Britain all of which were always uninhabited and
deserted (*semper desertae*), although sheep grazed on some of them. It has
been suggested that the isles with sheep were the Faeroes. At the end of the
ninth century, in the Old English version of Orosius' *Seven Books of History
against the Pagans* (see Chapter 7), the Norwegian Ottar described sailing
along the Norwegian coast, but he did not mention any islands north of
Britain.

Written Sources

The first sources to name Iceland and Greenland are a papal letter of 1053
and, about twenty years later, the *Gesta* of Adam of Bremen. In the eleventh
century, after the islands had been Christianized, accounts of their history
began to be written from the point of view of their inhabitants, and after
about 1130 sagas and chronicles on the subject were written and rewritten in
Iceland, but there are no contemporary sources for their earliest history.

The first known Icelandic historians lived at the end of the eleventh and
the beginning of the twelfth centuries. It is certain that Sæmund Sigfússon
(1056–1133), called the wise (*hinn fróði*), wrote a historical work, mention-
ing, among others, Olaf Tryggvason, king of Norway (995–1000), but his

writings are now lost, apart from some excerpts quoted by later historians. The earliest native history that has survived, *Íslendingabók*, or *Libellus islandorum*, was written in Icelandic between 1122 and 1134 by a priest, Ari Þorgilsson (1068–1148), also called the wise, who wrote it, as he says himself, for the Icelandic bishops: the first two bishops, Ísleif (1056–80) and his son Gissur (1082–1118), seem to have been his patrons. This remarkable work fills only a few pages in modern editions, but every sentence is important. Its contents give an idea of its range and depth: 1. On the settlement of Iceland; 2. On the first settlers and the imposition of law; 3. On the establishment of the *Alþing* (assembly for all—an administrative change made in the tenth century); 4. On time-reckoning; 5. On the division into quarters; 6. On the settlement of Greenland; 7. On the coming of Christianity to Iceland; 8. On foreign bishops; 9. On Bishop Ísleif; 10. On Bishop Gissur.

Ari was well versed in chronology, a central theme of his work. He scrupulously fixes every historical event in accordance with the Christian world-view, thereby giving northern Europe, Scandinavia, and Iceland a clearly dated history in a Christian European sense. He is largely concerned with the church, and for the most part he meticulously identifies his sources; however, the work ends abruptly with Ari's own genealogy traced through more than thirty-five generations, in which mythical ideas about a past peopled with heathen kings and semi-gods can be discerned. *Íslend-ingabók* thus reflects the triumph of Christianity and the rapid development of the church as a pow- erful factor in the newly established society of Ice- land, where nevertheless people's outlook was still moulded by the social and quasi-historical values of the Viking Age, when chieftains were dominant.

Another remarkable Icelandic historical source, *Landnámabók*, is only preserved in several late ver- sions of the thirteenth century, although it was probably first compiled in about 1100. It purports to name all the first settlers in Iceland, the so-called *landnámsmenn*, who arrived there more than 200 years earlier, and to give for each of them not only the extent of the land they took (*landnám*), but also the names of their descendants. Half-mythical genealogies, burial mounds, and pagan graves are referred to in order to prove titles to land.

Landnámabók describes the occupation of virtually all the lowlands of Iceland. The continuous sequence of settlements that forms its framework is divided into four quarters (*fjórðungar*), south, west, north, and east, cor- responding to the territorial division of Iceland when it was first compiled.

Facing: Remains of buildings of various dates on the Brough of Birsay, a tidal island that was probably the main residence of the Orkney earls in the eleventh century, and perhaps earlier. It was also the site of Orkney's cathedral until 1127 when the see was moved to a more central site in Kirkwall. The apse in the background is the east end of a twelfth- century church that was probably on the site of the first cathe- dral.

This bronze staff- head, in the form of a tau-cross, was found at Þingvellir, the site of the Alþing. It probably had an ecclesiastical function and has been dated c.1100.

Its various surviving versions have obvious additions and omissions, but these do not obscure its original aim of registering land titles at the beginning of the twelfth century. The alterations made in later versions reflect changes in landownership and political developments in Iceland during the twelfth and thirteenth centuries.

These later versions of *Landnámabók* also reflect political developments outside Iceland, in particular the growth of royal power in Norway. In the original *Landnámabók* powerful Norwegians, primarily King Harald Finehair and Earl Hákon Grjótgarðsson, were accused of tyranny, but in the later versions, dating from the end of the thirteenth century, an attempt was made to modify these accusations by describing King Harald as a law-giver who regulated land settlement. The claim of the Norwegian kings to own all the land ('all the *óðals* and all land, settled and unsettled, and even the sea and the lakes') in the Orkneys and Norway as described in Icelandic sagas of the twelfth and thirteenth centuries was obviously in conflict with the ideas of the early Icelandic chieftains and historians. But by the end of the thirteenth century the situation had changed. The Icelanders had, between 1262 and 1264, accepted the authority of the Norwegian king who did not then claim to own all the land, but who did claim the right to levy taxes and dis-

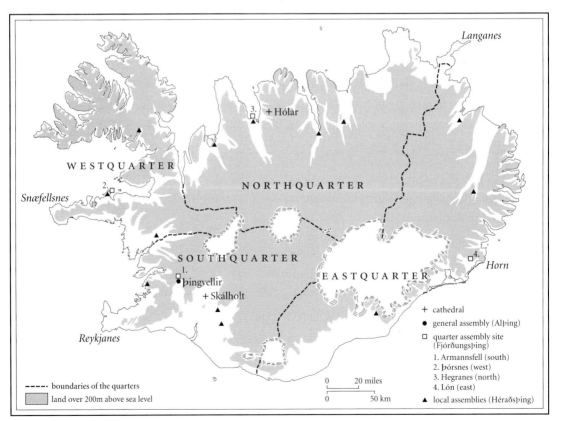

Langanes

+ Hólar

WESTQUARTER

Snæfellsnes

NORTHQUARTER

2.

SOUTHQUARTER

1.
þingvellir

+ Skálholt

EASTQUARTER

4.

Horn

Reykjanes

+ cathedral
● general assembly (Alþing)
□ quarter assembly site (Fjórðungsþing)
  1. Armannsfell (south)
  2. Þórsnes (west)
  3. Hegranes (north)
  4. Lón (east)
▲ local assemblies (Héraðsþing)

- - - - boundaries of the quarters

land over 200m above sea level

0   20 miles
0   50 km

pense justice, matters on which Icelandic leaders were prepared to negotiate.

Landnámabók is therefore a valuable historical source on the nature of Icelandic society at the end of the Viking period, reflecting to a greater extent than *Íslendingabók* the conservative and secular attitudes of the chieftains.

Another source of great importance for the history of the eleventh century is the treaty between the Icelanders and Olaf Haraldsson, king of Norway from 1015 to 1028. The treaty was agreed in, or soon after, 1025, but is preserved in the form that was confirmed under oath in about 1085, and some of its articles have been incorporated in later Norwegian and Icelandic law codes. Under this treaty the Icelanders secured their personal rights in Norway: on arrival they were obliged to pay a personal toll (*landaurar*) to the king and to support him in time of war; in return they gained full personal rights (*höldsréttur*) in Norway, including the right to inherit and to trade in accordance with the laws of seafarers and merchants, the *Bjarkeyjar réttur*. This traditional term for the laws of towns and harbours in Norway incorporates the name of the famous Viking town in Lake Mälaren in Sweden, *Bjarkey* (Latinized as *Birca*), 'birch island'. The laws regulating seafarers and merchants that were current in many parts of Scandinavia in the eleventh and twelfth centuries continued to be named after *Birca* even though it ceased to exist well before the end of the tenth century.

A miniature depicting ship-building from a medieval Icelandic manuscript of *farmannalög*, the law of seamen.

According to *Íslendingabók*, secular law was first committed to writing in Iceland in the winter of 1117/18. Manuscript fragments of *Grágás*, the record of law from the time of the Icelandic Commonwealth, date from about 1200, but the main texts preserved are from later in the thirteenth century. Christianity was accepted as law in Iceland, according to *Íslendingabók*, in the year 1000. The oldest surviving Icelandic ecclesiastical laws regulating the payment of tithe were agreed in 1096 or 1097. The so-called Old Ecclesiastical Law, *Kristinréttur forni*, was drawn up by the bishops, Þorlákur Runólfsson of Skálholt and Ketill Þorsteinsson of Hólar, with the advice and help of Archbishop Asser of Lund, between 1122 and 1133. These church laws cast light on the early development of Christianity in Iceland. Although secular law was put in writing, in Icelandic, early in the twelfth century, it was already influenced by Christian morality and ecclesiastical attitudes, and by the learned jurisprudence of southern Europe: Lombardic as well as Roman law can be discerned in *Grágás*, and Roman law also left its mark on the ecclesiastical laws.

Written law was one consequence of Christianity. Literacy was brought by seafarers and merchants who were used to some kind of *Bjarkeyjarréttur* and who were more familiar with Christianity than were the inhabitants of the islands. Thanks to the sea-routes the scattered societies of the islands were more accessible to the outside world than the traditional societies in Scandinavia, some of them far inland. This partly explains why the Icelanders accepted Christianity before some of the landlocked communities in Norway and Sweden.

For historians the Icelandic sagas are much more interesting as sources than as literature. Their origins and preservation pose many complex and debated problems. Most of them are only preserved in manuscripts of the fourteenth century and later, although many were apparently originally written in the twelfth and thirteenth centuries. People named in *Landnámabók*, and even whole chapters from it, often appear in the sagas; references to the coming of Christianity to Iceland are more likely to come from *Íslendingabók*, while many of the details given in the sagas about the missionary kings Olaf Tryggvason and Olaf Haraldsson were drawn from earlier sagas about these kings.

While it is reasonable to suppose that the Icelandic sagas were written and rewritten for chieftains and their followers, there is no doubt that many of the fourteenth-century saga manuscripts were made for powerful sheriffs or the royal prefect of Iceland, all of whom had bands of armed retainers. These royal knights were descendents of the chieftains of the Icelandic Commonwealth, the so-called *goðar*. In the sagas moralistic anecdotes and exciting stories are often set in Icelandic surroundings and periods that appealed to the taste and mentality of the chieftains and their armed followers. Christian chieftains and kings had their own favourite saints and heroic prototypes that changed with political and other developments, a point elaborated below.

Discovery and Emigration

The colonization of Iceland that began in the ninth century was made possible by the developments in shipbuilding and seamanship that are discussed in Chapter 8. Norwegians had long experience of voyaging along the 'North Way' to ship the valuable raw materials of the far north to southern markets. In Icelandic sagas of the twelfth and thirteenth centuries about Norway, for example the sagas of Sverri and of Egil, this long coast is the scene of events in which skills of seamanship, navigation, and naval tactics were tested. But navigation on the ocean to the Faeroes, Iceland, and Greenland demanded other skills than coastal pilotage.

Sailing directions for the North Atlantic are preserved in the thirteenth-century versions of *Landnámabók* and elsewhere. A version of *Landnámabók* in *Hauksbók* contains the following description of Atlantic routes:

Wise men say that from Stad in Norway it is seven days' sailing to Horn in eastern Iceland, but from Snæfellsnes [a peninsula in western Iceland] it is four days' sailing to Hvarf in Greenland. From Hernar in Norway one should keep sailing west to reach Hvarf in Greenland and then you are sailing north of Shetland, so that it can only be seen if visibility is very good, but south of the Faeroes, so that the sea appears half-way up their mountain slopes, but so far south of Iceland that one is only aware of birds and whales from it. From Reykjanes in southern Iceland it is three days' sailing south to Slyne Head in Ireland; but from Langanes in northern Iceland it is four days' sailing north to Svalbarði at the end of the ocean, but a day's sailing to the wastes of Greenland from Kolbeinsey [an island north of Iceland] to the north.

The treaty between the Icelanders and Olaf Haraldsson shows that, although ocean voyages were dangerous, they were also tempting; one

THE NORTH
ATLANTIC.
The place-names
include those
mentioned in the
sailing directions in
Hauksbók.

clause deals with those Icelanders who did not intend to go to Norway but 'were driven by sea to Norway and had been in Greenland or had ventured upon a voyage of discovery or had been torn out by storm from Iceland when moving their ship between harbours, then they are not obliged to pay *landaurar*'.

As can be imagined, stories were told about such adventurous long-distance voyages. Comparison of the more or less fictitious accounts of the discovery of Iceland in Icelandic and Norwegian texts written between the twelfth and fourteenth centuries, in which mythical naval heroes like Naddoddur the Viking, Garðar the Swede, and Flóki Vilgerðarson are named as the first discoverers, suggests that Sæmund Sigfússon had dealt with the discovery of Iceland in a similar way, although he does not seem to have identified the sailor who did it.

The methods used to explore unknown countries are described in several sources. When the voyagers arrived at a suitable landing-place, they erected temporary booths (*búðir*) or camps. Thus *Finnsbúðir* are mentioned in eastern Greenland, *Karlbúðir* in the northern part of western Greenland and *Leifsbúðir* in *Vínland*, a land discovered west of Greenland in about 1000. The explorations were undertaken in the summer; in the winter the explorers stayed in their camps. The description in *Landnámabók* of Erik the Red's exploration of Greenland over a period of three summers is typi-

These ruins of a medieval church surrounded by a churchyard are part of the remains of a large farm complex supposed to be Brattahlíð, now called Qassiarsuk, the site of Erik the Red's settlement in southern Greenland. Icebergs from the inland ice-cap are floating and melting in the fjord, now called Tungugdliarfik.

cal. In the Icelandic sagas about Greenland and the *Vínland* voyages, the crews are described as able and shrewd men, and as good carpenters able to repair their ships.

Adam of Bremen explains that *Vínland* was given that name because vines producing excellent wine grew wild there. The sagas about *Vínland* committed to writing by learned Icelandic clerks in the twelfth century seem to have been influenced by the description of the Fortunate Isles, *insulae fortunatae*, in the ocean given by Isidore of Seville (d. 636). *Vínland* and other more northerly lands in the west named in various sources as *Markland*, *Helluland*, and *Furðustrandir* must be sought somewhere on the east coast of the North American continent. They cannot be located with any accuracy, but there are many theories and an immense literature on their identification. In 1961 a remarkable archaeological discovery corroborating the Icelandic sources was made at L'Anse aux Meadows, near the northern tip of Newfoundland, where the remains of several Viking houses were found that have been dated to the eleventh century. It is tempting to interpret them as temporary booths and the site as a base for the exploration of the St Lawrence estuary. That such expeditions could be profitable is shown by the story in *Grænlendinga Saga* about Karlsefni's voyage from Greenland to Norway after a successful trip to *Vínland*: 'it is said that no richer ship has sailed from Greenland than the one he steered'.

Our knowledge of the first stages of the colonization of the Atlantic islands depends on archaeological discoveries as well as texts. Regrettably, neither type of evidence can determine when the eighteen isles that comprise the Faeroes began to be settled. Although the archaeological evidence is not entirely conclusive, it is a reasonable assumption that they were occupied by Scandinavians before the colonization of Iceland began. Rising sea-levels have probably destroyed some traces of the earliest settlements that were, presumably, close to the shore. Scandinavian settlers were well established by the tenth century, and towards the end of the Viking age a cathedral was established in the south, at Kirkjubøur on Streymoy, the largest island.

Greenland was settled from Iceland. Its east coast may be described as a desolate waste of ice, but the west coast is in many respects similar to Norway, not least in being a sea route to the far north with deep firths, sounds, skerries, and islands. The climate is, however, very different; the interior is covered by a massive ice-cap, thousands of feet high, and there are large quantities of drift-ice along the shore. All the Viking settlements in Greenland were on the west coast and may be easily recognized in archaeological remains and Icelandic sources. The richest settlement was in the south, and is known as the Eastern Settlement, in the district of Qaqortoq. It was there that Eric the Red built his farm Brattahlíð and the episcopal seat of Garðar was established in the twelfth century. Further north was a minor settlement, called the Midfirths, in the district of Ivigtut, and still further to the north there was the more substantial Western Settlement near the modern capital of Greenland, Nuuk.

The colonization of the North Atlantic islands must have been undertaken by Norwegian chieftains like Ottar who had their own ships and dependants. The interpretation of the emigration as essentially aristocratic is supported by twelfth-century evidence that it was the ship-owners who commanded the loyalty of numerous followers. It is therefore a reasonable assumption that chieftains and rich merchant farmers organized the settlement of the Faeroes, Iceland, and Greenland, and were also responsible for military expeditions to and the settlement of the Orkneys and Shetland. Confirmation of this view of the colonization process is provided by Ari's account of the settlement of Greenland. He dates its beginning in 985 on the basis of information given by a man who went there with Eric the Red. An article, apparently written by Ari, in one of the versions of *Landnámabók*, relates that when Eric the Red led his second expedition 'twenty-five ships sailed to Greenland from Breiðafjörður and Borgarfjörður, fourteen reached it, some were driven back and some were lost'. This last *landnám* of the Viking Age was apparently a naval expedition of chieftains, a convoy formed for mutual aid on an extremely dangerous voyage. It must have been much like earlier Viking expeditions, but on a smaller scale than most. A great fleet would have been able to conquer the Orkneys and Shetland in one expedition opening the way for settlers; that is the picture given by the twelfth-century *Orkneyinga Saga*. Iceland was, however, too large to be occupied in one operation. Its settlement must have been accomplished by many expeditions, large and small, that were launched from various places in Norway as well as from the Orkneys, Shetland, the Hebrides, and Ireland.

Scandinavians probably had various motives for emigrating to the islands. The Orkneys and Shetland offered good land for agriculture and were ideally located on the sea route from Norway to the western British Isles and beyond, sailed by both warriors and traders. The same could not be said about the Faeroes, Iceland, and Greenland. The first settlers were probably tempted by the prospect of easily gaining rich rewards by hunting and gathering, but those who had been familiar with agriculture in their former homes naturally attempted to farm these virgin lands. As these islands were in many respects similar to Norway, and were on the same latitudes, it is likely that the early experiments in farming were successful.

As we have seen, *Landnámabók* implies that one of the most important reasons for the settlement of Iceland was the tyranny (*ofríki*) of the Norwegian king. The word *ofríki* is revealing: it is also used in old Icelandic texts, for example *Elucidarius*, in connection with the attempt of the angel Lucifer to be God's equal and the price he had to pay for his pride and arrogance. Early in the twelfth century the Norwegian kingdom was regarded as politically and morally unjust by the Icelandic chieftains. There is, however, no reason to suppose that the ninth-century settlers of Iceland had the same opinion. The reason for the settlement of Iceland, and later Greenland, was simple: in the eyes of Norwegian stock-raising farmers, these newly discovered lands apparently offered immense opportunities that could be exploited with little effort.

Although it is difficult to obtain a comprehensive picture of the natural conditions in the North Atlantic islands when the first explorers arrived, modern scientific methods make it possible to describe some features, and additional information can be gleaned from archaeological evidence, place-names, and written sources. Ottar's account of his activities in northern Norway in the late ninth century shows very clearly that the prey coveted by Scandinavians in the Viking Age were whales, walruses, seals, reindeer, and birds.

The settlers probably began exploiting the fauna of Iceland by skimming off the cream. In *Egils Saga* there is a description of the golden age of the Icelandic settlement: 'Then whales also came frequently and could be harpooned at will, all the creatures remained still in the hunting-place as they were unused to man.' Two other large animals native to Iceland, the walrus and the great auk, were heavily exploited from the outset.

The walrus was valued for both its tusks and skin. Walrus-hunting is mentioned in the Old Ecclesiastical Law and walrus bones have been found in Reykjavík and elsewhere. A major peninsula in south-western Iceland, called Rosmhvalanes, 'walrus peninsula', must have provided ideal conditions for them in the absence of human settlement. Now it is only possible to imagine the rich hunting opportunities offered by abundant walrus colonies unused to humans, and the high value of catches when they were taken to markets in Europe. There is no reference to such a trade in the surviving historical sources and the walrus is no longer found in Iceland.

The great auk, the penguin of the north, must have been very numerous in Iceland since it had few natural enemies before the land was colonized.

This miniature showing a whale being cut up is from a medieval Icelandic legal manuscript. Whales were an important source of food and whaling was therefore subject to strict legal regulation.

Being a clumsy bird, unable to fly, it was easy prey and was naturally at first unafraid of man. Remains of great auks have been found in excavations in south-western Iceland, for example in Reykjavík. It is now extinct but could be found in Iceland, Greenland, and Newfoundland until relatively recently; in Iceland the last auks were caught early in the nineteenth century.

Settlement and Material Culture

The settlers in the islands had to adapt the natural circumstances they found to serve their own purposes. The domestic animals of the old world—dogs, cats, poultry, cattle, swine, horses, goats, and sheep—that were shipped to Iceland and Greenland by the Norse farmers, thrived. Stories in *Landnámabók*, for example about the cow Brynja that was lost but found again with forty descendants, or the settler Ingimund who lost ten pigs that were later recovered in a herd of a hundred, reflect the success of the early farmers in raising stock in a rich country.

The price of successful farming was that much of the natural vegetation was destroyed. Ari's comment that when the first settlers reached Iceland it 'was grown with wood between mountains and shores' implies that in his own day this woodland had been significantly reduced. Woods in Iceland and South Greenland originally consisted almost entirely of small birch (*betula pubescens*) with no conifers. These changes were perhaps not as rapid as in the animal kingdom, but in the long run they were no less dramatic. Pollen analysis shows that at least two species of large plants suffered heavily, birch and angelica (*angelica archangelica*), both of which were used by men and animals. The birch was cleared and burned to make way for hayfields, it was used for cooking food and heating houses, for building and carpentry, and it was the raw material for making the charcoal needed to produce iron. Pollen diagrams also make it possible to study the importation of plants to Iceland and Greenland, some of them weeds, others, such as barley, to be cultivated. The plant kingdom of the islands was thus conquered, tamed, and adapted.

With a few early exceptions, settlement in Iceland has always been confined to land near the coast less than 200 metres above sea-level. The interior of this great island is barren, with mountains, glaciers, and deserts. One of the characteristics of the Icelandic landscape is erosion, especially in the highlands and on the fringes of settlement. Geologists have shown that large-scale erosion started shortly after the settlement began. The settlers and their animals disturbed the natural vegetation, which in Iceland recovers very slowly. This allowed wind, often fierce, to erode soil that had previously been stabilized naturally, and blow it to create enormous 'dust bowls'; some of it settled in the lowlands, where layers of accumulated dust were in turn covered by layers of pyroclasts and tephra from volcanic eruptions. Iceland is volcanic and it is unusual for many decades to pass without an eruption occurring somewhere. They differ in scale and type, but in great eruptions volcanic ash (tephra) ascends many kilometres and is dispersed by the wind. As a result, sections through the soil in many places in Iceland look like a slice of cake, with alternate layers of eroded soil and volcanic tephra. This is the basis of what is known as tephrochronology, a method of relative dating developed by the geologists which can greatly assist the interpretation of changes revealed by pollen analysis and archaeology.

The dates of volcanic eruptions that have occurred since the twelfth century are known, thanks to chronicles and other texts, but as the Scandinavians who colonized Iceland were illiterate, there is no such written evidence for earlier eruptions. The chronology of earlier volcanic activity depends on measurements of radioactive carbon, C14, which can indicate when plants or animals died within a range, in this period, of several decades. The so-called 'settlement tephra layer' produced by an eruption that archaeological evidence suggests occurred just after the time of the first settlements, has been dated by this technique to the last decades of the ninth century.

Laugar, a deserted eleventh-century inland farm in southern Iceland. The ruins of a house can be seen in the foreground, with remains of the enclosure of the infield in what is now desert. Tephra from the nearby volcano Hekla, combined with erosion caused by the grazing of livestock, eventually made the place uninhabitable.

The Greenland ice-cap has been built up through the ages by precipitation. A core drilled vertically through the ice has enabled scientists to identify different volcanic eruptions by measuring the acidity of the annual layers. This increases after an eruption as gases and chemicals from the interior of the earth are poured into the atmosphere, mingle with snow, and are deposited on the surface of the ice. In this way the probable date of the eruption that produced the 'settlement layer' has been shown to be shortly before AD 900. This ice-core chronology, together with tephrochronology, C14 measurements, and archaeological evidence, corroborates Ari's claim that settlement began in about AD 870.

The archaeological evidence for the Viking period in the islands of the North Atlantic is important, though limited. Remains of human occupation were rarely intended to be preserved for posterity and their interpretation is often ambiguous: distribution can be unrepresentative, for example. Moreover, material remains are an uncertain guide to social and religious concepts without the aid of written sources, which pose problems of their own.

In the Orkneys, Shetland, and Iceland fewer than 400 pagan graves have been found, over 300 of them in Iceland. They are not significantly different from graves of the same period in Scandinavia and confirm that the islands were populated by heathens of Scandinavian origin.

In *Landnámabók* there are many tales involving pagan burial-places which seem to be connected with claims to land. They imply that pagan graves near some farms contain the remains of the ancestors of those who farmed that land in the twelfth and thirteenth centuries. The farms could be regarded as a kind of *óðal*, land inherited or rightfully acquired from ancestors. Remnants of such half-heathen legal ideas are widespread in Scandinavia, and involved kings as well as commoners. The kingdom itself could be regarded as the *óðal* of the king, who was sometimes said to have this *óðal* as a birthright. Magnificent burial mounds such as those at Uppsala in Sweden, Jelling in Denmark, and Vestfold in Norway were believed to contain the graves of the founders of dynasties. That such ideas survived in the Christian Middle Ages is evident from *Landnámabók* and Norwegian laws. In *Ynglinga Saga* Snorri Sturluson, the thirteenth-century historian, played with such beliefs and exaggerated them, making them seem ridiculous in Christian eyes. In this and some other sagas pagan forefathers are described as

An eleventh-century bronze statuette, found in Akureyri in north Iceland, has been supposed to represent the god Thor. It is, however, more likely to be a gaming-piece.

having some form of life in the burial mounds as shadows (*haugbúi*) or ghosts (*draugur*).

There are sometimes indications that Viking burial mounds were opened in the eleventh century or later. Such evidence can yield information about the attitudes of converts towards their heathen ancestors. There is, for example, a tale in *Landnámabók* in which it is related that 'Ásmund was buried in a mound and laid in a ship, and his slave with him who killed himself as he did not want to live after Ásmund was dead. He was laid in the bow of the ship.' There follows a report that the mound was later opened and the slave removed. There are several accounts in Icelandic sources of human bones being removed from their ancient graves to be buried in a churchyard. This custom seems to be reflected in archaeological finds in some places in Iceland, for example Austari Hóll and Ytra Garðshorn in northern Iceland, where heathen Viking graves, even whole cemeteries, have long ago been emptied of their human bones. The motive was apparently to ensure the salvation of ancestors. Some clauses in the early twelfth-century Old Ecclesiastical Law, concerning the moving of churchyards rule that all the bones are to be excavated and carefully collected from the old churchyard and reburied in the new one. This may have encouraged some people to remove pagan burials to Christian churchyards.

In undisturbed pagan graves that have been investigated in modern times males are usually buried with weapons or tools, personal belongings, and clothes, while women are normally buried with jewellery, other personal belongings, and clothes, together with equipment for preparing food or making clothes. Both men and women could be accompanied by a horse and in a few cases the corpse was laid in a boat or ship.

In *Íslendingabók* Ari states that before Scandinavians came to Iceland around 870 Irish Christians, *papar*, were living there, but that they went away when the Norsemen arrived. No archaeological trace has been found of *papar*, nor is there any scientific evidence of their presence. The report in *Landnámabók* that there were several Christian Norse settlers is highly suspect and may well be an invention of learned clerics. No Christian graves or churchyards earlier than the eleventh century have been found; Iceland was initially settled by pagan Scandinavians and there is no archaeological evidence to the contrary.

Excavations of houses and settlements of the Viking period have shown that most of the house types common in Scandinavia at that time were found in the North Atlantic islands. Indeed, they conform closely to the traditions of north European rural culture of the early Middle Ages. Archaeological evidence in Iceland and Greenland from the tenth to the thirteenth centuries shows that the basic unit of settlement in both places was the single farm, each with several houses or other structures. In addition to the main dwelling-house, *skáli* or simply *hús*, which could be rectangular or boat-shaped, there were smaller buildings for special functions, often connected to the main house. Some of these were at ground level, while others were sunk into the ground. Byres were normally placed some distance away from the main house, though, in mountainous regions they were connected with it. There were sometimes special winter shelters for sheep further away. Folds or pens for milking animals were common, often at some distance from the farmhouses.

The economic strategy of the stock-raising farmer was complex and resourceful: in areas where pasture was highly seasonal, scattered nomadic methods could be adopted and grazing found in the mountains or far away from the farm. But for animals that needed milking, temporary dwellings (shielings) had to be erected, and folds were also needed. This ancient shieling economy of European farmers is sometimes clearly reflected in the patterns of Viking settlement in the Atlantic islands, and can also be discerned in other archaeological evidence, as well as in place-names. In the northernmost islands, Iceland and Greenland, the sensitive seasonal vegetation suitable for grazing varied greatly from year to year. In harsh and cold years the shielings were abandoned and the number of animals reduced, but in good years the shielings were rebuilt and the animal population increased.

Archaeological evidence shows that the first colonists in Iceland tried to settle far inland, in valleys on the fringes of the highlands, where the vegetation was extremely vulnerable. They seem to have learned from bitter experience that this was unwise. One of the most remarkable silver hoards of the Viking period in Iceland was found at Sandmúli, a desolate inland site in the north-east, and a rich female grave with Arabic silver coins was found in Mjóidalur, a deserted valley in western Iceland. Investigations of the many ruins and settlement remains in the valley of Hrafnkelsdalur, far inland and high above sea level in eastern Iceland, have shown that early settlers attempted to adapt to the new environment.

Late in the Viking Age there were some changes in the method of heating dwelling-houses. Archaeological evidence and sagas show that originally, as in Scandinavia, houses were heated by fires in long hearths placed between benches set against the walls on either side. Here, people sat and slept. The seat of honour was placed in the middle of the north bench, facing south. It was apparently in the time of the Norwegian king Olaf Kyrre (1066–93) that the open hearths began to be replaced by stoves or ovens in royal farms in Norway. By the thirteenth century they were common in Iceland. The saga-writers of the twelfth and thirteenth centuries were well aware of the change. They called the traditional houses fire-houses (*eldaskálar* or *eld-*

hús), in contrast to the houses known as *skálar* or *stofur*, in which the open hearth had been replaced by an oven or stove, the normal type when the sagas were written.

After Christianity was accepted in the islands churches were needed. The first were very small, and, because many chieftains and landowners were converted at much the same time, there were many of them. *Eyrbyggja Saga* describes the building of the first churches at Helgafell and two other places by leading chieftains, and adds that: 'It was the promise of the priests that each man would have the right to a place in heaven for as many people as could stand in the church he had built.' The oldest church yet excavated, at Brattahlíð in Greenland, has standing-room for little more than a small household; its floor measured 2×3.5 metres. Churches built later tended to be larger and reflected the ecclesiastical hierarchy. The creation of a form of parochial system led to the abandonment of some small churches and the replacement of others by larger buildings. It was this reorganization during the eleventh and twelfth centuries that led to the regulation in the Old Ecclesiastical Law about moving churchyards, mentioned above.

In time, some of the major farms or manors (*aðalból*) acquired large timber stave-churches. Foundations at Brattahlíð suggest that such a church was planned there. *Laxdæla Saga* relates that the grandfather of the historian Ari, Gellir Þorkelsson, who died in 1073 in Denmark on his way home from a pilgrimage to Rome, built a new church at Helgafell, replacing the earlier one mentioned in *Eyrbyggja Saga*. The source of this information is said to be a poem commemorating Gellir by Arnór Þórðarson who also composed a poem praising Þorfinn, earl of the Orkneys (d. 1065). Þorfinn, who also went on a pilgrimage to Rome, built a church in his earldom at Birsay. There were stone churches at an early date in the Orkneys, but the great St Magnus cathedral in Kirkwall was not built until the middle of the twelfth century, some time after the Icelandic cathedrals at Skálholt and Hólar, the largest timber churches in the Atlantic islands, had been constructed.

In the National Museum of Iceland there are some fragments of carved wall panels depicting saints in the style current in late Viking period. They came from farms in northern Iceland which in the Middle Ages belonged to Hólar cathedral; according to Ari the first bishop of Hólar was consecrated in 1106. Unlike Skálholt cathedral, which was destroyed by fire in the Middle Ages, Hólar

Fragment of a large picture of Doomsday in Byzantine style that was probably originally in the twelfth-century cathedral of Hólar. In this part the serpents of the throne of Antichrist are delivering their prey to be judged.

cathedral survived until the seventeenth century when it was badly damaged by a violent winter storm. The building was demolished and the timbers reused in tenant farms of the bishopric. These apparently included the fragments now in the museum. Most remarkably, it has been shown that they originally formed part of an enormous depiction of the Last Judgement in Byzantine style, a striking reminder that in the eleventh century Icelandic chieftains had close contacts with southern and eastern, as well as northern, Europe.

The chieftains of the North Atlantic islands, some of whom had been both merchants and mercenaries, opened the way, not only for Christianity and the reception of Christian culture, but also, as archaeological evidence reveals, for innovations in material culture affecting clothing, weaponry, jewellery, and much else.

Social Structure and Politics

The text of the treaty between the Icelanders and King Olaf Haraldsson in the Codex Regius of *Grágás*. The initial I marks the beginning of the treaty: 'Icelanders shall have the rights of holds in Norway'.

What little is known about the social structure and politics of the North Atlantic islands in the Viking Age comes almost entirely from narratives written in Iceland, notably Ari's *Íslendingabók*, and the laws. In his interpretation of the past, Ari, like other historians, was influenced, to some extent unconsciously, by contemporary circumstances, for example by the Peace of God movement in eleventh-century Europe. Compilers of laws, in contrast, were consciously trying to realize social ideals, although the reality was perhaps very different. There was, of course, often some connection between historical and legal texts, which compounds the problem of using them as historical sources. It is not possible to give a comprehensive description of late Viking Age society in the islands on the basis of this meagre and difficult evidence; we can only hope to describe a few features at particular moments.

The earliest evidence for the social classification of Icelanders is in the eleventh-century treaty between the Icelanders and the Norwegian king. The first clause states that Icelanders were to have the rights of a social group called 'holds' (*höldsréttur*) in Norway. The early Norwegian laws provide for a hierarchy among free men, in which the wergeld (that is, compensation paid after a killing or injury to prevent a feud) varied with social rank, the holds ranking highest among freemen who were not royal agents. The fact that there is no evidence of such a hierarchy among free men in the collection of early Icelandic laws known as *Grágás* implies that Icelandic freemen were of equal rank, and were all considered to be holds. On the other hand, Ari tells of a man in Iceland who was guilty of murdering a slave or freedman (*þræls morð eða leysings*), a case supposed to have happened before law was committed to writing in Iceland. Ari's formula occurs in some early Norwegian laws, but not in *Grágás*, although it does include many references to slaves and slavery (*þrælar, þrældómur*). It seems reasonable to conclude that Ari was well acquainted with slavery in the North Atlantic islands at the end of the Viking period.

The societies of the islands had clear hierarchical characteristics, despite the legal equality of the freemen. The earls, *goðar*, and great farmers had the highest place; they were usually wealthy and ruled over both people and land. The social bonds of fidelity and submission between superior and subordinates were, according to *Grágás*, called *grið*. *Grið* was also used to describe the relations between the captain of a ship (*stýrimaður*) and his crew, and between the master of a household (*húsbóndi*) and his servants, who were called his *griðmenn*. A closely related meaning of the word was the legal domicile that everyone was supposed to have. Those who did not have such a *grið* were outlaws or vagabonds who lacked all rights. In another context the word was used in the phrase 'to set *grið*' (*setja grið*) when a truce was agreed in an armed conflict. These social bonds, *grið*, were an essential feature of every farm or ship, great or small. They affected the division of labour and everyday tasks, shaped relations between men and women, parents and children, and also, to a great extent, determined not only the right of masters to appropriate material goods, in particular land, but also their status and mutual relations. *Grið* thus had a political dimension.

It is difficult to define landownership on the basis of *Grágás*. It shows that land was inherited and that sons tended to inherit the great farms or manors (*aðalból*), while daughters were more likely to inherit the smaller tenant farms (*leiguból, leiguland*) and movables. There are also provisions for an extensive right to recover land (*landabrigði*), and especially manors, if they had been taken without lawful warrant (*heimild*). Thus a pattern of manorial structure can be discerned in the rural Icelandic settlements. The desire to keep the best land in the family, preferably in the male lineage, was general in medieval Europe. In Norway and the Orkneys land inherited or acquired lawfully by great farmers and chieftains was often called *óðal*. As suggested above, one of the main purposes of *Landnámabók* was to prove the legality of claims to such land.

Superimposed on these social relations there was a complex hierarchical organization in which the chieftains made law and dispensed justice. The oldest institution for this purpose was the *þing*, or assembly, in which the farmers gathered to make laws and give judgements. These assemblies also had a political function: Ari describes in *Íslendingabók* how the Icelanders held local assemblies before they instituted an annual general assembly for all Iceland, the so-called *Alþing*, in 930, and how the place for the *Alþing* was chosen in *þingvellir* in south-western Iceland. Thus a hierarchy was formed with many small local assemblies and one superior one, the *Alþing*, to which it was possible to appeal or to transfer major judicial questions. The *Alþing* was presided over by an elected law-speaker whose main function was to declare what was law. Ari also describes a violent dispute that, in about 962, led to the division of Iceland into quarters (*fjórðungar*) each with an assembly intermediate between the local assemblies and the *Alþing*, an innovation intended to make it easier for people to seek justice.

Grágás and *Íslendingabók* describe the legal and other proceedings of the *Alþing* in greater detail than can be discussed here. It is, however, worth making the point that the political and constitutional institutions of Iceland in the late Viking Age can cast light on contemporary developments in other parts of Europe.

Although the quarters had well-defined territorial boundaries, the authority of the *goðar*, the so-called *goðorð*, did not. In an ecclesiastical text of the twelfth century prohibiting the consecration of *goðar* to ecclesiastical office, their rights are treated as comparable with the privileges of the royal nobility (*lendir menn*) in Norway and the rights of counts to taxation (*greifaskattur*) in other countries. With the separation of secular and spiritual power in twelfth-century Iceland, the territories for the purpose of taxation and law enforcement were often called *ríki*, whether they were bishoprics or *goðorð*s. Spiritual and secular power in medieval Iceland thus gradually developed into something very similar to what was in early modern times called a state. The institutional development of the Icelandic Commonwealth or Republic, sometimes called the Icelandic Free State, which Ari shows was far advanced before the end of the Viking period, was admired by political theorists of the eighteenth and nineteenth centuries for its lack of a king, and for its liberty and equity.

The Conversion: Saints and Politics

Ari's main purpose in writing *Íslendingabók* was not to describe the early development of Iceland's political and legal institutions, but to give an authoritative account of its conversion and of the achievements of the first

native bishops. Both he and his predecessor, Sæmund Sigfússon, the first historians of Iceland, gave Olaf Tryggvason credit for the conversion of both Norway and Iceland, and Sæmund apparently claimed that Olaf was also responsible for the conversion of the Orkneys, Shetland, and the Faeroes. Neither mentions the conversion of Greenland, although according to Adam of Bremen, writing in the 1070s, the church had already been established there by then, apparently by Icelanders.

Ari's account of the conversion of Iceland is, briefly, that a missionary sent by King Olaf converted a few prominent people but was rejected by most Icelanders and eventually returned to Norway reporting failure. Olaf was angry and threatened to punish any Icelanders living in Norway. He was, however, persuaded to relent by two Icelandic converts, Gissur the White and Hjalti, who promised to renew the mission when they returned home. In the year 1000 they pressed the claims of Christianity at the *Alþing*, and after a heated argument it was eventually agreed to leave the decision to Þorgeir, the pagan law-speaker. The next day he declared that Christian law should be accepted, and that everyone should be baptized. Ari reports that there were some temporary exceptions allowing the clandestine worship of the heathen gods, the eating of horsemeat, and infanticide; he says nothing

Lund cathedral was consecrated in 1145, but the western part, seen here, was extensively reconstructed in the nineteenth century. When Lund was made an archbishopric at the beginning of the century, Markús, the Icelandic law-speaker, described it in a verse as 'for all people speaking the Danish tongue'.

129

about the evangelical methods used by King Olaf elsewhere. According to later sagas, some of which depend on a lost work by Sæmund Sigfússon, he used both persuasion and compulsion in Norway, but compelled the earl of Orkney to convert.

During the twelfth and thirteenth centuries several sagas were written in Iceland, not only about Olaf Tryggvason but also about Olaf Haraldsson, who continued the work of evangelism in Norway, and who was regarded as a saint soon after his death in the battle of Stiklestad, when he returned from exile to reclaim his kingdom. This series of royal sagas culminated at the end of the thirteenth century in compilations known as the Great Sagas devoted to each king. The roots of these accounts of the careers of the two kings can be traced back to the eleventh century when attempts were already being made to sanctify them. Even at that stage competing claims were made for them.

Olaf Tryggvason was the hero of Sæmund and Ari, and appears as a saint in several early Icelandic stories. In contrast, Adam of Bremen shows him no respect, calling him 'crow's foot' (*krákubein*) and an apostate. On the other hand, Adam treats Olaf Haraldsson with great reverence, describing his martyrdom and acknowledging him as a saint. He is, however, only mentioned twice in *Íslendingabók*, each time with the scornful nickname 'the fat' (*hinn digri*) and with no hint of his sanctity. There is a similar contrast in the treatment of Harald Hardrada, king of Norway (1047–66); Adam describes him as a mad tyrant whose fall, in the battle of Stamford in 1066, was a well-deserved fate. Icelandic sources represent him in much more favourable terms, and he is remembered as the donor of timber for the construction of the church at *þingvellir*. These differences were a consequence of the struggle for power in Scandinavia, and of the ecclesiastical politics of the period. These are discussed more fully in Chapter 7, but a brief account is needed here to explain the attitude of Ari and other Icelanders.

The archbishops of Hamburg–Bremen claimed ecclesiastical authority throughout Scandinavia, although the early papal privileges only referred to Danes and Svear. It was not until 1053 that Pope Leo IX explicitly named Norway, Iceland, and Greenland as being within the archbishop's jurisdiction. Hamburg–Bremen's ecclesiastical hegemony was threatened by English influence in Norway under Olaf Tryggvason, and in Denmark under Knut. Knut's claim to be overlord of Norway was, however, challenged by Olaf Haraldsson who was consequently considered to be an ally by the archbishop. After Olaf Haraldsson's death in 1030, Danish power in Norway increased for a short while, but five years later Olaf's son Magnus was recalled from exile and recognized as king. The Norwegians then not only expelled the Anglo-Danish regime established by Knut, but also threatened

Denmark itself, and in 1042, after the death of Knut's only remaining son, Harthaknut, Magnus Olafsson was also recognized as king by the Danes. With the support of the Danes and, according to sagas, the aid of his father St Olaf, Magnus and the Saxon duke defeated the Wends (Slavic neighbours of the Danes) in 1043. Magnus may also have had German support against Knut's nephew, Sven Estridsson, who claimed the Danish throne.

Magnus died in 1047 and was succeeded as king of Norway by his uncle, Harald Hardrada, while Sven Estridsson was at last recognized as king of the Danes. Conflict between Harald and Sven continued for several years, but peace was agreed between them in 1064. After Harald's death in 1066 cordial relations between the two kingdoms were reinforced by the marriage of his successor, Olaf Kyrre, to a daughter of Sven. The cult of Olaf Haraldsson was certainly not encouraged by Sven, and after the death of Magnus it was of no particular interest to his immediate successors as kings of Norway. Its main centre was, naturally, in Trondheim, where Olaf was buried. Outside Scandinavia Olaf's cult was observed in Saxony, in Baltic trading centres visited by German merchants, and in the British Isles, especially in southern England where it may have been particularly popular after the end of Knut's dynasty in 1042, in opposition to the claim of Sven Estridsson to be Knut's successor as king of England. The ecclesiastical consequences of the competition between Scandinavian kings were complicated by the so-called Investiture Dispute between Henry IV, the German emperor, and Pope Gregory VII in which the archbishops of Hamburg–Bremen supported the emperor, while the Danish kings generally supported the pope.

According to Ari, the first native bishop in Iceland, Ísleif Gissurarson, was consecrated in 1056, but Ari does not say by whom. Adam of Bremen reports that it was done by Adalbert, archbishop of Hamburg–Bremen, a see that is never mentioned in *Íslendingabók*. In 1080 Bishop Ísleif died and his son Gissur was elected to become his successor. Ari's account of the consecration of Gissur, his personal friend, is very revealing. He reports that in 1081 Gissur went from Iceland to Götaland in Sweden, and thence to Denmark in 1082, returning to Iceland as bishop in 1083. Gissur clearly avoided the archbishop of Hamburg–Bremen, who had by then been excommunicated by the pope as an ally of the German emperor.

Erik, son of Sven Estridsson, who succeeded as king of the Danes in 1095, was rewarded for his support of the papacy when his brother Knut, who had been killed by rebels in 1086, was declared to be a saint by the pope in 1101. He also induced the pope to establish the Danish see of Lund in 1104 as an independent archbishopric with Scandinavia as its province and Asser as the first archbishop. Markús Skeggjason, the Icelandic law-speaker and the friend of both Bishop Gissur and the historian Ari, composed a poem praising St Knut and another praising King Erik in which the establishment of a Scandinavian archbishopric is welcomed. The position of the Icelanders is therefore quite clear; they supported the pope and the archbishop of Lund against the emperor and the archbishop of Hamburg–Bremen.

The political situation at the beginning of the twelfth century left little room for St Olaf of Norway. In Denmark the newly proclaimed St Knut prevailed. A subtle indication of the changes that had occurred there is provided by the way the legend of a local Danish saint, Thøger of Jutland, was adapted. He was originally associated with St Olaf and opposed by King Sven, but the later development is reflected by the similarity of the proof of his and St Knut's sanctity; their bones could not be burnt. Thøger is also said to have been canonized by the pope. In Iceland it was Olaf Tryggvason that Sæmund and Ari wrote about and the poets praised, while in the Orkneys the patron saint was Earl Magnus, who died in 1117. In Norway the centre of St Olaf's cult was naturally at Trondheim where he was buried; elsewhere he had competitors, Hallvard in the south and Sunniva in the west.

Neither the emperor nor the archbishops of Hamburg–Bremen acknowledged an independent archbishopric in the north. In 1133 they had an opportunity to counter-attack by making the pope issue letters deposing Archbishop Asser and placing all his suffragan bishops under Hamburg–Bremen. However, these letters never went beyond Bremen and Asser remained archbishop of Lund. It was at about this time, and possibly as a response to this conflict, that Ari produced a revised version of *Íslendingabók*, the only one that has survived. Whether or not that is so, it is clear that the works of both Adam and Ari have to be interpreted in the light of the political and ecclesiastical developments of their own time.

When, in 1153 or 1154, the see of Trondheim was made an archbishopric, with a province that included the Norwegian colonies in the North Atlantic, the victories of St Olaf over Olaf Tryggvason and of Trondheim over Bremen were secured, but the Great Sagas of the two Olafs testify to the complexity of earlier political and ecclesiastical disputes in which they, and later their memory, had played a leading role.

In this period which lasted about 300 years, relatively stable Norse societies with deep roots in North European traditions were established in the North Atlantic islands. By exploiting natural resources, especially in Iceland and Greenland, the colonists were able to export to Europe valuable exotica, such as furs and falcons, walrus ivory and eiderdown, and occasionally a polar bear. The southernmost islands, the Orkneys, had fertile agricultural land, but in most of the others farmers raised stock, sustaining what was, for that period, a relatively large population. The new societies in these islands, even the remotest, were as quick as many parts of Scandinavia to accept Christianity and they soon absorbed a wide range of influences from the Continent and the British Isles. As a result, the twelfth century, when the Viking Age was over, saw the beginning of a period when culture flourished, above all in Iceland, no less than in other parts of Christian Europe.

6

SCANDINAVIANS IN EUROPEAN RUSSIA

THOMAS S. NOONAN

Scandinavians came to European Russia over the course of three centuries, *c.*750–*c.*1050, primarily from Sweden, but also from Denmark and Norway. They were active as explorers, adventurers, rulers, merchants, mercenaries, farmers, political exiles, and raiders. Some settled permanently and became part of what came to be called the Rus state. Others continued on to Byzantium or returned to Scandinavia, where they reported on their deeds in the 'east'. Any examination of the Scandinavian experience in European Russia needs to consider these diverse activities and the way in which they evolved over time. It must also keep in mind the environment the new arrivals found, as well as the developments taking place among the indigenous societies of the region.

There has been much debate about the meaning of the words Viking, Russia, Rus, and Varangian. The meaning of 'Viking' has been shaped mainly by events in the west, so to avoid endless debates about what constitutes a 'real' Viking it is preferable to use the term 'Scandinavian' when discussing the east. Russia did not exist during the Viking Age, nor does the Russia of today include all the areas where Scandinavians were active— Kiev, for example is in Ukraine, and Polotsk in Belarus. 'European Russia' is probably the best way of defining the entire area between the Arctic and Black seas and between Poland and the Urals.

There has been considerable controversy about the origins of the word Rus. Perhaps the best-known and most persuasive argument is that it derives from the West Finnic name for Sweden, *Ruotsi.* The Finns of northwestern Russia presumably used this term for the Scandinavians who appeared in their lands, and the East Slavs transformed it into Rus. Later, Rus was applied both to the Kievan state and to those Scandinavians and non-Scandinavians who became rulers of it, and ultimately came to include all the peoples of that state. After Vladimir's conversion to Orthodoxy in 989, Rus also began to mean someone who was an Orthodox Christian. The evolution of the word did not take place uniformly, so there is no necessary consistency in its meaning at any one time. The word Variagi/Varangians was also used for the Scandinavians in the east, but many argue that it appeared later than the term Rus, and was used primarily to designate those Scandinavians who entered the military service of the Rus princes and the Byzantine emperors.

The Scandinavians who penetrated the interior of European Russia encountered conditions far different from those facing the Northmen who pillaged the coasts of western Europe. Shallow-draught Viking boats could easily attack and plunder the rich towns and monasteries lying along the sea-coasts or river-banks of England and France, and make a successful get-away before local defences could be organized. But there were no lootable towns or monasteries along the coasts of Russia, while the routes inland involved crossing dangerous rapids and portaging substantial distances through virgin forests to go from one river system to another. Raiding on the inland seas was risky, for the Muslim auxiliaries of the Khazar *khagan* could block the escape route from the Caspian Sea, while Byzantine ships in the Black Sea attacked marauding Scandinavians with Greek fire.

Nevertheless, the Scandinavians who came to north-western Russia from the mid-eighth century onwards met far less organized resistance than did the Vikings in the west. There was a big difference between Finnic, Baltic, and East Slavic tribes on the one hand, and the Anglo-Saxon and Carolingian states on the other. The geography of European Russia rewarded trading far more than raiding. The Vikings in the west often did no more than take the treasure already accumulated in towns and monasteries. In European Russia, by contrast, the Scandinavians had to organize local systems to collect the natural wealth, and then establish trade centres and trading routes to market these goods.

The Peoples of European Russia

The most fundamental developments in European Russia after about AD 500 were growing economic diversification and the mass migration of peoples. Economic diversification produced greater wealth and security for many of the native populations, which in turn fostered political consolidation and the emergence of local élites. At the same time, mass migrations

Map labels:
R. Dvina
L. Ladoga
Beloozero
R. Viatka
Staraja Ladoga
R. Volkhov
Iaroslavl
V O L G A
Novgorod
Riurikovo Gorodishche
Rostov
Bulghar
Pskov
Murom
R. Oka
B U L G H A R I A
Polotsk
Gnezdovo
R. Don
Turov
Liubech
Listven
Chernigov
Shestovitsa
Kiev
R. Volga
Itil
R. Dnepr
K H A Z A R I A
Rapids
Caspian Sea
Caucasus
Black Sea
0   200 miles
0   400 km
Constantinople

completely altered the ethnic map. The Scandinavians who ventured into European Russia found that the indigenous peoples had dynamic societies which were undergoing significant changes.

There are three main geographic–economic zones in European Russia: the steppe, the forest steppe, and the northern forest. In the steppe zone, pastoral nomadism dominated, and the population was dependent on its flocks of sheep, horses, cattle, and other animals. Highly specialized pastoral nomadism was well adapted to the lush prairie lands of southern Russia and Ukraine. However, it was highly vulnerable to droughts, epidemics among the flocks, and other natural disasters, while over-specialization created a danger that nomads might become dependent on neighbouring sedentary peoples for goods they did not produce themselves such as crops, tools, jewellery, and weapons.

Shortly after the middle of the seventh century, the Turkic Khazars became the dominant power in the north Caucasian–Azov steppe. By the first half of the eighth century, their ascendancy stretched northwards into the forest steppe between the Volga and Dnepr rivers, westwards across the steppe towards the Danube, and into the Crimea. Numerous agricultural villages and a number of handicraft centres appeared throughout Khazaria. This diversification enabled the Khazar dynasty to maintain its control for over 300 years (*c*.650–*c*.965) and to create the Pax Khazarica that made the great trade between European Russia and the Islamic world possible.

Starting around the sixth century, Slavic migrants slowly moved north and east from the area of the lower Danube and lower Carpathians. A second wave of migration brought Slavs eastward from what today is Poland. The Slavic immigrants into European Russia became known as the East Slavs. During the course of their migrations, they drove out, exterminated, or assimilated the native Balts and Finns. As they left the rich black-earth lands of southern Russia and Ukraine, the Slavs had to modify their agrarian economy. It was not easy to survive on agriculture alone in the forest zone, where virgin forests had to be cleared using nothing but fire and axe; where soils were less fertile, the growing season shorter, and seeds low-yielding; where winters could be too cold and long and summers too dry and brief; and where draught animals had to be stalled in winter, consuming much of the scarce harvest. But the forest had its benefits. The trees provided the materials for homes and the fuel to heat them. There were numerous berries, mushrooms, and fish-filled streams. There were animals which could be hunted for food and for their pelts, which were used for warmth, for bartering, and for payment of tribute. The so-called East Slavic agriculturalist was in fact both farmer and forager.

Meanwhile, from about 750, Turkic-speaking peoples from Khazaria had been moving northwards from the Volga and Urals steppes. The Bulghars were the main group in this migration, and by the early tenth century they had established their domination over a large part of the middle Volga and many of its Finnic inhabitants. They soon developed a diversified economy based on stock-raising, agriculture, craft-production, and a thriving international trade in furs with central Asia.

Traditionally the northern forest zones of European Russia were occupied by hunter-gatherers, most of them Finno-Ugrians. In the centuries before *c*.900, agriculture spread rapidly. Handicrafts developed, and specialized artisans appeared. The one-time foragers of these regions raised more of their food and made more of their tools and weapons. The peoples of the Kama–Viatka region developed trade ties with central Asia, the Caucasus, and Byzantium. Iranian, Byzantine, and central Asian silverware and coins went north in exchange for furs. By the beginning of the Viking Age, central Asian merchants had become the key intermediaries in this commerce, and their annual caravans connected Khwarazm with the Bulghar markets of the middle Volga. The Scandinavians who came to northern Russia exploited the growing prosperity of many of its natives and capitalized on their long-established trade relations with the south.

The Origins of the Rus State

Between *c*.1050 and *c*.1120, several monks in Kiev's monasteries put together the first coherent account of the origins and early history of the Rus state. Called the *Russian Primary Chronicle*, it constitutes what might be called the official history of the Scandinavians in European Russia. It states that in 859 a group of Varangians attacked the Finns and East Slavs of north-western Russia and forced them to pay tribute. They were overthrown in 862, but the Finns and Slavs could not govern themselves and consequently invited another group of Varangians, called Rus and led by a certain Riurik, to come and rule over them. Riurik established himself in Novgorod and began to extend his rule over other lands in northern Russia. Several of his followers, led by Askold and Dir, left for Kiev, which was then dominated by the Khazars. After Riurik's death in 879, his successor, Oleg, led an expedition which seized control of Kiev. Novgorod in the north and Kiev in the south were thus brought under the same Rus ruling family, the Riurikids, who then launched a series of campaigns which eventually expanded their tributary domain from the Polish frontiers to the upper Volga.

The administration of this tributary empire lay in the hands of a grand prince in Kiev. He headed a loose-knit organization of relatives and retainers who had conquered the native peoples and extorted tribute from them. The *Chronicle* vividly describes the destruction of the Derevlianians, an East Slavic tribe who killed Grand Prince Igor in 945 when he tried to collect more than the normal tribute (usually one pelt per hearth) from them. His widow Olga systematically exterminated the Derevlianian prince, others of their ruling élite, and numerous rank-and-file members of the tribe before having their capital burned to the ground.

The booty from successful campaigns, along with the tribute paid, produced huge quantities of goods which, starting in the first half of the tenth century, were shipped to Constantinople. By 988, Rus and Byzantium had become so close that Grand Prince Vladimir decided to convert to Orthodox Christianity, and married the sister of the Byzantine emperor. Under Vladimir's son, Iaroslav the Wise, the Rus state reached its zenith.

The *Chronicle* is our most important source for the Scandinavians in

European Russia, but it is far from perfect. There is much truth in its account of the origins of the Rus state. But there is also much that is omitted, falsified, or distorted. Its compilers relied on flawed and incomplete information, much of which was second-hand at best. Above all, it must be remembered that the *Chronicle* was written for the princely patrons of the monasteries in which the authors resided. The monks were therefore entrusted with the task of legitimizing the rule of the Riurikids. For example, the grand princes of Kiev are not depicted as ruthless adventurers who had seized the lands of others and extorted tribute from them, but as the descendants of the semi-legendary Riurik, who had been invited by the indigenous peoples to 'come and rule over us'.

Fortunately there are a number of other written sources. Other Rus sources, such as Metropolitan Hilarion's sermons, the *Paterik* of the Kievan Crypt monastery, the Novgorod First Chronicle, and the earliest parts of the *Russkaia Pravda* (Russian Law), contain important evidence. The most famous Islamic source is probably Ibn Fadlan's *Risala*, a personal account of his 922 journey from Baghdad to the Volga Bulghars, where he encountered Rus merchants at first hand. A number of geographic works written in the ninth to the eleventh centuries, though sometimes confused and unreliable, describe the areas of the world, including European Russia, known to Islamic scholars. The best-known Byzantine source is the *De Administrando Imperio* of the Emperor Constantine Porphyrogenitus, written *c*.950, which provides a detailed description of the annual flotilla of Rus merchants going from Kiev to Constantinople, as well as of the collection of tribute within Rus. Unfortunately, the authenticity of the main Jewish sources (the *Khazar Correspondence* and the *Cambridge Document*) is disputed. The veracity of the Scandinavian sagas has also been seriously challenged in recent years. There are, though, runic inscriptions in different parts of Scandinavia and European Russia which report on Scandinavians who went to the east or testify to their presence there. Finally, several Latin sources, such as the *Annals of St-Bertin* and the writings of Liudprand of Cremona, contain valuable information on Scandinavians/Rus who visited Byzantium.

The thousands of settlements and graves excavated by archaeologists throughout European Russia

A toy horse (13 cm long) found in Staraja Ladoga.

provide a wealth of information on almost all aspects of the early Middle Ages. In particular, there are over 400 complexes with Scandinavian features or artefacts dating from the Viking Age. The numerous finds of Scandinavian brooches, pendants, iron neck-rings with pendants in the shape of Thor's hammer, knife sheaths, scabbard chapes, spearheads, iron shield bosses, smithy tools, some swords, and the remains of boat burials help archaeologists to trace where Scandinavians went within European Russia, when they were active in particular areas, and what activities they engaged in. In addition, hundreds of thousands of Islamic, European, Byzantine, and Rus coins have been reported from all parts of European Russia. This abundant numismatic evidence reveals much about the economic and political developments of the time. These diverse written and material sources provide the foundation for a more credible and more inclusive account of Scandinavians in European Russia than that found in the *Chronicle*.

Ladoga seen from the east bank of the River Volkhov. The buildings are on the site of the medieval castle which stood on the promontory formed by the confluence of the River Ladozhka and the Volkhov. The harbour was on the far side of the castle, in the Ladozhka.

The Beginnings of the Viking Age in European Russia

During the course of the eighth century new urban centres began to appear along the shores of the Baltic and North seas. These towns differed from earlier settlements, being hubs for international commerce and craft production. The best known is Ribe, in Denmark, founded early in the eighth century. While some scholars link these developments with the emergence of the Viking Age, others point out that similar settlements also began to

Aerial view of Riurikovo Goro-dishche. This was established by the mid-ninth century on an island in the River Volkhov where it divides into two branches close to its source in Lake Ilmen. The settlement of Novgorod, 2 km downstream, began by the mid-tenth century.

appear among the West Slavs who inhabited the southern coasts of the Baltic. Consequently, they suggest the existence of a new 'Baltic culture'.

Around 750, a small settlement was established at Staraja Ladoga (the Norse Aldeigjuborg), on the left bank of the Volkhov river, some 8 kilometres from its confluence with Lake Ladoga. Traders and raiders from Scandinavia had visited the shores of the south-eastern Baltic and Lake Ladoga for some time before this, and some had even established settlements in what are today Estonia and Latvia. Ladoga was the first town with Scandinavian residents in north-western Russia. Archaeological evidence shows that Scandinavians lived in Ladoga from its inception: a set of Scandinavian–Baltic smithy tools, including a talisman with the face of Odin, was found in a stratum of the 750s. One specialist has even suggested that their owner was from Gotland. The tools came from a large blacksmithing–metalworking–jewellery-making complex, which functioned between the mid-750s and the 770s.

The Scandinavians who visited Ladoga did not come to loot and raid. There were no other towns in the vicinity, monasteries did not exist, and the

141

Facing: Ruins of an
early shieling on the
fringes of highland
desert in Vesturdalur
in eastern Iceland.
Many early colonists
attempted to settle
very far inland.
Written sources,
place-names, and
ruins show that
shielings for summer
grazing were charac-
teristic of the early
phase of settlement.

Inset: These dramatic
rocks, known as
'The Giant and the
Giantess', are off the
north-west tip of
Eysturoy in the
Faeroes, but the stack
seen beyond the boat
is off the northern
point of Streymoy,
the main island. The
cliffs to the left,
which are over 300
metres high, shel-
tered the farm of Eiði
on the shore of the
sound between these
islands. Eiði had
shielings that have
recently been exca-
vated and dated to
the ninth century, the
earliest archaeological
evidence for settle-
ment in the Faeroes.

neighbouring burial mounds of the local peoples were very modest in their contents. There was little of value to steal here. Ladoga was created to facilitate access to the interior of European Russia, with all its natural wealth. The Scandinavians journeying there may originally have sought furs to be sold back in the Baltic. But they soon found that it was even more profitable to take the furs, and other goods obtained in northern Russia, to the Khazar capital of Itil, located at the mouth of the Volga. Here furs could be exchanged with Muslim merchants for Islamic silver coins, or dirhams. As trade with the Khazars grew, the Scandinavians found that they could also cross the Caspian Sea and then travel by camel along the famous land route to Baghdad. This arduous trip was well worth while, for both European Russia and Scandinavia lacked indigenous sources of silver, and western silver coins, such as those struck by the Carolingians, were very rare. Silver dirhams from the 'Russian' trade thus became the means by which enterprising Scandinavians gained wealth and power.

By the mid-780s, the earliest hoard of Islamic dirhams in all European Russia had been deposited in Ladoga, while a small dirham hoard dating from about the same period has been found in Gotland. In other words, Ladoga had already become a key town along the emerging trade routes which led from the Baltic across European Russia to the lower Volga and from there to Iran and Iraq. As this great Scandinavian trade grew over the course of the ninth century, so did Ladoga. More dirham hoards were deposited in and around the town. More craft shops appeared where tools, weapons, and jewellery were made from iron, bronze, bone, amber, and glass. These shops, as well as a number of warehouses, were connected with Ladoga's role as a service station for the eastern trade. A glass workshop, for instance, fabricated some of the beads exchanged with the native Finns for their best furs. In another workshop, amber was fashioned into jewellery used, in large part, for the same purpose. Recent excavations have uncovered considerable quantities of amber and many glass beads in the buildings of this period. Ladoga's craftsmen also constructed and repaired the sea- and river-boats used by the merchants passing through the city. The wood from seagoing ships arriving from the Baltic was even used to help construct Ladoga's dwellings.

Some of Ladoga's original Scandinavian inhabitants may have been only seasonal residents, perhaps returning home after the end of each year's commerce. As Ladoga grew, however, many if not most of its Scandinavians became permanent settlers. By the mid-ninth century, a purely Scandinavian cemetery—the only one in all European Russia, with a number of boat graves—had begun to function at Plakun, opposite Ladoga on the right bank of the Volkhov. Ladoga, however, was not an exclusively Scandinavian

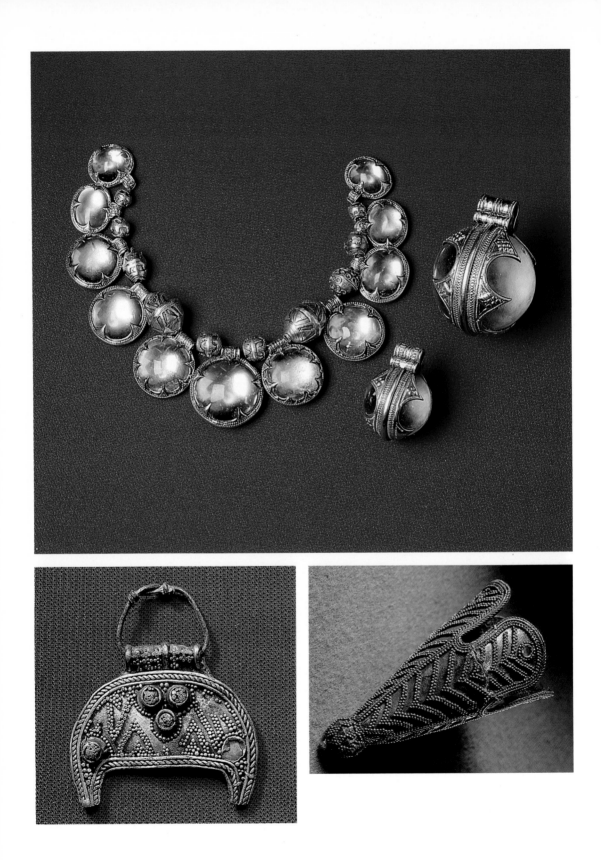

settlement. From the start, East Slavs and/or West Finns constituted a significant part of the town's population. Ladoga was a multinational centre of craft production and international trade.

Expansion and Settlement

Around the middle of the ninth century, significant new developments took place in the infrastructure of the trade routes across northern Russia. It was at this time, for instance, that a settlement called Riurikovo Gorodishche arose on the northern coast of Lake Ilmen. Like its later neighbour Novgorod, it was protected from Scandinavian raids by the presence of rapids along the Volkhov. While pilots could guide merchant ships safely through the cataracts, raiders found it impossible to launch a surprise attack. Ladoga's location made it vulnerable, as a major fire dated to about 860 suggests. Riurikovo was smaller than Ladoga, but fulfilled the same basic functions of craft production and service station for the long-distance trade. Moreover, it was located in an area of fertile soils better suited than those near Ladoga for farming, as the ninth-century hoard of farm implements discovered at the hill fort of Kholopyi Gorodok, 13 kilometres to the north, testifies.

The Scandinavians of Ladoga also began to penetrate into the interior of northern Russia. A small number of Scandinavian artefacts and graves, dating from the late ninth to the eleventh centuries have been found in the West Finnic cemeteries in the region south-east of Lake Ladoga. Some of the Scandinavian families here were no doubt traders who obtained furs from the natives in exchange for beads and other imported products. But it has also been argued that others were Swedish farmers who migrated to Russia in search of land and adapted to the local slash-and-burn agriculture. To the south-west of Ladoga, a Finnic–Balt settlement at Pskov perished in a fire of the early 860s. On its ruins between the late ninth and early eleventh centuries grew a town, inhabited by a multinational population of craftsmen, merchants, and warriors. Some Scandinavians pushed further east into the lands south of Beloozero (White Lake), where at least two craft and trade centres arose. At Krutik a settlement of the late ninth to the late tenth century which was active in the fur trade apparently hosted several itinerant Scandinavian blacksmiths. The settlement of Beloozero itself arose 40 kilometres to the north during the first half of the tenth century, and lived on after Krutik ceased to exist.

By the mid-ninth century a number of bases, primarily trading and handicraft centres used by Scandinavian merchants, began to appear on or near the major interior routes leading to Khazaria. The Scandinavians not

Facing, above: This necklace of rock crystal lenses mounted in silver foil was part of a hoard found in Gotland. Similar pendants have been found in other Gotland hoards. The decoration of the mounts is characteristically Slav but as similar pendants have not been found in Slav hoards it is likely that they were made late in the Viking Age in Gotland, reflecting the island's close contacts with eastern Europe.

Below, left: This crescent-shaped silver pendant, about 5 cm wide, was found in Sweden, but is of a type made in west Russia or Poland. The shape and granular decoration are characteristically Slav.

Below, right: This conical silver mount (6.6 cm high) was found in a tenth-century man's grave at Birka. It was attached to the point of a cap that was at least partly made of silk. The granulation is characteristic of the Dnepr region. The cap must have been made for a man of high status, possibly a retainer of the Prince of Kiev.

Three ninth- or tenth-century objects found in Riurikovo Gorodishche. The female, made of silver, was possibly a Valkyrie. A loop on the back suggests that it was worn on a necklace. The dragon's head, made of lead, was probably the head of a dress pin. Similar objects have been found in Birka and Hedeby. The bronze bridle mount is decorated in the same style as the mounts from Borre illustrated in Chapter 1.

only stayed at these sites while in transit, but some settled in them, either as merchants or agents or to service passing traders. These bases were multi-ethnic settlements, in which Scandinavians only constituted a small part of the population. The indigenous population along the upper Dnepr was Balt, while East Finns were the native inhabitants of the upper Volga. Significant East Slavic migration to central and northern Russia also occurred during the early Middle Ages. The Scandinavian burials in the cemeteries adjacent to these trading stations were normally dispersed rather than concentrated in one part, suggesting that the Scandinavians were integrated into the local society. They dealt on a daily basis with native trappers and merchants; they negotiated with the local tribal chieftains to ensure safe passage for Scandinavian merchants and access to local goods; and they were buried here with their families when they died.

The Scandinavian merchants who were active in European Russia should not be envisaged as law-abiding shopkeepers. They did not hesitate to use force and intimidation to interject themselves into local communities and compel the natives to provide the furs, slaves, and other products they wanted. When the native élites refused to co-operate the Scandinavians frequently destroyed them. But it was often possible to avoid conflict: the Scandinavian merchants, after all, also acted as agents, selling the goods which the local élites had extorted from their own peoples and supplying these élites with the prestigious imports that reinforced their status. In time, the exploitation of the native peoples was perfected. Furs and other goods were no longer extorted on a haphazard basis. Instead, bands composed of Scandinavian settlers and the native élites made an annual trip through their lands, usually in winter, to gather the year's tribute. The trading and handicraft towns thus began to function as centres for the collection of tribute from the local peoples.

The exact dating and ethnic composition of these bases is still the subject of discussion. Most seem to have started the transformation into multi-ethnic trading and handicraft centres some time during the ninth century, reaching their zenith during the tenth. One of the major bases along the upper Volga was Sarskoe, near Rostov. It originated between the sixth and eighth centuries as a Merian settlement. During the ninth century it developed into a multi-ethnic town and, by the tenth century, it had become a large trading and handicraft centre. Near Iaroslavl there are three large cemeteries, at Bol'shoe Timerevo, Mikhailovskoe, and Petrovskoe, with over 700 barrows or kurgans of the ninth to eleventh centuries. Nearby was a contemporaneous multi-ethnic village which apparently served as a centre for commerce and handicraft production. Excavators at Timerevo found in a male grave both a German 'Ulfberht' sword and a merchant's folding scale with an Arabic inscription on one of the pans. From the number of graves and the period over which the settlement functioned, it has been estimated that the average population of Timerevo was about 130. By contrast, the average population of Birka has been calculated at 500–600 and that of Hedeby at about 1,000. While some merchants no doubt travelled from the upper Volga bases to Khazaria via the Bulghar lands, the main route apparently went south via the Oka and Don river systems.

Another base was at Gnezdovo, some 10–12 kilometres west of Smolensk along the Dnepr. It was the great centre for merchants travelling between the Baltic and Black seas via the Volkhov and Dnepr rivers. The complex here originally consisted of over 5,000 barrow graves dating from the second half of the ninth to the first half of the eleventh century, as well as five settlements (two fortified sites and three craft and trade centres) of the same period. The combined population of these settlements probably averaged around 1,250 to 1,400. At least ninety graves contained Scandinavian artefacts.

The Eastern Trade

The bases at Ladoga, Riurikovo, Sarskoe, Gnezdovo, and elsewhere made possible a very profitable Scandinavian trade with the Islamic world via Khazaria. The development and growth of this trade can be traced through the hoards of dirhams deposited throughout European Russia and the lands around the Baltic. At present, there is information on over a thousand hoards containing five or more dirhams; the total number of coins in them was more than 228,000. Since many of the dirhams deposited in eastern and northern Europe were melted down, never reported, or are still buried, the actual number imported from the Islamic world was far greater. While not a perfect source, these dirhams constitute our best evidence for the history of the famous eastern trade of the Viking Age.

This coin evidence suggests that the eastern trade began in the 780s. Its scope was modest and somewhat erratic during the first half of the ninth century, corresponding with the period when Ladoga was first established and slowly began to develop. A marked increase in the volume of trade took place during the 860s to 880s. This growth in commerce stimulated the development of Riurikovo, the formation of interior bases along the upper Volga and upper Dnepr, and the expansion into the Finnic hinterland. It is no coincidence, for example, that a large hoard of some 2,700 dirhams dated to 865/6 was uncovered at the Timerevo settlement. The greater volume of commerce necessitated organized fur-collecting systems, as well as stations along the main water routes that supplied and serviced the merchants journeying to Khazaria.

By the late ninth century, Scandinavians had been active in European Russia for almost 150 years. Those who had settled down and intermarried with the native peoples slowly began to gain a new identity best expressed by the word Rus. But not all Rus were of Scandinavian origin: the term also encompassed many members of the local élites. At Shestovitsa, some 15 kilometres from Chernigov, archaeologists have unearthed a complex of six cemeteries, two fortified sites, and an open settlement. Shestovitsa appears to have been an armed camp of the local prince's retinue, which was composed of several Scandinavians and a much larger number of East Slavs. On the other hand, foreign commerce with Byzantium was almost entirely monopolized by those of Scandinavian descent as late as 945. The rate of assimilation was apparently dependent upon occupation. Nevertheless, because a growing number of Scandinavians were absorbed into Rus society, only new migrants will be referred to as Scandinavians from this point.

There was a brief decline in the eastern trade during the late ninth century, followed by major changes. First the Samanid state in central Asia became the chief supplier of dirhams to European Russia. Secondly, the volume of trade grew astronomically: 80 per cent of all the dirhams in the hoards were deposited between 900 and the 1030s. Thirdly, the routes by which the dirhams reached European Russia altered. In the

These tools were found, packed in a box, in the earliest, mid-eighth-century, occupation layer at Staraja Ladoga. They must have belonged to a craftsman who was both a black-smith and a jeweller, and who came from Scandinavia.

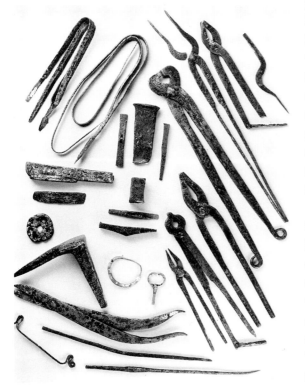

ninth century, the main routes led from Iraq and Iran across the Caucasus mountains or Caspian Sea to Itil at the mouth of the Volga. The main tenth-century routes went from Khwarazm and Transoxiana in central Asia across the steppe to Volga Bulgharia or Khazaria. Finally, the role of the Scandinavian/Rus merchants changed. In the ninth century, as we have seen, they would travel as far as Baghdad. In the tenth century, Rus and Islamic traders met at the great Volga markets of the Bulghars and Khazars, where they could conduct their business in a secure environment.

The tenth-century trade grew moderately until 940. At Ladoga, this steady expansion in commerce was reflected in a large complex of buildings built *c.*894 and used as the base and warehouse for an association of ten to twenty merchants. A similar building serving the same purpose appeared in the late 920s near the craft quarter of the town. The eastern trade reached its peak during the 940s and 950s, when a dramatic increase in dirham imports has been noted. One hoard from the Murom region of the upper Volga basin probably contained around 20,000 dirhams originally. Around 30 per cent of all the dirhams imported to European Russia and the Baltic were deposited in just these two decades. The huge influx of new dirhams was first evident in European Russia during the 940s and then became very notable in the Baltic in the 950s. The mid-tenth century was thus the heyday of the eastern trade of the Viking Age. It is not surprising that the bases at Gnezdovo, Timerevo, and Sarskoe all appear to have reached their zenith at this period. The earliest dated stratum of Novgorod also dates from this time. The booming commerce with central Asia led to the marked expansion and prosperity of the trading stations along the main routes.

The Rise of Kiev

While small settlements had existed at Kiev for several centuries, its emergence as a major town only began in the late ninth century. The podol, which became Kiev's main trade and handicraft centre, dates from about 887. The evidence of graves and artefacts suggests that Scandinavians constituted a small but discernible component of Kiev's élite. According to the *Russian Primary Chronicle*, Oleg and his band left Novgorod (Riurikovo/ Ladoga) for Kiev *c.*880 and killed two of Riurik's followers, Askold and Dir, who had moved there earlier. The archaeological evidence is thus consistent with the *Chronicle* account.

The establishment of the Riurikid dynasty in Kiev led to its emergence as the centre of the Rus state. Prior to the arrival of Oleg, the Khazars ruled Kiev and most of the middle Dnepr. Archaeological evidence points to a Khazar presence in the area since the late seventh century, while the absence

147

of both dirham hoards and Scandinavian artefacts suggests that Kiev had no appreciable role in the eastern trade for most of the ninth century. Under the Riurikids, it quickly became an active participant in the trade with the east. Traditionally Kiev's ascendancy has been linked with the creation of the Dnepr route to Constantinople, then the greatest city in all Europe. But there is good reason to believe that the eastern trade may have been more important in the early tenth century.

Kiev's new involvement with the eastern trade was based on over a century of Scandinavian relations with the Khazars. They regularly travelled through Khazar lands; they paid the *khagan* a tithe on the goods they brought to Itil; they settled commercial disputes in Khazar courts; they made deals with the *khagan* to raid Muslim towns in what is now Azerbaijan; and they even entered Khazar service, like those Swedes who acted as Khazar emissaries to Byzantium in 839. From the 830s the Khazars began to experience considerable problems with the Pechenegs, Magyars, and other enemies in the steppe, as a result of which they may have found it more difficult to maintain their domination of the middle Dnepr. Kiev thus became attractive to enterprising Scandinavians.

The Riurikids who established themselves there presumably worked out some *modus vivendi* with the Khazars, perhaps becoming *de facto* rulers of Kiev and the middle Dnepr, while acknowledging the *khagan*'s nominal overlordship. However, by the mid-tenth century, Kievan participation in the eastern trade had been brought to an end, apparently by growing tensions between Kiev and the Khazars during the 940s, noted by both the *Khazar Correspondence* and the *Cambridge Document*.

When the *Chronicle* was composed, a century or so later, the close relations between the Riurikids and the Khazars had been forgotten or, more likely, were conveniently omitted from the record. The Orthodox Rus princes of Kiev did not want to publicize their links with the nomadic Turkic Khazars, whose élite had converted to Judaism. In reality, ties between the Rus and the Khazars were so close that an early tenth-century Islamic source described the Rus ruler of (probably) Kiev as a *khagan*. Hilarion, the Orthodox, Kievan metropolitan of the mid-eleventh century, referred to the grand princes Vladimir and Iaroslav as *khagan*s of the Rus. The Kiev grand princes could not completely conceal the fact that they were widely seen as the legitimate successors of the Khazar *khagan*s as rulers of the middle Dnepr.

Having established themselves in Kiev, the Riurikids also set about developing trade with Constantinople. The Byzantines, however, were suspicious of the Rus. On several occasions, most notably in 860, bands of Scandinavians had attacked Constantinople as well as other Greek sites along the Black Sea coast. But Oleg persisted, and his attack on Constantinople (*c*.907–12) forced the Byzantines to conclude an agreement specifying the terms under which the Rus were allowed to trade in Constantinople. Kievan commerce with Constantinople continued to grow, and by about 950 large flotillas of merchant ships sailed annually from Kiev to the Byzantine capital, loaded with furs, slaves, wax, and honey. Despite the treaty, disagreements still arose. Between 941 and 945, for instance, a Rus fleet from Kiev raided Byzantine towns on the Black Sea until it was destroyed by the Byzantine navy. The precise reasons for this conflict are still debated. A new trade treaty was signed, which elaborated in great detail the conditions under which commerce was to be conducted. The Byzantines were still concerned that Rus raiders posing as merchants might gain access to Constantinople and its environs.

Between 750 and 1000, various Scandinavian adventurers had established themselves in different parts of European Russia. The descendants of Riurik formed only one of many Scandinavian families who aspired to rule here. In the Rus–Byzantine trade treaty (concluded between 907 and 912), for instance, reference is made to the great princes who lived in Chernigov, Polotsk, Rostov, Liubech, and other towns, and who were supposedly subject to Oleg. There is no other mention of these princes in the *Chronicle* and there is no reason to believe they were relatives of Oleg. In other words, local Rus rulers could be found in key towns located along the major water routes. Despite the tremendous territorial expansion of the Riurikid realm under Igor and Sviatoslav, independent Rus princes still existed in the last quarter of the tenth century. When Vladimir marched from Novgorod to Kiev in about 980 he detoured to take Polotsk, where Rogvolod ruled. The *Chronicle* notes that 'Rogvolod had come from overseas, and exercised authority in Polotsk just as Tury from whom the Turovians get their name had done in Turov'.

A woman's shoe from an eighth-century level in Staraja Ladoga. Similar shoes have been found in the Oseberg burial and elsewhere in Scandinavia.

The Riurikids were not among the pioneers who established the first Scandinavian settlements in European Russia or created the eastern trade. They only came to north-western Russia around the mid-ninth century when control over this region had become the subject of fierce competition among Scandinavian groups. Riurik's band defeated the other Scandinavians, subordinated the local Finnic and Slavic tribes, took control of Kiev, and created the Rus state. Some of the Scandinavian competitors of the Riurikids were killed, some left the Rus lands and either sought service in Byzantium or returned to the Baltic, and others entered the service of the Riurikids as servitors and retainers. The *Chronicle* ignores this 250-year struggle for power.

The main reason for the Riurikids' ultimate success was their control of Kiev. Kiev had an extensive merchant–artisan section located along the Dnepr, and a political–ecclesiastical quarter on a high plateau above the river. The steep cliffs gave the political centre some natural protection. Kiev also dominated the trade of the middle and upper Dnepr through its control over the river's traffic to Constantinople. It thus became the southern terminus of much Rus trade with Byzantium. The town lay some 10 kilometres north of the border between the forest and forest–steppe zones. While it was not immune to nomadic raids, the brunt of these attacks was borne by the Rus towns and settlements to its south. In sum, Kiev was ideally located—far enough south to regulate the trade to Byzantium and far enough north to have reasonable safety from raids.

Russia and the Baltic

While Kiev was becoming the centre of the Rus state, important changes were taking place in north-western Russia. During the late tenth and early eleventh centuries, Novgorod replaced Ladoga and Riurikovo as the locus of Rus power in the region. The earliest finds at Novgorod date to around the 920s, or some 170 years after Scandinavians first appeared in Ladoga. The transfer of political power very probably occurred in the aftermath of Vladimir's conversion. Ladoga was too vulnerable to be the political centre, while Riurikovo was situated very close to the pagan sanctuary at Peryn. Consequently the first local bishop no doubt wished to distance himself from such a heathen centre by locating his seat a little further to the north in the village of Novgorod. The local governor and the merchants soon followed, so that by the early eleventh century Novgorod emerged as the political, ecclesiastical, and commercial centre of north-western Russia.

The move from Riurikovo to Novgorod was part of a more widespread phenomenon taking place throughout the Baltic and European Russia in the late tenth and early eleventh centuries. In European Russia, Gnezdovo gave way to Smolensk, Timerevo to Iaroslavl, and Sarskoe to Rostov, while in the Baltic Birka was replaced by Sigtuna, Hedeby by Schleswig, and Paviken by Visby. It is not clear whether all these changes—sometimes referred to under the rubric 'paired' or 'twin' cities—were brought about by the same developments. In the case of Russia, it has been suggested that the new towns of the early eleventh century were more deeply rooted in the local economy and agricultural hinterland, and also served as the political and ecclesiastical centres for embryonic principalities.

The transformation of Novgorod into the major centre in north-western Russia took place at a time of significant changes in the international trade of European Russia. By the 960s, the volume of dirham imports had begun to decline, and by the eleventh century only relatively few dirhams were reaching European Russia. The flow ceased entirely in the 1030s. This decline was caused by the collapse of the Samanid state, along with the growing silver crisis in central Asia. High volumes of exports and the exhaustion of the existing silver-mines apparently led to a growing debasement of the new dirhams: a silver content of approximately 90 per cent in the year 1000 had declined to a silver content of about 5 per cent half a century later. Understandably, Rus merchants no longer wanted such coins. So by the early eleventh century, Novgorod's merchants had begun to look to the Baltic as their chief market for fur and their chief supplier of silver in the form of German and Anglo-Saxon coins.

A reconstruction of medieval Novgorod, seen from the west, partly based on archaeological evidence. The western part of the city was dominated by the eleventh-century kremlin or citadel and the cathedral of St Sophia. The 'Market Side' was on the east bank of the River Volkhov.

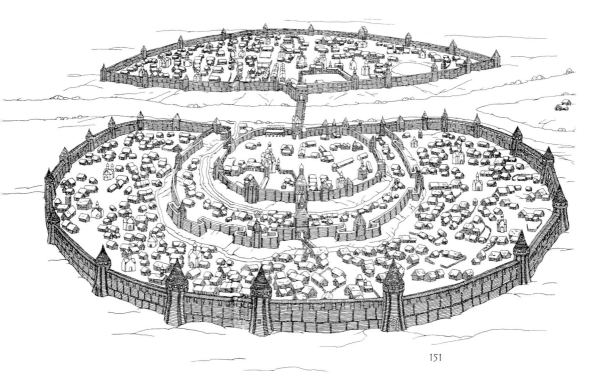

To appreciate the changes in Rus commerce with the Baltic, we need to examine the dirham hoards from the lands around it. Roughly 55 per cent of the dirhams reaching European Russia were re-exported to the Baltic. Consequently they tell us much about Scandinavian and West Slavic trade with European Russia. While dirhams are found in all the Scandinavian countries, relatively few come from Norway and only a modest number from Denmark. The vast majority were deposited in Sweden, including the island of Gotland. Indeed, Gotland possesses the largest single concentration of dirhams of any region in western Eurasia, a fact yet to be satisfactorily explained by historians. During most of the ninth and tenth centuries, Birka in Lake Mälaren was the primary Swedish market dealing with Russia, which explains why so many of the Scandinavian artefacts found in European Russia can be connected with central Sweden. No comparable centre in Gotland at this time is known.

The numismatic and archaeological evidence suggests very strongly that Swedes, most likely from central Sweden, played the major role in Scandinavian relations with European Russia. The trade was rather limited and somewhat erratic until the mid-ninth century. A definite increase took place during the 860s and 870s, but the volume then declined again towards the end of the century. The level of trade then grew steadily, reaching a peak in the 950s. The huge quantities of dirham imports into European Russia in the 940s reached Sweden during the next decade. From the 950s, the chronological composition of the Swedish dirham hoards becomes progressively older as fewer new dirhams reached Sweden. The flow declined, for unknown reasons, in the second half of the tenth century and ceased entirely in the 1010s. It was at this period that Novgorod emerged as the centre for Russia's new trade with the Baltic.

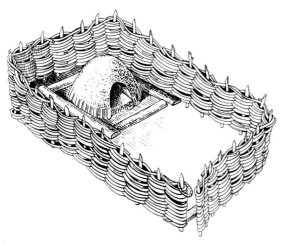

A reconstruction of tenth-century outdoor bread-ovens of a West Slav type found in Riurikovo Gorodishche.

Around 30 per cent of the dirhams from the Baltic lands come from what are now northern Germany and Poland, areas occupied by West Slavs in the Viking Age. The Baltic trade with the east thus involved far more than just Scandinavians, but the role of the West Slavs is relatively unexplored. One conjecture is that Scandinavians used dirhams to purchase grain and other products from the West Slavs. Another possibility is that the dirhams from north Poland and Germany were lost in Scandinavian raids on these lands. However, it seems most likely that West Slavic merchants were actively involved in the Baltic trade with north-western Russia, a circumstance which would also account for the West Slavic finds from the Ladoga–Riurikovo region. In other words, the West Slavs were competitors with the Scandinavians for the dirhams and natural riches of European Russia, and they too had their own infrastructure in towns such as Ladoga and Riurikovo. At some periods the Scandinavians were more successful and more dirhams ended up in Sweden. At other times, the West Slavs were highly effective and more dirhams reached northern Poland and Germany. On average, the Scandinavian share of European Russia's Baltic trade was over twice that of the West Slavs. Presumably the Scandinavians had a far bigger presence in the political structure of European Russia, giving them the greater competitive edge.

While dirhams were sent westward, a number of goods were imported into European Russia from the Baltic. Archaeological and written sources confirm that such products as amber, weapons (especially swords), tin and lead ingots, glass, and wine were all obtained from the Baltic. The West Slavs may also have exported grain to Ladoga. The imports of amber and swords must have been quite substantial, for an Islamic source notes that the Volga Bulghars supplied large quantities of these goods to Khwarazm in central Asia, along with furs from northern Russia. The growing wealth of its local élites made European Russia a good market for both oriental and European imports. Products such as dirhams and swords could either be used locally or re-exported abroad.

Besides their contacts with north-western Russia, Scandinavians were also active in the exploration of the White Sea and the Kola peninsula. By 880, Norwegians were sailing here regularly to gather furs and other local goods from the native Saami both through barter and the imposition of tribute. They encountered competition from other Scandinavian merchants and Finnic traders who came by land. By the tenth century, the Scandinavians also had to compete with the Volga Bulghars whose search for furs led them to the Arctic. In the eleventh century, the Rus of Novgorod began to create a tributary domain to their north among the Finns, Ugrians, and Saami. By the end of the Viking Age, the Scandinavians were facing stiff competition in the Arctic trade from the Rus and Bulghars.

The End of the Viking Age in Russia

As the Riurikids and their allies became established as rulers of the Rus state, they developed a somewhat schizophrenic attitude towards new Scandinavians entering European Russia. Many continued to arrive, for a variety of reasons including the growing lure of service in the Byzantine army. Scandinavian mercenaries had served in the Byzantine forces since the early

Toy wooden sword of the eighth or ninth century (14 cm long) found in Staraja Ladoga. It is a close copy of contemporary swords of Frankish type.

The Church of the Tithe in Kiev was built in stone for Vladimir by Byzantine craftsmen between 989 and 996 to serve as the ecclesiastical centre of the emerging Orthodox Rus state. It symbolizes the growing Byzantine influence on the Rus which was replacing the earlier Scandinavian influences.

tenth century, while the 945 Rus–Byzantine treaty specifically provided that the Kievan grand prince should send Scandinavian warriors to Byzantium when requested. The many Scandinavian mercenaries who returned home from Constantinople via the Dnepr–Volkhov route accounted for most of the Byzantine coins found in European Russia. Oleg, Igor, Vladimir, and Iaroslav had all invited Varangian auxiliaries from Scandinavia to help them in their campaigns against Byzantium and to fight their brothers in the struggles for the Kievan throne. However, these bands posed a potential threat to Riurikid rule of the Rus lands. The Riurikid attitude towards the new Scandinavians can be seen in Vladimir's actions at the start of his reign. As governor of Novgorod, he needed Scandinavian mercenaries from abroad to compete with his brothers for control of Kiev and the position of grand prince. But, having taken Kiev with Scandinavian help, Vladimir did

not want the mercenaries to loot his capital or challenge his rule. So he recruited a few into his service and sent the others on to Constantinople, informing the emperor that they were on their way. The Riurikids, in short, were by this time Rus rulers, concerned primarily with their position in the Rus lands. They increasingly saw new immigrants from Scandinavia as foreigners who potentially posed a threat to them.

Over the course of the ninth and tenth centuries the status of the Scandinavians who came to European Russia had changed. Formerly the creators of trade networks and tribute-collecting states, the newcomers were now increasingly mercenaries. They had served Vladimir well in his campaign to become grand prince, and they were crucial in Iaroslav's initial efforts to defeat his brothers and seize Kiev. But at the battle of Listven in 1024 Iaroslav's freshly recruited Scandinavian mercenaries were decisively beaten by his brother Mstislav's nomadic auxiliaries. Listven demonstrated the superiority of mobile cavalry forces over experienced foot-soldiers, and marked the point when nomadic auxiliaries became the mercenaries of choice within European Russia.

The last hurrah for Scandinavians in Russia came during Iaroslav's reign. His most famous house-guest was Harald Hardrada who had fled Scandinavia in 1031 and spent five years in Iaroslav's service (and married his daughter Elizabeth), before gaining fame first as a soldier in Byzantium and ultimately as king of Norway. Earlier, in 1029, Iaroslav had given refuge to St Olaf of Norway and his son Magnus. Iaroslav's wife was the Princess Ingigerd, a daughter of the Swedish King Olof Skötkonung. The sagas report that at their marriage he bestowed Ladoga upon her. She then appointed Jarl Rognvald of Sweden as her governor there. At Ladoga archaeologists have uncovered a number of eleventh-century Scandinavian Christian graves in the city cemetery. They may well be those of Jarl Rognvald's Swedish soldiers who died while serving in Russia. Finally, the Scandinavian expedition to the Caspian Sea (1036–41) led by Yngvar may have been undertaken with Iaroslav's approval.

While these events are often cited as evidence of enduring Riurikid ties with their Scandinavian homeland, they are, in reality, nothing more than a part of Iaroslav's systematic efforts to establish close ties with many of the ruling houses in Europe, a policy that may have been inspired by his stormy relations with Byzantium. Iaroslav's few important visitors and relatives were of far less long-term significance than the final eclipse of the Scandinavian mercenary in European Russia.

7

THE DANISH EMPIRE AND THE END OF THE VIKING AGE

NIELS LUND

The Danes and their Neighbours

Although our knowledge of Scandinavia before the eleventh century is imperfect, we have good evidence that for much of the Viking Age large areas were dominated by Danish kings. In 813, for example, they went to Vestfold, in southern Norway, described in the *Royal Frankish Annals* as 'the remotest part of their empire', to restore Danish authority, which had apparently collapsed in the civil war following the murder of Godfred, king of Denmark, in 810. It is likely that Danish kings also exercised a degree of overlordship over local rulers in western and northern Norway.

The extent and ways in which Viking activity in western Europe was influenced by the vicissitudes of Scandinavian kingship are open to conjecture. On the one hand there is clear evidence that some leaders of Viking expeditions were exiles, often members of royal families ousted from their homelands by more powerful rivals; on the other hand there are strong suggestions that in the first half of the ninth century reigning Danish kings were more deeply involved in the raids on Frankia than has previously been realized—at least the Frankish kings thought they could be held responsible. Little is known, however, about the power of the Danish kings in the second half of the ninth century when several Viking forces ravaged Frankia and Britain. The leaders of these forces may have been exiles from powerful kings, or they may have obtained the freedom to operate on their own during the reigns of powerless kings at home. We cannot tell.

It is clear, however, that by the end of the ninth century the power of the Danish kings had been greatly weakened, in part by rivals returning home

156

from successful Viking expeditions: for example, in 854 King Horik I was killed by a nephew who had resorted to piracy after his uncle had driven him into exile. Adam of Bremen, who in the second half of the eleventh century wrote a history of the archbishops of Hamburg–Bremen, attributed this loss of power to a signal defeat allegedly inflicted upon a Viking force by an East Frankish army under King Arnulf at the River Dyle in 891, thus suggesting a strong link between the kings of the Danes and the Viking armies active in western Europe, but the importance of this battle has been greatly exaggerated by Adam and other writers. It only involved part of a Viking army on its way to new winter quarters and the defeat did not stop them from wintering where planned.

Scandinavia in the Viking Age

The collapse was real enough, though, and exiles were tempted to go home. A dynasty that had spent some time in Sweden returned home and managed to establish itself for a couple of decades, only to be replaced by another dynasty returning from abroad. Before 900 Wulfstan, an English traveller in the Baltic, observed that Bornholm, which belonged to neither the Danes nor the Svear, had its own king, perhaps suggesting that what overlordship Danish kings might previously have claimed had now faded.

The clearest indication of collapse is perhaps provided by events in Norway. Unlike Denmark, Norway had never been united under a native king. Towards the end of the ninth century, however, Harald Finehair, a ruler whose own base was probably in the west of Norway, attempted to extend his power over the whole country. Tradition has placed him in Vestfold on the west side of Oslo fjord, but this tradition developed in the twelfth and thirteenth centuries when Danish kings were again pressing their claims to this area and when Norwegian propaganda therefore wished to represent it as the very heart of the kingdom of Norway. The famous battle of Hafrsfjord was also traditionally seen as the crowning effort in Harald's unification of Norway. In fact, it was a battle by which Harald extended his power from his base in the Bergen area southwards beyond the Hafrsfjord. He is unlikely ever to have controlled all Norway.

The Jelling Dynasty

The kings who restored Denmark to its leading position in Scandinavia belonged to the Jelling dynasty. In a runic inscription forming part of the magnificent monuments that this dynasty erected at Jelling, one of its members, Harald Bluetooth, boasts that he won for himself all Denmark and Norway and Christianized the Danes. Despite the study that has been devoted to the interpretation of this inscription, it is still far from clear what Harald achieved in reuniting Denmark; it is even highly debatable what 'Denmark' meant.

The name is first recorded in the description of a journey from *Sciringesheal* in Vestfold to Hedeby in the south of Jutland by the Norwegian chieftain Ottar. He told King Alfred and his learned company in Wessex that 'when he sailed there [i.e. to Hedeby] from *Sciringesheal* he had Denmark to port and the open sea to starboard for three days. Then two days before he arrived at Hedeby he had Jutland and *Sillende* and many islands to starboard. . . . On the port side he had, for two days, those islands that belong to Denmark.' Ottar's account was included in an Old English translation of Orosius' *Seven Books of History against the Pagans*, and its distinction between *Denemearc* and the islands belonging to it, and Jutland with *Sil-*

lende (south Jutland) and appurtenant islands, is matched by a distinction made elsewhere in the same translation between 'South Danes' inhabiting *Sillende* and Jutland, and 'North Danes' inhabiting the coastal regions of what are now south-east Norway, west Sweden, and the major Danish islands. If this is taken at face value the name *Denmark* applied to only part of the area that was inhabited by Danes and ruled by Danish kings. It is therefore significant that Harald's father Gorm was married to a princess, Thyre, who was described as 'the pride of Denmark'. This suggests that Gorm, based in Jutland, and therefore presumably a 'South Dane', had married a 'North Dane' from 'Denmark', thus paving the way for the unification of both areas under his son and heir Harald Bluetooth.

The archaeological record of the reign of Harald Bluetooth is very impressive. Besides the runic monument at Jelling, dedicated to the memory of his parents but devoted to recording his own achievements, he built two big mounds and a substantial wooden church. In the north mound he buried his father in a wooden chamber in 958; this date for the beginning of Harald's reign throws into question the tradition reported in later historical sources that he ruled for fifty years. As he died no later than 987, if he was king before 958 he must have been his father's co-ruler. No grave has been found in the south mound, which was completed more than a decade later. It may have been intended for Harald himself but not used for that purpose because he became a Christian, or it may have been intended for his mother

Aerial view of Jelling with its two mounds, church, and two rune-stones. Its history is still enigmatic. The smaller stone asserts that Gorm built a monument in memory of his wife and the larger one claims that Harald Bluetooth built it in memory of his parents. Gorm was probably first buried in the north mound in a chamber dendro-chronologically dated 958, and later transferred to a grave in the wooden predecessor of the present Romanesque church. There is no trace of Thyre. The south mound had no burial and was completed after 970.

159

Harald's rune-stone at Jelling has three sides. One has an inscription: 'Harald had these monuments erected in memory of Gorm his father and Thyre his mother, that Harald who won for himself all Denmark and Norway and Christianized the Danes'. The end of this inscription is on the other two sides of the stone; the claim to have won Norway is under a carving of a great beast and that about the Christianization of the Danes is under the crucifixion seen here.

Thyre. According to the smaller rune-stone at Jelling, she predeceased her husband Gorm and therefore ought to have been buried by him. However, on three inscriptions in the neighbourhood of Jelling one Tue, son of Ravn, claims to have built Thyre's mound, and that is most unlikely to have been the south mound at Jelling. Where Thyre was buried and by whom is therefore an enigma and a matter of much speculation. Having adopted Christianity, probably in 965, Harald removed his father's remains from the mound and reburied them in the timber church that was built between the mounds.

Many fortifications were constructed during Harald's reign. Hedeby and Ribe and possibly Århus were fortified with walls, and Danevirke, a complex of banks and ditches securing the boundary against the Germans that was begun before 700, was re-fortified in the 950s and new walls were built in the 960s to connect the main wall to the semicircular wall surrounding Hedeby. The most impressive monuments from Harald's reign, however, are the circular fortresses constructed *c.*980 at Trelleborg in west Sjælland, at Fyrkat in east Jutland, and Aggersborg in north Jutland, in Odense on Fyn, and, possibly, at Trelleborg in Skåne. They were previously thought to date from the reign of Sven Forkbeard and were interpreted in the context of his conquest of England. However, dendrochronology has now dated them to the reign of Harald: the timbers used for the construction of Trelleborg were felled between September 980 and May 981. This has reopened discussion about their purpose, or purposes. Some would see them as a means of coercion in Harald's unification of Denmark, others understand their function more broadly as royal strongholds serving a kingship trying to administer its country much more tightly than before, with the powerful Aggersborg, four times as large as the others, aimed at the control of Nor-

The circular fortress at Trelleborg, near Slagelse in Sjælland, was built in 980–1. Its strictly geometric design, with the houses outside the wall forming part of the overall layout, is a great tribute to the skill of the designer, but the reason the four gateways were placed at the points of the compass is unknown.

The houses in the circular fortresses all had curved side walls. This reconstruction is based on the excavation of the fortress at Fyrkat combined with pictures and carvings of Viking-Age houses.

way. This interpretation gains strength from a study of the finds made inside the fortresses and their houses. As only a minority of the houses had fireplaces, they were hardly intended to be winter quarters for even the toughest of warriors. In some houses traces of the work of craftsmen, including silver- or goldsmiths, have been found. The general impression is not that of garrisons. It has also been suggested that they were intended to serve as mobilization centres in the defence against Germany. Whatever their purpose may have been, they are strange monuments in almost every respect. Their strictly circular layout does not seem to serve any practical purpose and the model for it has not been found. At Trelleborg much trouble was taken to level the ground on which the fortress was built, for no obvious reason. The purpose of these fortresses was also short-lived: no repairs have been traced in any of them, and at Fyrkat part of the wall even collapsed during construction and was never repaired.

In addition to these structures Harald's reign saw much work on roads and bridges. At Ravning Enge south of Vejle the remains of a massive wooden bridge spanning 700 metres have been excavated and dendro-chronologically dated to 978. Impressive traces of road engineering at that time have also been found on Sjælland.

All these works suggest that Harald was a new type of Danish ruler, deter-mined to impose his will throughout his enlarged kingdom and to exploit its resources. When the circular fortresses were ascribed to Sven Forkbeard it was assumed that booty won in England financed the building—that Eng-land, in effect, paid for its own conquest. Harald is not known to have tapped foreign sources and therefore must presumably have made heavy demands on the Danes. Later sources hint that the Danes resented the tyranny of forced labour imposed on them by Harald, but this may be no more than a subsequent rationalization based on the rebellion against him by his own son and a memory of the great building enterprises of his reign.

Attempts to take Christianity to Denmark had been made since the early eighth century. Knowledge of Christianity must have been widespread in Denmark in view of its close contacts with the rest of Europe in this period, and one observer in the second half of the tenth century indeed claims that the Danes had long been Christians, although they still practised pagan rites. Churches were built in Hedeby and Ribe in the mid-ninth century, but Christianity was not officially accepted or permanently established in Den-mark at this time.

Responsibility for the evangelization of Scandinavia lay with Anskar's successors as archbishops of Hamburg–Bremen. This archdiocese was cre-ated in Hamburg in 832, and in 845, after a Danish attack on Hamburg, the diocese of Bremen was united with that of Hamburg, much to the dismay of Gunther and later archbishops of Cologne, from whose province Bremen was taken. More than a century later little progress, if any, had been made. The archbishop had no suffragans in Denmark or elsewhere and therefore his see could not function canonically. It was difficult to justify its existence, and Cologne wanted Bremen back.

It was Archbishop Adaldag's good fortune that the German kings and emperors now resumed an interest in mission combined with imperialism. Henry the Fowler (919–36) is said to have defeated the Danes in 934 and to have forced them to accept baptism. Even if this claim is true, which seems most unlikely, this conversion had no lasting effects. In 948, however, Otto the Great (936–73) appointed bishops to three dioceses in Denmark: Schleswig, Ribe, and Århus. These bishops may never have set foot in Denmark but their appointment gave Adaldag, who began his career in Otto's chancery and was archbishop c.937–88, the suffragans he needed so badly. He undoubtedly urged the king to support his mission in the same way that he helped spread the gospel to the Slavs. The German mission among the Slavs was inextricably bound up with imperialism; submission to Christ implied submission to the emperor whose efforts for the faith thus brought him considerable worldly rewards.

This lesson was bound to impress the Danes, and the likeliest explanation for Harald's conversion is that he realized that he could not resist the German champions of Christianity and therefore decided to convert,

Tamdrup church, near Horsens in Jutland, probably housed a shrine of Poppo that was covered with gilded plates depicting scenes from the conversion of Harald Bluetooth. This one shows Poppo wearing an iron glove to hold in a fire until it was red-hot, an ordeal to convince the king.

thereby depriving the emperor of any pretext for conquering Denmark. Contrary to what Adam of Bremen wants us to believe, this did not mean that close relations with Hamburg were established or, indeed, that the bishops appointed in 948 were admitted to their sees. Harald more probably wanted to appoint bishops of his own choice.

Harald is said to have been persuaded that Christ was the only true God by a missionary named Poppo, who allegedly underwent ordeal by fire. How important this was in comparison to the political arguments that swayed Harald remains open to conjecture, but it is remarkable that Poppo had no apparent connection with Hamburg. This was so embarrassing for Adam that he transferred the story about Poppo's ordeal to his account of the conversion of the Swedish king Erik the Victorious. Hamburg, of course, was part of the German imperial church, it had obligations towards the empire and the emperor claimed rights not only over Hamburg–Bremen itself but over its suffragan sees.

The historical record of Harald's reign is meagre compared to the archaeological evidence. Very little is recorded in writing before the second half of the eleventh century, when Adam of Bremen supplied some information, allegedly derived from his contemporary Sven Estridsson, king of Denmark from 1047 to 1076. Adam describes Harald as a model Christian king, personally very pious, a great friend of the archbishop of Hamburg–Bremen, and a supporter of the church in Denmark, who filled the country with priests and churches. Adam expresses the hope that Harald, having ended his reign as the victim of a pagan rebellion, will not be without the crown of martyrdom. Adam's account is, however, biased and far from trustworthy. His aim was to justify the existence and the position of his see, and he did not hesitate to distort the truth in service of this objective.

Crediting Harald's conversion to a missionary who was not from Hamburg—unfortunately we do not know where Poppo came from—may well reflect a negative attitude to that see because of its imperial connections. Such an attitude was certainly justified by subsequent developments. Harald adopted Christianity no later than 965, when the emperor issued a charter relinquishing imperial rights over the Danish dioceses, thereby acknowledging that Denmark had a Christian ruler. Otto's gesture, however, did not persuade Harald that German intentions were entirely friendly. He continued to re-fortify the Danevirke, and extensive works linking it to the wall round Hedeby were undertaken in 968, and in 974 after the accession of Otto II he even attacked the Germans. He lost this war and probably had to cede some land to the victors; he regained it, however, in 983 when, following Otto's defeat at the hands of the Saracens in Calabria, he attacked the Germans again. If, under such circumstances, Hamburg suffragans were admitted to Denmark, Harald is likely, like Sven Estridsson a century later, to have prevented them from attending synods in Germany. Adam's description of Harald's attitude to Hamburg–Bremen is propaganda for his own time, when Sven Estridsson was negotiating with the pope for the creation of an independent archbishopric in Denmark. Adam was keen to stress the ancient rights of Hamburg–Bremen and to prove the leading role of its archbishops in the Christianization of Scandinavia.

Denmark, Norway, and England

Harald Bluetooth's restoration of Danish power in Norway probably meant that he gained direct rule in the Viken area and was recognized as overlord in most other parts of Norway. The Norwegian king Harald Finehair probably died in the 930s and was succeeded by his son Erik Bloodaxe. Like his father, Erik tried to extend his rule over other parts of Norway, beginning in Trøndelag. However, he soon had to face a rival, his younger brother

This sword hilt from Dybäck in Skåne has guards of cast silver ornamented with gilding and niello. The grip was bound with gold wire. The ornament is late Jellinge–Mammen style with strong English influence. It was probably made in Denmark, but could be of English manufacture.

Håkon, nicknamed the Good, who had been fostered in England at the court of King Athelstan (924–39). Håkon's attachment to the court of Athelstan may suggest that Harald Finehair had sought the support of the English king against the Danes. Although England does not seem to have been troubled by Danish Vikings in the reign of Athelstan, there is some evidence that he formed an alliance with Otto the Great against the Danes. When Erik Bloodaxe was expelled from Norway by Håkon, with the support of the Trønder and their earl Sigurd of Lade, he went to Northumbria, where he was accepted as king of York, but was expelled, and killed, in 954 or, possibly, 952.

When Erik's sons—who were, if the tradition about their mother's descent is true, the cousins of Harald Bluetooth—rebelled against Håkon the Good, Harald supported them and helped one of them, Harald Greycloak, to power. Before long, however, he began to act more independently than the Danish king was prepared to accept and was opposed by a coalition of the Danes and the Trønder. After Harald Greycloak fell in battle in Limfjord, Harald Bluetooth was acknowledged as overlord of Norway, exercising his power through the earl of Lade.

Towards the end of his reign, again according to Adam, Harald's son Sven Forkbeard rebelled against him. Adam reports that Sven assumed the leadership of discontented elements in Denmark, among them magnates who had been forced to accept Christianity, and Sven is even represented as the leader of a pagan reaction in which the bishops loyal to Hamburg were expelled from Denmark. Harald Bluetooth was wounded in battle and sought refuge with the Wends in Jumne at the mouth of the Oder. Having died there from his wounds, he was taken to Roskilde and buried in a church that he himself had begun. According to Adam, Sven suffered divine punishment for his rebellion by being taken captive by his father's friends in Jumne in Pomerania and ransomed at a high price by the Danes, and then being driven from his ill-gotten kingdom by the Swedish king Erik the Victorious, and forced to spend fourteen years in exile in Scotland, among other places, having been denied refuge in England. In later sources his capture and ransoming are duplicated and even triplicated.

This is a very unlikely story. When, according to Adam, Sven was a miserable exile he was in fact leading Viking raids on England, and his father's Wendish friends are apocryphal. Harald Bluetooth had a Wendish wife, the daughter of the Abodrite prince Mistivoi, reflecting a political relationship between the two princes. Their common enemy was the Germans, against whom they joined forces in 983. It would have made good sense if, when faced with rebellion in Denmark, Harald had sought refuge among the Abodrites. Whether Jumne was at this time part of the Polish kingdom or was independent is not clear. In any case it would have been too dangerously close to the Poles for Harald to seek refuge there. The Poles were at that time on friendly terms with the Germans and were therefore the enemies of the Abodrites and presumably of the Danes as well. The Swedish king Erik the Victorious sought their friendship and married a Polish princess, doubtless in the hope of gaining support in resisting the Danes. What is more, no friend of Harald—Abodrite, Pomeranian, or Pole— would have given his body to the rebels for burial.

Sven Forkbeard: The Most Fortunate of Kings

A much more sympathetic account of Sven's career, although still biased, is given in the *Encomium Emmae Reginae*, written by an anonymous monk in Flanders *c*.1040. He describes Sven as 'practically the most fortunate of all kings of his time' who was undeservedly the victim of his father's envy and hatred. When his father publicly disinherited him, the army rallied around Sven to protect him. The encomiast goes on to describe how peacefully and well Sven ruled his country thereafter.

Little is known about Sven's domestic rule and equally little about the reasons for his attacks on England. Several explanations have been suggested. One is that he was impoverished after paying one or more ransoms to the Slavs, but, as there are good reasons for doubting that he was ever captured by them, this is unconvincing. Another suggestion is that he lost an important source of income when the flow of Arabic silver via the Russian rivers into the Baltic region dried up at just about the time that Sven succeeded his father. The flow of silver, however, stopped earlier, in the middle of the tenth century, and there is nothing to suggest that it was ever an important source of income for Danish kings. It is more likely that Sven's motive was to acquire wealth in England himself, and thus be better able to resist any challenge by rival Viking leaders who were also raiding England. He had no wish to suffer the same fate as Horik I. Sven could go on raids abroad because, unlike his father, he did not have to worry about the German threat.

For his final conquest of England in 1013 yet another explanation has been suggested. The encomiast claims that Sven made this expedition to punish Thorkell the Tall for defecting with part of the royal Danish fleet to serve the English king, Æthelred. Thorkell was the leader of a Viking force that arrived in England in 1009. They behaved like normal Vikings for three years, plundering, burning, and exacting tribute and ransoms from the English, and crowning their deeds of valour with the murder of Ælfheah, archbishop of Canterbury, in 1012, when he refused to be ransomed. After this Thorkell took service with Æthelred with part of his army, some forty-five ships, disbanding the rest of his forces.

The encomiast, who obviously wanted to depict Sven as an injured party with an impeccable reason to attack England, stresses Thorkell's position in the king's service and accuses him of defecting with part of the royal fleet. Other sources, however, are much more ambiguous about the relationship between the two. Thorkell was later connected with the legendary Jomsvikings, a highly disciplined body of warriors supposedly based in *Jomsborg* on the southern coast line of the Baltic. This stronghold, called Jumne by Adam, was said to have been founded by Harald Bluetooth, who took refuge there after his son's rebellion. Accounts of the Jomsvikings were probably elaborated in the twelfth and thirteenth centuries, but there may be a core of truth in the connection: as leader of a band of Vikings in the Baltic, Thorkell may have been employed by the ruler of Jumne. Excavations have shown that Jumne was no fortress, but a substantial town on the Oder estuary. It was commonly known as *Wolin*, and may have had as many as 10,000 inhabitants. Independent bands of Vikings were certainly active at this time, and Swedish runic inscriptions name a few chieftains who rewarded their followers with English money. It is possible that Thorkell was at some time forced to acknowledge Sven as his overlord, but his loyal support of Æthelred from 1012 to the king's death suggests that he was never Sven's man.

In 994 Sven led a raid on England, involving an unsuccessful attack on
London and plundering in the south of England. At the end of the campaigning season the army took winter quarters in Southampton, and while
it was encamped there Æthelred sent for one of its leaders, Olaf Tryggvason,
and offered him a separate peace and employment as a mercenary with his
followers. Olaf accepted this, and a treaty was drawn up to govern relations
between this army and the English population. Having served Æthelred for
some time Olaf returned to conquer Norway with the help of his English
money. He was first accepted as king in Trøndelag whose earl, Håkon Sig-
urdsson, had been murdered.

This was a strong provocation to Sven, as it was undoubtedly designed to
be. He had succeeded his father as overlord of Norway and was bound to
react strongly when Olaf began to seize power. From the English point of
view this was a calculated attempt to keep Sven busy in Scandinavia, and
apparently it was successful: Sven did not return to England until he had
defeated and killed Olaf in the battle of Svold in the year 1000.

Olaf Tryggvason has gone down in Norwegian history as the real founder
of Norway. Later historians made him a descendant of Harald Finehair, to
give him an impeccable claim to the throne, but their somewhat hagio-
graphical account of his childhood and youth shows that they knew nothing about his ancestry. Olaf obviously had some standing among the
chieftains of Norway when he followed his overlord to England, but his
claim to the throne was no better than that of any other chieftain.

In the battle of Svold, Sven had the support of Olof Skötkonung, king of
the Svear, the son of Erik the Victorious and his Polish queen, whom Sven
had married after Erik's death c.993. Sven thus became Olof's stepfather,
and Olof's surname, Skötkonung 'tributary king', presumably implies a
tributary relationship to the Danish king.

Adam of Bremen makes Sven the leader of a pagan reaction in which the
bishops were expelled from Denmark. It is no doubt true that Sven did not
welcome German bishops any more than his father did, but there is no evidence that he was an apostate. On the contrary, in his reign churches were
built in both Roskilde and Lund, and English missionaries operated in Denmark as well as in Norway. But, in Adam's view, to bring in English clergy
was even worse than apostasy.

Viking Armies and the Leding

The thirteenth-century provincial laws of Denmark describe a system of
military organization, the *leding*, under which the population of Denmark
was obliged to furnish fighting ships and to find crews for them. The system

was based on landholding, and theoretically a fleet of about a thousand ships, each with a crew of about forty, could be mustered. It has sometimes been claimed that Sven Forkbeard must have been able to draw on this system in order to muster the forces necessary to conquer England, as he did

swiftly and convincingly in 1013. Sven may well deserve admiration for his generalship, but it is very unlikely that the system documented from the thirteenth century already existed in the tenth. It was in fact probably not introduced before the second half of the twelfth century.

Sven's armies were recruited in the way that was customary in the Viking Age, when many men were eager to serve because of the rewards that could be earned in successful campaigns. An overlord could expect his subordinates, some of whom might themselves be kings, to join him in his campaigns or to fight for him on their own. Thus the earl of Lade furnished a contingent for Harald Bluetooth's war with the Germans, while his raids in Götaland and even Russia were probably made on behalf of his Danish overlord. Sven's own forces were not conscripts. The encomiast stresses that Sven 'had rendered them submissive and faithful to himself by manifold and generous munificence'. They formed a traditional military following and expected to be rewarded and well maintained by their lord. Their typical attitude is reflected in several runic inscriptions which also show that some came from parts of Scandinavia that were not directly under Sven's lordship. Several Swedish inscriptions commemorate Swedes participating in expeditions led by Sven's son, Knut. Chieftains who led expeditions to the west and to the east on their own behalf are also mentioned on runic stones, a reminder that the kings of the Danes were not the only Viking commanders, although some of those who went west may have acknowledged Sven's authority, as at the peak of his power he controlled an empire comprising most of Scandinavia. This is probably the light in which we should see Thorkell the Tall, not as the commander of part of the Danish *leding*. The force to which he belonged may have had an independent role in the 980s when they took Harald Bluetooth's side against Sven and, possibly, fought a famous battle at Hjørungavåg against Håkon, earl of Lade, in revenge for his support of Sven.

The Accession of Knut the Great

Complicated problems of succession arose when Sven died at Gainsborough on 3 February 1014. He had been acknowledged as king of England by the English magnates shortly before Christmas 1013 while Æthelred had sought refuge in Normandy. The English chose to recall their former lord rather than to acknowledge Sven's son Knut, who was elected as Sven's successor by the Danish army in Gainsborough. That did not, however, make him king of Denmark. Sven was succeeded there by Knut's elder brother Harald, who had probably been left in charge when Sven set out for England. The situation seems to have been rather ambiguous for Knut had dies cut in England as if he expected to strike coins in his own name in Denmark immediately, and according to the encomiast he also claimed a share in the Danish kingship, which Harald denied him.

In this situation Knut probably had two options: he could fight for Denmark against his brother, the ideal option from the English point of view, or he could return to claim England. He chose the latter and recruited a new army, like his father's from across Scandinavia, returning to England in 1015. However, the situation held great potential dangers for the Danes. Sven's control of Scandinavia crumbled in the hands of his sons. First, the English once again supported a Norwegian chieftain to cause trouble in that part of the Danish empire. Olaf Haraldsson, who had been with Thorkell the Tall in England, went to Norway with English support in a bid to seize power and attacked the earls of Lade, the brothers Erik and Sven Håkonsson, who had been loyal supporters of Sven Forkbeard. Earl Sven was defeated in the battle of Nesjar and died soon afterwards, while Erik joined Knut. Olaf began the task of winning the rest of Norway.

Danish influence in Sweden was also eroded. Olof Skötkonung did not automatically transfer his loyalty from his stepfather Sven to his uterine brother Harald; indeed, he seems to have taken the opportunity to free himself from the Danish yoke. He married a daughter to Olaf of Norway, and sent for a bishop from Hamburg–Bremen, thus seeking friends among the enemies of the Danish kings. A story that Knut sent the sons of Edmund Ironside to Olof in Sweden to be murdered and that Olof refused to comply with Knut's instructions and sent the boys to Russia and Hungary suggests

Facing: Narrative sources only name the most famous Viking leaders. This rune-stone from Yttergärde in Uppland, commemorates Ulf of Borresta who won tribute in England three times, under an otherwise unknown leader called Tostig as well as under Knut and Thorkell. It shows that not all Knut's warriors came from Denmark.

that Knut expected Swedish loyalty to be transferred to him. Olof's son Anund who succeeded him in about 1022 followed a similar anti-Danish line.

Extremely little is known about the reign of Knut's brother Harald and his possible involvement in Knut's bid for England. His death is not recorded, but in 1019 Knut, having meanwhile been formally accepted as king of England, paid a visit to Denmark, presumably to take power there as well. Knut was later known as 'the Great' in acknowledgement of the empire that he eventually established. It was, however, not so extensive as his father's had been, but as king of England he was a wealthy ruler, and his status in Scandinavia, although important, was not his first concern.

Knut, King of England

After Knut had won England, he retained Wessex in his own hands, but appointed earls to run the rest of the country. Erik Håkonsson of Lade was rewarded with the earldom of Northumbria. Eadric Streona, whose treachery ensured Knut's success, retained control of Mercia, but was soon executed. Thorkell the Tall was made earl of East Anglia.

It is not clear when Thorkell came over to Knut. He was still in Æthelred's service when the king was recalled from Normandy after Sven Forkbeard's death, but in the first years of Knut's reign he occupied a very trusted position in England. A letter Knut addressed to the English from Denmark in 1020 suggests that Thorkell had in effect been left as regent in England during Knut's absence. This is remarkable, bearing in mind that Thorkell had vigorously opposed Knut's father. He seems, indeed, to have been so powerful that Knut could not afford to ignore him, and, although he was exiled in 1021, he was restored to favour a couple of years later.

One of Knut's first concerns as king of England was to protect his new kingdom against fresh Viking attacks, possibly by former members of his own army who had been paid off and had returned to Scandinavia. He retained the service of forty ships, and in 1018 was able to destroy a fleet of thirty ships that attacked England. Two years later he assured the English that he had taken such precautions against future dangers from Denmark that they would be safe as long as they supported him loyally. It is uncertain what these precautions were. It may be that one was the appointment of his brother-in-law Ulf, who was a member of a powerful Danish family, as his regent in Denmark. Ulf witnessed two English charters in about 1022, but may have done so during a short visit to England.

On his accession Knut apparently made several promises regarding his government of England, and subsequently issued a code of law on both ecclesiastical and secular matters that was largely a repetition of earlier English laws. It was greatly influenced, and may have been compiled, by Archbishop Wulfstan of York, who had drafted several of Æthelred's laws and continued until his death in 1023 as legal adviser to Knut.

This, combined with Knut's obvious eagerness to accept and fill the role of a Christian king, has created the impression that his conquest did not mark a break with England's past, that all was continuity. This was not true in all respects, however. In the first place, Knut's campaigns had been very bloody, and cost the lives of many English ealdormen and thegns; the witness lists of Knut's charters show that the higher classes of English society were largely replaced by new men, including numerous Danes who appear as king's thegns. Much land must also have changed hands, as new owners took over the land of dead magnates and, possibly, also of ecclesiastical institutions that had not survived the wars. There is, however, no evidence that large numbers of Danes settled in England during Knut's reign. He retained a number of ships and their crews in his service and maintained a force of housecarls, most of them probably Danish; some of these were rewarded with land and entered the thegnly class. New Danish immigrants, although apparently not numerous, were an appreciative audience for the new Anglo-Danish style of sculpture that Knut encouraged, a fine example of which has been found in Winchester.

Remains of clothing were found on the man buried in the richly furnished grave at Mammen near Viborg in Jutland, that has been dated dendrochronologically 970–1. This reconstruction, however, is based on the costume of King Knut in the picture reproduced on p. 177.

Knut's Scandinavian Empire

Knut's impact as king of Denmark is only manifest in two areas. First, he tried to introduce a coin system on the English pattern and began to strike coins modelled on his own English coins and those of his predecessor. Whether types were changed at regular intervals as they were in England is doubtful, but Knut certainly intended that to happen.

The other area was church policy. Knut initially had the same attitude to Hamburg–Bremen as his father and grandfather. He brought in ecclesiastics from England rather than Germany and encouraged Danish ecclesiastics to seek education in England. Church organization may, in fact, be the only area in which Knut actually sought to integrate his dominions into one empire. Adam of Bremen reports that Unwan, archbishop of Hamburg–Bremen, captured Gerbrand, bishop of Roskilde, when the bishop was returning to Denmark from England and kept him prisoner until he promised Unwan obedience and fidelity in the future. Gerbrand had been consecrated in Canterbury by Archbishop Æthelnoth, and it is likely that Knut was planning to elevate Roskilde to archiepiscopal status under the metropolitan authority of Canterbury. This would explain Unwan's drastic action, which was combined with an appeal for help to the German king Conrad II. It would also explain the enormous grants of land that the bishop of Roskilde seems to have received in Knut's reign. What is more, a stone cathedral was begun in Roskilde at that time, and, although nothing is left of it, the same gang of builders in the 1030s also built another church in Roskilde, St Clemens, which was clearly the work of English stonemasons.

Knut had probably abandoned his policy towards Hamburg–Bremen by 1027 when he attended the imperial coronation of Conrad II in Rome. During that visit he negotiated some concessions for his subjects and also arranged for the marriage of his daughter to the emperor's son when they both came of age.

Knut's journey to Rome followed a serious crisis in Scandinavia. In 1026 he faced a coalition of the kings of Norway and Sweden, Olaf Haraldsson and Anund Jacob. They were apparently joined by Ulf, Knut's brother-in-law, who, until his rebellion, seems to have been ruling Denmark on behalf of Knut's little son Harthaknut. Knut brought an army from England to Scandinavia and fought his enemies in a battle, the outcome of which has been the subject of controversy. According to the *Anglo-Saxon Chronicle*, Knut's opponents kept possession of the battlefield, while contemporary poetry has, probably mistakenly, been cited as evidence that Knut won a splendid victory. Whatever happened Knut was able to visit Rome a year later. In a second letter to his English subjects, written on his way back from Rome via Scandinavia, he makes it clear that his enemies had failed to rob him of his dominions, but apparently he could not dictate terms, and had to negotiate before he could return to England.

The frieze from which this early eleventh-century fragment came probably formed part of the ornamentation of the Old Minster at Winchester that was scrapped when that building was demolished in 1093–4. It shows a scene from the saga of Sigmund and the wolf. Sigmund was regarded as the ancestor of the kings of both Wessex and Denmark. The frieze apparently underlined Knut's legitimacy as king of England.

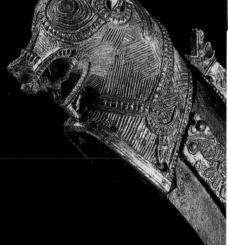

Above: The Imperial Crown was probably made for the coronation of Otto I in 961. The arch and cross were added for the coronation of Conrad II in Rome in 1027, a ceremony attended by Knut.

Left: The terminal of one of the two harness bows found in refuse from a smithy at Mammen, mounted on modern wood. The almost identical terminals are decorated in Jellinge style and hold gripping beasts in their mouths. Harness bows placed on the backs of horses served to secure the reins.

Ulf's role in the rebellion cost him his life. There are contradictory stories about the circumstances, but there is little doubt that Knut had him liquidated. It is significant that Ulf suffered *damnatio memoriae*: his son was very rarely called Sven Ulfsson, but was usually given the matronymic, Estridsson.

After these events Knut turned against Norway, where Olaf Haraldsson had greatly extended his authority, often violently, but also through alliances with powerful local chieftains. Knut, however, regarded Olaf as a usurper. He styled himself king of Norway before 1028 when, at last, he succeeded in expelling Olaf. He did this not by pitched battles but simply by persuading, or bribing, the Norwegian chieftains to abandon Olaf, who had proved to be a harsh ruler. Deprived of support, Olaf sought refuge with the prince of Novgorod, another traditional enemy of the Danes.

Knut appointed as his agent in Norway, Håkon, son of Erik Håkonsson, who had been earl of Lade under Sven and later, under Knut, earl of Northumbria, thus restoring the traditional practice by which Danish overlordship in Norway was exercised through a native chieftain. Unfortunately Håkon died on his return to Norway having travelled to England to fetch his bride. This tempted Olaf to return with Russian and Swedish support, but he was killed in the battle at Stiklestad on 29 July 1030 by Norwegian opponents. Knut now made a crucial mistake. Rather than choose another native agent, he sent Sven, his son by Ælfgifu of Northampton, and Ælfgifu herself to rule Norway. Their regime may have been no harsher than that of Olaf Haraldsson, but rule by foreigners soon became very unpopular. Olaf was soon revered as a saint, and when his son Magnus returned from Russia the Norwegians rallied round him and—possibly even before Knut's death in 1035—drove out Sven, who died soon afterwards, and his mother.

Knut claimed to be king not only of Norway but also of 'part of the Swedes'. Various attempts have been made to identify the Swedes who acknowledged him. Coins struck in his name in Sigtuna, which have often been regarded as evidence that he was recognized as king by the Svear were, in fact, all struck from a single die which was copied from a coin of Knut, just as other Sigtuna coins are in the name of Æthelred, king of the English. These coins are therefore not evidence that Knut ruled the Svear. A number of runic inscriptions commemorating thegns and drengs in Götaland do, however, identify Swedes who served Sven Forkbeard or, more probably, Knut. It is likely that Knut attempted to re-establish Danish authority in Sweden in much the same way as he did in Norway, by securing the allegiance of as many magnates as he possibly could.

Knut's death revealed the fragility of his empire. There is, indeed, little to suggest that Knut or his advisers consciously thought of his dominions as a

Facing: The fortress at Fyrkat in Jutland, reconstructed after excavation. Although this fortress cannot be dated with the same exactitude as Trelleborg, it was certainly built at much the same time. The south-west quadrant (nearest the camera) has been left unexcavated, and thus preserved for future study.

unity. The conjectural plan to create an archdiocese in Roskilde subordinate to Canterbury is the only hint of such a conception. No joint assemblies of Danish and English magnates, for example, seem to have been held.

Before he became king of England Knut had a relationship with Ælfgifu of Northampton, the daughter of Ælfhelm, ealdorman of Mercia. She bore him two sons, Harald and Sven. Having conquered England, however, political considerations prompted Knut to take Æthelred's widow, Emma of Normandy, as his wife. They made an agreement that only their joint issue could succeed to the kingship, thus excluding Emma's sons with Æthelred and Knut's with Ælfgifu. By this agreement Harthaknut, the son of Knut and Emma, should have succeeded Knut as king of England. But when Knut died Harthaknut was in Denmark and so severely threatened by Magnus of Norway that he was unable to claim England for at least four years. In his absence his half-brother Harald, nicknamed Harefoot, had been accepted, with some reluctance, as king of England, supported by his

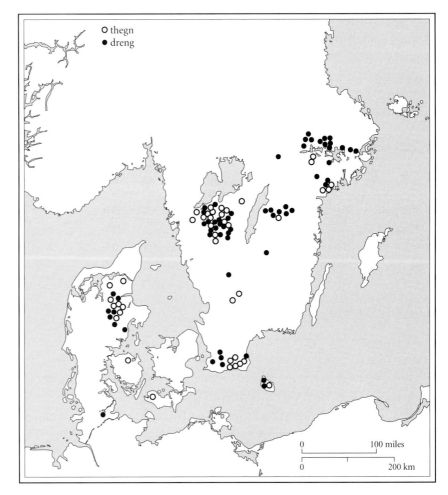

○ thegn
● dreng

Runic inscriptions commemorating thegns and drengs.

0   100 miles
0   200 km

powerful English kinsmen. Emma sought refuge in Flanders. It was only after Harald's death in 1040 that Harthaknut was able to make good his claim to England.

Harthaknut's reign in England was short. He died in 1042, and the English reverted to their old dynasty, electing Edward, son of Æthelred and Emma of Normandy. Knut's nephew Sven Estridsson claimed the Danish kingship, but the Danes recognized Magnus of Norway as their king. It was only after Magnus died in 1047 that Sven Estridsson was accepted as king in all parts of Denmark, but for many years he had to struggle against Harald Hardrada, uncle and successor of Magnus in Norway. Danish imperial ambitions were in abeyance but not forgotten, and the dream of uniting England and Denmark under one king was revived after William of Normandy conquered England.

Harald Hardrada: The Last Viking

Sven Estridsson may have cherished a claim to England, but he made no attempt to assert it during the reign of Edward the Confessor, or immediately after Edward's death, when Harold Godwinesson was elected king by the English. The next Scandinavian to claim England was the Norwegian king Harald Hardrada. In alliance with Tostig, the exiled earl of Northumbria and brother of Harold Godwinesson, he invaded Northumbria in 1066, but was killed in the battle of Stamford Bridge against Harold Godwinesson.

William of Normandy was more successful, but his conquest was not accepted as final, either by all the English or by Sven Estridsson, whose claim as the nephew of Knut was as good as that of William, and perhaps better.

In 1069 rebellious English leaders called for Danish help and Sven Estridsson sent a fleet, allegedly of 240 ships, led by three of his sons and his brother Osbeorn. This venture was no mere old-fashioned Viking raid, even if loot was taken; it was a serious attempt to drive William out of England.

The English and Danes joined forces and seized York, but the Danes were reluctant to confront William's main army and, when he approached York, they withdrew and spent the winter in the Humber where, in the words of a contemporary chronicler 'the king could not get at them'. They were, nevertheless, a destabilizing influence and William agreed to pay them tribute. They eventually withdrew, abandoning their English allies. In 1075 two of William's Norman earls rebelled and appealed to the Danes for help, but the fleet arrived after the rebellion had been crushed and had to be content with plundering York.

St Knut's Plan to Conquer England

Ten years later William faced a much more serious challenge. According to the *Anglo-Saxon Chronicle*, in 1085 people in England 'said and declared for a fact, that Knut, king of Denmark, son of King Sven, was setting out in this direction and meant to conquer this country with the help of Robert, count of Flanders, because Knut was married to Robert's daughter'. Although this has often been regarded as no more than a romantic attempt to revive the good old Viking days, William, who was in Normandy when these rumours reached him, took the threat very seriously. He recruited an exceptionally large force of mercenaries and billeted them on his vassals, and 'had the land near the sea laid waste, so that if the enemies landed, they should have nothing to seize on so quickly'. Colchester Castle was apparently hastily given a crenellation one storey lower than originally intended. William was clearly alarmed by news of the planned invasion. In 1084 he had levied a very heavy Danegeld on England and it is possible that this action was also prompted by the threatened attack. An invasion on this scale must have required a long period of planning and preparation, and rumours of it probably reached William before 1085.

The invasion was never launched, and in the following year Knut was killed by rebellious Danes. What caused this rebellion has been the subject of prolonged debate. Some contemporaries regarded his murder as the just fate of a tyrant who encroached on the liberty of the free peasants and imposed unfair burdens on his subjects; others denounced it as the most shameful betrayal of a saintly king and pious champion of the Christian faith and church. Modern historians are still discussing the true character of Denmark's only saintly king. It is, however, arguable that the rising was, in fact, caused by the first attempt to impose on the Danes the *expeditio*, the public burden of military service or payments in lieu, known as *lethang wite*, the equivalent of the Frankish *herebannus*.

The projected attack in 1085 was not the first time that Knut had been involved in hostilities against William the Conqueror: he was one of the leaders of the expedition in 1075. Nor was it the first time that William had faced an alliance of Danes and Flemings. The *Chronicle* reports that when the Danish fleet left England in 1075, it proceeded to Flanders. Knut left three children, two daughters and a son, by his Flemish queen Adela; the marriage is therefore unlikely to have been contracted very long after his accession in 1080. It may, indeed, have been discussed during Knut's visit to Flanders in 1075 and could conceivably have been contracted before he became king.

Knut's father-in-law Robert was the brother of Maud, William the Conqueror's queen, but relations between Robert and William deteriorated after the battle of Cassel in 1071, by which Robert usurped power in Flanders at the expense of his nephew Arnulf. As Robert was reconciled with the French king Philip I very soon after Cassel, and afterwards loyally supported his attempts to curb his powerful Norman vassal, relations between the rulers of Flanders and Normandy were naturally hostile. In 1072 Edgar the Atheling, the English prince who was a focus for opposition to the Norman conqueror, was given asylum in Flanders when William forced the Scots to expel him, and in 1079 Robert gave refuge to Robert Courteheuse, William's rebellious son. When Knut planned to invade England, for whatever motives, Count Robert was, therefore, an obvious ally.

Knut was a very ambitious king. His marriage alliance had wider aims than those of any of his predecessors with the exception of Knut the Great, and it is no coincidence that his son, later Count Charles the Good of Flanders, was named after Charlemagne, the most famous member of his maternal family, the first member of the Danish royal family with that name. Knut's ambitions may have given his younger brothers cause for concern and even led them to actively oppose policies which threatened to bar their path to the throne.

Knut's brief reign saw a vigorous attempt to increase royal power in Denmark. He claimed royal prerogatives that were probably previously unknown there, including the claim to own common land, the right to wrecks, and the right to be the heir of strangers and people without kinsfolk. Like contemporary European princes, he also tried to enforce his own peace and exacted heavy penalties if it was broken. He was also a zealous champion of the church; discounting the exaggerations of hagiographers, there is no reason to doubt that he issued laws to protect the weak, orphans, widows, and strangers, a Christian ideal, and that he also tried to enforce the payment of tithes.

Knut's fleet dispersed without having set sail for England. He was detained in south Jutland when he was due to join the fleet in Limfjord in

The eastern wall of Colchester castle shows clear traces of crenellation one floor below the present top of the wall. The explanation is probably that in 1085, when it was feared that the Danish king Knut planned to invade England, the walls had not reached their intended height and were crenellated as an emergency measure, and raised to their full height after the crisis.

the north. Contemporary sources offer contradictory and untrustworthy reasons for his delay, but it is likely that he feared the intervention of the German emperor Henry IV. Knut appears to have supported Henry's rival, the anti-king, Count Herman of Salm. He also gave refuge to German bishops who supported Pope Gregory VII against Clement III, the anti-pope sponsored by Henry. This would have given Henry cause to put pressure on Knut, but the emperor may also have been alarmed by the alliance between Knut and Count Robert of Flanders, who was Henry's enemy. After Cassel, and Robert's reconciliation with the French king, Henry had supported the claim of Baldwin, count of Hainault, to be count of Flanders. It is tempting to speculate that Henry deliberately tried to prevent Knut's invasion of England. If Robert and Knut had succeeded, Henry would have been faced by much more formidable enemies in both Flanders and Denmark, and therefore had very good reasons to try to thwart the planned invasion.

Henry's role is, however, hypothetical. All we do know is that Knut was prevented from leaving Schleswig to join the fleet in Limfjord. When the fleet grew impatient, envoys were sent to Knut to persuade him to join it or to appoint his brother Olaf as its leader. Olaf was himself one of the envoys and Knut, fearing a conspiracy, had him arrested and sent to Flanders. Knut then allowed the fleet to disperse, and the leaders promised him that it would reassemble in a year's time.

However, before this could take place, a rebellion broke out in Jutland, ending on 10 July 1086 with Knut's death before the altar of St Alban's in Odense, martyred by his enraged subjects.

Knut's failure marked the end of the Viking Age. No more Scandinavian plunderings or invasions of Britain, France, or Germany occurred. The classic Viking activity, however—raids, tribute-taking, and even the conquest of kingdoms, all normal forms of foreign relations—did not stop. In the Baltic numerous expeditions, some of them under the crusading banner, took place in the twelfth century against the Wends, who had themselves exploited Danish weakness and civil wars to ravage the Danish coasts. One of the leaders of these campaigns was Absalon, bishop of Roskilde (1158–91) and archbishop of Lund (1177–1202), and the contemporary historian Saxo reports that no sooner had he been appointed to his see than he took up the career of a Viking, no less than that of a bishop.

8

SHIPS AND SEAMANSHIP

JAN BILL

Although shipbuilding traditions in Viking-Age Scandinavia were not fundamentally different from those in other parts of northern Europe, archaeological evidence shows that Viking ships were lighter, slimmer, faster, and thus probably better sailers than the heavier vessels used by the English and, presumably, the Franks at that time.

There are two main reasons for these differences. The first is geographical. In Scandinavia waterways and access to the sea were more important factors in determining the location of settlements than they were in other parts of northern Europe. In Norway and Sweden most people lived near the coast or around large lakes, while the forests and mountains were very sparsely settled. Inland waterways were not only sheltered; they were also routes to the sea. No part of Viking-Age Denmark was far from the sea; it was virtually an archipelago, joined to the Continent by a narrow strip of land, and separated from the interior of the great Scandinavian peninsula by a deep barrier of forest. These natural features also meant that the authority of many rulers in Viking-Age Scandinavia, unlike that of their contemporaries in Europe, to a large extent depended on ships and control of the sea. The extensive empire that Danish kings ruled at the end of the eighth century was to a significant degree based on naval power.

The second reason is historical. Scandinavia was sufficiently remote from the Romans and, later, the Franks for its political and religious life to flourish relatively unaffected by the transformations that occurred in other parts of Europe in the first millennium AD. One feature that survived was the central role of the ship as both a religious and secular symbol, a role that is illustrated by the fact that Bronze-Age stone ship-settings and metal representations of ships were already well developed over a thousand years before Christ. The symbolic significance of ships naturally led to refinements in their construction: a fine ship conferred prestige on its owner. In the clash between Christian and Nordic culture that occurred in the Viking Age, ship burials were more frequent than they had previously been, implying that ships had acquired even greater significance as a religious symbol, at least among the pagans who resisted the advance of the new religion.

The symbolic and practical importance of ships in early Scandinavian society resulted in such improvements in ship design that Scandinavians were well equipped in comparison with other north Europeans. The contrast was all the greater because in many parts of Europe one of the main functions of ships had long been to carry cargoes, a purpose for which speed and elegance were not highly prized qualities. On the Atlantic and the North Sea Viking ships met the same challenges as the ships of the English, Frisians, and Franks, but they did so for different reasons.

The Earliest Ships

The development of ships in Scandinavia was greatly influenced by the importance of their role in gaining or maintaining power, and the fact that they operated in relatively sheltered waters. From the war canoes of the Bronze Age to the longships of the Vikings, Scandinavian vessels were slim and lightly constructed, and were not dependent on the wind. It was frequent Atlantic voyages and, later in the Viking period, the growing trade in bulk goods that made sailing-ships necessary.

The earliest Scandinavian plank-built vessel is the Hjortspring boat from Als in south-west Denmark. It was a war canoe about 19 metres long and 2 metres wide. Its bottom is the trunk of a lime tree, hollowed out and expanded. The sides are each formed of two broad planks that overlap a little, and were sewn with bast. It is the first known example of clinker construction, which was to be the dominant technique in the whole of the northern Europe well into the Middle Ages. Its ribs were lashed to cleats left when the bottom and side planks were shaped. Each rib was additionally held in place by a thwart with room for two men; the space between each rib being exactly 1 metre. The canoe was propelled by twenty-four paddles, and there was room for up to four other men with steering-oars in the prow and stern. The stems were sewn on and have the distinctive two-pronged profile familiar in Bronze-Age rock carvings. The Hjortspring boat, however, is not as old as that. It was sunk in a lake, together with the equipment of defeated warriors, as a sacrifice in about 350 BC.

Several of the features of the Hjortspring boat are also found in three boats from a similar sacrificial deposit made early in the fourth century AD at Nydam in south-west Denmark. They too are clinker-built and have sewn ribs. The planks were, however, not sewn together but are fastened by iron rivets, clenched on the inside by hammering out the point over a small metal plate. Other differences are that the double-pronged stems have been replaced by simple rabbetted pieces of curved timber, and that the wood used is not lime, but oak or, in one of the boats, pine.

The most important change, however, was in the method of propulsion. The paddles have been replaced by oars, making possible larger vessels with more freeboard. The largest of the Nydam boats is about 23.5 metres long, 3.5 metres broad, and 1.2 metres deep and has fourteen pairs of oars. There were also changes in the method of steering. In the stern the steering-oar has been replaced by a fixed side rudder. Pictures of ships from the fifth and sixth centuries show that a steering-oar continued to be used at the prow, and a single find from the seventh century shows that this technique had not been completely abandoned by then.

Although Nydam has yielded the earliest rowing-boats known in Scandinavia, it should be emphasized that they date from 600 years later than the Hjortspring boat and that there are almost no finds of boats made in the intervening period. Many of the new features observed in the Nydam boats could therefore have been used much earlier. It is, though, likely that the Germans first seriously developed seagoing ships after the Romans extended their empire to the Rhine. In AD 98 the Roman author Tacitus reported that the Svear, in what is now eastern Sweden, were still using paddles, but there is no reason to believe that innovations in ship design were adopted simultaneously throughout Scandinavia. In every area there must

The Nydam boat, as seen by Magnus Petersen, the artist who recorded the find in 1863. The vessel had disintegrated when it was found, but was quickly restored after the excavation. Recent excavations have revealed more parts of the boat that have been dendrochronologically dated 310–20.

have been a need for a new technology before it was adopted. The sail is probably a good example of this.

The Introduction of the Sail

Sidonius Apollinaris, a Gallo-Roman aristocrat, refers to a raid by Saxons on the coast of Gaul in a letter to a friend written in about AD 473. According to him their ships had sails. This is the earliest, if only an indirect, hint that some Scandinavian ships may also have had sails by then. As Jutes and Angles from the Jutland peninsula mounted raids against the Roman empire at the same time as the Saxons, and were active in the Wadden Sea, the stretch of coastal water, much of it sheltered by islands, from Blåvandshuk on the west coast of Jutland to Texel, it is difficult to believe that they did not take advantage of the same shipping technology as their western neighbours. The Wadden Sea was, in fact, a centre for pioneering developments in shipping for many centuries to come.

The testimony of Sidonius contrasts with that of the picture-stones of Gotland, a distant part of Scandinavia. They show clearly that the sail was not used there until the seventh century; the pictures from the fifth and sixth centuries only show rowing-boats. The ship found at Sutton Hoo in East Anglia was probably also a rowing-boat, although there is room for some doubt because this can only be deduced from impressions left in the soil. It is, however, remarkable that the ribs of the Sutton Hoo ship, like those in the boat of approximately the same date found in Denmark at Grestedsbro at the northern end of the Wadden Sea, were fastened to the planks by trenails, not by lashing. That method was first used widely in Scandinavia several centuries later, which suggests that by the seventh century the Saxons and Anglo-Saxons were using different shipbuilding techniques than were current in the Scandinavian peninsula.

The first Scandinavian sailing-ship, the best-preserved Viking ship so far discovered, was found in a burial mound at Oseberg, west of Oslo fjord. It has been dated by dendrochronology to about AD 820, and is 21.5 metres long, 5.1 metres broad, and its depth amidships from gunwale to keel is 1.4

The Sutton Hoo ship, built c.600, was an impressive craft, about twenty-seven metres long with twenty pairs of oars. It was found in a lavishly equipped burial in East Anglia, but the only remains of the boat were nails and faint traces of wood and tar.

metres. The mast is mounted on a keelson placed just ahead of the middle of the ship, and held in place by a mast partner at the level of the deck which, thanks to its shape, was known as a *kløften* (literally, 'the fork'). In comparison with later ships the Oseberg keelson is very short; it extends over only two of the ribs that are about 1 metre apart. The forked mast partner also seems to have been inadequate; it split and was repaired with an iron band. The mast partner had two functions, to guide the mast when it was raised and lowered, and to support it when the ship was under sail. It was, however, no substitute for shrouds, the ropes that supported the mast laterally. In a ship found at Gokstad, about 20 kilometres south of Oseberg, built between 895 and 900, this construction was greatly improved. The keelson is longer and extends over four ribs, while the mast partner is a massive piece of timber with a channel in which the mast was raised. At first sight it appears that the mast partner in the Oseberg ship was a primitive device and that in the next hundred years there was a great improvement. That is, however, hardly right. The keelson and mastfish in the Oseberg ship were inadequate because that vessel, which was used for a queen's burial, was exceptionally large, and its builders were not used to coping with the forces that the mast and rigging in a vessel of that size had to withstand. The key to this problem lies in the length of the keelson. In Scandinavian vessels, from the Hjortspring boat to the end of the Viking period, the distance between ribs remained the same, about a metre, because it was the ideal distance between thwarts and the oarsmen who sat on them. The keelson was intended to spread the pressure of the mast over a relatively large part of the hull. The Oseberg keelson, covering two ribs, would have been suitable in a smaller vessel, but was entirely inadequate in the Oseberg ship. Shipwrights quickly realized this and later used much longer keelsons in large ships.

The adoption of sails resulted in very significant developments in ship design. While the largest of the Nydam boats and the later Sutton Hoo ship were long, narrow, and low, with low, raking stems, the Oseberg ship was broader, deeper in relation to its length, and had high stems. A corresponding change can be observed in the Gotlandic picture-stones at the beginning of the seventh century, where we see the earlier long, crescent-shaped rowing-vessels being replaced by vessels with steep stems and relatively deep hulls. A detailed examination of the rib system in the Oseberg ship shows that not only had the shape of the hull been altered, but that there had also been a fundamental constructional change.

In ships earlier than Oseberg, the ribs extend from gunwale to gunwale, whether they were lashed to the hull, or fastened to it by trenails. The resulting cross-sections were either arcs of circles or, towards the stems, V-shaped. The ribs could be formed from naturally shaped pieces of wood. A

Facing: The Oseberg ship, very well preserved in its mound of clay, was in use for several years before it was repaired for the last time and used for the burial of a woman of very high status, presumably a queen, in ninth-century Norway. It was probably one of the largest and most imposing Scandinavian ships in its day.

hull of that type had relatively poor lateral stability but great potential speed. In the Oseberg ship stability was improved by deliberately creating a transition between the bottom and sides. The ribs no longer consisted of single pieces of wood, but were frames made of several pieces. A floor timber was lashed to cleats in the bottom planks, and two knees were fastened firmly to the upper planks of the hull, and to a cross-beam, called a *bite*, placed on, but not attached to, the floor timbers. An exceptionally strong strake (that is, a line of planks joined endwise from stem to stern) at the junction of the bottom and the sides, called a *meginhúfr*, spread the strain exerted by the tops of the floor timbers.

There was yet another innovation in the Oseberg ship. Instead of rowlocks on the gunwale the oars passed through oarports that could be closed when under sail. This enabled the oars to reach the water at a suitable angle, despite the greater size of the ship and its higher freeboard. The Oseberg ship, launched early in the ninth century, thus displays all the key features that distinguished Viking ships for the next 200 years.

Different Types of Ship

During that time numerous improvements were made in ship design, incorporating lessons learned on many Viking voyages. Lashed floor timbers were still used in the small ship from Tune on the east side of Oslo fjord, which was made no later than AD 910. The length (23 m.) and breadth (5.2 m.) of Gokstad's ship are a little larger than Oseberg's, but it is considerably deeper, 1.8 metres excluding the deep keel. The oarports are in the second, not the top, strake, and the *bite*s and *meginhúfr* are also lower in the hull; there is no doubt that this was a ship built for Atlantic voyages. Two ship burials of about the same date, that is, shortly before or after 900, have been found in Denmark, at Hedeby and at Ladby on Fyn. Both were princely burials in long, slender warships that could be sailed. The Hedeby ship was 17–20 metres long, 2.7–3.5 metres broad and its keelson extended over four frames. The Ladby ship was 20.6 metres long and 3.2 metres broad, and the excavators found iron rings that were used to fasten the shrouds. Despite the poor preservation of these finds, they show that already by the end of the ninth century specialized types of ships were being made in Scandinavia. Some were slim, fast warships for use in the sheltered waters of south Scandinavia, while the Gokstad ship represents the more robust seagoing vessels. These variations were not regional; Norwegian magnates undoubtedly had very fast warships, while Danish kings needed ships that could cross the North Sea and other open seas.

Specialized cargo boats were apparently developed later. The vessel

Hedeby coins with representations of ships. Some of the earliest Danish coins, minted in the first half of the ninth century, display ship motifs. They are more detailed than the Carolingian coins on which they are modelled, and are, thus, sources of information about contemporary shipbuilding in Scandinavia.

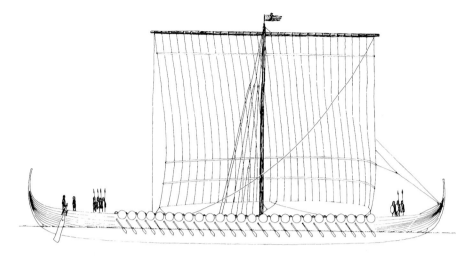

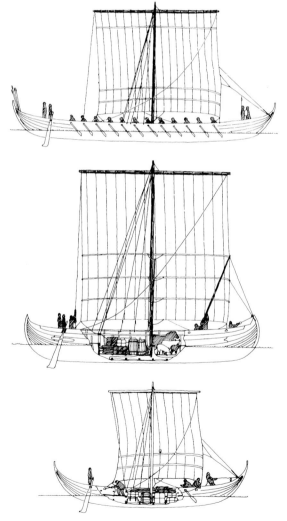

Reconstructions drawn to the same scale of four eleventh-century ships found at Skuldelev, Denmark. Two, *left and immediately below,* were warships (wrecks 2 and 5) and two cargo ships (wrecks 1 and 3).

found at Klåstad in Norway, dated about 990, is the earliest firmly dated example of a Viking ship that was built primarily as a sailing-ship but which was also equipped with a limited number of oars to facilitate manœuvres near the shore. It was smaller than the Gokstad ship (21 m. long, 5 m. broad and 1.6–1.7 m. deep) but with much the same proportions. However, it had rowlocks instead of oarports, and the shape of the hull was also different: the *meginhúfr* was lower, on the bottom, creating the characteristic double-angled cross-section of ships designed to carry heavy loads. At the same time the *bite*s were lower, making the hold larger.

When the Klåstad ship was excavated remains of its last cargo, a small heap of whetstones, was found in the bottom of an otherwise empty wreck. It is naturally tempting to think of this as a cargo ship built for the growing trade in heavy or bulky goods, such as iron, soapstone, and whetstones, towards the end of the Viking Age. It is, however, likely that more important factors in the development of specialized cargo ships towards the end of the tenth century were the improved security provided by increasingly effective royal authority, and the transport needs of the Norse settlements on

Facing: The form and
decoration of the
stem post of the
Oseberg ship, includ-
ing the upper part
which was broken off
in the grave, was
carefully copied in
this replica.

the Atlantic islands. In such circumstances a ship did not need a large crew
for protection. Several cargo ships of this period, or a little later, have been
found; at Äskekärr in Göta Älv in west Sweden, at Skuldelev in Roskilde
fjord, and in the harbour of Hedeby.

The normal term used in Norse sources for ships that made Atlantic voyages in the Viking and early Middle Ages was *knarr*, and in modern discussions that name has been particularly linked with a type of ship that was first
discovered in Roskilde fjord at Skuldelev.
That find comprised five ships that were
sunk on two separate occasions to block a
channel leading to Roskilde. Five different types of eleventh-century ship were
found, making it the richest source of
knowledge of ships of the period. The vessel that is now thought of as a *knarr* was
16.3 metres long, 4.5 metres broad, and 2.1
metres deep, bluff-bowed and strongly
built. It apparently came from Norway; at
least, this is indicated by the large amount
of pine used in its construction, as pine
was not common in Viking-Age Denmark. It was part of the first phase of the
blockage and was therefore roughly contemporary with another boat from the
same phase that has been shown by dendrochronology to have been built in 1040.
The *knarr*, referred to as Skuldelev 1, had a

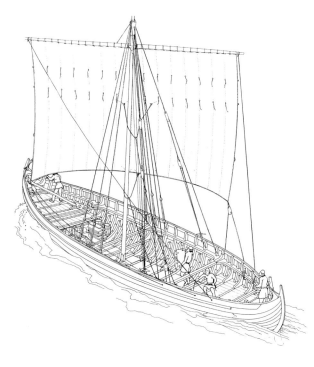

cargo capacity of up to 24 tons. Another *knarr*, found in Hedeby harbour
and dated 1025, was, to judge by the parts so far recovered, even larger; about
25 metres long, 5.7 metres broad, and 2.5 metres deep, with an estimated
capacity of about 38 tons. A third vessel of this kind has been found at
Äskekärr: it has the same proportions as Skuldelev 1 (16 m. long, about 4.5
m. broad, and 2.5 m. deep) and dendrochronological analysis shows that it
was built between 950 and 1050, although its date has not been determined
more closely.

A reconstruction of a
large *knarr*, based on
finds from the har-
bour of Hedeby. The
size and capacity of
such ships might be
considered evidence
for the growing bulk
trade in the eleventh
century, but is per-
haps better under-
stood in the context
of ever more frequent
voyages between
Scandinavia and the
settlements on the
North Atlantic
islands.

These ships with their broad prows, strong construction, and high freeboard are the most seaworthy vessels of the period that have been found,
and it is difficult to believe that Scandinavian shipbuilders of the time could
have made much better seagoing ships. That is the most convincing reason
for thinking that they were what Norse authors called *knarr*. Before the
eleventh century that word was only used for warships. It is therefore sig-

GOKSTADSKIBET

nificant that the construction of Skuldelev 1 is very similar to that of the Klåstad ship, which in its turn had much the same proportions as the Gokstad ship. It is by no means impossible that all these ships, and Oseberg as well, would have been called *knarr*s by contemporaries.

A second type of cargo ship was also found at Skuldelev, and is numbered 3. It is only 14 metres long, 3.4 metres broad, and 1.4 metres deep. It was clearly designed to carry goods—its six oars cannot have been the normal means of propulsion—but the hull was sharply built, and could only carry 4.5 tons. It was more probably a ship used by a landowner for his own journeys and for local trade than a cargo boat designed for long voyages. The fact that it has many features in common with the small longship Skuldelev 5, which was built in 1040, probably in Sjælland, suggests that it was built for local use. The builders of Skuldelev 5 were so markedly economical in their use of material that it has been suggested that it was made under compulsion, possibly for the king, or to strengthen local defences at the expense of the men of the district under the guidance of the local shipwright. One sign of the builders' cheeseparing approach is that several parts are made from reused timbers taken from other ships. The gunwale, for example, came from a rowing-boat in which the ribs were closer together than in the new ship, making it necessary to close most of the old oarports and cut new ones.

Skuldelev 5, with thirteen pairs of oars, is the smallest vessel that could be called a longship. It may be contrasted with the much larger longship that was built in 982 and used as a fire-ship in an attack on Hedeby. Its remains, found in Hedeby harbour, show that it was up to 28 metres long with between twenty-one and twenty-four pairs of oars, and that it was made of

Facing: The Gokstad ship, built in Norway between 895 and 900 was, like the Oseberg ship, preserved because it was buried in a mound sealed with clay. The broad, sturdy hull was clearly intended for open waters, and several replicas have crossed the Atlantic—the first one a thousand years after the original ship was built.

A model of the small longship Skuldelev 5. Sea trials of a full scale replica have demonstrated that it was well adapted to operate in the fjord system north of Roskilde, but not in open water where it was vulnerable to large waves.

Skuldelev 2, the
largest longship yet
found. This ship was
built in Dublin, but
served many years in
Danish waters before
it was used to enlarge
the underwater barri-
er in Roskilde Fjord.
Shipbuilding in
Dublin was much the
same as in other
Scandinavian areas,
but the flat and
rather closely spaced
floor timbers are not
common features in
contemporary Nordic
ships.

finest wood, with planks of a size and quality unparalleled in any other known Viking ship. Being only 3 metres broad and correspondingly low, it cannot have been sailed in the open sea, but in the sounds and belts of Denmark and in the south-west Baltic it must have been a formidable craft. The date of its construction is so close to that of the Danish ring-forts that it is tempting to see this ship as belonging to the Danish king, or possibly as evidence of the threat that caused him to build those forts. Viking longships had many names. In poetry they were often praised as dragon-ships or snakes, with reference not only to their speed and the flexibility of their hulls, but also to the 'bite' of their crews of well-armed warriors. A common term for a longship, especially in the early Middle Ages was *snekke*, which in Sweden and perhaps in Denmark too was associated with *leding* ships. A surprisingly large number of places that were sheltered natural havens in the Viking period and early Middle Ages have names incorporating that word.

The largest longship that has been found so far is also from the Skuldelev barrier. It was made in 1060 in or near Dublin. After reaching Denmark it was used and repaired for several decades before being sunk to reinforce the barrier in Roskilde fjord, probably in about 1133. Skuldelev 2, as it is known, is poorly preserved, but enough survives to show that it was about 30 metres long and probably had thirty pairs of oars. That was possible because the distance between the ribs was unusually small, little more than 0.7 metres. It could have transported about 100 warriors and must have been among the

largest warships of the period. According to later evidence, the Danish levy fleet (*leding*) then consisted mainly of twenty-*sessere*, that is, ships with twenty pairs of oars, and that the largest were thirty-*sessere*.

In addition to large cargo ships and warships, Scandinavian waters in the Viking period were teeming with smaller boats, for travel, fishing, and other local purposes. It was above all such boats that were used in the thousands of boat graves that were made in Viking-Age Scandinavia, especially in Norway and Sweden. These boats are almost always so badly preserved that only a few rusty rivets survive. There are, however, exceptions. Boat burials in Uppland in central Sweden have yielded interesting information about the use of these small craft. By comparing the size of the boats with the scale of the rivers on which the cemeteries stand it has been possible to demonstrate a link between the navigability of rivers and the size of the boats. This clearly proves that boats were specially built for use on smaller streams.

Shipbuilding

Thanks to the systematic attempts that have been made by the Viking Ship Museum in Roskilde to build replicas, we now know a great deal about the way Viking ships were built. In order to ensure that the copies are as close as possible to the originals, not only in appearance but also in performance, efforts have been made to use to use the original building methods as far as they can be deduced, for example, from tool marks, or from the choice of timber and the ways it was worked. The most significant difference between shipbuilding in the Viking Age and later is the way the planks were made. Although the Romans had introduced the saw to northern European ship-builders, it was forgotten when the western empire collapsed and was not used again in northern Europe before the thirteenth century. The technique used instead was to form the planks by splitting tree trunks. In south Scandinavia, which was rich in oak woods, large trunks were split radially, a technique that required trunks at least a metre in diameter and with few knots. Planks produced in this way are very strong because they follow the grain of the wood. What is more, as they dry they do not shrink or warp much. This was important because builders always used freshly felled trees, which can be worked more easily than weathered timber. Further north, where the timber was mainly pine, trunks were split in two and each half was trimmed

Before being used in a boat-burial at Årby in Uppland, this lightly built vessel (3.8 m long) navigated the small rivers leading from the central Swedish farmlands to Lake Mälaren and Birka. In Norway and Sweden especially, the inland waterways were important arteries for transport and communication throughout the Viking Age.

The construction sequence of a small Viking-Age cargo ship, Skuldelev 3. Although the 'shell-first' technique demanded an almost sculptural approach to the shaping of the hull there was nothing haphazard about it. The design was carefully planned in advance and key measurements were recorded and probably used in building other ships.

to make a broad plank. This method was also used to make exceptionally wide planks of oak or other types of wood.

The framing timbers, stems, and other curved or angled pieces were, as far as possible, made from naturally bent pieces of wood. In this way the dimensions, and consequently the weight, of the ship could be reduced to a minimum. One of the main aims of Viking shipwrights was to make the construction light, flexible, and strong. The floor timbers were often shaped to be narrow and deep over the keel but flat and broad at their upper ends where the demand for flexibility was greatest.

Studies of Skuldelev 3 have shown that before they began to build a vessel shipwrights had a clear idea of the intended design. This ship had a large, hollow stem with lines incised on each side that correspond to the strakes of the completed ship as they joined the stem, continuing the line of each one at the correct angle. Complete stem- and stern-posts were sometimes, perhaps normally, stored under water for a while to reduce the risk of cracking and warping later. Finished but unused stem-posts that have been found, well preserved, in marshes have similar lines or steps. Detailed analysis of Skuldelev 3 has shown that the design of the stem was based on segments of circles with different diameters determined by the length of the keel. The shipwright must have had some rule of thumb and a simple method, possibly using a length of rope and a piece of chalk, that enabled him to determine the form and shape of the ship from the outset.

The method of construction was also a well-established routine. Scandinavian ships, like most other ships built in northern Europe before the fifteenth century, were 'shell-built': the keel and stems were laid first, and the strakes were then built up one by one. As they reached suitable heights the internal elements were put in place: the frames and *bite*s when the bottom was ready, and when the sides were high enough the upper cross-beams and other internal fittings were added. A clinker-built shell was itself a strong construction, with every plank fastened by rivets to its neighbours. The frames, although slight, provided the necessary reinforcement against the lateral pressure of waves and the rigging without making the hull rigid. The construction of Skuldelev 3 shows clearly the importance of flexibility. The top ends of the floor timbers, for example, are jammed under, but are not nailed to two internal reinforcements along the length of the ship known as stringers, a pattern that is repeated with the *bite*s. As in all Viking ships great care was taken in this and other ways to reduce the strain in the critical area at the top of the floor timbers.

Tools and Shipyards

Viking ships were built with simple tools. Trees were felled and roughly trimmed with long-shafted axes with short edges, but the planks were trimmed with short-shafted, T-shaped broad axes such as are depicted in the Bayeux Tapestry, and have been found in London, Hedeby, and elsewhere. Tree trunks were split with wedges driven in by hammers or mallets. The first stages in the preparation of planks were presumably carried out where the tree was felled; there was little point in transporting whole tree trunks, many of them huge, to the shipbuilding site. Planks were not normally planed—an experienced craftsman could produce a sufficiently smooth surface with an axe—but planes were used to trim the overlapping edges, the lands, that had to be a close fit. The groove that housed woollen yarn to make the joint as watertight as possible could be cut with a special tool known as a mould scraper, which could also be used to incise decorative patterns on the planks and other parts of a ship. Holes were made with a spoon-shaped bore that could be rotated while being pressed against the surface by means of a breastplate; the brace and augur were later inventions. Nothing is known about measuring instruments, but there is little doubt that shipwrights used plumb-lines together with staves and strings on which various standard measurements were marked.

Replicas of the two cargo ships from Skuldelev under sail. The reconstruction of such vessels has greatly enhanced modern understanding of the technical and navigational skills of the Vikings.

Special tools were also necessary to make the hundreds of rivets that were needed. Approximately five rivets were used to fasten each metre of plank in a Viking ship; in a small vessel such as Skuldelev 3 well over 1,000 were used. Rivets did not require advanced smithing techniques, but anchors did. A well-equipped ship needed a large iron anchor, of the kind found in Ribe and the Ladby ship burial. These must have been the largest objects made by smiths in the Viking Age.

Ironwork is often the only surviving indication that a place was once

195

used to repair or make ships. One very good example is Paviken, a Viking-
Age trading centre in Gotland, where thousands of rivets and many simple
tools have been found. Paviken yielded an exceptional quantity of rivets,
but smaller numbers are found virtually everywhere that Vikings are known
to have landed. Traces of ship-repairing are commonly found near the ship-
shelters called *nausts*, large numbers of which have been excavated in Norway. This is not surprising; shipbuilders did not need special facilities and
most repairs could be done by any craftsman used to working with wood
and iron. There is, therefore, no reason to suppose that Viking shipbuilding
was concentrated in shipyards, although such places did exist.

Remains of one from the end of the Viking Age have been excavated at
Fribrødre Å on Falster, an island in south Denmark. The finds were mainly
planks and other parts of ships that had been broken up, but the discovery
of unused rivets suggests that ships may also have been built there. The ships
that were broken up and many of the objects found came from the Slav territory south of the Baltic, and some place-names on Falster suggest that
there was some Slav settlement there. Two *snekke* names near the site imply
that it was also a haven for longships. It is therefore possible that the ships
that were broken up had been captured from the Slavs, although it is also
possible that it was the base of an exiled Slav chieftain who was responsible
for local defence in the service of the Danish king. The huge quantity of
material found shows that the activity was on too large a scale for the site to
be interpreted as only a repair yard for a few warships.

Harbours and Landing-places

Snekke-havens were one type of place where ships assembled and were
repaired; coastal market-places were another. During the Viking Age several permanent and relatively large trading centres or proto-towns were
established in Scandinavia, notably Ribe, Hedeby, and Birka. All certainly
had harbours, but it is only in the latter two that clear evidence of harbour
installations has been found, both having a palisade set in the water surrounding the harbour. They also had jetties. Dendrochronological analysis
has shown that the first jetty was constructed at Hedeby as early as 725, but
was replaced by several new ones immediately after the site was systematically regulated and divided into tenements in 836. In 885 a much more substantial jetty was added. Later, as rubbish from the settlement accumulated
in the harbour, all these jetties were lengthened. The 885 jetty may have been
made extra strong to support a building; the discovery of exceptionally large
quantities of coins and weights under it suggests that it was there that the
king's agents collected toll and other fees from newly arrived ships.

Hedeby, like the contemporary Frankish/Frisian harbour of Dorestad, had numerous separate jetties; so too did Schleswig after it took over Hedeby's functions in the eleventh century. This suggests an individual relationship between each owner of a jetty and the landlord, the king; towns as independent corporations with common harbour facilities were a later development in Scandinavia.

It is likely that there were many more Viking period jetties and harbours than have so far been discovered, but they were not generally needed for Viking ships that had a shallow draught and could be landed on any open coast with a suitable beach of sand or gravel. It is, however, likely that large harbours were only constructed in places where the scale of traffic justified the expense. Harbours served military as well as commercial purposes. The Kanhave canal, constructed in 726, is a good and very early example. It bisected Samsø, an island that commands two of the major Danish water-ways, Storebælt and Lillebælt. The canal, which was 11 metres wide and several hundred metres long, linked the excellent harbour on the east of the island with the open west coast, making it possible for a fleet based in the harbour to control traffic through both belts.

Navigation

The navigational techniques of the Vikings were developed in the relatively sheltered waters of Scandinavia by seamen who, for centuries, had travelled along the coast from landmark to landmark, normally in daylight and in fair weather. They used the same methods as they extended their voyages to other parts of Europe. The observations made on these journeys were committed to memory, and contributed to what was in effect a sea-chart of the known world that was not the less reliable for being remembered and not drawn. When travelling in unknown waters it was an advantage to have the advice of someone who had already made the journey, but information could naturally be passed on by word of mouth. One means was with the help of descriptive place-names, such as *Hjelm* (Helmet), the name given to a steep-sided island in Kattegat. Another example is *Kullen* (the Hill), the name of a high headland jutting out from the low-lying coast of Skåne.

Scandinavians used the same methods of navigation on their more extensive voyages into distant waters, first to the islands north of Britain and later to Iceland, Greenland, and North America. It is true that they could be out of sight of land for several days, but by sailing, as far as possible, in the same approximate direction they could have a good idea of where they were, on the basis of observations made earlier by themselves or others. There were various ways in which experienced sailors could detect where there was land, and even how far away it was, although it was not visible. There is a good illustration of this in a medieval description of the route from Norway to Greenland:

From Hernar in Norway one should keep sailing west to reach Hvarf in Greenland and then you are sailing north of Shetland, so that it can only to be seen if visibility is very good; but south of the Faeroes, so that the sea appears half-way up their mountain slopes; but so far south of Iceland that one only becomes aware of birds and whales from it.

This text is from *Hauksbók*, a fourteenth-century version of *Landnamabók*, but it is an excellent illustration of Viking methods of navigation. Hernar is where the fjord on which Bergen lies reaches the open sea, and Hvarf is now called Cape Farewell, the southern tip of Greenland. The advice to sail directly west does not mean that a compass was used; that device first reached Europe long after the Viking period; it was, however, possible to know approximately where the main points of the compass lay with the help of the sun and the stars.

If the Shetlands were invisible, their presence, like that of Iceland later in the voyage, was revealed by sea-birds. *Hauksbók* mentions another way in which birds could help locate land. It claims that Flóki Vilgerðarson, the discoverer of Iceland, had three ravens, one of which, when released, flew in the direction of Iceland, showing Flóki where to sail. This is obviously a reworking of the biblical story of Noah's doves, but birds are known to have been used as navigational aids in other parts of the world, and the idea may not have seemed strange to people skilled in observing and interpreting the flight of birds. The appearance of whales was also instructive, revealing the presence of rich feeding-grounds that occur where the nutritious water from deep levels of the sea is forced up to the surface near land masses, such as Iceland, or where major sea currents meet. The description of the appearance of the Faeroes depended on the knowledge that distant objects, such as ships or landmarks, disappear under the horizon, but that does not mean that the Vikings thought that the world was a sphere.

The Vikings thus had a number of methods of navigating that required no more than experience and careful observation. They also accumulated a great deal of information about the prevailing winds and currents in the North Sea and North Atlantic that enabled them to forecast the weather a few days in advance and plan their routes accordingly.

There has been a great deal of discussion about navigational aids that the Vikings may have had, but the only one for which there is any convincing evidence is the lead. Wulfstan reports than on his voyage from Hedeby to Truso he sailed both night and day. That implies that a lead was used to enable the ship to keep a safe distance from the shore in the dark. It has been claimed that the 'sunstone' (*sólarsteinn*) mentioned in *Hauksbók* and in other Icelandic texts was a device used by Viking sailors. It has been suggested that it was felspar, a mineral found in Iceland that polarizes light, enabling the position of the sun to be determined even when it is completely obscured by cloud. As that requires some clear sky, the device would have been useless in overcast conditions. It is therefore difficult to see that it had any practical value as a navigational aid. A small wooden board with a central hole, apparently for a pin, found in a Greenland monastery has been interpreted as both a bearing-dial and a sun-compass. The latter suggestion is based on the supposition that lines incised in the surface mark the points of the compass and that the central pin is a gnomon casting a shadow. This has generally been dismissed as fanciful, not least because the lines are irregular. There is, in fact, no reliable written or archaeological evidence that the Vikings used any navigational aid other than, probably, a lead.

Viking Influences

Clinker-built boats were used in many parts of northern Europe before the Viking Age. The expansion of the Anglo-Saxons and other Germanic tribes certainly brought the clinker-building tradition to England, and probably to Frisia and Frankia as well. Later developments in shipbuilding in some of these areas resulted in such medieval types of ship as the cog and hulk, but

This section of the Bayeux Tapestry, which was made in the late eleventh century, illustrates the construction of the fleet with which William, duke of Normandy, invaded England in 1086. This evidence is consistent with the tool marks and constructional details of the Skuldelev ships. The designer of the tapestry must have been familiar with Nordic shipbuilding tradition but it is not possible to say whether this knowledge was gained in England or Normandy.

in Normandy and the British Isles shipbuilding was greatly influenced by
the Vikings. The Norman ships depicted in the Bayeux Tapestry at the end
of the eleventh century are virtually identical with contemporary Scandinavian ships. In England a distinctive type of clinker construction was in use
until the tenth century. Later this was merged with Viking and Norman tradition, the result being the so-called 'English keel'. Numerous finds on the
waterfront of Dublin have shown that from the early tenth century there
was little difference between ships built there and in Scandinavia. The
Dublin excavations have provided evidence of ships built not only there but
also at other places bordering the Irish Sea, and show that they were remarkably similar. Dublin, as an international harbour from the tenth to the thirteenth centuries, especially after the Normans conquered the city in the
1170s, might reasonably have been expected to yield evidence of a much
greater variety of ships. Viking shipbuilding tradition may also have left its
mark further afield. It has been suggested that the Vikings who were active
in Galicia in north-west Spain in the eleventh century introduced the technique of building clinker boats that still flourishes there today.

In the east, it is clear that the Slavs, who occupied the coastlands of the
south-west Baltic between the seventh and ninth centuries, in large measure
adopted Scandinavian shipbuilding techniques. Before that their settlements were inland and they therefore had no independent shipbuilding
tradition. But after they gained control of the coastal region, they soon
began lively contact with Scandinavians, in coastal markets and elsewhere.
Numerous finds of Slav ships show that they were very similar to those of
the Scandinavians, although they were generally smaller, less elaborately
decorated, and their planks were mostly fastened by small trenails.

There was a tradition of clinker boats further east in Finland, the Baltic
lands, and in Russia. The Finno-Ugrian tribes obviously adopted the clinker
technique, and developed their own somewhat different traditions. This
apparently happened as Scandinavians began to be active in north Russia. It
is interesting that the rivets found in Staraja Ladoga and in a boat grave at
Gnezdovo were from vessels in this Finnish rather than the Scandinavian
tradition, which suggests that on the Russian rivers the Vikings used locally
built boats rather than ones they had made themselves.

After the Viking Age

With the progress of Christianization and the gradual establishment of
kingdoms of a west European type, ships gradually lost the privileged status
that they had had for centuries in Scandinavian consciousness. The concepts of value changed; so too did ideas about what was worth paying for. By

This eleventh-century
vane from Heggen,
Norway, is 28 cm
long. Contemporary
depictions suggest
that it probably deco-
rated the stem of a
Viking ship, showing
not only the direction
of the wind, but also
the identity and
status of the ship
on which it was
mounted.

the early thirteenth century, when the development of towns and of a market economy were well advanced, these changes started to become clearly
apparent in shipbuilding. Unnecessary subtleties, elegant shapes, and richly
carved details disappeared to be replaced by more solid structures, larger
cargo holds, and cheaper building methods. The ship became a tool of trade
rather than a reflection of its owner's social and political status. And soon
Scandinavian ships began to resemble the large ships—cogs and hulks—
familiar in other parts of northern Europe. The old traditions nevertheless
survived in smaller ships and boats, especially in areas remote from the pop-
ulous and economically dominant region of south Scandinavia. Square-
rigged fishing-boats with many of the characteristics of Viking ships
continued to be used in north Norway to the end of the nineteenth century.
And, even more recently, the boats that were used on rivers and inland lakes
in Scandinavia were hardly distinguishable from the small boats that
accompanied a Norwegian chieftain in his burial-ship at Gokstad more
than 1,100 years ago.

9

RELIGIONS OLD AND NEW

PREBEN MEULENGRACHT SØRENSEN

Adam of Bremen

'Some very ferocious peoples'. This, Adam of Bremen's description of the
Scandinavians, is the continental European, Christian view of pre-Christian Scandinavia that has prevailed until recent times, even in Scandinavia
itself. However, if we want to understand pre-Christian society on its own
terms it is not satisfactory to treat it as a primitive form of society that was
gradually being civilized. We must accept Scandinavian pagan culture as
being equal to Christian cultures, although completely different from them.

Adam wrote his *History of the Archbishops of Hamburg* in about 1070, not
long after the official adoption of Christianity in Scandinavia. In Denmark
this happened in the second half of the tenth century, in Iceland in the year
1000, in Norway gradually in the early eleventh century, in Sweden some
decades later, and in Finland later still. The archdiocese of Hamburg (which
later incorporated the see of Bremen) had been created in 832 with the purpose of evangelizing the pagan lands to the north and east, and in Adam's
time the whole of Scandinavia still belonged to this north German ecclesiastical province.

Much of Adam's work is devoted to the history of the Scandinavian
countries, and the concluding fourth book, *A Description of the Isles of the
North*, is a detailed geographical and ethnographical account. It is therefore
one of the most interesting sources for the history and culture of the Viking
Age, even if its information must be used with caution, for Adam saw Scandinavia with an unsympathetic and intolerant eye.

Although they were Christian, the Scandinavians were strange in the eyes
of the learned German. He generally describes even Scandinavians of his
own day as barbarians and sometimes even as pagan, reporting that there

were still idol-worshippers in Bornholm and in Skåne, and that in the latter province Bishop Egino had chopped up a famous idol of Freyr. The situation was particularly bad in Sweden, where furious persecutions of the Christians raged in about 1066, and in Uppsala a famous sanctuary devoted to Odin, Freyr, and Thor still flourished. Each god had its own special characteristics: Freyr, who was endowed with an enormous phallus, gave men peace and joy, and offerings were made to him at weddings; Odin, the god of war, was depicted with weapons; Thor had his hammer, described by Adam as a sceptre. He was master of thunder and lightning, storm and rain, fair weather and crops, and the pagans sacrificed to him when threatened by hunger or disease. According to Adam's informant major sacrifices were made in this sacred place every nine years: nine males of all living species, both animals and humans, were killed, and their bodies suspended in a grove. Everyone was obliged to take part in these celebrations; Christians had to pay to be exempted.

Although Adam based this famous account of pagan cult on hearsay, he presents it as that of an eyewitness. It appears to be reasonably authentic, and the account of the gods and their functions largely corresponds with the information found in Old Norse literature. However, Adam's ethnographic account grows increasingly fantastic as he describes more distant regions, and his extreme east is peopled with imaginary beings such as Amazons, cyclops, dog-headed men, and cannibals.

We must believe that Adam intended to give as truthful an account as he could, but his work reflects not only contemporary Christian ideology but also his own sympathies and continental ecclesiastical politics. This is particularly evident in his treatment of rulers who promoted the influence of the Anglo-Saxon church in their kingdoms. We are told that Sven Forkbeard, the Danish king who conquered England and favoured English missionaries, persecuted Christians in Denmark. Olaf Tryggvason, who in the Norse sagas is presented as the great evangelizer of Norway and Iceland, is virtually a pagan in Adam's account. Olaf was probably baptized in England and was accompanied by English ecclesiastics when he took Norway from the pagan Jarl Håkon. This brought him into conflict with the missionary policies of Hamburg, and Adam put him in his place by reporting that some people said he was an apostate, and that all were agreed that he practised witchcraft and took auguries from birds.

Adam's description of the religious conditions in Scandinavia offers us a picture of a period of transition when pagans and Christians lived side by side. As a new religion, Christianity experienced some setbacks in Scandinavia, and bishops and missionaries had to combat pagan cults; but in most places and during most of the long transition from one religion to another

Facing: On Gotland, from the fifth century to the twelfth, stones were ornamented with symbols or scenes from myths or epics to commemorate the dead. Over 400 are now known, but only thirty are as large and elaborate as this two-metre high stone from Ardre which was made early in the Viking period. The upper field apparently depicts a hero arriving at Valhalla on Odin's horse. The lower field has scenes from the legend of Wayland the smith, whose forge is in the centre. Others depict Thor, who is shown under the sailing ship fishing for the World Serpent.

Below: A tenth-century soapstone mould for both a Thor's hammer and crosses, found at Trendgården in Jutland.

peaceful conditions probably prevailed. Long before the beginning of the Viking Age Scandinavians travelling in Europe must have become acquainted with Christianity, and even in the first centuries of the Christian era there were contacts between Scandinavia and Rome, although we do not have exact details of how or where these took place.

Pagans and Christians

As early as the first or second century AD Scandinavia had its first script—runes—probably inspired by Mediterranean, particularly Italian, alphabets. The runic script was newly developed in northern Europe, probably in southern Scandinavia, but it did not initiate a proper written culture in the north comparable to the classical cultures in the south. It is, however, a somewhat neglected fact that whoever created this new script must have been familiar with the alphabets that inspired it, and therefore also with the literature written in those alphabets. The originators of the runes must have been able to write and read Latin or other written languages.

They must also have been capable of transmitting the ideas of classical culture and Christian religion to the oral culture of the north, which was to retain its oral traditions for centuries to come. The fact that Scandinavians of that time did not avail themselves of writing to any greater extent cannot have been because they were incapable of doing so. There was nothing to stop them from learning to use parchment and ink, or from hiring people who did. The reason they retained an oral culture must have been that it was well suited to their life style. We can safely assume that Christian ideas and motifs were borrowed at an early stage, but we must also assume that they were utilized in a purely pagan context. No dominant Christian impact on rites, ethics, or social organization is perceptible in Scandinavia until the closing years of the first millennium AD.

During the ninth and tenth centuries many Scandinavians who settled in Christian countries were converted to the new religion. There must have been a lively exchange of ideas and views between pagans and Christians, and while the Christians were obliged to accept the dogma and commands of their church to the letter, the pagans were at liberty to adopt Christian ideas, rites, and elements of myth if they found them useful in their own religious context. Such borrowings, however, did not make paganism Christian; we should, rather, talk about loans than about Christian influence on paganism. As long as Christianity coexisted with paganism it was subjected to an *interpretatio norræna*, a Nordic, pagan interpretation. The two religions were fundamentally different, as were the societies to which they belonged; and if the pagans adopted Christian elements in their cult or their myths, these had to be transformed and gain significance in an entirely different context. Only when Christianity triumphed as the official religion was there a radical change. Pagan ideas, customs, and concepts of all kinds were then banned and branded as demonism, even though some of them survived in a Christian form.

For posterity the proscription of everything pagan by the church has meant a loss of knowledge. Christianity brought the Latin alphabet and a new technique of writing. For a long time it was the church that decided to what uses this writing might be put, and it did not want pagan knowledge to be preserved. Adam's work is an example of this attitude. As a member of the cathedral chapter in Bremen he must have had first-hand knowledge of the pagan religion that still flourished within the archdiocese, but he records practically nothing about pagan beliefs and customs, apart from his description of the Uppsala temple, which he only includes to give us an abominable example. In the view of the church paganism had no place in history; Adam expresses this view when, towards the end of his account of Uppsala, he mentions that during the sacrifices many obscene songs were sung but that it is best not to speak about them.

In spite of this we have a relatively comprehensive knowledge of the old Nordic religion, especially of its mythology, thanks partly to contemporary evidence from the Viking period preserved in archaeological finds, runic inscriptions, place-names, and the comments of foreign visitors, and partly to the literature written by medieval Scandinavian authors about the Scandinavian past. It is in this literature that we find those interpretations and syntheses that enable us to put the other evidence in its context.

Myths in Poetry and in Snorri's Edda

A remarkable coincidence of favourable circumstances led to the production of this literature. In twelfth-century Europe a new interest in the past developed, not least in its poetry and language, and this early renaissance had powerful effects in Scandinavia, where Christianity was only a few generations old, and poems and stories from the Viking Age were still preserved by word of mouth. This interest, and the liberal spirit accompanying it, encouraged scholars to put these oral traditions in writing. This happened in both Norway and Denmark, but first and foremost in Iceland where a new kind of prose, the *saga*, came to form the framework of what medieval scholars recorded from the past and what they composed themselves.

Two main types of Viking-Age poetry—eddic and skaldic—are preserved in Icelandic manuscripts. It is important to understand that this poetry had a far greater importance in oral, pre-Christian society than literature has today: it was the principal way in which knowledge of ethics, religion, history, and political ideology, were transmitted in Scandinavian society.

Eddic poetry is known from the *Codex Regius*, written in about 1270, which contains ten poems about gods and nineteen about heroes; three more poems about gods are preserved in other contexts. Some of these poems are didactic dialogues revealing mythological knowledge. Some relate a complete myth, but in most cases knowledge of the myth is taken for granted, and used in the larger context of the poem. The eschatological vision *Vǫluspá*, (The Prophecy of the Sibyl), with which the editor of the *Codex Regius* opens his collection, describes in magnificent scenes the history of the world from its creation to its end in *Ragnarǫk* (the extinction of the gods), and the subsequent emergence of a new world.

The eddic poems on the gods are exceptional; there is nothing comparable in European literature. Their age is debatable, and they probably underwent change and re-creation in the course of oral transmission. We can, however, assume that their content is genuinely pre-Christian.

The first skaldic poetry was composed in Norway around the beginning of the Viking Age, but from the eleventh century and until the decline of the genre towards the end of the thirteenth century it was above all cultivated by Icelandic skalds. It was a highly developed, complex, and subtle art-form that appealed first and foremost to kings and their retinues, or *hird*s. The skalds made good, even extreme, use of periphrases, the so-called kennings, many of which had a mythological basis. A good knowledge of mythology was therefore necessary to understand their poetry, which is probably one of the main reasons why the myths, and the poems preserving them, were

Above: Many elaborately carved wooden objects were found in the Oseberg burial, including a cart that was apparently made specially for the burial. Its round-bottomed body rested on a pair of cradles, the upper ends of which are carved in the shape of heads; one is illustrated here.

Left: This tenth-century picture stone from Lärbro in Gotland illustrates scenes from Nordic mythology. It displays an excellent example of the rhomboid sail pattern and extremely complicated sheet system shown on many picture stones. These features have not yet been satisfactorily explained.

Right: One of seven embossed, gilded plates from Tamdrup church in Jutland, made *c.*1200, illustrating the conversion of King Harald Gormsson by Poppo. They may have originally been attached to a reliquary of Poppo. This one shows the king's baptism.

Below: This eleventh-century representation of Christ crucified, but triumphant, is from Åby church, near Århus in Jutland. It is the earliest-known crucifix from a Scandinavian church.

still remembered two or three centuries after the advent of Christianity. The twelfth-century renaissance awakened a new interest in skaldic poetry in Iceland, Norway, and Orkney because it was regarded as the finest expression of pre-Christian Scandinavian language and world-view. It became fashionable to take the old skaldic tradition up again, and in Iceland Snorri Sturluson composed his *Edda* in about 1220 as a poetics of skaldic verse, which retells the Scandinavian myths in a complete mythography. Snorri's *Edda*, together with the eddic poems and skaldic poetry, form our most important sources of knowledge about Nordic mythology.

In Denmark Saxo Grammaticus composed his great *Gesta Danorum* (The Deeds of the Danes), in about 1200. He gives ingenious Latin translations of old Danish poems about heroes and gods and recasts myths into historical accounts about the oldest times; Snorri used the myths in the same way in his history of Norway, *Heimskringla*, from about 1230.

Are these written sources reliable? Scholars have long been sceptical about them and have held that most of the information about pre-Christian Nordic religion transmitted to us by medieval authors consists of learned constructions with no reliable basis. Similarities between Christian literature and the descriptions of pre-Christian myths and rites that have been recognized have been thought to show that Christian historians and mythographers like Snorri Sturluson shaped pagan religion on the model of Christianity. On this assumption, the myth of Thor's battle with the World Serpent was based on the account of Christ's battle with the sea-monster Leviathan; the god Baldr was modelled on Christ, and the accounts of pagan sanctuaries and sacrifices were based on Christian and Jewish rites. It is obvious that medieval authors interpreted paganism in the light of their own experience, just as we do in the light of ours, but it would be a gross exaggeration to explain all similarities with Christianity as simply Christian reconstructions.

Medieval authors themselves clearly understood the relationship between pagan and Christian world-views. Snorri explains this in the prologue to his *Edda*, in which he describes pre-Christian cosmology and mythology. In agreement with the theology of his own time he says that after the Creation men forgot God's name and the true faith, but that God let them retain their intelligence. They therefore began to reflect on natural phenomena, and invented their own deities to explain all they saw. 'They understood everything in a worldly sense, for the spiritual had not been bestowed on them', says Snorri. On this basis Snorri and his like in the high Middle Ages describe pre-Christian religion. It was idolatry, of course, but as long as this was remembered Christians could study it as part of the culture of their ancestors without risk or prejudice.

In Europe only two pre-Christian mythologies, the Greek and the Norse, have been preserved as coherent ideologies. If the Nordic mythology appears as a whole, it is due primarily to Snorri's account of it, and most of the myths now known have only been preserved as complete entities in his retelling of them. His mythography in the *Edda* follows the main outline of *Vǫluspá*, but in contrast to the poem, Snorri's presentation is logical and systematic. This reflects an important difference between pre-Christian and medieval approaches to description. Snorri, like modern structuralists, wanted to depict the pagan view of the world as a coherently structured system, a body of teaching comparable with Christianity. The poems of the Viking Age never do that; in them the myths are fragmentary, enigmatic, and changeable.

This, however, does not mean that Viking-Age religion was obscure and 'primitive'; it was simply based on premises and forms that differ from our own. The poems must have presupposed a generally accepted conception of the world in which divine powers had well-defined properties and functions, and where mythic patterns of behaviour and action might manifest themselves by being combined in stories and pictures, or be invoked by key

words in the kennings of the skalds, or represented by iconographical features in the work of artists and craftsmen. In oral tradition the myths did not have any final definition as they do in Snorri's *Edda*. Their regular elements, both persons and objects, could be combined creatively to express the ideas and modes of thought that made up the Nordic world-view. It is these ideas and thoughts, rather than the

An iron axe-head, 17.5 cm long with gold and silver inlay, from the burial of a man of very high status at Mammen in Jutland. This pagan grave has been dated 970/1 by dendro-chronology, a few years after the conversion of the Danish king Harald.

myths themselves, that are repeated with variations in Viking-Age poetry, as poets and other interpreters worked to translate the myths into concepts that would make sense of life and its problems.

This implies that it does not always make sense to seek the oldest or original version of a myth. One example is the myth of the death of Baldr, the most important expression of the idea of the collapse of the world of the gods. The gods could not prevent Baldr's killing, because their own circle incorporated an element of deceit and destruction, personified by Loki, a trickster and mediator, whose father was a giant and whose mother was a goddess. Loki epitomizes the duality of Nordic mythology: he is Odin's sworn brother, but sides with the powers of chaos in *Ragnarǫk*; he creates problems and solves them. It is he who, by a clever stratagem, brings about Baldr's death.

This myth appears briefly in *Vǫluspá*, where the soothsaying sibyl (*vǫlva*) tells the story in a series of striking images: the bloody god; the piece of mistletoe that becomes a deadly arrow; Hǫðr, who shoots this arrow and kills his brother; the third brother, who is born to avenge Baldr, 'one night old'; Frigg, Baldr's weeping mother; and, finally, the sibyl's vision of a fettered figure in a sinister-looking place, which, we are told, 'looks like Loki'.

Snorri relates this myth in detail. In his version Frigg makes all and sundry swear not to harm Baldr the Good; only the weak mistletoe is not asked to swear. All the gods then shoot at Baldr, thinking he is proof against wounds; Loki makes an arrow of mistletoe and gives it to Hǫðr, the blind god, who kills his brother with it. Snorri adds a magnificent description of Baldr's funeral, which he knew from the skaldic poem *Húsdrápa* (the House Poem), composed in about 980, which describes mythological pictures in the hall of an Icelandic chieftain. Snorri goes on to relate Hermóðr's journey to the underworld where he asks its mistress, Hel, to let Baldr return. Treacherous Loki prevents even that, and the end of the story is that the gods capture him, tie him to three pointed rocks, and suspend a poisonous serpent above his head. He is to lie there until *Ragnarǫk*, but Sigyn, his wife, collects the dripping poison in a bowl, and the poison only drips into Loki's face when she leaves to empty it. This makes him shiver so violently that all the earth trembles; and that explains earthquakes.

Saxo's *Gesta Danorum* offers a third version. Saxo incorporates Hǫðr and Baldr into the history of Denmark and turns the myth into a crime of passion over Nanna who, according to Snorri, is Baldr's wife. Saxo, like *Vǫluspá*, has the story about the third brother who was born to avenge, and he relates that Odin begat him by stratagem with a Russian princess. This element was also known to Icelandic skalds; with them, however, the princess from a remote land is a giant's daughter.

Several Viking-Age poems mention the death of Baldr, but we would hardly be able to comprehend the myth as a coherent story if we did not have Snorri's interpretation. Pre-Christian sources each use part of it. Only *Vǫluspá* has the complete sequence, but in the broken and enigmatic form characteristic of Viking-Age myth. The skalds wove these myths into their enigmatic periphrases: in the eddic poems giants and sibyls disclose secrets about the beginning and the end of the world, but they do so obscurely and incompletely. Viking-Age man, who availed himself of technical knowledge so rationally, who organized complex expeditions, and established new communities, also understood that the deepest reasons and purposes of life could only be encompassed in myth and art.

Our understanding of Nordic mythology is obviously imperfect compared to our understanding of the Viking Age itself. This is so because the
sources yield limited information, and because with our radically different
mentality we find it difficult to comprehend mythical concepts. To deny
any possibility of forming a relatively reliable picture of the world-view and
the gods of pre-Christian culture would, however, be as naïve as to accept all
that the written sources tell us as authentic expressions of Viking-Age
mythology. The difficulties lie rather in our capacity to understand than in
the sources. The following account rests on this assumption.

Mythology

Pre-Christians believed that they lived in the middle of the world. The
world-picture of the myths is a projection of the farmer's land and the
sailor's horizon. The inhabited part of the world is called *Miðgarðr*, 'the
fenced world in the middle', within which is the world of the gods, *Ásgarðr*
(the fenced world of the Æsir). where each god has a residence. Thor lives in
Þrúðheimr (world of might), Odin in *Valhǫll* (hall of slain warriors), Frejya
in *Folkvangr* (battlefields), Frigg in *Fensalir* (marsh halls), Baldr in *Breiða-
blik* (broad splendour), and Heimdall in *Himinbiǫrg* (heavenly mountains).

Yggdrasill, the World Tree, grows in the middle of *Ásgarðr*; its top
reaches the sky and its three roots encompass all the world: one is where the
human race lives, another in the world of the giants, and beneath the third
is the Otherworld. Yggdrasill is the axis of both time and space. It stands by
a spring called Urðr's Well. Together with Verðandi and Skuld, Urðr
decides fate, that is to say, what time will bring. The names Verðandi and
Skuld are derived from verbs meaning, respectively, 'be' and 'must'. These
three women carve the fate of men on wooden sticks, or spin and weave it.
In the farms of men the World Tree is paralleled by the tree in the middle
of the farmyard, which made for continuity from one generation to the
next.

Outside the inhabited world with its orderly societies and cultivated
fields lay the dangerous wilderness. In the myths this is the world of the
giants. Snorri employs the term *Útgarðr* (the world outside), about these
parts, but in the eddic poems they are simply called *Jǫtunheimar* (the worlds
of the giants). Thus, in Snorri's view, the pagan world-picture is circular,
with the gods in the middle and the giants on the periphery towards the sea.
He attempts, like modern students of myth, to visualize this world-picture
as a parallel to the concentric cosmos of the Bible and antiquity. However,
the pagan cosmos was based on a dimension running from the near to the
distant. It had its point of departure wherever people lived; the distance to

the wilderness, whether in reality this was the sea, the mountains, or the deep forests, implied a transition from the secure to the dangerous. In mythical terms it meant the difference between the world protected by the gods, and those worlds that were dominated by the enemies of gods and man. In the myths these enemies generally live far to the east and north.

There were many different powers in the pre-Christian Nordic world, in nature as well as in domestic life; but cosmology was dominated by the antithesis of gods and giants. The Æsir were the superior, culturally creative powers that protected life, while the giants were dangerous, huge and coarse, but also wise and knowledgeable. The relationship between the two opposite powers is, however, more complicated and subtle than just the contrast of order and chaos, culture and nature, or, from a Christian point of view, good and evil. Gods and giants represent the fundamental dialectic in the pagan world-picture. The world is born and comes to an end in the battle and interplay between these forces.

Time was strongly emphasized in pagan thought. Even the World Tree is described as something changeable and perishable. The women of fate sit at its foot planning the future. A worm bites at its roots, and four deer bite at its leaves. In *Vǫluspá* the sibyl begins by saying that she remembers when Yggdrasill was still only a seed in the ground. After the creation of the world by the gods she says: 'from it [the tall tree] comes the dew that falls in the valleys. It stands always, green, over the well of Urðr.' But in her vision of *Ragnarǫk* she speaks of 'the old tree', that trembles and howls. At the end of the poem the world rises afresh and the sons of the gods choose a new World Tree.

Vǫluspá describes the cosmic sequence in those four phases, the Creation, the time until the end of the world, *Ragnarǫk*, and the new world. Before creation there was nothing, only a huge space of chaos called *Ginnungagap*. In a late manuscript (*c.*1430) of Adam of Bremen's description of the north this name is applied to the frozen, misty ocean beyond that place in the utmost north referred to by Greek authors as Thule. Experiences in these parts, to which the Northmen sailed, may have contributed to their ideas of the universe before the creation of the world. The word *Ginnungagap* may be interpreted as 'the immense empty space' or as 'the immense space full of powers'. Both interpretations are compatible with myths about original chaos.

According to *Vǫluspá* the gods lifted the earth from *Ginnungagap*. Before this, however, Ymir (the roaring), had been created by the powers in chaos. This primordial being is paralleled in the mythology of other cultures, for example in the Indian Yama and the Iranian Yima. In Scandinavia it was an immense hermaphrodite, a chaotically proliferate creature. From under its arm a man and a woman sprang, and one foot was procreating children with the other. Thus the family of giants was created. Another primeval being was the cow Auðhumbla. Its udder fed Ymir. The cow licked salt rocks and in three days it licked forth a human-like creature, Búri, who got a son, Borr.

This creation myth is characteristic of the pre-Christian Nordic way of understanding, explaining history as meetings of opposites. The two original families are united through a marriage between Borr and the giant's daughter Bestla, whose sons were Odin, Vili, and Vé, names that may be translated 'Intellect', 'Will' and 'the Sacred'. They were the first Æsir, and they created the cosmos. They killed Ymir and shaped the world from his body. His flesh became the earth, his bones the mountains, his blood the ocean, his skull the firmament, and his brain the clouds. Ymir's family, the giants, who were also the maternal family of the gods, thus became their enemies. The gods created order. They gave the sun, the moon, and the stars their permanent orbits and divided time into day and night. They invented tools and built smithies and temples.

'They lacked nothing of gold', says *Vǫluspá*. This concludes the account of the beginning of the world. The gods have created an ideal condition, comparable to the Greek idea of a Golden Age and the Jewish–Christian Garden of Eden; but mankind has not yet been created. The second part of the sequence explains how the originally static cosmos was made dynamic when the world of the gods was invaded by three young giant women. This twin element of feminine sex and giant power starts fresh activity. Modern research has often interpreted the three giant women from a Christian point of view as a destructive, 'evil' element that destroyed the ideal world of the gods. But in the poem their arrival is followed by creativity, as well as fate, and death. Man is created, time starts, and the whole process that leads to *Ragnarǫk* begins.

In *Ragnarǫk* everything disintegrates; brother fights brother; the gods fight against the monsters of chaos, and perish; the world burns; the earth is swallowed by the ocean, and the firmament cracks. But *Vǫluspá* concludes with the vision of a new world that emerges from the cosmic sea, where a new generation of gods will rule, and mankind live happily. Snorri accepted this conclusion to the cosmic sequence in his prose account of the myths. In modern times it has been interpreted as a vision of eternal life coloured by Christian views. The most recent research in the history of religions has, however, provided good reasons for regarding the myth of the recreated earth as genuinely pre-Christian.

It is not difficult to find parallels to the Christian view of the world in Norse mythology, and *Vǫluspá* in particular seems to have borrowed from

Christian ideas. These have, however, been inserted into a mythology with an essentially different interpretation of life and the world, an interpretation that in some respects may appear to people nowadays to be as advanced as the Christian one. This applies not least to the recognition of everything in the cosmos as a necessary part of it. The epitome of this wisdom is the World Serpent, the giant sea-monster. In *Ragnarǫk* it goes ashore and kills Thor, described in the poems as 'the protector of mankind'; but until then the serpent lies far out in the ocean as a uniting band round the lands, a part of the cosmos. It is at once necessary and destructive.

The similarities between pagan and Christian myths should not be interpreted as evidence that Christianity and its world-view was gradually gaining a foothold in Scandinavia before the official change of religion. Christian ideas were absorbed into the Nordic world-picture without changing its basis. In the Viking Age in particular, Christianity was certainly a source of inspiration to the poets who were the custodians of the Nordic myths.

This stone from Hørdum in north Jutland depicts Thor's expedition with the giant Hymir to catch the World Serpent. The strain was so great that he forced his foot through the bottom of the boat. Hymir frustrated Thor and possibly saved the cosmic order by cutting the line.

Cults and Symbols

We know much less about pre-Christian cult than about the myths. The Christian church saw pagan rites as devilry, and medieval authors hardly took the same interest in them as they did in the myths. In the works of contemporary foreign authors, both Christian and Muslim, and in medieval historical literature, there are accounts of pagan rituals. These sources are important, but they pose many problems of interpretation. In addition place-names and archaeological discoveries provide valuable evidence.

The most important difference between pagan and Christian worship was that pagan cults did not have the regular organization of the Christian church. Religion was not a separate institution with special temples and priests. It was part of ordinary life and maintained by individual members of society, that is, by yeomen and housewives, and the rituals were performed in the homes of farmers and chieftains. One of the few authentic impressions of pagan cult comes from a couple of lines composed by Siggvatr, St Olaf's skald. According to Snorri, in 1019 the king sent Sighvatr on a diplomatic mission to the earl of Skara in Västergötland. One night during their journey he and his companions sought shelter in a farm, but they were turned away because a sacrifice to the elves was being made, an offering to powers connected, as far as we know, with ancestors and fertility. In a couple of lines about the encounter he relates how he had to bow to put his head through the door, and was refused admission by the woman in the farm:

> 'Go no further,
> wicked man', said the woman,
> 'I dread Odin's wrath,
> we are pagan here.'
> The odious woman,
> who resolutely turned me away,
> as if I were a wolf,
> was sacrificing to the elves on her farm.

This gives the impression of a small farm and a ritual celebrated by a woman. The gods must have been worshipped locally in this way, but there are also reports of major public rituals. I have already mentioned Adam of Bremen's account of the offerings at Uppsala. In the early eleventh-century chronicle by the German bishop Thietmar of Merseburg there is a similar account of human beings and animals being sacrificed a hundred years earlier to the gods at Lejre on the Danish island of Sjælland.

This account is coloured by Christian propaganda against paganism. Neutral and detailed accounts of sacrifices in chieftains' halls are found in the sagas. The sacrifice was called *blót*, word that may be translated as 'strengthening'. The offering was intended to strengthen the gods and thus dispose them favourably towards mankind. According to the sagas animals, particularly horses and pigs, were sacrificed: they were killed and cooked in a deep pit, and their blood sprinkled on walls and idols. As part of the ritual the participants ate the meat and drank the sacred beer. This is the description Snorri Sturluson gives in *Heimskringla* of a sacrificial feast that took place in Trøndelag in the middle of the tenth century. Snorri also relates that the chieftain blessed the drink and the food. The participants drank to Odin for victory and power to the king, then to Njord, and finally to Freyr for fertility and peace. Later they drank to the ancestors in their mounds.

These saga accounts have been doubted by modern scholars, who denounce them as medieval fantasies. We do know, however, that learned historians like Snorri possessed a comprehensive knowledge of the pre-Christian past, and we have no reason to doubt their desire to give truthful accounts of it, as far as possible. In all probability these accounts are a more or less free rendition of oral traditions that are otherwise unknown to us.

The archaeological evidence and place-names have an entirely different character, providing direct and authentic information about pre-Christian times. It is, however, often very difficult to interpret this information in the context of cultural and religious history. The place-names can give some idea of the extent of cults and their social significance, and archaeology does not always support the evidence of texts. For example, no archaeological confirmation of Adam of Bremen's description of the temple at Uppsala has yet been found.

Archaeological discoveries are best understood when they can be interpreted in the light of poetry and medieval historical writing, enabling us occasionally to have some idea of the relationship between these types of evidence. The potential value of combining material finds with literary evidence is well illustrated by the thin, tiny sheets of gold found in many parts of Scandinavia. They are often no greater than 1 centimetre square and are embossed with reliefs depicting one or two persons. As they are too light and fragile to have served as currency, their significance must have been symbolic and religious. A common motif is a man and a woman facing and embracing each other, a love scene. Gold plaques of this kind have been found in Denmark, Norway, and Sweden, but not outside Scandinavia. A considerable number have been found in dwelling-houses, close to or under posts, in some cases the post that supported the high seat in a king's or chieftain's hall. They have been found in centres of power, at Gudme in Denmark, Mære and Borg in Norway, and Helgö in Sweden. Perhaps they were deposited at the high seat when the king or chieftain celebrated his wedding, and may thus symbolize the connection between family and farm and the mythical origins in the cosmos of gods and giants. The couple on the plaques has been connected with the eddic poem *Skírnismál* about the love of the god Freyr for the giant maiden Gerðr and his attempts to win her by means of presents, threats, and, finally, magic. There are good reasons for believing that the couple do indeed represent that pair and thus symbolize the sacred wedding, *hieros gamos*, to which *Skírnismál* is the overture.

What is distinctive about this Nordic myth is that the marriage unites opposites, god and giant woman, and thus encompasses the whole cosmos. The religious historian Gro Steinsland has shown that this sacred marriage is fundamental to mythology and rites and thus to pre-Christian social ideology. In *Heimskringla* Snorri Sturluson claims that the marriage between the god and the giant woman was the origin of the legendary Swedish dynasty, the Ynglings, from which Norwegian medieval kings also descended. The idea that gods were the ancestors of kings is familiar in many religions, but the first ancestress of these Scandinavian dynasties was, remarkably, from the race of giants. This use of cosmic contrasts is, as we

Small pieces of very thin gold foil, less than a centimetre square, with embossed figures have been found in many parts of Scandinavia, apparently deposited as votive offerings before and during the Viking period. Many, like this one from Gullmarsberg in Bohuslän, Sweden, depict a man and woman embracing. They have been identified as the god Freyr and the giant maiden Gerðr, whose marriage symbolized the mythical origin of the royal dynasty.

215

have seen, fundamental in the Nordic world view. In *Vǫluspá* it sets fate,
human life, and the course of the world in motion.

The story of Freyr and Gerðr is an example of the way myth was realized
in history. Both before and after the change of religion in Scandinavia, history was interpreted according to mythical models. In Christian historiography the Bible was the model, and the birth and death of Christ the
watersheds that repeat themselves in the history of each kingdom and king.
Pre-Christian man availed himself of other models, the most important of
which was the fateful meeting of the god and the giant woman. It is repeated
in medieval historical writing in accounts of the king's connections with a
remote, mysterious woman. The Norse kings' sagas thus relate that the
Norwegian king Erik Bloodaxe was married to the beautiful Gunnhild who
lived in the farthest north with people skilled in magic. In another tradition
Gunnhild is said to be the daughter of the Danish king Gorm.

Death and Burial

Death is one of the facts of life that confronts us most clearly in the sources
for the Viking Age. In the Old Norse literature it is the goal of life in an
entirely different way than in later Christian ideology. In pre-Christian
times it was important to live in such a way as to have a good posthumous
reputation. It was this that made the manner of death so important: nothing was worse than a shameful death. 'Cattle die, kinsmen die, a man dies
likewise himself / One thing I know that never dies: the verdict over each
dead man.' Thus run the famous lines of the eddic poem *Hávamál*, which is
presented as the words of Odin. A good earthly reputation, not heavenly salvation, was the most profound aim of life and death.

Burial finds suggest a belief in life after death. It was usual for the well-to-
do to bury their dead with objects; men with their weapons and maybe their
tools, women with their jewellery and utensils. Remains of food and drink
are also found in graves.

What was the point of these grave goods? Mythology mentions lands of
the dead. There is dismal, dark *Hel* (which in Christian times was interpreted as *Helviti*, Hell, 'the punishment by the goddess of death'). The sagas
tell of a life after death in the company of dead kinsfolk inside the holy hill.
An eddic poem refers to a land of the dead belonging to the goddess Freyja,
and towards the end of the Viking Age we hear about Odin's Valhalla, 'the
hall of the slain warriors'. In the tenth century some Scandinavian men were
buried with horses and riding-gear. These finds have been interpreted in the
light of the Valhalla myth, which says that those who die in battle will live in
the hall of Odin until *Ragnarǫk*, when they will fight on the side of the gods

against the mighty powers of chaos. Some have seen Christian ideas of Paradise in this myth. It is perhaps as likely (though speculative) to see it as inspired by Muslim ideas of Paradise, with which Scandinavians could have become acquainted in the Near East.

In the most richly furnished grave excavated in Scandinavia, in the Oseberg mound in south Norway, two women, probably a queen and her maid, were interred in a richly decorated Viking ship that was just over 21 metres long. It contained everything the dead might need, as if they were still living. There are utensils for housekeeping and cooking, beds and bed-linen, looms, pots and vessels, and objects of art whose meaning eludes us. There is a cart and sledges, thirteen horses, six dogs, and two oxen. The grave undoubtedly also contained jewellery and other treasures that have been taken by grave-robbers.

We must interpret this grave and others like it, though less magnificently furnished, as implying that the dead were symbolically, not literally, sent on a journey. There are other ship-burials, but more often raised stones symbolically mark the contours of the deceased's ship. In some places, for example at Lindholm Høje near Aalborg, there are large grave-fields with numerous stone settings of this kind. At Old Uppsala in Sweden and Borre in Norway there are groups of large grave-mounds that presumably marked

Many of the graves in this Viking-Age cemetery at Lindholm on Limfjord in Jutland are marked by stones arranged in the form of a ship, a substitute for the Scandinavian custom of ship-burial.

the status and continuity of royal dynasties. In Denmark Harald Bluetooth
had a monument with two huge mounds erected in about 960 at Jelling, a
royal centre. These mounds were built on top of an older ship setting and
thus marked a break with the earlier burial custom. Shortly after the com-
pletion of this monument, however, Harald converted to Christianity and
had a church built between the mounds. Archaeological excavations have
revealed that the chamber in the north mound was emptied soon after it was
used for a burial, and that the skeleton of a man was interred in the choir of
the wooden church. An idea which immediately suggests itself is that after
he himself had been baptized, Harald transferred his father Gorm to the
church to give him a Christian burial. The large rune-stone in front of the
church, with depictions of a beast and a crucifixion, has an inscription
recording that Harald erected it memory of his father Gorm and his mother
Thyre, and that Harald himself 'made the Danes Christian'. Jelling is thus a
spectacular monument to the religious change in Denmark.

The Politics of Conversion

The change of religion in Scandinavia had a different political background
in each country. It happened at the same time as radical changes in social
and political organization and was itself a consequence of these changes. In
the first place, as the kingdoms were unified, new structures of power and
new forms of government developed. Secondly, Christianity was intimately
associated with the revolution in methods of communication, the transition from a predominantly oral to a written culture, that made the new systems of power possible. Thirdly, the church implemented a comprehensive
programme of ethical, cultural, and religious education to teach people to
understand their place in the new centralized order.

The late introduction of Christianity in Scandinavia, centuries after its
adoption in Ireland, England, and continental Europe, reflects the very different situation in these different parts of Europe. For Christian rulers it was
a matter of course that their subjects were Christian, but neither the
Romans nor the Franks conquered any part of Scandinavia. Charlemagne's
empire stopped at the southern border of Denmark, and his programme of
Christianization extended no further. It was his son, Louis the Pious, who
first sent missionaries as part of his attempt to extend Frankish supremacy
over the Danes. Louis supported the exiled Danish king Harald, and he in
return paid homage to Louis and was restored with Frankish help. In 823
Ebo, archbishop of Reims, preached the gospel in Denmark and three years
later Harald became the first Danish king to be baptized. After the ceremony, which took place in Mainz, Harald returned to Denmark, accompa-

nied by Anskar. He was, however, driven into exile once again a year later, and it was some twenty years before Anskar was able to resume his mission to the Danes in earnest.

In about 830 Anskar, who was later made archbishop of Hamburg, travelled to Birka in Sweden. According to Rimbert, who wrote Anskar's *Vita* in the 870s, he had a church built there. In the middle of the century he was also able to establish churches in Hedeby and Ribe in southern Denmark, and Rimbert reports that he bought Danish boys to educate them in the Christian faith. Despite these efforts, Anskar achieved no permanent results.

Although we have very little evidence for the first phase of Christianity in Scandinavia, there is enough to show that English missionaries had an important role alongside the Germans. There are two accounts of the conversion of Harald Bluetooth. The oldest is Widukind's, in his *Saxon Chronicle* written in about 970. According to him a priest called Poppo convinced the king of the power of the Christian God by a miracle. He underwent an ordeal by fire, grasping a piece of hot iron for as long as the king wished without harming his hand. About a century later Adam of Bremen claimed that Harald's conversion was brought about under pressure from the German emperor. This is a typical example of ecclesiastical political propaganda. Had the emperor introduced Christianity in Denmark it would, according to Christian imperial ideology, have implied the submission of the Danish king to the emperor. In the face of such a threat, Harald's claim on the Jelling stone that he had 'made the Danes Christian' was a significant political statement, an assertion of Denmark's independence. Under Harald's successors, Sven Forkbeard and Knut the Great, the English church won greater influence in Denmark, but in the long run the links with Hamburg–Bremen were the stronger.

Norway was converted in several phases, all of them involving English missionaries. Harald Finehair, the pagan king who, according to the sagas, first united Norway, sent his son Håkon to England to be fostered by the Christian king Athelstan (924–39). This story, which is probably reliable, is remarkable. It shows not only that the first sole king of Norway wanted to have diplomatic contacts in the west, but also that he was far-sighted enough to realize that Christian ideology would provide valuable support for the new kingship.

Håkon did not succeed in converting Norway. He died an apostate in 960. In *Heimskringla* Snorri explains the background in a masterly manner, illustrating the clash between the king and the Norwegian farmers by two episodes. First in the account of ritual sacrifice in Trøndelag, mentioned above, where the king was forced to participate in pagan rites, and secondly in a meeting of the assembly or *þing*, in which the leader of the farmers presented their case in a speech linking power and religion. He argued that if they adopted the king's faith, they would also have to submit to a new type of power and claimed that the religion of the king would turn them into slaves. Half a century later Olaf Tryggvason sailed from England to Norway with his fleet. He set out to convert the country by the sword, and used Christianity as an instrument of power politics in his attempt to subdue the people. He died long before the task was finished, but a generation later St Olaf effectively completed the change of religion in Norway by a combination of evangelization, force, and legislation. After his death in the battle of Stiklestad in 1030 there was no longer any vigorous Norwegian opposition to the new faith.

A third variant of the religious change is found in Iceland. Here too we can observe how religion was adapted to the established order. Iceland had no king but was governed by an oligarchy of large-scale farmers and chieftains. It was these leaders who, by a majority vote in the *Alþing* adopted Christianity in Iceland. Our most important source for this event is *Íslendingabók* (The Book of the Icelanders), written by the learned Ari Þorgilsson in the third decade of the twelfth century. We are told here that Olaf Tryggvason sent his missionary Thangbrand to Iceland, but did not succeed in converting the Icelanders. Like Harald Bluetooth on the Jelling stone, Ari asserts the independence of the country by stressing that the decision to change religion was taken, not by a foreign ruler, but by the lawful representatives of the Icelanders themselves

Pagan Reactions

The introduction of Christianity did not take place without pagan reactions. Ari writes that the decision of the *Alþing* was accompanied by certain exceptions, among others that sacrifices to the pagan gods were still permitted provided they took place privately. Towards the end of the tenth century Håkon Jarl led a pagan revival in Norway, even though he had been baptized in Denmark. By his baptism he had acknowledged the overlordship of Harald Bluetooth, and Harald could boast on the Jelling stone that he had 'won for himself all Denmark and Norway'. By his apostasy Håkon Jarl asserted his political independence.

In Sweden Christianity began to gain a foothold in about the year 1000 and in the following century many magnates adopted the new faith. There were, however, setbacks in its progress, for pagan beliefs were deeply rooted in many parts of the country.

Generally speaking the young Christian church remained weak for a long time and had to set about its task cautiously. In about 1120 Ælnoth, an

This stone, 2.8 m high, erected in the eleventh century at Dynna in Hadeland, Norway, depicts scenes from Christ's nativity, including the three kings and their presentation of gifts to Mary in the stable, with the crib in the centre.

Odense priest of Anglo-Saxon origin, wrote a history of Denmark centred on the life of St Knut, with an introduction in which he commented on religion in other parts of Scandinavia. He wrote:

The Svear and the Götar, however, seem to honour the Christian faith only when things go according to their wishes and luck is on their side; but if storm winds are against them, if the soil turns barren during drought or is flooded by heavy rainfalls, if an enemy threatens to attack with harrying and burning, then they persecute the Christian faith that they claim to honour, and with threats and injustice against the faithful they seek to chase them out of the land.

Things were hardly better in the other parts of Scandinavia. In letters to the Danish king Harald Hen (1076–80) Pope Gregory VII had to admonish him to protect poor widows, orphans, and priests. In a letter of 1080 the pope reproached the Danes for 'blaming unseasonable weather, storm damage, and all sorts of corporal diseases on the clergy'. Six years later rebellious farmers killed Harald's successor Knut (1080–6) in the church of St Alban in Odense.

Church and king supported each other, and slowly both gained in strength. All over Scandinavia churches were built, at first of wood, but in Denmark and parts of Sweden from the twelfth century onwards also in stone. The organization of the church as well as its spiritual power was strengthened. In political terms the most conspicuous expression of the new alliance between church and royal power was the creation of the archbishopric of Lund, then part of Denmark, in 1103 or 1104. Until then the churches of Scandinavia were in the archbishopric of Hamburg–Bremen. Sven Estridsson had endeavoured to escape German ecclesiastical domination, and very nearly succeeded in the 1070s, but it was first under his son Erik that the papacy recognized the ecclesiastical, and consequently the political, independence of Scandinavia in relation to Germany.

Conversion and Cultural Change

In Denmark, Norway, and Sweden the change of religion was effected from above, under royal leadership, and often by brute force. In Iceland the conversion was the chieftains' decision under pressure from the Norwegian king. It was primarily a political change; but what did it mean to individuals? How could it be effected at all?

It has often been claimed that the change took place because paganism had outlived its day and collapsed for internal reasons when confronted by Christianity, a religion that was stronger in both organization and ideology. There is, however, nothing to suggest that the religion of the Viking Age was not vital and capable of functioning to the last, or that its view of life and associated ethics were not sufficient in non-Christian societies.

The Norse word for the religious change, *siðaskipti*, shows us how contemporaries understood the conversion. The second element is cognate with the English word shift, and *siðr* means 'ways and customs', more or less what we now call 'culture', and the meaning of the word also encompassed the religious sphere. The introduction of Christianity implied a thorough change of culture, even if it did not take place overnight. The whole way of life was changed. Pre-Christian religion was an integral part of society and life in all respects. Religion and society merged, and the religion only collapsed because society changed. The change of power demanded a new religion with an ideology that could legitimize centralized power, and this ideology was supplied by the Christian church.

The most important tool of the church was the book. This was revolutionary, as it made it possible to preserve and transmit knowledge from remote parts and times. Knowledge no longer depended on the comprehension and memory of individuals, and changeability was no longer, as in oral culture, a natural consequence of communication. The church was a powerful international organization, and with writing the Europeanization of Scandinavia began. Books gave access to immense treasures of foreign poetry, philosophy, and history that were adopted in Nordic culture, and changed it. Writing also created an interest in the native oral poetry and traditions. These began to be committed to writing, and people were made conscious of pre-Christian times as an era distinct from the Middle Ages.

Latin script was treated with great respect, as, of course, the pagan runic script had been. The runes had a divine origin, being Odin's gift to man. Christianity, however, was inextricably bound up with Latin script in a different way. It is a literate religion, based on the Bible, Holy Scripture. The message of the church, as well as its theology and moral doctrines, was deeply rooted in the written word.

The new script created a new form of consciousness, because written culture implied a new conception of history. Previously time had been counted

in generations, and ordinary people hardly had concrete ideas about more than the last two or three of these. Now the concept of the long chronological sequence of history was introduced. It became possible to see oneself in relation to the remote past stretching back to Adam and Eve, and the individual had to reconcile himself with the equally remote prospect of a future Doomsday. In this long perspective both individuals and kingdoms had their place. The emphasis was shifted from the kin and the home, and power was taken from the farmers and their assemblies.

While we can trace the importance of this religious change in political, cultural, and social terms it is difficult to understand what happened in the minds of individuals. The church called on individuals to fear God and lead a pious life. It offered salvation in the form of eternal life in Paradise after death, and threatened damnation in the fires of Hell. It demanded that men should serve and honour one god alone, and do so unconditionally, expecting nothing but grace in return. It was this that turned traditional religious and ethical norms upside down.

The relationship with the pagan gods had been a sort of friendship, a contract by which man sacrificed to the gods and was entitled to their support in return. A man could withdraw his allegiance to a god who did not support him well enough. Thus, in his poem *Sonatorrek* Egil Skalla-Grímsson rebukes Odin because his son was drowned: he regarded this as a breach of friendship by the god. Pre-Christian Scandinavians worshipped a pantheon in which the new Christ could be included without immediate problems. This explains why Anskar was permitted to build churches in Viking-Age towns. Christ was one among several gods there. The Icelandic *Landnámabók* (The Book of Settlements) relates that Helgi inn Magri, who settled in Iceland in about 900, believed in Christ but invoked Thor when in distress at sea. He also asked Thor to show him where to build his new farm, but he named it after Christ.

Christianity implied a greater distance from God and a new kind of morality. It influenced all walks of life, and its moral doctrine was reflected in ecclesiastical legislation that regulated everyday habits, not least those connected with food and sexuality. Times of fasting were fixed, and the eating of horsemeat was banned. Rules about whom you could marry were introduced: polygamy and extramarital sexual relations were forbidden. The church even interfered in married life. The Norwegian *Gulating Law* forbade sexual intercourse in the nights before Sundays, Wednesdays, and Fridays, and before fast days and church festivals.

The consequences of sin now began to regulate life. Most church law was not based on human relationships, but on man's relationship with the invisible God. God was the injured party, and punishment belonged to him.

Facing, above:
A nineteenth-century lithograph of Gamla (Old) Uppsala, the most renowned cult centre in pre-Christian Scandinavia. The three large grave mounds are of the fifth and sixth centuries. The church in the background was originally the cathedral, established after pagan rituals here ended in about 1080.

Facing, below:
Midwinter Sacrifice, a detail from the large and controversial painting made in 1911 by the Swedish artist Carl Larsson for the National Museum in Stockholm, based on a story in Snorri Sturluson's *Heimskringla*. This part shows how King Domaldi of Uppsala, after a severe famine, was sacrificed naked to the gods in front of the pagan temple to secure good crops.

The concept of sin was new. In pre-Christian times people were responsible to each other, and their deeds were governed by norms of honour and shame; judgement and revenge lay with fellow human beings. Now fear of shame was replaced by fear of sin, and what in pagan society had been a right and a duty—first and foremost of revenge—was now made an offence against God and the king. What is more, the church introduced the hitherto unknown concept of 'original sin', which implied that no one could avoid being in God's debt, and all must fear eternal damnation.

For the individual as well as for society as a whole the change of religion implied distance. The world was enlarged and power was more distant; in many respects it was transferred from farm, family, and local assemblies to the king and clergy. The practice of religion was removed from the hall of the farm to special houses of God. God himself was remote and, strangely, the meaning of life was shifted from life itself to death. For women the change was dramatic; the church regarded them as subordinate to men and associated them with what was mortal and sinful. Before Christianity they could lead the cult; that leadership was now the preserve of men. Women were put under tutelage. On the other hand, the church insisted in principle on a woman's right not to marry against her will, and by elevating virginity as an ideal the church offered her an alternative way of life as a nun.

This wooden sculpture of the Madonna, from Appuna church in Östergötland, Sweden, was made towards the end of the twelfth century. She is represented as a queen, with a gilded crown, not as the innocent virgin familiar in later medieval representations.

10

THE VIKINGS IN HISTORY AND LEGEND

LARS LÖNNROTH

The medieval writers who first recorded the activities of the Vikings saw them from the point of view of their victims, and it is thus natural that they did not give a very flattering picture of them. The barbaric brutality of the Vikings was simply taken for granted by some early writers, particularly in western Europe. The Arabs also saw the Scandinavians as barbarians, as can be seen from Ibn Fadlan's detached but terrifying eyewitness account, dating from *c*.930, of a Viking ship burial on the Volga, with its graphic descriptions of violence, filth, drunkenness, and offensive sexual behaviour.

The Heroic Age of Scandinavia

When the Scandinavians themselves, however, started to record the exploits of their Viking ancestors, they painted a much more glorious picture of what they had accomplished as warriors, seafarers, settlers, and pioneering explorers of foreign lands. In the twelfth and thirteenth centuries, when the classical Old Norse sagas and skaldic poems were committed to parchment, the Viking era began to be regarded as the heroic age of Scandinavia. A fascinating literature developed, particularly in Iceland, but also to some extent in Norway and Denmark; it is this literature, more than anything else, that has formed later ideas about Viking life, even today, and not only in Scandinavia.

It is practically impossible to make a clear distinction between 'history' and 'fiction' in these early Norse texts, since most of them contain some of each without separating one from the other. In that respect they may be compared to American Westerns about legendary heroes such as Jesse James or Wild Bill Hickock. It is also, in most cases, difficult to determine how much of the narrative material was based on genuine oral tradition and how much was 'reconstructed' or simply invented by medieval writers. This is, in fact, one of the major problems of Old Norse scholarship.

Gráskinna ('the Grey Skin'), an Icelandic saga manuscript of about 1300. Many Icelandic saga manuscripts have a raw and rustic quality which suggests that they were made in ordinary farmhouses. Most were, however, written by priests for wealthy farmers and chieftains.

Most experts agree, however, that the skaldic poems, some of which undoubtedly date from the Viking period, contain the earliest and most reliable testimonies, since they seem to have been carefully remembered and preserved more or less literally for several generations. This kind of poetry, composed in very complicated metres and in an ornate metaphoric language which would have been mastered only by a small intellectual élite, was designed to celebrate particular kings or chieftains in a rhetoric worthy of their great exploits. But although the sophisticated wordplay of these artful verses is a delight to connoisseurs, the factual information they convey is often disappointingly slight; in most cases we only learn, after having straightened out the inverted syntax and deciphered all the intricate metaphors, that some great ruler, attended by brave warriors, defeated his enemies at such-and-such a place, thus making the life of local corpse-eating wolves and ravens a little happier.

The epic narrative of the sagas appears to be much more straightforward, factual, and 'objective' in its presentation, but it is nevertheless more open to suspicion from a modern historian's point of view, since no sagas were written or composed in their present form until the twelfth century, although some of them are evidently based both on ancient skaldic poetry and on oral tales. The king sagas (*konungasögur*) were the first to be recorded (from about 1150) and are also the ones that contain the most ambitious presentations of major historical events involving the kings of Norway, Denmark, and Sweden. The family sagas (*Islendingasögur*) are generally later (thirteenth century); they have become particularly famous for their dramatic and amazingly realistic stories—admired by anthropologists as well as by literary critics—about ordinary Viking feuds involving Icelandic farmers and their families. The mythical–heroic sagas (*fornaldarsögur*), on the other hand, most of which were not written down before the fourteenth century, are more openly fantastic and obviously based on folk-tales, romances, and mythical–heroic poetry of the eddic type.

Although these late sagas are nowadays more often read by folklorists and literary scholars than by historians, they were used as important historical sources by nationalistic Swedish antiquarians of the seventeenth century.

Saxo Grammaticus and Snorri Sturluson

Among all the medieval texts of Scandinavia, however, two monumental works of historiography achieved more authority than the rest and became particularly influential in the Nordic tradition. These are *Gesta Danorum*, a Latin history of Denmark written by the Danish cleric Saxo Grammaticus (d. *c.*1220) and *Heimskringla* (History of the Norwegian Kings), a collection of king sagas written in Old Norse by the Icelandic chieftain Snorri Sturluson (d. 1241). Both were compiled in the first half of the thirteenth century on the basis of earlier (and partly lost) sources in verse and in saga prose. Many of the legendary stories told by later generations in Scandinavia about the Vikings can be traced back to these two celebrated works, which for several centuries were regarded as national monuments.

Although basing their histories on similar narrative material, the style and historical philosophy of Saxo and Snorri are vastly different, and they have, through the centuries, appealed to different kinds of reader. Saxo is a superb Latinist, who knows how to use the classical rules of rhetoric and the Roman models of heroic conduct to make a rough Viking chief appear as a noble statesman of grand proportions. His goal is to convince the learned world of Europe that the early kings of Denmark were equal to the exemplary rulers of the Roman empire. This he tries to do by describing their virtues, as well as the vices of their enemies, in a high-flown emotional language, emphasizing the moral to be drawn from each story that he relates. His *Gesta Danorum* was particularly admired in the sixteenth and seventeenth centuries, when it provided Shakespeare with the dramatic story of Hamlet and the royally appointed

The title-page of *Gesta Danorum*, published in Paris in 1514, is a magnificent example of Renaissance art. The Viking heroes and Norse mythical figures of Saxo Grammaticus' Danish history, written in imitation of classical Roman historiography, are here displayed in classicist style as if they were Roman knights and creatures from Roman mythology.

historians of Denmark and Sweden with a lot of colourful material for patriotic boasting.

Snorri, on the other hand, is totally committed to the concise and seemingly objective style of the Icelandic sagas. He is a master of understatement and will rarely give his own opinion or express a direct value judgement, even though he obviously shares Saxo's admiration for some of the famous Viking rulers. He writes not only for learned clerics but for unlearned laymen, and instead of preaching to his readers he holds them in suspense by cleverly building up a sequence of dramatic scenes in which the heroism of the Viking Age is convincingly demonstrated. His *Heimskringla* was at first thought to be less elegant than Saxo's work, but since the nineteenth century he has generally been regarded as the more accomplished writer of the two, and his sagas of the Norwegian kings have reached a much wider audience in modern translation.

The saga of King Olaf Tryggvason (d. 1000), as told by Snorri, may serve as a typical example of the Old Norse tales about Viking rulers that have been particularly admired until the present day; it is certainly one of the most influential stories of its kind. Olaf's father, King Tryggvi, is killed while Olaf is still a child, and his mother has to leave the country with him in order to escape the murderous plans of Tryggvi's enemies, Queen Gunnhild and Earl Håkon. Their ship is boarded by pirates in the Baltic, and the boy Olaf is separated from his mother and sold as a slave in Estonia. He shows his mettle at an early age by killing the pirate who sold him, and he is shortly afterwards adopted by the king of Russia, where he grows up and performs various heroic deeds, charming everyone around him with his bravery, good looks, and charisma. He is, in other words, a typical 'lucky man' (*gæfumaðr*), the kind of hero that sagas present as destined for success.

Nobody knows what Snorri Sturluson, the great Icelandic saga-writer and politician, looked like, but nationalistic artists in Norway and Iceland have tended to picture him as a wise and venerable farmer. This woodcut by Christian Krohg has been used as the frontispiece in numerous Norwegian editions of Snorri's *Heimskringla* ('History of Norwegian Kings').

Somewhat later Olaf manages to collect a host of brave warriors and sail with them to Germany and the British Isles, where he makes huge Viking conquests, wins enormous wealth, and marries a couple of beautiful foreign women (who conveniently die, one after the other). Although he is a heathen he does not want to worship the pagan gods, and soon becomes a devout Christian before deciding to return to Norway. By a strange coincidence, the Norwegian farmers of Trondheim have at this very moment decided to get rid of their present ruler, Earl Håkon, and Olaf is accepted as their new king. He then rules Norway successfully for some years and converts his countrymen to the new faith.

After this success story, the second part of the saga is devoted to Olaf's tragic decline and fall, when his luck changes and fate turns against him. The decline starts when he angrily strikes and insults his most recent lady friend, the proud Swedish queen Sigrid, because she does not want to become a Christian. She then plots a conspiracy against him, involving both the Swedish and Danish kings together with the son of Earl Håkon. Olaf's famous dragon ship, *The Long Serpent*, is insidiously attacked by an enormous navy at Svold in the southern Baltic as it returns from a visit to the land of the Wends. Olaf and his men are heavily outnumbered, but defend themselves valiantly against hopeless odds. The bowstring of the *Serpent's* great archer, Einar, is finally destroyed by the enemy; when Olaf asks: 'What broke?' Einar answers: 'Norway out of your hands, King!'—a laconic reply that marks the end of Olaf's rule in the typical understated style of the best sagas. Realizing that his time is up, Olaf dives into the water and is never seen again. Some people are reported to have testified that he survived the battle and escaped to some foreign country, but Snorri himself puts his faith in contemporary skaldic verses, saying that he did indeed drown in the waves at Svold.

Although many elements in this saga are mythical—some are obviously borrowed from folk-tales, heroic poems, and even from foreign romances—it is told in such a factual and convincing manner by Snorri that it was accepted as history for several centuries. Many of its basic literary motifs, for example that of the hero's early exile, his valiant childhood deeds, his marvellous luck and charisma, his ability to endure hardship, his refusal to workship pagan gods, his tendency to express himself in few but salty words, and his eventual fated downfall in a major battle, became part of an established pattern for interpreting the lives of great Viking leaders. Important characteristics of such leaders in the sagas are usually their restraint, common sense, balance, and strong sense of honour, which make them respected by their men and fortunate in their undertakings—until they start to act rashly, often provoked by less balanced kinsmen or lovers. Chaos and tragedy are almost always caused by emotional mistakes of this kind.

Heroes and Villains

It is an interesting fact, however, that such noble Viking heroes are never called 'viking' (*víkingr*) in the sagas. This term seems to have been tainted by a certain amount of disapproval and is normally reserved for brutal and unpleasant characters, for example berserk thugs or heartless pirates of the sort that sell Olaf as a slave in his childhood. To go on a Viking expedition (*fara í víking*) may, on the other hand, be considered not only a legitimate but almost an obligatory experience for a true saga hero, provided that it is confined to an early stage of his career, after which he is supposed to settle down on his farm to a more peaceful and respectable way of life.

There is thus an inherent contradiction in the saga presentation of the Vikings, and this contradiction prevails in literary narratives even to this day. On the one hand they are the greatest heroes; on the other they are not heroes, but problematic characters—or even villains—if they devote too much of their life to typical Viking activities such as warfare, piracy, and plundering. This contradiction becomes particularly obvious in the ambivalent presentation of some saga characters such as the controversial Icelandic skald Egil Skalla-Grímsson of *Egils Saga*, one of the most realistic family sagas. Egil is, at different stages of his life and sometimes even simultaneously, a family man and a raving lunatic, a tragic hero and a comical, uncouth rabble-rouser, a defender of noble values and a ruthless avenger.

At the age of 12 he is reported to have composed a poem in which he expresses his dream to become a Viking in lines that have become a classic expression of 'Viking mentality':

> That mentioned my mother,
> My ship they should buy me,
> A fleet one, fair-oared one,
> To fare out with Vikings;
> Stand up in the stem there,
> Steer the dear sea-steed,
> Hold on to her haven,
> Hew this man and that man.

> (trans. Gwyn Jones)

The structure of this short poem, with its idyllic, almost romantic beginning and brutal twist at the end, mirrors the saga as a whole. Later in life Egil is ironically described in situations where, among other things, he throws beer in the face of one enemy, pulls out the eye of another, and bites off the throat of a third. Typically these things happen when he is far away from home on one of his legendary journeys. At home on the farm in Iceland, on the other hand, he is generally pictured with empathy and respect, for example defending the honour of his family or grieving at the death of his son. Even as an old man, however, he can suddenly reveal his Viking mentality at home and at a meeting of the *Alþing* become a nuisance to his kinsmen, for example when he proposes to throw out the silver treasure he has brought home from England just for the pleasure of seeing people fight over his wealth.

While Olaf Tryggvason and Egil Skalla-Grímsson represent two principal types of masculine Viking hero in the sagas—the charismatic leader and the tough, wild, and not-so-noble fighter—Guðrún Ósvífrsdóttir in *Laxdæla Saga* may be said to represent the typical Viking heroine. She is presented as an immensely proud, strong, and beautiful woman who is married several times and also has lovers out of wedlock, but who will not take second place to any of her men when it comes to independence, toughness, and authority. When her lover Kjartan leaves Iceland she wants to go with him, but he refuses to take her on board, since she has young brothers to care for, and asks her instead to wait for him three years. Guðrún does not want to promise anything, and when Kjartan returns she has married his best friend, Bolli; Kjartan therefore marries another woman and settles down. He is soon regarded as one of the greatest men in Iceland, but Guðrún, who secretly loves him but is too proud to admit it, is jealous and generally dissatisfied with her own marriage.

A tragic feud now develops between the two families, instigated by Guðrún, and she finally goads her husband Bolli to kill Kjartan. When Bolli returns after the killing she greets him with the following cool words: 'Morning tasks differ. I have spun yarn for twelve ells of cloth, and you have killed Kjartan.' Not until the end of her life, when all her men are dead, is she prepared to tell the truth about her passionate feelings for Kjartan: 'I was worst to him that I loved the most.'

Towards the end of the middle ages, Iceland became a Danish colony and its population was impoverished. It was in such circumstances that this leaf of parchment from a manuscript of *Sturlunga saga* was used to make a pattern for a child's shirt.

Although it is stories such as these, composed in thirteenth-century Iceland by the period's best writers, that have in later years formed the educated reader's view of life in the Viking Age, they were at first not very well known except in west Scandinavia. Even in Iceland, that remote corner of the Scandinavian world, they seem to have been largely forgotten towards the end of the Middle Ages, when chivalric romances and ballads replaced sagas as the favourite literature of the upper classes. When interest in the Vikings started to flourish again in Scandinavia in the sixteenth century, it was largely a patriotic and antiquarian interest prompted by the intellectual leaders of the emerging national states of Denmark and Sweden, who wanted to demonstrate to the world that their countries had a longer and more glorious history than most other countries of Europe.

The Gothic Revival

In order to achieve this goal, several Scandinavian historians, especially in Sweden, felt they had to go much further back in history than the Viking Age and show that their countries were venerable and respected even in the time of the Greeks and the Romans. They also tried to base their arguments on the Latin authorities that were available to the learned world of Europe and generally recognized as trustworthy. For this reason, histories such as Saxo's *Gesta Danorum*, first published in Paris in 1514, were at first of greater interest to the patriotic antiquarians than the Old Norse texts, which were still unpublished and which few people in those days could read or understand.

Among the most influential of these antiquarians were the Swedish brothers Johannes and Olavus Magnus, who both lived in Rome after the Reformation, exiled by King Gustav Vasa for their refusal to abandon their Catholic faith in favour of Lutheranism. Challenged by Saxo's impressive achievement, the elder of the two brothers, Johannes (1488–1544), wrote *Historia de omnibus gothorum sveonumque regibus* (History of all the Gothic and Swedish Kings, published posthumously in 1554), in which he argued that the Gothic people of early European fame had really come from Sweden, thus making the Swedes an even more glorious people than the Danes and the Viking Age a mere revival of military policies successfully implemented in the Roman era. The younger brother, Olavus (1490–1557), wrote *Historia de gentibus septentrionalibus* (History of the Nordic Peoples, 1555), enthusiastically describing the ancient and noble culture as well as the daily life of the Scandinavians in minute detail, derived partly from Latin authorities (including Saxo) and partly from his own experience.

The patriotic historiography of Saxo and the Magnus brothers was carried on in the seventeenth century by scholars such as Ole Worm (1588–1654) and Thomas Bartholin (1659–90) in Denmark, and Olof Rudbeck (1630–1702) in Sweden. An intense and sometimes bitter competition between the Danes and the Swedes made both sides eager to make the most of their respective histories. During this period the runic inscriptions from the Viking Age, as well as the Icelandic sagas, came into more frequent use as historical sources and were finally printed in scholarly editions with parallel translations in Latin. Early medieval manuscripts of Snorri's *Heims-*

kringla and other saga texts were transferred from Icelandic farms to the archives of Copenhagen and Stockholm, where they were compared to Latin texts and often became the objects of extremely imaginative interpretations which made the past of Denmark and Sweden increasingly glorious. These scholarly efforts culminated in Olof Rudbeck's notorious four-volume masterpiece *Atlantica* (1679–1704), in which the learned author tried to prove that Sweden was not only the cradle of all Greek and Roman culture but was in fact identical with Atlantis, the wonderful island that was supposed to have sunk into the sea according to an ancient myth related by Plato.

It should be noted, however, that even though Rudbeck and the other seventeenth-century antiquarians were very much inspired by Old Norse sources that either dated from the Viking Age or described that period at great length, they were not at all interested in 'Vikings' in the sense of rough and barbaric sea-warriors. On the contrary, these learned men wanted to demonstrate to the world that their ancestors had not been barbarians at all, but wise and noble human beings with a great civilization that had originated many centuries before the Viking Age. Admittedly, these ancestors had been used to a rough and simple life in their cold northern climate, and they were for this reason tenacious and good at overcoming difficulties when circumstances forced them to leave their homes and go to other parts of Europe. But they were at the same time cultural heroes who had brought civilization to the countries they visited.

Enlightenment and the Nordic Renaissance

The enlightened eighteenth century brought a (temporary) end to this kind of historiography and also to the Great Power status of both Sweden and Denmark. Historical scholarship became more rational and pragmatic in the works of such historians as the Dane Ludvig Holberg (1684–1754) or the Swede Olov Dalin (1708–63), who tended to identify civilization with the Enlightenment of their own age. Neither Vikings nor Gothic conquerors were their particular heroes, and the chauvinistic theories of Olof Rudbeck were summarily rejected. The Icelandic sagas were still used as important historical sources for the earliest periods, but the Viking Age was not regarded as a golden age but rather as a barbaric and uncivilized period in the history of the Nordic countries.

In the latter half of the eighteenth century, however, the Vikings again became fashionable, this time not as cultural heroes but exactly *because* they were considered barbarians, hostile to modern civilization and enlightened culture. The time of Rousseau and the Noble Savage had come, and the

Viking was soon admired as a delightfully wild and romantic person, capable of the sublime passions which the polite rationalists of the Enlightenment had neglected. This admiration became one of the driving forces of the so-called 'Nordic Renaissance', which did not start in Scandinavia but on the European continent and in England, appealing particularly to young intellectual rebels involved in art and literature.

Sublime art was now defined by these young rebels as the art that violated the conventional rules of harmony, correct measure, and balance. It should be terrible, violent, and awe-inspiring like thunderstorms, enormous threatening mountains, endless deserts, nightmares, madness, divine revelations, and visions of Hell. The most sublime poetry was the barbaric and archaic verses of wild and primitive people like the Celts, the Scyths, or the Scandinavian Vikings, people who had not been tamed, domesticated, and corrupted by modern civilization. In order to experience the sublime, upper-class man had to leave his comfortable, cultivated, and enlightened environment to seek out wild and archaic nature and rediscover his primitive passions; one had, in short, to become rejuvenated, transformed into the original, genuine state of mankind.

Inspired by such ideas, the Nordic Renaissance movement introduced the Old Norse poetry of the *Edda* and the Icelandic sagas to the literary scene of western Europe. This renaissance should not, however, be understood as a revival of genuine Old Norse ideals, but rather as a systematic adaptation or reinterpretation, and partly a distortion, of those ideals in the light of the new aesthetic theories. As a result of this process, the mythical lays of the *Edda*—together with the Celtic songs of Ossian, Scandinavian folk-ballads, and various other mythical texts of supposedly barbaric origin—were thought to possess shattering powers of a special and mysterious kind, derived from nature and from wild, illiterate bards, not from the cultivated art of educated poets.

The first important figure of the Nordic Renaissance was Paul-Henri Mallet (1730–1807), a Swiss citizen of Geneva employed in the 1750s as Professor of French at the University of Copenhagen. In 1755 he published his *Introduction to the History of Denmark*, where he characterized Old Norse poetry in general accordance with the ideas of Ole Worm and other Scandinavian antiquarians of the seventeenth century: as a very sophisticated form of art, based on strict rules and presenting intellectual puzzles or enigmas to its readers. In the second edition of the same work, however, published in Geneva in 1763, Mallet changed his description of this poetry to conform to the new ideas of the sublime and make it more interesting to the faddish young literati of Europe. Now he characterized the poetry of the *Edda* and the Icelandic skalds as 'sublime but obscure', and continued:

The soaring flights of fancy may possibly more peculiarly belong to a rude and uncultivated, than to a civilized people. The great objects of nature strike more forcibly on rude imaginations. Their passions are not impaired by the constraint of laws and education. The paucity of their ideas and the barrenness of their language oblige them to borrow from all nature, images fit to clothe their conceptions in. How should abstract terms and reflex ideas, which so much enervate our poetry, be found in theirs? . . . If it be asked, what is become of that magic power which the ancients attributed to this art? It may well be said to exist no more. The poetry of the modern languages is nothing more than reasoning in rhyme, addressed to the understanding, but very little to the heart. No longer essentially connected with religion, politics or morality, it is at present, if I may say so, a mere private art, an amusement that attains its end when it hath gained the cold approbation of a few select judges. (trans. Thomas Percy, 1770)

In its insistence on the emotional, irrational, barbaric, and magical imagery of great poetry, this statement is quite typical of the new aesthetics of the sublime. It was through inflammatory appeals of this kind that Mallet's presentation of Old Icelandic poetry had an enormous effect on young intellectuals all over Europe. People like Thomas Gray (1717–71) and Thomas Percy (1729–1811) in England, James Macpherson (1736–96) in Scotland, and Johann Gottfried Herder (1744–1803) in Germany all became enthused with the powers of such poetry and tried to collect it, translate it, imitate it, and present it to the world as a sublime and, at the same time, patriotic alternative to the classicist poetics of polite education. Admiration for the primitive but noble souls of one's rustic ancestors became the starting-point and the inspiration for a new and more romantic kind of nationalism, one that emphasized nature and the 'folk spirit' rather than civilization or military conquest.

It took several decades before this kind of thinking reached Scandinavia, but when it finally did, towards the end of the eighteenth century, its influence was far-reaching and profound, and it led to a complete revaluation of the Viking Age, which now for the first time appeared as the true golden age of all the Nordic countries, a time when Scandinavian culture was in perfect harmony with nature and the folk spirit. But although the ideology of the Nordic Renaissance was largely populistic, it was at first accepted only by a fairly small intellectual élite, who saw themselves as the chosen representatives of this folk spirit. Such ideas spread from Germany to academic circles in Copenhagen, Uppsala, and Stockholm, and from there eventually to a large segment of the Scandinavian middle class.

This new enthusiasm for the Vikings became particularly intense in Denmark and Sweden after both countries suffered humiliating military defeats during the first decade of the nineteenth century, Denmark through the

British bombardment of Copenhagen in 1807, Sweden through the loss of Finland in a war against Russia in 1809. Educated people of both nations became convinced that it was now time to regain the power, vitality, and self-respect that the Scandinavians had possessed during the Viking Age. The Nordic Renaissance was gradually transformed from a primarily aesthetic trend among intellectuals to a more general nationalistic revival movement with political overtones.

Denmark's two most prominent Romantic writers, Adam Oehlenschläger (1779–1850) and N. F. S. Grundtvig (1783–1872), thus wrote their earliest poetry, based on a strange combination of Old Norse myth and esoteric German philosophy, for a small circle of literary admirers, but they both became national figures with a strong influence on political ideology. Oehlenschläger's poem *Guldhornene* (The Golden Horns, 1803) eulogizes two precious artefacts from Denmark's archaic past as symbols of a mysterious glory that had once been given by the gods but had since disappeared; this text was interpreted in nationalistic terms by generations of Danish schoolchildren, although it was probably not originally intended to be read in that way. Grundtvig's poetic interpretations of Old Norse mythology eventually provided the ideological basis for the Scandinavian folk high schools.

The Gothic Society, Geijer, and Tegnér

Nationalistic sentiments in Sweden, combined with interest in the Viking-Age and Old Norse literature, led in 1811 to the founding of a patriotic society, *Götiska förbundet* (the Gothic Society), by a group of young academicians and officers in Stockholm who liked to drink mead from horns, address each other by ancient saga names, recite poems from the *Edda*, and perform other Viking rituals in the optimistic hope that such activities would rejuvenate and strengthen their country in future conflicts with Russia. The intellectual leader of the society was Erik Gustaf Geijer (1783–1847), who was to become Sweden's most influential historian and one of its most admired poets. He edited the society's journal *Iduna* (named after the Old Norse goddess who provided Valhalla with the apples of immortality), publishing not only antiquarian articles about various aspects of Viking culture but also patriotic editorials and poems or songs in (considerably modified) Old Norse style.

Two of the poems that Geijer published in *Iduna* during its first year, *Vikingen* (The Viking) and *Odalbonden* (The Yeoman Farmer), soon became seen as classic expressions of true 'Viking spirit', and were often recited or sung at patriotic gatherings and later in many Swedish schools. In

This silver drinking-horn was presented to the Swedish historian and poet Erik Gustaf Geijer in 1816 by his admiring students. The horn was decorated by the artist Bengt Fogelberg with mythical scenes from the *Edda*, illustrating the divine origin of poetry and history. The romantic idea behind this gift is evidently that Geijer should drink skaldic mead from the horn and thus be inspired to write poetry in Old Norse style as well as a truly heroic history of the Viking Age.

Vikingen we hear a shipwrecked sea-warrior relate the story of his wild youth: how he runs away from home at the age of 15, roams the seas restlessly and desperately in search of adventure and glory, loses everything he has gained, and finally prepares to die as a famous hero in the cold waves at the age of 20. In the second poem, *Odalbonden*, skilfully built up as a contrast to the first one, we hear about a farmer who stays at home to defend his no less heroic way of life:

> Though not allured by honour's name,
> My heart well knows its worth.
> I harvest not the field of fame,
> I reap my own good earth.
>
> I love not noise and vain display;
> Great deeds are never loud.
> Few traces mark the tempest's way
> When fades the flaming cloud.
>
> Each sickness wails in its degree
> But health needs no such brawl,
> And therefore no one speaks of me
> Or thinks of me at all.
>
> The mighty lords midst shriek and groan
> Spread ruin all around;

The silent ploughman and his son
They till the reddened ground.

(trans. C. W. Stork)

By thus presenting the Viking and the farmer as heroic representatives of two alternative and opposite lifestyles existing simultaneously in Old-Norse society—a dramatic trick learned from Snorri Sturluson's *Heimskringla*—Geijer makes the Viking Age attractive to people of different political persuasions. Comparing the two heroes and arguing in favour of one against the other became for a while one of the most common exercises in Swedish classrooms. The expected outcome of these scholastic exercises was usually that both heroes were equally necessary and good for the country, although the yeoman farmer has gained in political correctness at the expense of the Viking in the modern Swedish welfare state.

In his *Svenska folkets historia* (History of the Swedish People, 1832–6) and other historical works, Geijer used similar contrasts to present Viking-Age Scandinavia as a model society. In his opinion, the harmony of that society depended on a delicate balance between, on one hand, great kings and, on the other hand, the rural *þing*s, or assemblies of free farmers. The Viking kings provided leadership and military prowess, while the assemblies provided sound judgement, folksy common sense, and a certain amount of democracy. The absence of a real aristocracy made it possible for the people to be close to their kings and for the kings to be close to their people. According to Geijer, this balance was destroyed by the Catholic church and the feudal aristocracy during the Middle Ages, when the assemblies lost their power and the farmers most of their ancient freedom. A strong, free, and independent Scandinavian state such as Sweden should therefore, in his view, not seek its roots in the Middle Ages but rather in the pagan Viking Age and its Old Norse customs and institutions. This view of cultural development in Scandinavia strongly appealed to the Protestant and patriotic spirit of nineteenth-century Sweden, and it became more or less accepted by nationalistic historians for almost a century. A very similar view of the Viking period as dominated by free and proud farmers, irrepressibly speaking their minds to their king at the local assembly, may be found in many other Scandinavian writings of the nineteenth century, for example in the Norwegian histories of Rudolph Keyser (1803–64) and P. A. Munch (1810–63). It is a view that may ultimately be traced back to Snorri Sturluson, but it suited the political climate of the nineteenth century—in which farmers were struggling for more power—exceedingly well.

Although Geijer was by far the most influential member of *Götiska förbundet* during his own lifetime, another member, Bishop Esaias Tegnér

Right: Egil Skalla-Grímsson, the violent tenth-century Icelandic poet and Viking hero, is here shown as he appears in an Icelandic saga manuscript of the seventeenth century. According to the saga, Egil had 'a broad forehead, heavy eyebrows, a short and very thick nose, beard growing all over his face, an extremely broad chin and heavy jaw; he had such a thick neck and such broad shoulders that he was immediately noticed among other men, and he looked tough and cruel when he was furious'.

Left: The death of Baldr, the noblest and most beautiful of the Norse gods, is a motif which often appears in Scandinavian art and literature. This picture was made in the 1760s by an Icelandic country priest and shows how the evil god Loki fools the blind god Hǫðr into piercing Baldr with an arrow made of mistletoe. All three gods are dressed in contemporary Icelandic costumes.

(1782–1846), became even more famous outside Sweden through the publication of *Frithiofs Saga* (1825), a poetic romance in twenty-four epic songs about a Viking hero and his love, based on one of the mythical–heroic sagas from Iceland. Through its brilliant blend of Byronic verse, Romanticism, and Old Norse myth *Frithiofs Saga* became Sweden's first major international success on the literary market, translated into several foreign languages, including English, French, German, Russian, Hungarian, and Croatian. It was therefore Tegnér's version of the Viking Age that became the most well-known in the educated homes of Europe. His hero, like so many Icelandic saga heroes before him, vacillates between the role of *Vikingen* and the role of *Odalbonden*. In his wild youth he behaves like a Byronic Viking hero, after having lost his true love Ingeborg, and his 'Viking's Code' is a romanticized nineteenth-century version of some famous misogynous stanzas in the *Edda*:

> Now he swept o'er the seas, now he roamed far and wide, like the hawk
>   in his airy abode:
> For the warriors on board he wrote rules and decrees. Shall I tell you the
>   Wanderer's Code?
>
> 'Pitch no tent on the ship, in a house never sleep: in the hall none but
>   enemies stand;
> With the sky for his tent, let the Viking-brave sleep on his shield with his
>   sword in his hand . . .
>
> 'When the storm waxes fierce, hoist the sail to the top, it is blithe when
>   the wind blows a gale:
> Let it go, let it go, they are cowards who furl, rather founder than take in
>   thy sail.
>
> 'Leave the maid on the land, let her come not on board, were it Freja she
>   yet would deceive;
> For her dimples are pitfalls, her locks are a net, in her smiles it is woe to
>   believe.'
>
> (trans. L. A. Sherman, 1877)

Towards the end, however, when he is reunited with his Ingeborg (who, needless to say, has loved him faithfully all along) it is time for Frithiof to become a stable and responsible *odalbonde*:

> And as a bloody shadow sank his Viking's life
> With all its angry conflicts and adventures wild

Tegnér thus adjusts the Viking experience to the edifying pattern of the German *Bildungsroman*, in which an immature hero lives a stormy and

Facing: Ribe lies about 6 km from the west coast of Jutland. It developed from the emporium established early in the eighth century on the north bank of the river (among the trees). The medieval town grew up around the cathedral on the other side of the river.

unhappy life away from home during his youthful *Wanderjahre*, but then gradually becomes a more mature person, preparing him for his trumphant homecoming and ultimate success as a wise, reconciled, and thoroughly educated member of society. This is probably one of the main reasons why *Frithiofs Saga* became a success not only with Swedish educators, who made the text obligatory reading in schools, but also with the pious court circles of Victorian England, including Queen Victoria herself, to whom one of the English translations was dedicated. As one British scholar has put it: 'Here was just the Scandinavian tale to encourage Victorian matrons, shocked by Sarah Bernhardt's Cleopatra, to cry "how *very* like the home life of our own dear Queen".'

Grundtvig's Viking Revival

Although *Götiska förbundet* was dissolved after some decades, its ideas lived on for more than a century, inspiring large numbers of educators as well as artists, poets, and politicians. Even more influential, however, was N. F. S. Grundtvig's campaign to infuse the Danish school system with large doses of Viking spirit. In the 1830s this charismatic priest and visionary poet, whom his followers saw as a prophet, presented a new educational pro-gramme aimed at abolishing grades and examinations and replacing Latin grammar with a mixture of Christian revivalism and Old Norse mythology. Grundtvig, who was a passionate enemy of bookish learning and despised traditional academic education, wanted to preach 'the Living Word', by which he meant not only the word of God in the gospels, but also the songs of the *Edda* and all kinds of oral folk traditions that he felt had been neglected by the conventional school system. His utopian vision of a new, free, humanistic, and voluntary school system for the common man, in which the Living Word prevailed over dead learning, inspired the Danish farmers' movement in their ultimately successful struggle against the con-servative upper classes. With the help of the farmers, Grundtvig's followers in the 1860s established the first folk high schools, where students listened to pious sermons about Valhalla and learned to sing patriotic songs about their Viking ancestors.

The folk high school movement soon spread to the other Scandinavian countries. Although the emphasis on Old Norse culture was eventually scaled down in the curriculum, it was at least partly because of these new schools that, during the latter half of the nineteenth century, the Vikings became a major concern not only for a nationalistic élite but also for many ordinary farmers and to some extent for the liberal urban bourgeoisie. For the first time, the Vikings were exploited commercially by various Scandi-

navian companies, which used the names of Old Norse gods and saga heroes as brand names for their products. A rather anachronistic and romanticized 'Viking style' became fashionable in architecture, design, and interior decorating as well as in social gatherings and various types of social events. Artists painted romantic pictures of Old Norse gods and famous saga heroes. Politicians tried to speak like Viking kings to their constituents. Restaurants offered mead in drinking-horns and arranged Viking parties where people turned up in horned helmets and rattled their toy weapons. Public buildings, ships, furniture, and household articles were adorned with fancy dragon's heads, runes, and other symbols of the Viking Age.

On a more limited scale, this enthusiasm for the Vikings also spread to Victorian England, where not only Bishop Tegnér's *Frithiofs Saga* but also more genuine Icelandic sagas were translated into English and ambitious Old Norse programmes were started at both Oxford and Cambridge. Even more important was the fact that some of the Old Norse scholars and saga translators in Britain were prominent national figures such as Samuel Laing (1810–97) and William Morris (1834–96). Laing's interest (like that of some other Scottish intellectuals) clearly had something to do with the fact that he saw himself as a descendant of Viking settlers in Orkney. William Morris's enthusiasm, on the other hand, seems to have developed out of a more general interest in the arts and crafts of the Middle Ages. A third well-known British saga translator, George Webbe Dasent, made flattering comparisons between the Vikings and his own Victorian contemporaries:

Swedish high society dressed as Vikings for a fancy-dress ball organized in Stockholm in 1869.

The interior of
Bravalla, a Swedish
private home of the
Victorian era,
designed, furnished
and decorated in
Romantic 'Viking
style'.

242

They [the Vikings] were like England in the nineteenth century: fifty years before all the rest of the world with her manufactories and firms—and twenty years before them in railways. They were foremost in the race of civilisation and progress; well started before all the rest had thought of running. No wonder therefore that both won.

Also in the Scandinavian countries similar comparisons were made between the Viking spirit and the enterprising spirit of modern entrepreneurs, travellers, scientists, politicians, and so on. The very idea behind the imitated 'Viking style' in art, literature, commerce, and interior decorating was obviously to promote nineteenth-century Scandinavians as true descendants of the Vikings. Such lofty comparisons and pompous imitations, however, were soon ridiculed by many younger intellectuals in the cities, where modern life seemed to have little in common with the Viking Age. During the last decades of the nineteenth century, usually seen as the 'Modern Breakthrough' in Scandinavian art, literature, and industry—and also as the beginning of social democracy—the Viking enthusiasm of earlier generations was again rejected and sometimes openly scorned by radical intellectual leaders such as the Danish critic Georg Brandes (1842–1927) or the Swedish dramatist and novelist August Strindberg (1849–1912). Historians in these two countries also began to be more critical in their attitude to the heroic stories told of the Vikings in the sagas, and the Grundtvigian folk high schools had to tone down some of their romantic enthusiasm for anything Old Norse.

In Norway, Iceland, and the Faeroe Islands, however, the provincial culture had always preserved some genuine traits of the Old Norse period. Vikings were also associated with the time when these west Scandinavian nations had been independent of Denmark and Sweden. Especially the Icelanders and the Faeroese, but also some Norwegians, spoke a language similar to Old Norse, and traditions from the *Edda* and the sagas still survived in local folklore. On the other hand, it took quite a while before such academic intellectual trends as the Nordic Renaissance or the Grundtvigian Viking revival were imported from Copenhagen to these remote and old-fashioned shores. When this finally happened, it coincided with the rise of the national independence movements. For a patriotic citizen in any of these three countries, returning to the Viking Age became more or less equivalent to a return to political independence. The Vikings thus gradually became a major concern for west Scandinavian nationalists and remained so long after the Modern Breakthrough.

Yet it was hardly the most ultra-Romantic or 'sublime' stories of the Vikings that appealed to Norwegian, Icelandic, or Faeroese readers, not even during their struggle for national independence, but rather the tough and understated heroism of the family sagas or of Snorri's *Heimskringla*. It is characteristic that Snorri's Icelandic sagas about the Norwegian kings became a major national classic during the nineteenth century not only in Iceland but also (and particularly) in Norway, where it has been retranslated and reprinted over and over again ever since, often with marvellous woodcut illustrations by some of Norway's most prominent realist artists of the Modern Breakthrough: Christian Krohg (1852–1925), Erik Werenskiold (1855–1938), and others. It is also characteristic that these illustrations have tended to emphasize not so much the splendour, charisma, and wealth of the great Viking chiefs, but rather the hard struggle of poor and tough Norwegians to survive under difficult circumstances in their cold fjords and high mountains. A similar realist spirit, inspired by the Icelandic family sagas, is found in some early stories and plays about the Viking period by Henrik Ibsen (1828–1906), Bjørnstjerne Bjørnson (1832–1910), August Strindberg, and other writers of the Modern Breakthrough, for example Ibsen's play *Hærmændene på Helgeland* (The Vikings of Helgeland, 1858).

The Norwegian enthusiasm for the Vikings increased considerably towards the end of the century as two stately Viking ships were found and excavated in large burial mounds near the Oslo fjord—the Gokstad ship in 1880, the Oseberg ship in 1904. Not only were these discoveries in themselves spectacular and the circumstances of their discovery in many ways sensational, but they also happened to coincide with the last stage of Norway's struggle for independence, which was finally achieved in 1905. It was thus natural that these ships would become treasured national symbols, prominently displayed in the centre of the new Norwegian capital of Oslo.

Vikings in America

For the Scandinavians emigrating to North America in the course of the nineteenth century the Viking heritage also acquired an important national significance, particularly cherished in their initial struggle to assert themselves in relation to other immigrant groups in the United States or Canada. Many of these emigrants, many of whom settled in midwestern states such as Minnesota or Wisconsin, strongly identified with the Viking farmers who had once settled in the North Atlantic islands and in *Vínland*, settlements that are vividly described in the sagas. It was unavoidable that the Scandinavian Americans would choose as their particular hero Leif Eriksson, the legendary Norwegian Viking who was supposed to have discovered America centuries before Columbus. It was also unavoidable that they would write about the Vikings—fact as well as fiction—in their ethnic pub-

244

lications (some of which even had Old Norse names) and eagerly welcome any evidence that could convince the world that the Scandinavians were indeed the first to arrive in America. This opened the way for forgeries such as the Kensington Stone, said to have been 'discovered' in the soil of Minnesota in 1898 with an amateurishly concocted inscription supposedly made by fourteenth-century descendants of Viking settlers. The Kensington Stone actually became a major ethnic symbol for at least half a century, and there are still some Minnesotans who believe in its authenticity. Of greater significance in the long run, however, was the fact that the Scandinavian community in the United States encouraged several American universities to start ambitious academic programmes in Viking history and Old Norse culture.

Wagner and the Nazis

Meanwhile in Germany enthusiasm for the Vikings took a more romantic, extreme and, ultimately, dangerous course. The tone had been set by Richard Wagner (1813–83) in the *Ring des Nibelungen* (1852–74), a stunning operatic extravaganza based on Old Norse and Early Germanic mythology. In Wagner's dramatic and musical recreation of these myths, interpreted in the fascinating but obscure light of Romantic philosophy, they achieved a new religious significance for the entire German nation. Siegfried is presented as the tragic Germanic hero destined to fall in his attempt to save the gods and the world from cosmic forces of greed, evil, and destruction. He and his passionate but self-destructive mistress, the Valkyrie Brünnhilde, are gradually both revealed to be the chosen heirs of Wotan himself, the incarnation of the world-spirit, and also of Erda, the Earth Mother, symbol of divine nature. The whole cycle of the *Ring* appeared to its audience as a sublime manifestation of the German spirit, and its performance at Bayreuth, originally sponsored by the king of Bavaria, became a sacred national ritual of gigantic proportions.

A German businessman in Valhalla, a caricature from the 1920s by the radical artist George Grosz. The drawing is evidently meant to satirize the kind of German middle-class enthusiasm for the Vikings and Norse mythology that later culminated in Hitler's national socialism.

When, towards the end of the nineteenth century, this Wagnerian mystique merged with Nietzsche's élitist philosophy of superman, imperialist ambition, and newly developed racist ideas of German supremacy it did not take long before some Germans began to see themselves as *Herrenvolk* and the Vikings as their own racial forebears and role models, destined to defeat their inferiors in other countries. During the first decades of the twentieth century such racist thinking resulted in a flood of uncritical German appreciations of the Viking Age and of Old Norse literature, the texts of which were often read as sacred expressions of a purely Germanic *Blut-und-Boden* philosophy, rooted in the home soil of one's family and the whispers of the blood inherited from heroic Viking ancestors. This kind of semi-religious thinking also found its way to England and Scandinavia, although it never became as influential or militant there as in Germany.

A few decades later, after Germany's humiliating defeat in the First World War, such ideas were turned into party politics by Adolf Hitler and his followers. When the National Socialists came to power in 1933 they started a crusade against 'decadent' modern culture, systematically replacing it with their own version of 'Aryan' culture, based on the heritage of the

A German *Dingspiel*, a semi-religious form of Germanic theatre organized by the Nazis and performed in large outdoor arenas reminiscent of the Old Norse Thing meetings. The plot was often taken from the *Edda* or the Viking world, and the idea was to create a large collective manifestation of the Aryan spirit.

Vikings, Old Norse mythology, Wagner, and German peasant culture. The Nazis particularly encouraged a new and supposedly Germanic form of drama, called *Dingspiel* ('thing play'), huge collective manifestations of the 'folk soul', with much parading and collective chanting of political slogans, performed in majestic outdoor arenas made to look like the places where, according to the sagas, Norse farmers held their *þing* meetings. During the German occupation of Norway and Denmark (1940–5), the Nazis were particularly eager to use the Vikings in their propaganda. 'Viking' was, for example, the name given to an infamous regiment of Nazi soldiers recruited among Norwegian volunteers and set against the Russians on the eastern front towards the end of the war. One typical poster from this period shows an SS soldier shaking hands with a young, blond Norwegian standing in front of a huge Viking ship carrying the following message: 'With Waffen. SS and the Norwegian Legion against their common enemy . . . Against Bolshevism.'

This kind of Nazi propaganda does not seem to have had much effect on ordinary Scandinavians. As a matter of fact, Viking symbols were also used by the Resistance movement in its underground war against the German occupation. One legendary Resistance group in southern Denmark, for example, was named Holger Danske after a famous Old Norse saga hero. Its members mainly consisted of farmers who had grown up in the Grundtvigian folk high school tradition and therefore found it quite natural to be inspired by Norse mythology in their struggle against the German enemy, casually (and often jokingly) referred to in their daily conversations as 'the Fenriswolf' or 'the Midgard Serpent'.

Modern Attitudes

When the war ended in 1945 the Nazi form of Viking enthusiasm naturally came to an end, at least temporarily, and the Viking heritage in general lost much of its appeal not only in Germany but also in the Scandinavian countries, particularly among academics and intellectuals. A more radically critical attitude to the Old-Norse sources, originally introduced in the early twentieth century by historians such as Lauritz Weibull in Sweden (1873–1960), finally prevailed in most Scandinavian and British universities, making the national romanticism of earlier Viking histories obsolete. Modern historians and archaeologists have generally not tried to present the Vikings as great national heroes or as glorious leaders of exciting military adventures, but rather as competent but fairly unglamorous tradesmen, colonists, shipbuilders, craftsmen, mercenaries, or (alas) plunderers.

This certainly does not mean that the Vikings lost their popularity after

the Second World War. On the contrary, they have become more and more
popular all over the world, and particularly in the mass media, even in
countries where they have only ever been seen as plunderers and hooligans.
Yet one can say that they have, during the last fifty years, been relegated
from 'high culture' to 'low culture' Nowadays they are rarely the heroes of
serious novels or ambitious poems, but rather the popular anti-heroes of
comic strips such as *Asterix* or *Hagar the Horrible*. Their dragon ships and
horned helmets have commercial value and the power to attract large
crowds of people, but such emblems of Viking culture are today considered
funny rather than romantic or heroic. And the real Viking fans are today
more often found among uneducated football supporters than within the
intellectual avant-garde.

The most popular modern novel about the Vikings is probably *Röde Orm*
(The Long Ships, 1941–5) by the Swedish author Frans G. Bengtsson (1894–
1955) which has been translated into many languages, including English; the
book has also been made into a musical and a Hollywood movie. It is a novel
that still deserves to be widely read for its exciting adventures, its brilliantly
ironic style, and its many entertaining episodes. What makes the text particularly interesting from a literary historian's point of view is the fact that it
represents a transition from an older way of understanding the Vikings to a
more modern one. On one hand, Bengtsson is an old-fashioned Viking
admirer who has learned much from the sagas and from conservative histories where the Vikings are still pictured as heroes. On the other hand, he is
also a modern intellectual who treats all kinds of exalted heroism or romantic posturing (especially of the Wagnerian or Nazi kind) with a good deal of
sarcasm. The male protagonists of his story, the Viking companions Orm
and Toke, are shown to be real heroes in their dealings with the enemy, but
they are also rather funny in their homely style and unblushing, but very
human, concern for simple material pleasures such as beer and pork. After
escaping from a long imprisonment by the Muslims in Spain, the two companions manage to be invited to the Yule celebrations of King Harald Bluetooth in Denmark, where they demonstrate their prowess in battle against
some particularly unpleasant Viking thugs. But weaker sentiments, which
Orm and Toke have carefully concealed under their tough appearance, are
suddenly revealed when one of the king's servants starts handing out their
food:

They sighed blissfully as he lifted out fine pieces of shoulder pork to put on their
plates, reminding each other how long it was since they had last eaten such a dinner,
and marvelling that they had managed to survive so many years in a country where
no pork was allowed to be eaten. But when the blood-sausage arrived, tears came
into their eyes, and they declared that they had never eaten a meal worthy of the

248

name since the day they had sailed away with Krok.

'This is the best smell of all,' said Orm in a small voice.

'There is thyme in it,' said Toke huskily.

(trans. Michael Meyer)

It is scenes like this, rather than the more conventional Viking adventures and battles, that have made *Röde Orm* a modern Viking classic. Orm and Toke, like Hagar the Horrible, seem to have become popular as comic heroes exactly because they do not possess any refinement and sophistication whatsoever. They will never become educated and civilized like Tegnér's Frithiof. Like modern working-class heroes, these Vikings have made a virtue of their simple tastes, rough exterior, and blunt manners. Naturally, their hearts are made of pure gold.

During the last decades of the twentieth century, the Vikings have become more popular than ever. Viking fairs and Viking festivals are celebrated each summer in the Scandinavian countries as well as in Britain, Germany, and the United States. Gallons of mead and thousands of horned helmets are usually sold at such occasions along with Viking jewellery such as Thor's hammer, Viking bread, Viking swords, models of Viking houses, and many other remarkable products. Young people are learning to build Viking ships and sail them over the ocean. Viking plays are performed, and Viking battles fought in commemoration of Maldon, Stamford Bridge, Stiklestad, and various other famous events of the Viking era. Some enthusiasts have even started new sects for the celebration of the Old Norse gods. Yet only small groups appear to take the Vikings completely seriously; the fact that some of them use Viking symbols in imitation of the Nazis to promote racist ideas has occasionally provoked well-meaning educators into saying that it is now about time to forget the Vikings altogether, since they do not seem to be entirely compatible with the progressive, liberal, and multicultural ideals of the modern Scandinavian welfare state. History should teach us, however, that the Vikings can be understood in many ways and exploited both for good and for evil.

11

THE VIKING LEGACY

PETER SAWYER

Our knowledge of Viking activity in western Europe largely depends on texts written by churchmen. Archaeological evidence, coins, and place-names provide a great deal of additional information, much of it unobtainable in any other way, but that evidence is all the more instructive when set in the framework provided by the chronicles, charters, laws, and other texts produced in the churches and courts of the Christian West.

The value of such conventional historical sources is underlined by comparison with eastern Europe where the only contemporary texts to help interpret the abundant archaeological and numismatic evidence were produced by Muslims and Byzantines, not by the peoples who were directly affected by the Scandinavian invaders. A few of these texts, notably those by Ibn Fadlan and Constantine Porphyrogenitos, include information gained at first hand, but our understanding of the role of Scandinavians in the east is inevitably much more conjectural than of their role in the west.

The Fury of the Northmen

Clergy, monks, and nuns had good cause to fear the Vikings, for their churches were the most attractive targets for the raiders. They were, at least at first, undefended and many had large quantities of precious metals and gems adorning their altars and shrines, book-covers, and vestments. In all parts of western Europe churchmen regarded the Viking attacks as God's judgement, which they certainly did not minimize when describing the destruction wrought by the raiders. In 841, according to the *Annals of St-Bertin*, Danes who attacked Rouen 'plundered the town with pillage, fire, and sword, slaughtered or took captive the monks and the rest of the population and laid waste all the monasteries and other places along the banks of the Seine, or else took large payments and left them thoroughly terrified'.

The impression given by such catalogues of disaster that the Vikings were exceptionally violent is reinforced by later accounts, such as the twelfth-century Irish *Cogad Gaedel re Gallaib* (The War of the Irish with the Foreigners), which contains an extravagant account of Viking destructiveness that has often been quoted:

In a word, although there were an hundred hard steeled iron heads on one neck, and an hundred sharp, ready cool, never-rusting, brazen tongues in each head, and an hundred garrulous, loud, unceasing voices from each tongue, they could not recount, or narrate, or enumerate, or tell, what all the Ghaedhil suffered in common, both men and women, laity and clergy, old and young, noble and ignoble, of hardship, and of injury, and of oppression, in every house, from these valiant, wrathful, foreign, purely pagan people.

Some modern historians have echoed such judgements, claiming for example that 'all the abbeys and towns of the west from Hamburg to Bordeaux had been put to the sack and great tracts of country, especially in the Netherlands and north-western France were converted into desert', or that the Vikings caused 'political disintegration and social chaos in the Atlantic coastlands of Europe', bringing commerce and industry to a halt and making agriculture impossible.

One of the aims of this book has been to provide a more balanced picture. The Vikings undoubtedly destroyed much and caused widespread disruption, but there is no reason to believe that they were any more brutal and ruthless than the peoples of western Europe. The Franks, English, Irish, and others behaved in much the same way against their neighbours or in their internal conflicts. In 841, for example, the *Annals of St-Bertin* report that in the course of the civil war following the death of Louis the Pious, his eldest son, Lothar, in going from Sens to Le Mans ravaged 'everything with such acts of devastation, burning, rape, sacrilege and blasphemy that he could not even restrain his men from damaging those whom he was planning to visit. He lost no time in carrying off whatever treasures he could find deposited in churches or in their strongrooms for safe keeping'. There were, however, two important differences between the Vikings and their victims. First, they came by sea, giving them the advantage of surprise when attacking coastal regions, and a relatively safe means of retreat. Secondly, the first generations of Vikings were pagans. We should not put much weight on this religious difference, although some contemporaries did. Churches were not immune from attack by Christian kings, and Christians in their conflicts with one another could be as ruthless, cruel, and destructive as any Viking.

The armies of Christian kings, like most armies, could be as much a terror to their own people as to their enemies.

The main purpose of the Viking raids, at first the only one, was to acquire treasure by plundering, extorting protection money or tribute, and by ransoming captives. Huge sums were occasionally paid to free captives of high rank. In 858 the abbot of St-Denis was ransomed for more than had been paid in 845 to spare Paris. In 994 raiders who sailed up the Elbe captured the count of Stade and his brother, and demanded 7,000 marks for them. Most ransoms were much smaller. In 841 the abbey of St-Wandrille in the Seine valley paid 26 pounds of silver for the release of sixty-eight prisoners.

The abundance of treasure in Frankia is probably the reason the Vikings do not seem to have sold captives taken there into slavery: it was simpler, and perhaps more rewarding, to ransom them. In Ireland, where the churches had very little gold and silver, the Vikings were more interested in selling their captives. Slave-trading was even more important in eastern Europe. In the eighth century there was virtually no silver or gold in the forest region, but Scandinavians soon discovered that they could acquire treasure indirectly by selling slaves, furs, and other produce to Muslim merchants in exchange for silver. It may be, as suggested in Chapter 6, that furs were bought from native trappers, but it is likely that most were obtained as tribute, as the princes of Kiev, Novgorod, and other centres did later. In the tenth century the large quantities of silver that were being accumulated in Russia were as attractive to Vikings as the church treasures of western Europe had been earlier, and it is likely that much of the silver that reached Scandinavia from the east in the tenth century was gained by raiding.

The effect of Viking raids in western Europe varied. In Frankia many monasteries had widely scattered estates to which the brethren could retreat with their relics, treasures, books, and archives when an attack was threatened until the danger had passed. In this way, although churches and monastic buildings might be destroyed, many communities in the heart of Frankia survived with at least some of their most valued possessions. Those in the coastal regions were not so fortunate. The efforts made by Charles the Bald to defend the central part of his kingdom meant, in effect, that the lower reaches of the Seine and Loire and other coastal regions were abandoned to the mercy of the Vikings. A natural consequence was that most religious communities and bishops soon sought safety in other parts of the kingdom. No bishops are known to have existed for the sees of Avranches, Bayeux, Évreux, or Lisieux for some time after the early 870s; the bishop of Coutances sheltered in Rouen, where a Frankish count retained some semblance of power, and the bishop of Nantes abandoned his see. In Normandy successive dukes in the tenth century encouraged the restoration of diocesan organization, but the monastic revival was slower, only gathering pace in the eleventh century.

Nowhere in the British Isles was there a safe refuge from the Vikings. Alfred may not have exaggerated much when he described the period of Viking invasions as a time when everything was ransacked and burned, although, as Simon Keynes points out in Chapter 3, there is little reliable evidence for the fate of any monastery. Some may have been permanently destroyed, but there is no means of telling how many. In areas that remained under English control or were quickly recovered, some communities survived or were soon revived.

In England, as in Frankia, the main disruption was in the areas conquered and colonized by the Danes. Much of the land acquired by the settlers had belonged to religious communities. This threatened their survival more than the destruction of buildings and the loss of treasures. Physical damage could be made good, but the loss of estates deprived them of the resources on which they depended. As a result, by the end of the ninth century there were few monasteries left in England between the rivers Tees and Welland, or in East Anglia. Diocesan organization was also disrupted by the Scandinavian conquest, although the archbishops of York stayed in their see, and at least two of them actively co-operated with the Scandinavian rulers of York. The conquest was in fact to their advantage for it enabled them to recover Lindsey, which had once belonged to their diocese.

The survival of monasteries in Ireland, even near Dublin and Cork, may have been partly because Scandinavian settlement there was much less extensive than in England, but the fact that, as Donnchadh Ó Corráin explains in Chapter 4, many survived in all parts of Ireland despite being attacked, some of them repeatedly, does cast doubt on the claim that monasticism in England was virtually undermined by the Vikings. It is true that later monastic reformers looked back on early tenth-century England as a 'monastic desert', but that was because the religious communities that did survive were irregular and were therefore, in the eyes of the reformers, not true monasteries. It is certainly not evidence that the Vikings had extinguished English monasticism. Even in the ninth century Alfred's biographer Asser complained that there were many monasteries but that they 'were not properly observing the rule of this way of life'.

Political Consequences

Vikings were responsible for many political changes. Several of the bases they established in Ireland retained some measure of independence for a while and were a complicating factor in Irish politics at least until the

Facing, above:
A reconstruction of
the medieval farm-
house at Stöng in the
deserted valley of
Thórsárdalur in
southern Iceland.
This relatively large
and rich farm was
abandoned in the
early thirteenth
century because of
deteriorating climate,
erosion, and repeated
eruptions of the
volcano Hekla.

Facing, below:
One of three stone
panels, carved in the
early twelfth century
with scenes from the
Crucifixion and
Resurrection of
Christ, now mounted
in the walls of
Forshem church, in
Västergötland,
Sweden. It shows the
three women arriving
at the tomb to find it
empty, and an angel
waving an empty
shroud, while Christ
is seen, crowned, to
the right. These
panels doubtless
originally formed
part of a sepulchre in
the church, which
was dedicated to the
Holy Sepulchre. It
was presumably
founded by a
magnate who visited
Jerusalem after the
first crusade.

twelfth century. Vikings also established coastal bases in several parts of Frankia, but all were sanctioned by Frankish rulers, at least in theory, and only Normandy proved permanent. The changes in England were more substantial. Two kingdoms were conquered, Northumbria and East Anglia, and a third, Mercia, was undermined, leaving the kings of Wessex as the only surviving native dynasty. Their successful opposition to the invaders greatly enhanced their prestige, enabling Alfred to claim to be the true representative of all Anglo-Saxons thus preparing the way for his children and grandchildren to extend their authority and eventually unify the kingdom. The forts or boroughs (*burhs*) that Alfred constructed were controlled by royal agents and proved to be an important factor in strengthening the power of English kings. As Alfred's successors gradually gained control of the areas that had been conquered by the Danes, they extended this network of boroughs as far north as Chester and York, and during the tenth century mints were established in many of them, producing a royal coinage that was closely controlled, symbolizing the unity of the kingdom.

The changes brought about by Vikings, directly or indirectly, in Frankia, England, and Ireland were dwarfed in scale by the development of the principality of Kiev and the establishment of its hegemony over much of eastern Europe. As is made clear by Thomas Noonan in Chapter 6, this was not an exclusively Scandinavian achievement, but the princes of Kiev and several of the rulers within their empire were of Scandinavian descent, as were many of their retainers.

In contrast, the colonization of the Atlantic islands was almost entirely a Scandinavian enterprise. The descendants of the Scandinavians who settled in England, Ireland, Frankia, and Russia were quickly assimilated, but in the previously uninhabited Atlantic islands Norwegian colonists and their descendants continued to speak their own language. So too did those who settled in Orkney, Shetland, the Hebrides, and the Isle of Man. This was a huge, and largely permanent, extension of the Scandinavian world that remained in such close contact with Norway that much of it was eventually incorporated into the Norwegian kingdom.

Settlement and Economic Changes

The number of Scandinavians who emigrated in the ninth and tenth centuries is not known. Archaeological evidence for Scandinavian settlers is more abundant in Russia than in western Europe, but that is because pagan burial customs lasted very much longer in the east than the west. Most estimates of the scale of Scandinavian colonization have been based on the evidence of Scandinavian place-names, but these reflect the influence of

Scandinavian speech on the language spoken locally, and certainly do not indicate where Scandinavians settled. The fact that there are many more Scandinavian place-names in England than in Normandy or Ireland is only partly due to differences in the density and extent of settlement. Another factor was the length of time a Scandinavian language was spoken in any one place. For example, Scandinavian influence on the names of minor features in the landscape is greater in western than in eastern Normandy because Danish speech survived longer there than around Rouen. The arrival in England of new groups of settlers for at least forty years after the original settlement in 876 ensured that Scandinavian speech survived in some districts well into the tenth century. An even more important factor was that in the ninth century the Danish and English languages were very much more closely related than Danish or Norwegian were with either French or Irish. As a result, Scandinavian speech influenced language in England much more than elsewhere. A large number of Scandinavian words were borrowed into English, at first in the dialects of the areas in which Scandinavians settled. Many of these loanwords were later adopted throughout England, for example *take, call, window, husband, sky, anger, low, scant, loose, ugly, wrong, happy*. As a Danish scholar has remarked, 'an Englishman cannot *thrive* or be *ill* or *die* without Scandinavian words: they are to the language what *bread* and *eggs* are to the daily fare'.

There were certainly many more Scandinavian settlers in England than in either Normandy or Ireland, but the Scandinavian place-names give a very misleading impression of the difference. In England place-names certainly indicate the areas that were most influenced by Scandinavian speech. It is, however, likely that the main areas of settlement are indicated by the densest concentrations of Scandinavian place-names, for example, in the Lincolnshire Wolds or east of Sleaford. It is significant that most of the brooches, rings, and other ornamental metalwork of the tenth and eleventh centuries decorated in Scandinavian styles that have been found in Lincolnshire come from these areas.

Although trading centres proved remarkably resilient in the face of repeated plundering—Dorestad was raided at least seven times between 834 and 865—in many regions of western Europe the raids must have caused a serious decline in trade. It was some compensation that the Vikings later stimulated the economies of the parts of Frankia, England, and Ireland that they had conquered.

In Ireland many of the coastal strongholds established by Vikings in the mid-ninth century soon became active trading centres as well as continuing as bases for raids by land and sea. The wealth accumulated in them attracted

Facing: By the eleventh century Dublin was expanding west of the original settlement. Excavations in this area (along High Street) uncovered this late eleventh-century wooden path and remains of several houses with walls made of wattles woven around upright posts set in the ground.

Irish kings, who made great efforts to 'protect' them, a point underlined by the Irish historian Francis Byrne: 'The Irish provincial king who could milk Dublin, Waterford or Limerick for tribute was far more powerful than his peers who extorted allegiance from twenty tribal kings.'

In England and Frankia Viking conquests were more extensive than in Ireland, and in these areas much of the produce that had previously been extracted by agents of English or Frankish kings and by monasteries and other major landowners remained in the hands of the producers. The Scandinavian rulers and their leading followers demanded some, but in total probably less than their predecessors. Thanks to this larger surplus, farmers, Scandinavian settlers as well as natives, were well placed to profit from the increased demand as the economy in many parts of Europe expanded in the tenth century.

Scandinavian settlers themselves contributed to that expansion by redistributing—and spending—the treasure they had acquired. Their loot included gold and gems, but the bulk was silver in the form of coins, jewellery, and plate. The Viking leaders probably retained the most valuable items and used the silver to reward their men. Viking hoards of silver containing English and Frankish coins, rings, ingots, and occasionally pieces of jewellery have been found in many parts of the British Isles, especially in areas that remained outside the control of English kings who, in their own territory, converted most treasures of that kind into coin. Although most of these hoards are small, their owners had greater purchasing power than most of the natives who remained in the areas ruled by Scandinavians. The presence of numerous relatively wealthy people must have stimulated local economies and contributed to the revival of York and Lincoln that began after Vikings began to settle in their neighbourhoods. The rapid expansion of these and other English towns towards the end of the tenth century had other causes, but the initial stages were in large measure due to the Vikings. In Frankia, as Janet Nelson argues in Chapter 2, the Viking contribution to economic development was far less significant. The urban expansion that began in the ninth century, especially in the valleys of the Rhine and Meuse, continued after the disruption of the Viking raids. It was only in Normandy that the wealth of Scandinavian settlers could have stimulated urban development as it did in England, contributing to the revival of Rouen and to the emergence of Caen and other new towns.

Scandinavia

Scandinavia was radically transformed during the Viking Age. By the end of the eleventh century the process of Christianization was well advanced in most regions. New methods of government made the authority of Danish and Norwegian kings more effective, enabling them to convert unstable hegemonies into relatively stable kingdoms, and by the beginning of the twelfth century most of the medieval towns of Denmark and Norway had been firmly established. The Vikings contributed to these changes, but so too did traders, missionaries, and royal envoys.

Two of the most fundamental developments—the conversion to Christianity and the creation of the medieval kingdoms—were closely related. From the middle of the ninth century Christian missionaries were able to preach in many parts of Scandinavia. One result was that some Scandinavians were prepared to accept that Christ was a god, if not the only one. As the tenth-century German chronicler Widukind remarks: 'the Danes have long been Christians but they nevertheless worshipped idols with pagan rituals.' The toleration of missionaries prepared the way for the next stage of Christianization, the formal acceptance of the exclusive claims of the Christian god, which meant the abandonment of traditional cults, or their reduction to mere superstitions, a dramatic break with the past that required the support of rulers.

The first king to be baptized in Scandinavia was the Dane, Harald Gormsson, but there are indications that at least one Norwegian king publicly acknowledged Christianity earlier than he did. Håkon, the son of Harald Finehair, was fostered in the court of the English king Athelstan. Although this arrangement was apparently made for political or diplomatic and not religious reasons, it had important religious consequences when Håkon eventually succeeded his father. He was remembered as the first king actively to encourage Christianity in Norway and there may be some truth in the later tradition that he invited English missionaries to Norway. Snorri's claim that Håkon abandoned Christianity is supported by the poem *Hákonarmál*, composed in his memory, which implies that Håkon had, at least for a while, accepted Christianity personally, but had not made any serious effort to impose it on his people. The early progress of Christianity in Norway has been obscured by the emphasis later put on the role of Olaf Tryggvason, who was undoubtedly an active supporter of the new reli-

The rune-stone at Risbyle in Täby parish, Uppland, is a good illustration of Christian influence in eastern Sweden in the eleventh century. It ends 'God and God's mother help his spirit and soul, grant him light and paradise'.

257

The lower coin, minted in Sigtuna for Olof Skotkonung, was modelled on English coins of the 'Long Cross' type, one of which is illustrated here. Coins with a 'Long Cross' on the reverse were issued in England between c.997 and 1003, and were copied in Sigtuna before the end of the century.

gion. It does, though, seem likely that his missionary activity in Norway consolidated a process that had begun decades earlier.

In Sweden Olof Skötkonung, who was later generally recognized as the first Christian king, was issuing Christian coins by 995 from his mint at Sigtuna. However, it was not until about 1080 that pagan cults ceased to be celebrated at Uppsala. Over 650 Christian rune-stones and many pagan burials show that in Svealand Christians and pagans lived alongside each other throughout the eleventh century.

Before Christianity was publicly accepted, missionaries must have depended on the protection and hospitality of rulers and magnates who were well disposed to them. Later, when kings were Christian, a royal retinue would normally include a bishop to perform liturgical functions and advise the king. It was some time before ecclesiastical organization in Scandinavia conformed to the pattern elsewhere, with bishops permanently based in their cathedral churches, ruling dioceses with settled boundaries. This happened first in Denmark where, by about 1060, all the medieval sees had been established. Norwegian sees began to be established about ten years later, first in Nidaros, where St Olaf was buried, on the Isle of Selja, which was soon transferred to Bergen, and in Oslo. The early development of the Swedish sees is obscure. The first was Skara, founded by the mid-eleventh century, but by the year 1100 there were probably cathedrals in Linköping and Sigtuna as well, although diocesan boundaries were not then fixed.

By the end of the eleventh century Christianity had begun to affect all levels of Scandinavian society. Numerous churches had been built, many of them by landowners. The first churches were timber structures that have left few traces, but many were rebuilt in stone in the twelfth century. The church introduced a new language, Latin, and a new script, the Roman alphabet, that were used for centuries alongside Scandinavian languages and runes. It brought new forms of worship, and churchmen also introduced a vast and varied literature, including the Bible, the lives of saints, letter collections, chronicles, and other forms of historical writing that were used to educate future clergy and eventually provided models for native literature.

Most of the early bishops in Scandinavia were foreigners, many of them from England or Germany. Some, who had experience of the workings of royal government in Christian kingdoms, eventually taught Scandinavians to use documents as evidence of grants or other transactions. They were also largely responsible for the compilation of the first written laws, and began to modify traditional customs in accordance with the law of the church, although church law was not always, or in all parts of Scandinavia, accepted.

These laws only survive in versions that were compiled or edited after 1100, but there is no reason to doubt that some changes were already being made under the influence of Christian advisers before then.

The main beneficiaries of the process of Christianization that gathered pace in eleventh-century Scandinavia were the kings, especially of the Danes and Norwegians. Their government was made more effective by such innovations as written law and royal diplomas, and their status was enhanced by the ideology of kingship and the rituals that the church introduced. What is more, new forms of political organization were developed in which bishops were not only royal counsellors but also literate royal agents.

One of the most important results of conversion was the increasingly close contact with the papacy. Knut's visit to Rome in 1027 had little effect in Scandinavia, but fifty years later reforming popes had begun to claim direct authority there and to demand obedience to the law of the church as they interpreted it. In 1100 a second Danish king, Erik Ejegod, visited the pope, partly to prepare for the elevation of Lund to an archbishopric, and partly to obtain papal confirmation of the canonization of his brother, Knut, who had been assassinated in Odense in 1086, and was already recognized as a martyr in Denmark. It was to serve the shrine of this royal saint that Erik invited monks from Evesham Abbey in England. This was the beginning of a new and, before long, important network of religious communities and monastic orders that helped to bind Scandinavia ever more closely to other parts of Europe.

Increased royal power was also reflected in the economic developments that occurred towards the end of the Viking Age. The huge quantity of treasure that reached Scandinavia thanks to the Vikings was, as in England, widely dispersed among many people, but it did not automatically stimulate economic change or lead to the growth of towns. Until the eleventh century most of it was kept in hoards, some of them large, to be used for major transactions, such as the payment

The earliest surviving Swedish charter, concerning a dispute over the endowment of the Cistercian monastery at Viby, near Sigtuna. It was issued between 1164 and 1167 by Stefan, the first archbishop of Uppsala, and witnessed by King Karl Sverkersson, with the seals of both king and archbishop.

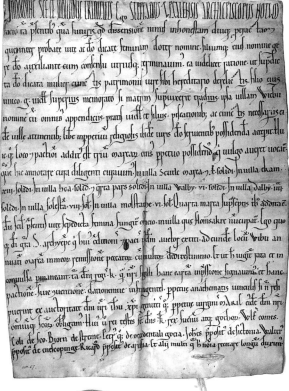

of dowries, ransoms, and tributes, or to buy farms or ships. The earliest hoards to contain numerous small fragments of silver suitable for everyday purchases date from the late tenth century in Denmark, and imply an increase in local marketing. It was in the same region that urban expansion began, under the protection of Danish kings and their agents, who could provide the security that traders and craftsmen needed; significantly, it was at this time and in the same part of Scandinavia that the first sailing-ships designed to carry large cargoes were made, a development discussed in Chapter 8.

In the middle of the tenth century the only towns in Scandinavia were found in Denmark: Ribe, Hedeby (later succeeded by Schleswig), and Århus; Birka was then rapidly declining and did not last much longer. By the end of the century Lund, Odense, Roskilde, and Viborg had been founded in Denmark and Oslo and Trondheim in parts of Norway that, before 1015, had for most of the time been under the control of Danish kings or of jarls who acknowledged them as overlords. In Sweden royal power developed

Towns in Scandinavia *c.*1200 with the bishops' sees established by then in the archiepiscopal provinces of Lund, Nidaros, and Uppsala. There was also a cathedral at Garðar in Greenland.

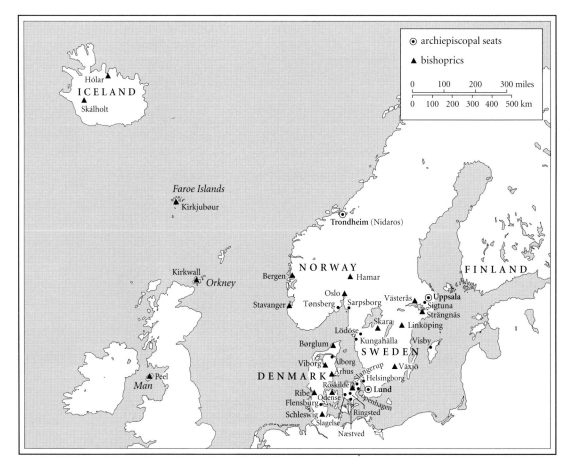

260

more slowly, and so too did urbanization. In the year 1000 there was only one town, Sigtuna, which had been founded in about 975 and was the base from which Olof Skötkonung and later eleventh-century kings attempted, with limited success, to assert their authority over the Svear.

By the end of the eleventh century few, if any, Scandinavians could either hope to find new homes in the British Isles or the Atlantic islands, or realistically expect to repeat the exploits of their forefathers in gathering treasure in west or east Europe by force. They could, however, profit from peaceful trade, earning not silver but such useful produce as cloth, cereals, flour, and beer, as well as ornaments and furnishings for churches and wealthy laymen. The rapidly expanding towns of western Europe needed timber and other raw materials as well as the preserved food that Scandinavia could supply. In the early twelfth century, and probably much earlier, Norwegians were exporting what was later to be their most important product, dried cod, that could supplement the food supply, especially in towns, during the winter and spring months. The large number of twelfth-century stone churches in Denmark and southern Sweden, many of which must have been built by foreign craftsmen (there was no native tradition of building in stone), suggest that many landowners in those parts of Scandinavia, as well as in Norway, benefited from the trade that continued to flourish after the Viking Age, as it had before.

FURTHER READING

1. The Age of the Vikings, and Before

General surveys

Although the general works listed here contain comments and additional information on many of the topics discussed in this book, they are not repeated in the further reading suggested for later chapters.

PETER FOOTE and D. M. WILSON, *The Viking Achievement* (2nd edn, London, 1980), the fullest account in English of Scandinavian society in the period 800–1200.

JAMES GRAHAM-CAMPBELL, *The Viking World* (2nd edn, London, 1989), a well-illustrated introduction.

GWYN JONES, *A History of the Vikings* (2nd edn, Oxford, 1984), a vigorous account.

JOHN HAYWOOD, *The Penguin Historical Atlas of the Vikings* (Harmondsworth, 1995), an up-to-date survey with helpful maps.

ELSE ROESDAHL, *The Vikings* (Harmondsworth, 1991) is concerned with Scandinavians at home as much as abroad.

ELSE ROESDAHL and DAVID M. WILSON, *From Viking to Crusader: Scandinavia and Europe 800–1200* (Copenhagen, 1992), the very instructive and lavishly illustrated catalogue of an exhibition held in Paris, Berlin, and Copenhagen in 1992–3, with short articles by experts on a great range of topics as well as detailed descriptions of, and comments on, all the objects exhibited.

P. H. SAWYER, *The Age of the Vikings* (1st edn, London, 1962) questioned many assumptions then generally accepted about the Vikings.

P. H. SAWYER, *Kings and Vikings* (London, 1982), a survey taking account of the discussion provoked by *The Age of the Vikings*.

The eighth century

MOGENS BENCARD, *Ribe through 1000 years* (Ribe, 1978), a popular and well-illustrated account.

HELEN CLARKE and BJÖRN AMBROSIANI, *Towns in the Viking Age* (Leicester, 1991) includes brief accounts of the earliest trading places in north-west Europe, Scandinavia, and the Baltic region.

ULF NÄSMAN, 'Vendel Period Glass from Eketorp-II, Öland, Sweden: On Glass and Trade from the Late 6th to the Late 8th Centuries AD', *Acta Archaeologica*, 55 (1984), 55–116, an important article, of much wider significance than its title suggests, surveying and discussing the archaeological evidence for the early development of trading links between western Europe and the Baltic region.

IAN WOOD, *The Merovingian Kingdoms 450–751* (London, 1994) includes (Ch. 17) an authoritative discussion of the early development of trading places in north-west Europe that began in the late seventh century.

2. The Frankish Empire

The first three items are translations of some of the most important, and frequently cited, sources.

Janet L. Nelson, *The Annals of St-Bertin* (Manchester, 1991).

Timothy Reuter, *The Annals of Fulda* (Manchester, 1992).

B. W. Scholz, *Carolingian Chronicles* (Ann Arbor, 1970) includes the Royal Frankish Annals.

Albert D'Haenens, *Les invasions normandes en Belgique au ixe siècle* (Louvain, 1967), a critical study of the sources for the region that became Belgium.

George Duby, *The Early Growth of the European Economy*, trans. H. B. Clarke (London, 1974), a brilliant essay.

Margaret Gibson and Janet L. Nelson, *Charles the Bald, Court and Kingdom* (2nd edn, Aldershot, 1990) contains many relevant articles, including one by Richard Hodges on 'Trade and Market Origins in the Ninth Century'.

F. Donald Logan, *The Vikings in History* (2nd edn, London, 1994), particularly useful for the Vikings in the Loire valley.

Rosamund McKitterick (ed.) *The New Cambridge Medieval History*, ii (Cambridge, 1995), includes chapters by Simon Coupland on 'The Vikings in Francia and Anglo-Saxon England' (pp. 190–201), and by Janet L. Nelson on 'Kingship and Royal Government' (pp. 383–430).

Janet L. Nelson, *Charles the Bald* (London, 1992), discusses Viking activity and reactions to it against the background of the other concerns of the West Franks in this reign.

Neil S. Price, *The Vikings in Brittany* (London, 1989), a detailed account of Viking activity in the region.

T. Reuter, 'Plunder and Tribute in the Carolingian Empire', *Transactions of the Royal Historical Society*, 5th ser., 35 (1985), 75–94, puts Viking activity in context.

3. The Vikings in England, *c.*790–1016

Sources and general works

J. Campbell (ed.), *The Anglo-Saxons* (Oxford, 1982), essential reading for understanding of the wider context of Viking activity in England.

N. Hooper and M. Bennett, *Cambridge Illustrated Atlas: Warfare: The Middle Ages 768–1487* (Cambridge, 1996), useful maps which make it easier to visualize and to follow the course of events during the reigns of Alfred the Great (pp. 18–25), his successors in the tenth century (pp. 26–30), and Æthelred the Unready (pp. 36–9).

S. Keynes and M. Lapidge, *Alfred the Great: Asser's 'Life of King Alfred' and Other Contemporary Sources* (Harmondsworth, 1983), a collection of the most important primary sources for the reign of King Alfred, in translation.

H. R. Loyn, *The Vikings in Britain* (London, 1977), a judicious discussion which brings the study of different regions into relation with each other.

J. D. Richards, *English Heritage Book of Viking Age England* (London, 1991), especially strong on those aspects of the subject which turn on the examination of archaeological evidence.

F. M. Stenton, *Anglo-Saxon England* (3rd edn, Oxford, 1971), first published in 1943, and now dated in various respects; but still of great value for its analytical narrative, and for its general discussion of Scandinavian settlements in England.

D. WHITELOCK (ed.), *English Historical Documents c.500–1042* (2nd edn, London, 1979), contains translations of and comments on many of the primary sources, including the *Anglo-Saxon Chronicle*, law-codes, charters, letters of Alcuin, and Archbishop Wulfstan's *Sermo ad Anglos*.

Viking raids in the eighth and ninth centuries

M. BIDDLE and B. KJØLBYE-BIDDLE, 'Repton and the Vikings', *Antiquity*, 66 (1992), 36–51, a preliminary account of the remarkable discoveries at one of the bases used by the Vikings in the 870s, pending the appearance of the definitive publication.

N. BROOKS, *The Early History of the Church of Canterbury: Christ Church from 597 to 1066* (Leicester, 1984), essential not least for its discussion of the impact of Viking activity on the English Church.

A. P. SMYTH, *Alfred the Great* (Oxford, 1995), contains some useful discussion of Alfred's struggles against the Vikings, but the value of the book as a whole is compromised by the author's determination to impugn the authenticity of Asser's *Life of King Alfred*, for reasons which many will find unconvincing.

Scandinavian settlements in the Danelaw

R. N. BAILEY, *Viking Age Sculpture in Northern England* (London, 1980), a detailed analysis of the corpus of Anglo-Scandinavian sculpture, which demonstrates the historical and cultural importance of this material.

K. CAMERON (ed.) *Place-Name Evidence for the Anglo-Saxon Invasion and Scandinavian Settlements* (Nottingham, 1975), contains reprints of Cameron's seminal papers on the evidence of place-names.

M. GELLING, *Signposts to the Past: Place-Names and the History of England* (London, 1978), further guidance on the evidence of place-names.

R. A. HALL, *English Heritage Book of Viking Age York* (London, 1994), an excellent survey of the material excavated from sites in Coppergate and elsewhere in York, set most effectively into a general account of the development of the city as a whole.

N. LUND, 'King Edgar and the Danelaw', *Medieval Scandinavia*, 9 (1976), 181–95, an interesting paper which seeks to elucidate the history of the Danelaw against the changing background of political events.

ORDNANCE SURVEY HISTORICAL MAP AND GUIDE, *Viking and Medieval York* (Southampton, 1988), instructive and decorative.

A. P. SMYTH, *Scandinavian York and Dublin: The History and Archaeology of Two Related Kingdoms* (2 vols, Dublin, 1975–9), important in its conception of the subject, but in other respects controversial.

Viking raids during the reign of King Æthelred (978–1016)

D. SCRAGG (ed.), *The Battle of Maldon, AD 991* (Oxford, 1991), essays commemorating various aspects of the Battle of Maldon, with text and translation of the famous Old English poem.

4. Ireland, Wales, Man, and the Hebrides

BO ALMQVIST and DAVID GREENE (eds), *Proceedings of the Seventh Viking Congress* (Dublin, 1976), critical essays on language, history, place-names, art, and archaeology by D. Greene, L. de Paor, Magne Oftedal, J. Graham-Campbell, and other experts.

JOHN BRADLEY, 'The Interpretation of Scandinavian Settlement in Ireland', in John
  Bradley (ed.), *Settlement and Society in Medieval Ireland* (Kilkenny, 1988), 49–78,
  an important and illuminating survey.

B. G. CHARLES, *Old Norse Relations with Wales* (Cardiff, 1934), very detailed, if
  dated.

HOWARD CLARKE (ed.), *Medieval Dublin: The Making of a Metropolis* (Dublin,
  1990), reprints of important papers on Viking Dublin by H. B. Clarke, P. F. Wal-
  lace, E. Curtis, B. Ó Ríordáin, and A. Simms.

BARBARA E. CRAWFORD, *Scandinavian Scotland* (Leicester, 1987), the best general
  account of Scottish–Viking relations.

WENDY DAVIES, *Wales in the Early Middle Ages* (Leicester, 1982), a succinct and
  critical discussion in the context of Welsh history generally.

A. J. GOEDHEER, *Irish and Norse Traditions about the Battle of Clontarf* (Haarlem,
  1938), an important study of Clontarf in history and literature.

FRANÇOISE HENRY, *Irish Art during the Viking Invasions (800–1020 AD)* (London,
  1967), the classic account of Irish art, now somewhat dated.

POUL HOLM, 'The Slave Trade of Dublin: Ninth to Twelfth Centuries', *Peritia*, 6
  (1986), 317–45, a well-documented discussion of an important topic.

A. T. LUCAS, 'Irish Norse Relations: Time for a Reappraisal', *Journal of the Cork Historical and Archaeological Society*, 71 (1966), 62–75, a significant stage in the
  reassessment of Viking-Irish contacts.

CARL MARSTRANDER, *Bidrag til det norske sprogs historie i Irland* (Kristiania [Oslo],
  1915), the classic account of linguistic relations by a truly great philologist.

D. Ó CORRÁIN, *Ireland before the Normans* (Dublin, 1972) surveys the Viking period
  in the context of general Irish history, now somewhat dated.

D. Ó CORRÁIN, 'High-kings, Vikings and Other Kings', *Irish Historical Studies*, 21
  (1979), 283–323.

E. RYNNE (ed.), *North Munster Studies* (Limerick, 1967), essential studies of Viking
  monastic raiding and the rise of Dál Cais.

HAAKON SHETELIG, *Viking Antiquities in Great Britain and Ireland* (6 parts, Oslo,
  1940–54), now dated because of subsequent major excavations but still fundamental.

A. P. SMYTH, *Scandinavian York and Dublin* (2 vols, Dublin 1975–9), an important
  study of a most significant aspect of Viking Ireland.

J. TODD (ed.), *Coghadh Gaedhel re Gallaibh: The War of the Gaedhil with the Gael*
  (London, 1867), the work that shaped the Irish perception of the Vikings for centuries, and still does.

E. WAMERS, *Insularer Metallschmuck in wikingerzeitlichen Gräber Nordeuropas*
  (Neumünster, 1985), and briefly 'Some Ecclesiastical and Secular Insular Metalwork found in Norwegian Viking Graves', *Peritia*, 2 (1983), 277–306, an authoritative discussion of the proceeds of raiding recovered in Scandinavia.

5. The Atlantic Islands

COLLEEN E. BATEY, JUDITH JESCH, and CHRISTOPHER D. MORRIS (eds), *The Viking
  Age in Caithness, Orkney and the North Atlantic: Select Papers from the Proceedings of the Eleventh Viking Congress . . . 1989* (Edinburgh, 1993) includes several
  contributions dealing with the Faeroes.

The Book of Settlements: Landnámabók, trans. Hermann Pálsson and Paul Edwards
  (Winnipeg, 1972), a translation of the Sturlubók version.

JESSE L. BYOCK, *Medieval Iceland: Society, Sagas and Power* (Berkeley and Los Angeles, 1988).

JÓN JÓHANNESSON, *A History of the Old Icelandic Commonwealth: Islendinga Saga*, trans. Haraldur Bessason (Winnipeg, 1974).

GWYN JONES, *The Norse Atlantic Saga*, (2nd edn, Oxford, 1986), includes translations of several Icelandic texts, including *Íslendingabók*, and an account of the discoveries made at L'Anse aux Meadows.

KNUD J. KROGH, *Viking Greenland* (Copenhagen, 1967).

Laws of Early Iceland—Grágás: The Codex Regius of Grágás with Material from Other Manuscripts, i, trans. Andrew Dennis, Peter Foote, and Richard Perkins (Winnipeg, 1980).

Orkneyinga Saga: The History of the Earls of Orkney, trans. Hermann Pálsson and Paul Edwards (Harmondsworth, 1981).

DAG STRÖMBÄCK, *The Conversion of Iceland: A Survey*, trans. Peter Foote (London, 1975).

PREBEN MEULENGRACHT SØRENSEN, *Saga and Society: An Introduction to Old Norse Literature*, trans. John Tucker (Odense, 1993), a translation of a work published in Danish in 1977.

6. Scandinavians in European Russia

BJÖRN AMBROSIANI and HELEN CLARKE (eds), *The Twelfth Viking Congress: Developments around the Baltic and the North Sea in the Viking Age* (Stockholm, 1994), includes a contribution by Thomas S. Noonan on coin evidence for contacts between Scandinavia and Eastern Europe.

M. BRISBEIN (ed.), *The Archaeology of Novgorod, Russia: Recent Results from the Town and its Hinterland* (Lincoln, 1992) includes a good study of Riurik Gorodishche by E. N. Nosov.

JOHAN CALLMER, 'The Archaeology of Kiev to the End of the Earliest Urban Phase', *Harvard Ukrainian Studies*, 11 (1987), 323–53, a revealing study of the emergence of Kiev and the role of Scandinavians in the city's early history.

CONSTANTINE PORPHYROGENITOS, *De Administrando Imperio*, ed. Gy. Moravcsik, trans. R. J. H. Jenkins (Budapest, 1949), includes (Ch. 9) an account of the journey by Rus merchants from Kiev to Constantinople.

H. R. ELLIS DAVIDSON, *The Viking Road to Byzantium* (London, 1976), one of many general books on 'The Vikings in the East'.

SIMON FRANKLIN and JONATHAN SHEPARD, *The Emergence of Rus, 750–1200* (London and New York, 1996), an excellent introduction to the early medieval history of European Russia with much attention given to Scandinavians, Rus, Volga Bulghars, and other key peoples of the Viking Age.

NORMAN GLOB and OMELJAN PRITSAK, *Khazarian Hebrew Documents of the Tenth Century* (Ithaca, New York, 1982), a good recent analysis of what Khazar written sources may tell us about the Rus.

HERMANN PÁLSSON and PAUL EDWARDS (trans.), *Vikings in Russia: Yngvar's Saga and Eymund's Saga* (Edinburgh, 1989), texts that show why many scholars are very sceptical about the value of sagas as sources of information about Scandinavians in Russia.

The Russian Primary Chronicle: Laurentian Text, ed. and trans. Samuel H. Cross and Olgerd P. Sherbowitz-Wetzor (Cambridge, Mass., 1953), the fundamental text for Scandinavians in early Russia; the introduction and notes provide valuable background.

K. R. Schmidt (ed.), *Varangian Problems* (Copenhagen, 1970), an important collection of articles with several stimulating studies of the Scandinavians in Russia.

Anne Stalsberg, 'The Scandinavian Viking Age Finds in Rus: Overview and Analysis', *Bericht der Römisch-Germanischen Kommission*, 69 (1988), 448–71, a good introduction to the Scandinavian finds from European Russia and their significance.

Alexander A. Vasiliev, *The Russian Attack on Constantinople in 860* (Cambridge, Mass., 1946), a detailed study of the earliest Scandinavian activity in the Black Sea.

7. The Danish Empire and the End of the Viking Age

Janet Cooper (ed.), *The Battle of Maldon: Fiction and Fact* (London, 1993), papers from a millenary conference.

Encomium Emmae Reginae, ed. Alistair Campbell (Royal Historical Society, London, 1949), text and translation with a most valuable and detailed discussion of its historical value.

Simon Keynes, *The Diplomas of King Æthelred 'the Unready' 978–1016: A Study of their Use as Historical Evidence* (Cambridge, 1980), the fundamental study of the reign of Æthelred.

Sten Körner, *The Battle of Hastings, England and Europe 1035–1066* (Lund, 1964).

M. K. Lawson, *Cnut: The Danes in England in the Early Eleventh Century* (London and New York, 1993), a new study of Knut, somewhat uneven but useful.

Niels Lund, 'Scandinavia, c.700–1066', in *The New Cambridge Medieval History*, ii, ed. Rosamund McKitterick (Cambridge, 1995), 202–27, an account of political events in Scandinavia.

J. Niles and M. Amodio (eds), *Anglo-Scandinavian England: Norse-English Relations in the Period before the Conquest* (Lanham, New York and London, 1989), a collection of papers discussing, among other things, Anglo-Scandinavian relations in the late Viking Age.

Alexander R. Rumble (ed.), *The Reign of Cnut, King of England, Denmark and Norway* (London, 1994), articles on various aspects of Knut's reign.

Birgit Sawyer, Peter Sawyer, and Ian Wood, *The Christianization of Scandinavia* (Alingsås, 1987), report of a seminar held on the topic in 1985.

D. G. Scragg (ed.), *The Battle of Maldon AD 991* (Oxford, 1991), an edition and translation of the poem with articles on its historical and literary background.

Pauline Stafford, *Unification and Conquest: A Political and Social History of England in the Tenth and Eleventh Centuries* (London, 1989), a thoughtful and stimulating study.

8. Ships and Seamanship

Niels Bonde and Arne Emil Christensen, 'Dendrochronological Dating of Three Viking Age Ship Burials at Oseberg, Gokstad and Tune, Norway', *Antiquity*, 67 (1993), 575–83.

Niels Bonde and Ole Crumlin-Pedersen, 'The Dating of Wreck 2 from Skuldelev, Denmark', *Newswarp*, 7 (1990), 3–6.

A. W. Brøgger and Haakon Shetelig, *The Viking Ships: Their Ancestry and Evolution* (Oslo, 1951), although somewhat outdated, this is still the most significant monograph in English on the Norwegian ship finds.

Ole Crumlin-Pedersen (ed.), *Aspects of Maritime Scandinavia AD 200–1200: Pro-*

ceedings of the Nordic Seminar on Maritime Aspects of Archaeology, Roskilde, 13th–15th March 1989 (Roskilde, 1991), the contributions highlight various aspects of Scandinavian seafaring and adaptation to a maritime environment before and during the Viking Age.

OLE CRUMLIN-PEDERSEN and BIRGITTE MUNCHE (eds), *The Ship as Symbol in Prehistoric and Medieval Scandinavia* (Copenhagen, 1995), in which historians of religion and maritime archaeologists discuss the role of the ship in Scandinavian religious beliefs from the Bronze Age to the Middle Ages.

OLE CRUMLIN-PEDERSEN and MAX VINNER (eds), *Sailing into the Past: The International Ship Replica Seminar, Roskilde 1984* (Roskilde, 1987), a valuable, if no longer up-to-date, introduction to the rapidly expanding field of experimental ship archaeology.

DETLEV ELLMERS, *Frühmittelalterliche Handelsschiffahrt in Nord- und Mitteleuropa* (Neumünster, 1972) contains the best catalogue yet available of ship finds from the Viking Age and adjacent centuries from Northern Europe, together with important, but not unchallenged, theories on harbour sites and the development of trade in those centuries.

NIELS LUND (ed.), *Two Voyagers at the Court of King Alfred: The Ventures of Ohthere and Wulfstan together with the Description of Northern Europe from the Old English Orosius* (York, 1984), this competently commented translation of the reports of Ohthere's and Wulfstan's voyages offers an insight into what are perhaps the two most important written sources for Viking seafaring.

MICHAEL MÜLLER-WILLE, *Bestattung im Boot: Studien zu einer Nordeuropaischen Grabsitte* (Neumünster, 1970), although 25 years old, this work is still the authoritative study of the Scandinavian custom of boat burial, with a comprehensive catalogue of boat graves and related types of grave monument. A very condensed English version is in the *International Journal of Nautical Archaeology and Underwater Exploration*, 3, 187–204.

OLAF OLSEN and OLE CRUMLIN-PEDERSEN, 'The Skuldelev Ships', *Acta Archaeologica*, 38 (1968), preliminary, but detailed, reports on the five late Viking-Age ships found at Skuldelev in Denmark.

9. Religions Old and New

ERIK MOLTKE, *Runes and their Origin: Denmark and Elsewhere*, trans. Peter Foote (Copenhagen, 1986).

SVEN B. F. JANSSON, *Runes in Sweden*, trans. Peter Foote (2nd edn, Stockholm, 1987), two works that provide a good introduction to the evidence of the runic inscriptions in Scandinavia.

JÓNAS KRISTJÁNSSON, *Eddas and Sagas: Iceland's Medieval Literature*, trans. Peter Foote (Reykjavík, 1988), a traditional history of Old Norse literature.

MARGARET CLUNIES ROSS, *Prolonged Echoes: Old Norse Myth in Medieval Norse Society, i: The Myths* (Odense, 1993), a sociological and anthropological approach.

GRO STEINSLAND, *Det hellige bryllup og norrøn kongeideologi* (Oslo, 1991), a detailed analysis of a myth in its social context, including the thesis that kings descended from gods and giants.

GRO STEINSLAND and PREBEN MEULENGRACHT SØRENSEN, *Mennesker og makter i Vikingenes verden* (Oslo, 1993), a survey of Viking society, religion, culture, and art.

PREBEN MEULENGRACHT SØRENSEN, *Saga and Society: An Introduction to Old Norse Literature*, trans. John Tucker (Odense, 1993), emphasizes the sociological aspects of the topic.

E. O. G. TURVILLE-PETRE, *Myth and Religion of the North: The Religion of Ancient Scandinavia* (2nd edn, Greenwich, Conn., 1977), a comprehensive and traditional work.

E. O. G. TURVILLE-PETRE, *Scaldic Poetry* (Oxford, 1976), a good introduction to this poetry.

10. The Vikings in History and Legend

SVERRE BAGGE, *Society and Politics in Snorri Sturluson's Heimskringla* (Berkeley and Los Angeles, 1991), the most recent work on Snorri's historiography.

THOR J. BECK, *Northern Antiquities in French Learning and Literature (1755–1855): A Study in Pre-Romantic Ideas*, (2 vols, New York, 1934).

ANTON BLANCK, *Den nordiska renässensen i sjuttonhundratalets litteratur: En undersökning av den 'götiska' poesiens allmänna och inhemska förutsättningar* (Stockholm, 1911), a classic work in Swedish about the discovery of Norse literature in the eighteenth century.

ÚLFAR BRAGASON (ed.), *Wagner's Ring and its Icelandic Sources* (Reykjavík, 1995), a collection of essays about the use of Old Norse myth in the works of Wagner and other nineteenth-century German artists.

FRANK EDGAR FARLEY, *Scandinavian Influences in the English Romantic Movement* (Boston, 1903).

BO GRANDIEN, *Rönndruvans glöd: Nygöticistiskt i tanke, konst och miljö under 1800-talet* (Uddevalla, 1987), an excellent survey of Norse themes and 'Viking' motifs in nineteenth-century Scandinavian art.

KURT JOHANNESSON, *Gotisk renässens: Johannes och Olaus Magnus som politiker och historiker* (Stockholm, 1982), about the origins of Gothic historiography in sixteenth-century Sweden.

INGEMAR KARLSSON and ARNE RUTH, *Samhället som teater: Estetik och politik i Tredje riket* (Stockholm, 1983), a brilliant discussion in Swedish of Nazi aesthetics and its use of Viking symbols.

JOHAN MJÖBERG, 'Romanticism and Revival', in *The Northern World*, ed. David M. Wilson (London, 1980), 207–38.

JOHAN NORDSTRÖM, *De yverbornes ö* (Stockholm, 1934), a classic study of nationalistic historiography in seventeenth-century Sweden.

MARGARET OMBERG, *Scandinavian Themes in English Poetry, 1760–1800* (Uppsala, 1976).

STEFANIE VON SCHNURBEIN, *Religion als Kulturkritik: Neugermanisches Heidentum im 20 Jahrhundert* (Heidelberg, 1993), a fascinating dissertation about modern fundamentalists who worship Vikings and the Old Norse gods.

ELSE ROESDAHL and PREBEN MEULENGRACHT SØRENSEN (eds), *The Waking of Angantyr: The Scandinavian Past in European Culture* (Århus, 1996), a collection of essays by scholars from several countries and disciplines about the Viking heritage and Old Norse studies in Western Europe.

ERICA SIMON, *Réveil national et culture populaire en Scandinavie: La génèse de la höjskole nordique 1844–1878* (Uppsala, 1960), a very thorough dissertation about the rise of the Grundtvigian folk high school and its use of Old Norse Viking symbols.

Erik Wahlgren, *The Kensington Stone: A Mystery Solved* (Minneapolis, 1958), an entertaining description of the patriotic Scandinavian–American milieu that produced 'Viking' forgeries such as the notorious Kensington Stone around the turn of the century.

Andrew Wawn (ed.), *Northern Antiquity: The Post-Medieval Reception of Edda and Saga* (Enfield Lock, Middlesex, 1994), a collection of literary essays by British and Scandinavian scholars.

11. The Viking Legacy

Birgit and Peter Sawyer, *Medieval Scandinavia: From Conversion to Reformation c.800–1500* (Minneapolis and London, 1993) discusses the main changes in Scandinavia brought about by contacts, peaceful as well as hostile, between Scandinavians and Europeans during the Viking Age.

CHRONOLOGY

822/3	Pope Paschal I authorizes Ebo, archbishop of Rheims, to evangelize 'in northern parts'
823	Archbishop Ebo leads a mission to the Danes
	The Danish king Harald appeals for Frankish help against Godfred's sons
826	Harald and his wife are baptized at Mainz, with Louis the Pious as sponsor. He returns to Denmark accompanied by Anskar whose task was to strengthen the king's faith and evangelize the Danes
827	Harald expelled from Denmark
829–31	Anskar's first missionary journey to Birka
832	Anskar consecrated bishop of the newly created see of Hamburg which the pope converts into an archbishopric
833	Louis the Pious deprived of power by his sons, the eldest of whom, Lothar, encourages the exiled King Harald to attack Frisia
834	Louis restored to power, but Lothar continues to oppose him
834–7	Annual raids on Dorestad
835	The Isle of Sheppey in the Thames estuary raided
836	West Saxons defeated by Vikings at Carhampton in Somerset
	Raids extend to the interior of Ireland
	The monks of St-Philibert abandon Noirmoutier and seek permanent refuge on the mainland, finally settling in 875 at Tournus in Burgundy
837	In Ireland large fleets on the rivers Boyne and Liffey
839	Svear 'who were called Rus' arrive at the court of Louis the Pious, sent by the Byzantine emperor
	A fleet on Lough Neagh plunders the surrounding region
	Vikings attack the Picts
840	Civil war in Frankia after the death of Louis the Pious
	A Viking fleet winters on Lough Neagh in Ireland
841	Lothar grants Walcheren to 'the pirate Harald' as reward for his help against Louis the Pious
	The Seine valley raided
	A fleet winters in Dublin
842	Quentovic and *Hamwic* sacked
	The first recorded Viking–Irish alliance
843	Nantes is sacked
	Louis's sons agree to divide the empire in three, the youngest, Charles the Bald, ruling the western kingdom
844	Raids on Toulouse, Galicia, and al-Andalus
	A fleet on Lough Ree plunders monasteries in midland Ireland
845	Paris ransomed for 7,000 pounds of silver
	Hamburg is sacked by a Danish fleet
	A pagan revolt leads the missionaries to abandon Birka
845–8	Several defeats of Vikings by Irish kings
848	Bordeaux seized by Vikings after a long siege
848/9	Anskar is given the see of Bremen to hold jointly with Hamburg

849	Périgueux sacked
	A new fleet arrives in Ireland
c.850	Horik I, king of the Danes, allows Anskar to build churches in Schleswig/Hedeby and Ribe
851	A Viking fleet winters on Thanet
	Canterbury and London stormed by Vikings who were then defeated in battle by the West Saxons at *Aclea*
	Danes challenge the Norwegians in Ireland
852	Vikings winter in the Seine valley
	Raids on the Welsh coast begin
	Anskar returns to Birka to revive the mission
853	Vikings winter in the Loire valley
	The abbey of St-Martin, Tours, attacked
	Vikings in Ireland submit to Olaf, son of the king of *Laithlinn*, and the Irish pay him tribute
854	Horik I is killed in battle against returning Vikings and is succeeded by a kinsman, Horik II
859	A Danish fleet enters the Mediterranean, and attacks Nakur in North Africa
	A Viking base established in the Camargue on the south coast of Frankia
	A Viking fleet active in the Somme valley
	The traditional date for the first exaction of tribute from north-west Russia by 'Varangians'
860	The Vikings from the Somme attack Winchester and then return to Frankia
	Rus attack Constantinople
862	The traditional date of the invitation by the Finns and Slavs to Riurik and the Rus to rule over them
862–6	A fortified bridge constructed at Pont-de-l'Arche to prevent Viking ships reaching Paris
864	Horik II sends gifts to Pope Nicholas I
865	The abbey of St-Benoit, Fleury, attacked
	Vikings based on the Loire burn Poitiers
	The first part of the 'great army' lands in East Anglia, forcing the East Anglians to 'make peace', that is, pay tribute
	Anskar dies and is succeeded as archbishop by Rimbert
866	The 'great army' occupies York
	Vikings from the Loire, allied with Bretons, sack Le Mans
	Vikings are expelled from their bases in the north of Ireland and at Youghal in the south
	Vikings from Ireland and Scotland exact tribute from the Picts
867	Osbert, king of the Northumbrians, and his rival Ælle join forces in an unsuccessful attempt to recover York, and both are killed. Leaving Egbert, a native, to rule Northumbria as a subordinate king, the army leaves York to winter in Nottingham

868	The Mercians, with West Saxon support, besiege Nottingham, but are forced to 'make peace', and the Vikings return to winter in York
869	The 'great army' returns to East Anglia. Edmund, king of the East Angles, opposes them, but is defeated and killed on 20 November
	Olaf plunders Armagh
870	Dublin Vikings capture Dumbarton, capital of Strathclyde
c.870	Scandinavians begin to settle in Iceland
871	The 'great army' attempts to conquer Wessex. The West Saxons, under King Æthelred and his brother Alfred, prevent this but are forced to 'make peace'. Æthelred dies in April and is succeeded by Alfred
871–4	The 'great army' winters successively at London, Torksey, and Repton
873	Charles the Bald besieges Vikings who had occupied Angers, and forces them to submit and leave
	Death of Ivar, 'king of the Northmen of all Ireland and Britain' (i.e. the Hebrides, Scotland, and Strathclyde)
874	After driving Burgred, king of the Mercians, into exile, and establishing Ceolwulf in his place, the 'great army' splits. One part under Half-dan returns to Northumbria and winters in the Tyne valley. The other part, under three kings, moves to Cambridge and winters there
875	The Vikings from Cambridge invade Wessex, successively occupying Wareham and Exeter, but make peace with Alfred and, for the first time, surrender hostages
877	The Vikings withdraw from Wessex and winter in Gloucester. They take control of north-east Mercia and begin to settle there. Ceolwulf remains king of 'English' Mercia, extending from the Welsh frontier to London
878	Vikings under Guthrum invade Wessex but after some initial success are defeated by Alfred at Edington. Guthrum and his leading companions accept baptism and withdraw to Cirencester
	A new large army assembles at Fulham on the river Thames
	Vikings winter in Dyfed
879	The army that wintered at Fulham crosses the Channel to campaign in the Meuse–Lower Rhine region
	Guthrum's force moves to East Anglia and begins to settle there. Before his death in 890 Guthrum, as king of East Anglia, agrees a treaty with King Alfred, defining the boundary between English and Danish territory
c.879	In Russia, Riurik dies and is succeeded by Oleg
880	The East Franks inflict serious losses on the Viking army at Thiméon; the survivors fortify the royal palace at Nijmegen and winter there
c.880	Oleg gains control of Kiev
881	Liège, Utrecht, Aachen, and many places in the Rhine valley including Cologne, ravaged
882	The Franks besiege Vikings in their fortification at Asselt on the Meuse, but the Emperor Charles the Fat agrees to pay them tribute, and grants territory in Frisia to Godfred. Sigfred continues campaigning in west Frankia

885	Godfred tricked by the Franks and killed; the army divides, one part returns to England and unsuccessfully besieges Rochester, the other, under King Sigfred, unsuccessfully besieges Paris
886–8	The Vikings pass Paris and spend two years campaigning in the central part of west Frankia, besieging Sens and raiding many places, including Troyes, Verdun, and Toul
890	Vikings from the Seine valley defeated by the Bretons at St-Lô
c.890	In Denmark the established royal dynasty is replaced, at least in south Jutland, by Olaf, probably a returning exile, who was succeeded by his son and grandson
892	After being defeated in a battle on the river Dyle near Louvain, the remnants of the army cross to England from Boulogne. Soon afterwards a fleet from the Loire, led by Hasting, arrives in the Thames estuary
893–6	The Vikings vainly attempt to extend the Scandinavian conquests in England
895x900	The Gokstad ship is built
896	The Viking army in England disbands, some settle in England, others return to Frankia
	Sihtric, son of Ivar, is killed in the course of a dispute between factions among the Dublin Vikings
899	Alfred dies and is succeeded by his son Edward the Elder
c.900	By winning the battle of Hafrsfjord, Harald Finehair extends his power in Norway
902	Vikings expelled from Dublin
910	Danes settled in eastern England raid Mercia but are badly beaten in the battle of Tettenhall
911	Vikings led by Rollo raid the Seine valley, are defeated at Chartres but are allowed to occupy Rouen and the lower Seine valley to help Frankish defences
912–20	The West Saxons and Mercians regain control of most of the territory occupied by the Danes south of the Humber
c.913–45	Igor, prince of Kiev
914	Ragnald, grandson of Ivar, defeats the English and the Scots at Corbridge on the river Tyne
	Vikings from Brittany establish a base at Waterford
c.915	In Denmark Olaf's grandson is replaced by another returned exile whose son and successor was Gorm 'the Old'
917	Ragnald's fleet arrives at Waterford and his kinsman Sihtric gains control of Dublin
917–1042	Descendants of Ivar rule Dublin until 1042, but after 944 are subject to Irish kings most of the time
918	Ragnald leaves Ireland, sacks Dunblane in Scotland, and defeats the English and Scots again on the river Tyne
919	Ragnald conquers York and is recognized as king there
919–c.950	Ragnald's kinsmen are intermittently kings of York, although few are independent for long. Most submit to, and are expelled by, English kings
920	After submitting to Edward the Elder, Ragnald dies and is succeeded at

*c.*980	Trelleborg and other circular forts in Denmark are constructed
983	The Danes recover the land lost to the Germans in 974
*c.*985	The settlement of Greenland begins
986/7	Harald Bluetooth dies of wounds received in a rebellion against him, and is succeeded by his son Sven Forkbeard
988	Vladimir sends Varangians to assist the Byzantine emperor
989	Sihtric Silkenbeard becomes king of Dublin under Mael Sechnaill
	Vladimir accepts Christianity
*c.*990	The Klåstad ship is built
991	Vikings attack East Anglia, defeat the English at Maldon, and are paid 10,000 pounds of money
*c.*993	Olof Skötkonung succeeds his father as king of the Svear
994	A fleet led by Sven Forkbeard, Olaf Tryggvason, and others besieges London forcing the English to pay a tribute of 16,000 pounds
	Vikings raid the Elbe valley and capture several notables, including the count of Stade
995	Olaf Trygvasson allies with Æthelred and after being confirmed, with the English king as sponsor, returns to Norway to challenge the Danish overlordship
997	Mael Sechnaill and Brian Bórama divide Ireland between them, making Brian overlord of Dublin
997–1002	Annual raids on England, leading to the payment of 24,000 pounds as tribute
999	Revolt by the Dubliners crushed by Brian and Mael Sechnaill in the battle of Glenn Máma
	Sihtric retains the kingship of Dublin under Brian
	Viking raiders kill the bishop of St David's
1000	In Iceland the Alþing accepts Christianity
	Olaf Tryggvason is killed in the battle of Svold against Sven Forkbeard, who thus re-establishes Danish overlordship over Norway
*c.*1000	*Vínland* discovered
1002	Æthelred orders the killing of all Danes in England
1003–5	Sven Forkbeard campaigns in England
1006	A large fleet invades England and is paid 36,000 pounds as tribute in 1007
1009	A large fleet led by Thorkell begins campaigning in England. Æthelred orders elaborate religious rituals to gain God's help
1012	Thorkell's army takes Canterbury and kills archbishop Ælfheah. A tribute of 48,000 pounds is paid and Thorkell agrees to serve Æthelred with 45 ships
1013	Sven Forkbeard invades England, drives Æthelred into exile in Normandy and is recognized as king by the English
1014	Sven dies at Gainsborough on 3 February; Æthelred is reinstated and forces Sven's son, Knut, to return to Denmark
	Leinster and Dublin, threatened by Brian, gather support from Orkney, the Hebrides, and Man, but are defeated by Brian and Mael Sechnaill on 23 April at Clontarf. Brian is killed in the battle

Olaf Haraldsson, who accompanied Æthelred on his return from Normandy, leaves to claim the kingship of Norway and challenge the Danish overlordship

1015   Knut returns to England and begins an extensive campaign of conquest

1016   Æthelred dies and is succeeded by his son, Edmund Ironside. After Edmund's defeat in battle at *Assandun* England is partitioned between Knut and Edmund, who retains Wessex. After Edmund's death on 30 November Knut is recognized as king by the English, who agree to pay a tribute of 82,500 pounds

1019   Knut succeeds his brother Harald as king of the Danes

*c.*1025   Treaty between Olaf Haraldsson and the Icelanders

1026   Denmark is invaded by a coalition of Norwegians and Svear under Olaf Haraldsson and Anund Jacob, and are opposed by Knut in the battle of the Holy River

1027   Knut visits Rome and attends the imperial coronation of Conrad I

1028   Knut expels Olaf Haraldsson from Norway

1029   Olaf Haraldsson and his son Magnus are given refuge in Novgorod by Iaroslav

1030   Olaf Haraldsson returns to Norway, and is killed at Stiklestad on 30 June; Knut's decision to send his son Sven and Sven's mother, Ælfgifu, to rule Norway is unpopular

1035   Knut dies in Winchester and is succeeded in Denmark by Harthaknut, his son by Emma; Magnus, son of Olaf Haraldsson, is recognized as king of Norway

1037   Harald, Knut's son by Ælfgifu, is finally accepted by all as king of England

1040   Harald, king of England, dies and is succeeded by Harthaknut

1042   Harthaknut dies, and is succeeded as king of England by Edward the Confessor, son of Æthelred; the claim of Sven Estridsson, Knut's nephew, to be Danish king is frustrated by the recognition of the Norwegian Magnus as king by the Danes

1047   Magnus of Norway dies and is succeeded in Norway by his uncle, Harald Hardrada; Sven Estridsson succeeds as king of the Danes

1052   Diarmait, king of Leinster, seizes Dublin

1053   Pope Leo IX formally gives the archbishopric of Hamburg-Bremen authority over Norway, Iceland, and Greenland as well as over the Danes and Svear

1056–80   Ísleif, the first Icelandic bishop

*c.*1060   Skuldelev 2 is built in or near Dublin

The division of Denmark into regular dioceses is completed

The first regular Swedish see is established at Skara in Västergötland

1066   Edward the Confessor dies; Harald Hardrada claims the succession but is killed on 25 September in the battle of Stamford Bridge; Harold Godwinesson is killed in battle near Hastings on 14 October; on 25 December William, duke of Normandy, is crowned king of the English

1069   Sven Estridsson sends a fleet to support English resistance to William, but the Danes are unwilling to confront him

Olaf Kyrre, son of Harald Hardrada, becomes sole king of Norway

1070   The Danish fleet leaves England

*c.*1070   The first regular Norwegian sees are established in Nidaros, on the Isle of Selja (soon moved to Bergen), and Oslo

1072   Diarmait described as 'king of Wales and the Isles and of Dublin' dies and is succeeded by Tairdelbach, grandson of Brian. Tairdelbach's son Muirchertach is made king of Dublin

1073   Vikings attack St David's, and do so again in 1080 and 1091

1075   A Danish fleet is sent to England to support a rebellion against William, but arrives too late and only plunders York

1076   Sven Estridsson dies and is succeeded by five sons in turn

*c.*1080   The celebration of pagan cult at Uppsala ends

1085   An invasion of England is planned by Knut, king of the Danes, and Robert, count of Flanders, but is never launched

1086   Tairdelbach dies and is succeeded by Muirchertach, who keeps Dublin as his capital

King Knut is killed in Odense

1098   The first expedition by Magnus Barelegs, king of Norway (1093–1103), to Orkney, the Hebrides, and Anglesey. His overlordship over the Isles is recognized by the Scottish king

1102–3   Magnus Barelegs spend the winter with Muirchertach, and they campaign jointly in Ulster, where Magnus is killed

1104   The see of Lund is made an archbishopric

ILLUSTRATION SOURCES

The editor and publishers wish to thank the following who have kindly given permission to reproduce illustrations on the following pages:

2 Den Antikvariske Samling/Rita Fredsgaard Nielsen, Ribe, Denmark

4 Antikvarisk-Topografiska Arkivet, Stockholm/Jan Norman

5 (*left*) Nordam-Ullitz/Torkild Balslev, Denmark; (*right*) Forhistorisk Museum, Moesgard, Denmark

9 University Museum of National Antiquities, Oslo

16 State Hermitage Museum, St Petersburg

20 British Library, Cotton Tiberius C xi, fo. 137

21 National Museum, Copenhagen

22 Nationalbibliothek, Vienna/AKG, London

26 Bibliotheek der Rijksuniversiteit, Utrecht

33 M. Müller-Wille, *Berichte über die Ausgrabungen in Haithabu* (1978)

36 British Museum, PS272528

43 Rijksdienst voor het Oudheidkundig Bodemonderzoek, Netherlands

45 A.F. Kersting

46 Musée départementaux de la Seine-Maritime/Yohann Deslandes

49 English Heritage

55 Martin Biddle, Oxford

56 Cambridge University Collection of Air Photographs

57 British Museum, BM Acq.479 1896 4.4.63 & 4

58 Cambridge University Collection of Air Photographs

60 Ashmolean Museum, Oxford

70 Ted Spiegel

71 Prof. Else Roesdahl, University of Åarhus

74 The Master and Fellows of Corpus Christi College, Cambridge

75 Museum of London

79 The Master and Fellows of Corpus Christi College, Cambridge

80 British Museum, 1955.7.8.81

82 University Museum of National Antiquities, Oslo

84 National Museum of Ireland

87 Bergen Museum, Norway/Ann-Mari Olsen

90 National Museum of Ireland

92 National Museum of Wales

96 National Museum of Denmark

99 Manx National Heritage

102 Ted Spiegel

104 Department of Arts, Culture and the Gaeltacht, Dublin

107 Ted Spiegel

108 Antikvarisk-Topografiska Arkivet, Stockholm

111 National Museum of Iceland

113 Stofnun Árna Magnússonar, Iceland

116 Ted Spiegel

119 Stofnun Árna Magnússonar, Iceland

121 Prof. Sveinbjörn Rafnsson

122 National Museum of Iceland

125 National Museum of Iceland

126 National Museum of Iceland

129 AKG, London

139 State Hermitage Museum, St Petersburg

140 Prof. Kirpichnikov, St Petersburg

141 Prof. Nosov, St Petersburg

144 State Hermitage Museum, St Petersburg

146 State Hermitage Museum, St Petersburg

149 State Hermitage Museum, St Petersburg

151 Mark A. Brisbane (ed.), *The Archaeology of Novgorod, Russia* (Society for Medieval Archaeology monograph ser., no. 13, Lincoln, Nebr., 1992)

152 Mark A. Brisbane (ed.), *The Archaeology of Novgorod, Russia* (Society for Medieval Archaeology monograph ser., no. 13, Lincoln, Nebr., 1992)

153 State Hermitage Museum, St Petersburg

154 Zdenek Vana, *The World of the Ancient Slavs* (Wayne State University Press, 1983)
159 Biofoto, Denmark
160 National Museum of Denmark
161 Nordam-Ullitz/Torkild Balslev, Denmark
162 Werner Forman
164 National Museum of Denmark
166 Antikvarisk-Topografiska Arkivet, Stockholm
170 Antikvarisk-Topografiska Arkivet, Stockholm
173 National Museum of Denmark
174 Winchester Excavation Committee/John Crook
177 British Library, Stowe MS 994, fo.1
180 Colchester Museums
184 National Museum, Copenhagen
185 British Museum, PS109025
186 University Museum of National Antiquities, Oslo
188 Antikvarisk-Topografiska Arkivet, Stockholm
189 Viking Ship Museum, Roskilde, Denmark/Martin Gothche
190 Archäologisches Landesmuseum, Schloss Gottorf, Schleswig
191 Archäologisches Landesmuseum, Schloss Gottorf, Schleswig
192 Viking Ship Museum, Roskilde, Denmark/Werner Karrasch
194 Antikvarisk-Topografiska Arkivet, Stockholm
195 Jan Bill
199 Giraudon, Paris
201 University Museum of National Antiquities, Oslo

204 National Museum of Denmark
205 Antikvarisk-Topografiska Arkivet, Stockholm
208 National Museum of Denmark
213 National Museum of Denmark
215 Antikvarisk-Topografiska Arkivet, Stockholm
217 Ted Spiegel
220 University Museum of National Antiquities, Oslo
222 Det Kongelige Bibliotek, Copenhagen
224 Antikvarisk-Topografiska Arkivet, Stockholm
226 Stofnun Árna Magnússonar, Iceland
227 Det Kongelige Bibliotek, Copenhagen
228 Gothenburg University Library
231 Stofnun Árna Magnússonar, Iceland
237 Johan Paues, Stockholm
241 Stockholms Stadsmuseum
242 Gunnar Källström, Stockholm
245 George Grosz, *Ecce Homo* (1923) ©DACS
246 Ullstein Bilderdienst
257 Antikvarisk-Topografiska Arkivet, Stockholm
258 Gabriel Hildebrand, Stockholm
259 Antikvarisk-Topografiska Arkivet, Stockholm

In a few instances we have been unable to trace the copyright-holder prior to publication. If notified, the publishers will be pleased to amend the acknowledgements in any future edition.

Picture research by Charlotte Ward-Perkins.

INDEX

Page numbers in *italics* refer to black-and-white illustrations or maps and their captions. Map references are given first. Colour plates (which are unpaginated) are located by reference to the nearest page of text and are indicated by **bold**.